RIVALS

The Offbeat Guide to the 92 League Clubs

Geoff Harvey and Vanessa Strowger

AP

AESCULUS PRESS LTD

Managing Editor – David Ikerrin

Editor – Anna Middleton

Cartoons – Wiz Middleton

Additional material – Kevin Hughes and Diane Dekuysscher

Design and layout
Mouse House Print Shop

First published in Great Britain in 2004
Aesculus Press Limited, PO Box 5276
Swadlincote, Derbyshire DE11 9ZT

Copyright © 2004

ACKNOWLEDGEMENTS

Thank you to the hundreds and hundreds of people who provided information via the Aesculus online questionnaire, through message boards and interviews. Particular thanks for detailed contributions go to:

Ian Baker, Martin Baker, Tim Barlow, Tom Blackburn, Jannus Bodker, Martin Brodetsky, Andy Burton, James Corner, Dick Dale, Adam Davies, Andrew Davies, Charles Eacott, Paul Farrington, Mike Field, Tom Finney, Robert Ford, Michael Gillespie, Vinny Goodfield, Hazel (?), Paul Howard, Phillip Hughes, Keith Lewis, Mick McNeill, Kev Monks, Stephen Nicholson, Jonathan Oliver, Matt Osborne, Keith Palmer, David Proctor, Dave Radford, Mat Roper, David Southworth, Bob Stonehouse, Steve Stuart, Peter Sweeting, Matt Tomiak, Nigel Trotter, Tim Trueman, Andrew Turton, Neil Vaughan, Michael Wood.

Special thanks to the following for putting up with the authors during this project:
Carole Bates, Juliet Downs, Nina Emefiele, Kelly Irvine, Angela Morris.

Suggestions and corrections for future editions can be sent to rivalsbook@hotmail.com

Background cover photo: Yeovil fans at their first league game at Rochdale © www.ciderspace.co.uk

The Offbeat Guide to the 92 League Clubs

'Rivals' is simply a directory of stuff that we thought fans really wanted to know about the 92 League clubs, without wading through reams of dull histories, player biographies and inconsequential stats. It is also an attempt to assess the strength of virtually every single one of the huge web of rivalries, from the well-publicised rows between the two Manchester clubs to the more obscure, but probably equally passionate, bad feeling between the likes of Wycombe Wanderers and Colchester.

In completing the book, we canvassed the views of hundreds of fans through questionnaires, written submissions, telephone and face to face interviews. A pattern quickly emerged revealing not so much the differences between the supporters of football clubs but their staggering similarity. However, fans of opposing clubs generally dislike each other with a vengeance. In this book, many take their chance to vent their spleen.

The biography of the average football fan generally started when his Dad took him to watch Glumsville Town, or whoever, at around seven years old. Sometime during the afternoon, a permanent and irreversible electro-chemical change occurs in the youngster's brain that turns him into a lifelong supporter. After 23 years of going week in, week out, and with one Freight Rover Trophy final appearance to show for his dedication (lost to Bristol Rovers by a disputed 78th minute penalty), he has a child of his own, who he alarmingly bounces around on his shoulders in his mini size Glumsville Town replica shirt (price £39.99), waiting for the day when the poor child experiences the same moment of conversion - starting the whole grim cycle off again.

Though this is a common pattern, the fact that more of us are zipping around the country after jobs, houses and semi-decent schools means that only a minority of a club's supporters actually live in the town that the club is named after. Fans of all teams are spread far wider than is generally acknowledged. Charles Koppel, the man responsible for moving Wimbledon to Milton Keynes, claimed that only 10% of the club's season ticket holders lived in the London borough of Merton, the area where 99% of fans wanted them to return to. The figure appeared as if it might have been the product of an over-active imagination at the time, but from the authors' experiences, it has the air of reality about it. There are Manchester United fans in virtually every city, town and village in the British Isles. But equally, the city of Manchester itself is a melting pot as well, with fans of Newcastle, Tottenham, Yeovil…you name it…largely keeping a low profile in the sea of red and light blue. Although the figure is totally unscientific, we reckon that if you asked everyone in the home section of a medium-sized club where they lived, over half of them would give you an answer that didn't include the name of the club's town - assuming, unlike Port Vale, there is such a town.

One interesting characteristic of the fans we contacted was their wilful dismissal of the League tables, unless of course it was their club who were actually on top. As far as they are concerned, their team is clearly the best in some respect - their fans are less fair-weather; the ground is better; they haven't bought their way to success; they have bought their way to success (and that's why everyone else is jealous); their youth policy is superior; the pies have more meat - anything to grab a piece of the moral high ground.

Some clubs are definitely more chilled-out than others. Keeping the company of a fan whose formerly great team has hit the buffers takes some endurance. His mind is in turmoil. A win at Bury and the world is perfect. The club has turned the corner and is defiantly on its feet again. They're going to be taking 40,000 to the San Ciro in just a couple of years. That'll teach them to write us off.

And then disaster. Three days later, Tranmere grab a late equaliser and the black mist descends. The back four are a bunch of overpaid journeymen, the manager is a floundering bufoon and the chairman (who has pumped £4 million of his own money into the club) must leave the town immediately and make a full apology.

In contrast, the clubs with the most laid-back fans tend to have had low expectations historically but are tasting, or have tasted, a modicum of success in recent years. The prime examples are sides such as Charlton and Crewe Alexandra, and, although their Premiership escapades were a while back, we were struck at how level-headed Barnsley fans were.

Supporters we spoke to had a tendency to see absolutely no wrong in their club in general. The players might be awful, but they can always be dispensed with. We asked fans for any particularly witty or relevant chants that they had witnessed against their club. The vast majority found this an impossible task, as if they couldn't believe that anyone else was unable to recognise that their team were the greatest in the universe.

Without exception, every fan we spoke to had absolutely no interest in football violence. In some ways we found this surprising, sensing that at least some, though not actively involved, might derive titillation from the darker side of fanaticism. Though it isn't clear why, the media are fascinated with the concept of the middle-class hooligan, who it is breathlessly reported, likes to organise trouble on his 'mobile phone', suggesting that the reporter imagined that semaphore or smoke signals were the preferred method of fans' communications. As far as we can tell, this social phenomenon simply doesn't exist. A bored journalist, hoping to scare the wits out of his predominantly middle-class readership, has simply used some artistic licence in reporting the prosecution of a hospital orderly or an accounts clerk. By the time the piece hits the breakfast table, the two drunken hooligans have been promoted to consultant of obstetrics and senior partner in Price Waterhouse.

KEY TO CLUB PAGES

AKA / ANAGRAMS

Most of the 'akas' are in common usage with supporters of their rivals, though sometimes we have used some judgement in choosing the best. Crystal Palace are more commonly known as Crippled Parlarse than Crippled Alice, but the latter got our vote. Some are more widely used than others. In desperation, we had to cajole Leicester City fans to try and think of a derogatory name for Coventry. Their selections were mostly unprintable. Where we could find no record of any unofficial nickname, we have reverted to completely juvenile anagrams and assorted quips so nobody feels left out.

RECOMMENDED WEBSITE

Five years ago, the internet football culture was thriving. Not any more. Much of the independent spirit has been sucked out of the internet - swamped in a barrage of pop-ups, ads you can't get rid of and things you click on that download various nasties onto your hard-drive. The web presence of football clubs largely boils down to three 'networks'. Clubs' official sites are presently mostly controlled by Premium tv who own a clutch of media rights for clubs and the Football League itself. You have to register your personal details, to 'assist in the provision of services/products to you'. Great. Not one fan we spoke to had a good word to say for the official sites. The 'Footy Mad' and 'Rivals' (no relation) networks provide the platform for previously independent fans' sites. Rivals' sites allow users to flip between the clubs' message boards effortlessly, leading to a lot of scurrilous cross-posting which tends to end in rows. There are gripes about the amount of flashy advertising, but some have excellent content and deserve to feature in our 'recommended' list. The number of truly unofficial, non-revenue generating sites seems to be diminishing by the day, but a few excellent ones remain. Our top 10 are listed in the back.

WHO ARE YA?

A brief, condensed and possibly, totally unfair summary of the club - a mixture of the significant and totally trivial. The changes in the names of the Leagues and cup competitions are a major headache for compilers of football history. In general, we have tried to ignore the name of sponsors completely, sticking to the 'League Cup' rather than bothering with all its horrible variants over the years. However, some of the micky mouse competitions can only be identified using the sponsors' names. The changes in the names of the Leagues are a farce that everyone has to work round somehow. Before 1992, the divisions were named One to Four. Then in 2004, as the book was in its final stages, the Football League decided on another completely unnecessary re-branding, artificially promoting everyone in Division Three to League Two, Division Two to League One and Division One to The Championship. This was more than most fans could bear and makes historical comparisons almost impossible. The compromise we've settled on is to use the names:

Premiership, *Level One*, *Level Two* and *Level Three* usually regardless of what the divisions were called at the time. These reflect the divisional names before the 2004 change. So, for example, a reference to a team being promoted from Level Three to Level Two in 1979 would, at the time, have seen them go up from Division Four to Division Three. A team who is pushing for promotion from Level One in 2004 means that they are currently in the Championship. The only exceptions are when we are referring to teams in the past who were in the top division, what we now call The Premiership. We call this the *old First Division*. Rarely, phrases like 'Third Division South' creep in, which don't really correspond easily to the current divisional structure.

CELEBRITY FANS

These were surprisingly difficult to collate because, as far as ordinary fans are concerned, celebrity and football don't mix. Many are subject to hot debate. Being a famous fan of any club can be a risky business. Anyone who does publicly express an allegiance had better make sure that they attend plenty of games (and not just at home), and empty their pockets if the club runs into trouble. Whatever they do, on no account should they ever be seen associating with another side.

IN AND AROUND

Non-footballing nuggets from the locality.

POST-1960 LEAGUE POSITION

Each team's graph charts its League position from 1960, a starting date arrived at somewhat arbitrarily, representing the limits to which most current fans will have had personal experience. The team's average position is plotted, taking into account all seasons since 1960 where it competed in the League. Where a team entered the League after 1960, the values that make up its average start at the point of entry. Any side who dropped out of the Leagues for a spell, only to return later, has been given a value equivalent to finishing in last place in Level Three for the seasons it spent below the four main divisions. Within each graph the four divisions are colour-coded.

The 'yo-yo' rating is a measure of a side's volatility of League position, so those that have changed Leagues the most have a rating towards 100. Those who have remained the most static have values towards nil.

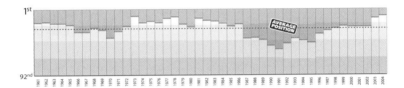

PROGRESS REPORT

A summary of the graph, often with an assessment of whether the side appears to be treading water, sinking like a stone, or storming towards glory.

ODDMENTS

Football factoids ranging from the important to the totally stupid.

NUTTER RATING

An assessment of a club's fans' propensity towards violence and mayhem based on published arrest figures and banning orders. One 'nutter' is awarded to the fans least likely to cause trouble, with five 'nutters' for the worst offenders. Instead of assessing raw arrest figures, they have been compiled by looking at the arrest rate compared to the club's average attendance. So a club with 40 arrests who only manages to pull in 4,000 at the turnstiles will have a higher nutter rating than a club with 80 arrests and an average attendance of 10,000. The full rankings are shown in the back.

RIVALS

There is an assumption that football rivalries are quite fixed, festering slowly. In fact, they are like shifting sands and very sensitive to the current positions of the clubs. They are also a phenomenon that exists entirely in fans' heads, so it is not surprising that there is very little agreement. Some fans can get quite heated over the subject of who is their biggest rival, i.e. Arsenal. Some regions are particularly complicated (the Lincolnshire-Humberside patterns of rivalries can be quite involved), and others are just plain difficult (Plymouth is especially tricky). Each rivalry's skull and crossbones rating works from one (tepid, transient and of minor interest) to five (intense, long-lasting and probably violent).

Rivalries come and go depending on how fans see the status of their team. The trick with identifying your rivals is generally to pick on a side that is reasonably local, but also in a slightly better League position than you. If fans of one club set their heights too high (for example, if Brentford named Chelsea as their biggest rivals), they are likely to get a curt rebuff from the opposition to the effect that they are not interested in such a tiny little club. This leads to endless posturing, along the lines of 'you are our rivals, you just don't admit it'.

Readers will find plenty to disagree with here. Our final ratings of the rivalries are extremely subjective and often amount to no more than a broad attempt to reflect what fans of the clubs have told us. In many cases, we're none the wiser. Some told us that the Everton/Liverpool derby is a matey affair with supporters mingling together in harmony. Others swore that the Merseyside 'friendly' rivalry was a complete media-inspired myth and that actually Liverpool was in the grips of a vicious civil war.

We have tried to avoid a blow-by-blow account of hooligan incidents except where they are necessary to illustrate key moments in rivalries. Hooliganism is generally something you can avoid. It is rare for those not seeking trouble to be victims of it. As such, we haven't adopted a 'what is the matter with fans these days?' tone, or at the other extreme, descended into long, florid narrative accounts of violent incidents with associated medical details.

FANS V.F.M

An assessment of a club's current 'feel-good factor' based on the standard of its facilities within its League, its current position compared to where it has been in the past, and its trajectory. (Those on an upward trend get more points). Again the full ranking is printed in the back.

PERFORMANCE AGAINST RIVALS

A pie chart of how a team has performed against its main rivals since 1960, including all meetings in the major domestic competitions.

YOUR GROUND'S TOO BIG FOR YOU

A measure of whether a club is able to fill its ground based on the ratio of stadium capacity to average attendance. A high rating indicates that tickets are scarce but there'll be a good atmosphere. A low rating indicates rows of empty seats and very little chance of much noise. Full ranking in the back.

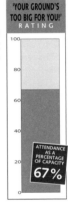

LOVE/HATE

Notable loves and hates for each side - some current, others going back a while.

CHANTS

Any particularly relevant, wounding, clever or ridiculous songs, mostly sung by the side's fans in question, but sometimes, totally unfairly, chants that have been directed at them.

DOH

An assortment of a cock-ups associated with each club.

ARSENAL

Recommended website: **www.arseweb.com**

WHO ARE YA?

Exactly how good are this lot? Labelled with a 'boring' tag for a substantial part of their recent history (not helped by probably the lowest TV camera gantry in senior football, making Highbury's matches look flat and one-dimensional), Arsenal surprised many when, at the turn of the millennium, they were crowned the 'team of the century'. They were promoted to the old First Division in 1919 and have stayed there ever since, making them the longest serving top-flight team and helping them maintain a 20th century average position of 8.5, just beating Liverpool's of 8.7. But it is what's happened in the few years since the turn of the 21st century that has had everyone except hardened Gunners' haters cooing. Arsène Wenger's record of winning the double twice and effortlessly achieving the longest unbeaten run in the history of League football is only tempered by Arsenal's decidedly mixed record in the Champions League.

CELEBRITY FANS
JOHN LYDON
Ex-Sex Pistols
OSAMA BIN LADEN
Cave dweller
RORY BREMNER
Impressionist

Wenger remained suitably tight-lipped on the subject of how long Arsenal's 49-match unbeaten spell, starting in 2003, was going to last. His reticence to make predictions was from bitter experience. A casual remark in 2002 that he would not be surprised if they "go unbeaten for the whole season" was the sort of curse the players didn't need. They went on to lose six matches, being overhauled by Manchester United on the final day, after one leading bookie had already paid out on Arsenal.

IN and AROUND

Woolwich Arsenal's role in weapons' development is more up-to-date than some might realise. Britain's first nuclear bomb was developed at the site in the 1940s, with the nose cones and electronics assembled at the not so aptly named Ha-ha Road.

If Arsenal were forced to stay at their current home much longer, they would be facing the prospect of playing in front of half the gates achievable by Manchester United. Highbury's capacity is only 38,500 and local residents have put up stiff resistance to any expansion of the facilities, hence the building of a new stadium at Ashburton Grove. London has traditionally been the capital of the floating supporter, eagerly rooting around in order to latch onto the merest whiff of success. This coupled with Nick Hornby's clarion call to the football middle classes, *'Fever Pitch'*, go some way to explaining why Highbury has a large proportion of the 'new breed' of supporters, unwilling to contribute to anything resembling a cauldron-like atmosphere. Taunts of 'Highbury is a library' have become commonplace with visitors.

Football fandom collided with conceptual art when Michael Landy staged his 'Breakdown' installation in an empty Oxford Street store. Destroying every single possession he owned, including, controversially, a collection of art works worth a small fortune, Landy hung on until the very end before putting his beloved Arsenal scarf in the crusher.

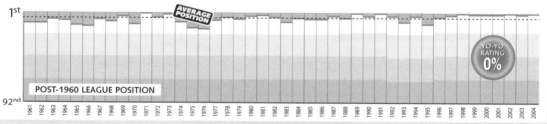

1st

AVERAGE POSITION

POST-1960 LEAGUE POSITION

YO-YO RATING 0%

92nd

1961 1962 1963 1964 1965 1966 1967 1968 1969 1970 1971 1972 1973 1974 1975 1976 1977 1978 1979 1980 1981 1982 1983 1984 1985 1986 1987 1988 1989 1990 1991 1992 1993 1994 1995 1996 1997 1998 1999 2000 2001 2002 2003 2004

PROGRESS REPORT

Taking League positions since 1960, Arsenal still have a bit to do to overhaul Liverpool, who have maintained an average finishing position of fourth. A Premiership win in 2004-05 would leave the Gunners with a post-1960 position of 6.09. Manchester United would need to finish below seventh place in order for Arsenal to move into second place in the roll call of the greatest clubs in recent history.

```
...Though popularly known as Highbury, the ground's official name is the Arsenal Stadium...
    ...Former manager Herbert Chapman got the name of the London Underground station,
                   Gillespie Road, changed to Arsenal...
...First team to win two domestic competitions in one season, the FA and League Cup, in 1993...
```

RIVALS

The phrase 'a history between the clubs' is often used to justify rivalries, even when there is scant evidence of much to divide fans in the past. Arsenal v Spurs is one of a surprisingly few derby matches where there was genuine bad feeling from the start. The Gunners moved from Plumstead, southeast London, in 1912, the first time a club had been moved outside its local area. Tottenham were, and remain, apoplectic at the outsiders parachuting into their patch. In the uncertainty surrounding the FA's plan to increase the size of the divisions, folklore has it that Arsenal were involved in some very sharp practices to achieve promotion from Division Two in 1919, despite only finishing fifth in the table. Their rise was at the expense of Tottenham, who'd ended up at the foot of the First. Arsenal's retort is that the FA rightly gave them the nod as it was they who had supported the League structure all along, whereas Spurs had originally put their faith in their competitors, the Southern League.

TOTTENHAM

Things became even more bitter following Arsenal's double winning season of 1971, in which the Championship was won with a Ray Kennedy header at White Hart Lane. Up to that point, Spurs could justifiably be seen as London's top dogs, having been the first side in the 20th century to pick up the League and FA Cup double. Arsenal then appeared to come along and dismantle all their records. Overall, Spurs contented themselves with the label of being attractive and entertaining, whilst Arsenal were dogged and defensive. Spurs were not thrilled as that long-standing characterisation of the two clubs went out of the window. Their appointment of Christian Gross as head coach in 1996 was seen at Highbury as a deliberate copycat move, aping the importation of the relaxed continental approach of Wenger a year earlier. The fact the move went horribly wrong for Spurs was treated as a symptom of their desperate game of catch-up.

MANCHESTER UNITED

The status of the Tottenham rivalry compared to that with Manchester United has become quite a fractious issue. There are two conflicting views on who Arsenal's main rivals are. Traditionalists are horrified that the Spurs' derby has been downplayed in favour of the constant bad mouthing of Manchester United. The naming of Ferguson's lot as number one rivals is seen in some quarters as a manufactured phenomenon in the minds of younger fans who never get to see football apart from Sky broadcasts – instead they should all be united in their hatred of the enemy down the road. Naturally, the reply is that all the Spurs' stuff should be consigned to the history books as they can hardly be seen to be anything more than minor players, even on the London scene.

CHELSEA

PERFORMANCE AGAINST RIVALS

MANCHESTER UNITED

WON 38%

LOST 37%

DRAWN 25%

SUPPORTERS' **VFM** **94%**

LOVE/HATE

Arsenal's heroes run to many pages, though special mention goes to *Ian Wright* who is largely seen as responsible for heralding the club's modern day revival. Whilst Alex Ferguson is an obvious target, his place in the hall of infamy could soon be taken by Chelsea boss *Jose Mourinho*, whose undiplomatic interview style is threatening to win him new enemies.

CHANTS

The craze for chants to the tune of The Pets Shop Boys/Village People '*Go West*' is typified by

'*1-0 to the Arsenal*',

though West Brom claim their

'*Go West....Bromwich Albion*'

came first.

DOH!!

Saudi Arabian Emirates Airlines will pay an estimated £3 million a year for the naming rights to Arsenal's new Ashburton Grove Stadium. Perhaps unaware that most fans loathe such sponsorship deals, the company and the club are expecting the new ground to be known as '*The Emirates Stadium*' for 15 years. To which many utter '*fat chance*'.

'YOUR GROUND'S TOO BIG FOR YOU!'

R A T I N G

100

80

60

40

20

0

ATTENDANCE AS A PERCENTAGE OF CAPACITY **99%**

ASTON VILLA

Recommended website: **www.thevillan.co.uk**

WHO ARE YA?

In the 60s, the fact that a fairly anonymous sounding borough of Britain's second city had its own university seemed quite strange to some. By 1981, it had gained fairly unlikely League Champions, and by 1982, it also could boast the winners of the European Cup. During the late 90s, Villa again seemed only a whisker away from the elite of British football. If you draw two lines across Britain, one bisecting south Manchester, the other through north London, the most successful side to occupy the 150 miles in between is Aston Villa.

Universally known as 'Deadly' Doug Ellis, the Villa Chairman has ploughed on, totally regardless of the fact that he is public enemy number one amongst his own club's supporters. Traumatising a string of ex-managers, he came to Villa having put Wolves into voluntary administration in 1982. His reputation for being reluctant to wipe the dust from his chequebook causes fans to accuse him of using the club as his mini-fiefdom, though he might point to the fact that the club has enjoyed relative stability and success under his autocracy.

CELEBRITY FANS
PRINCE WILLIAM
JIM LEWIS
Owner of three times
Gold Cup winner, Best Mate
FLOELLA BENJAMIN
Play School

IN and AROUND

The Aston Expressway joins the M6 at Spaghetti Juntion, Britain's most curvaceous motorway interchange. Hidden under the twisted concrete, alongside a canal, there is a small beach. Sun-seekers might like to arrange a tetanus booster before making a day of it.

With John Gregory at the helm, Villa gained a reputation for short-sighted foreign signings, the most disastrous being Alpay Ozalon, whose explosive spell at Villa consisted of a catalogue of appalling fouls, laughable errors and on-field fisticuffs with team-mates. Threatening to become England's number one hate figure following his boneheaded finger pointing at David Beckham during a European Championship qualifier in Turkey in 2003, Villa made a swift decision to release him to the peaceful waters of the South Korean league. Whilst at Villa, Alpay maintained a bi-weekly blog, variously titled 'It's great to be a group leader' and 'My telephone has been stolen'.

The faithful had only just got over the saga of Savo Milosevic, signed on the basis of his performance for Yugoslavia in Euro 2000. 'Miss-a-lot-evic' comes high on the all-time roll call of hopeless Premiership players. Disliked by fans, the feeling appeared to be reciprocated when, following a 5-0 defeat, he theatrically spat in the direction of Villa supporters. Still unable to shake off the 'dodgy signing' tag, £9.5 million Juan Pablo Angel is only semi-tolerated.

Refreshingly, fans don't appear to suffer from 'big-clubitis'. All West Midlands supporters have a good reputation for witty stoicism, and the Villa faithful haven't succumbed to anything approaching the arrogant swagger that certain other Premiership fans exhibit.

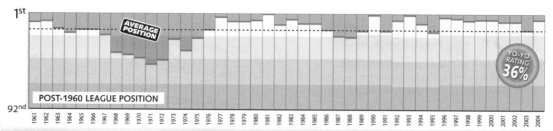

1st

AVERAGE POSITION

POST-1960 LEAGUE POSITION

YO-YO RATING 36%

92nd

1961 1962 1963 1964 1965 1966 1967 1968 1969 1970 1971 1972 1973 1974 1975 1976 1977 1978 1979 1980 1981 1982 1983 1984 1985 1986 1987 1988 1989 1990 1991 1992 1993 1994 1995 1996 1997 1998 1999 2000 2001 2002 2003 2004

PROGRESS REPORT

Founder members of the football league, Villa clocked up six Championships before 1910, including the 2nd ever double. Not a lot followed until promotion to the old First Division in 1975, since when they've cemented their standing as solid top flight long-termers. Aside from a one season spell back in Level One in 1987-88, they have managed to avoid too many relegation scrapes. Between 1996 and 2002, they boosted their long-term average further by finishing no lower than 8th place during the seven seasons, though they've slipped below realistic European contention since. Villa are second only to Liverpool with their tally of five League Cups.

```
    ...JR Tolkien struck upon his wizard, Gandalf, by inverting the name of his
                    favourite Villa player of the 1930s, Alf Gand...
    ...Villa were the original 'claret and blue' club. West Ham and Burnley copied them...
```

RIVALS

Success, measured in terms of Premiership status, has been reasonably shared out amongst the Birmingham/West Midlands teams in recent years. But with Villa consistently top of the local pile, their rivalries have undergone minor readjustments as they have been joined, sometimes fleetingly, by their local adversaries.

BIRMINGHAM

Without a top division meeting in 16 years, Villa's rivalry with Birmingham was rekindled in 2002, with a 3-0 defeat. But the sense of historical superiority Villa's fans enjoy is plain to see: "They are more irritants than rivals. Up till promotion, they were just little people who bleated on about what an unfair existence they had. Since promotion, the above still applies, but now they think they are God's chosen ones and the best team in the world. They think Europe is a possibility, when, sadly, the closest they will get is the Burberry induced 18-30 holidays they take to sunspots. They have a tendency to appear when they win and we lose. To them, the time before their promotion to the Premier League has been erased. They seem to have thousands of fans who claim they were season ticket holders in the darkest days".

Such is the indistinct geographical boundary between the two clubs, the rivalry tends to split families down the middle à la Liverpool/Everton. Some areas are roughly 50-50, providing much fuel for school and workplace rows.

WEST BROM

SUPPORTERS' VFM 65%

PERFORMANCE AGAINST RIVALS
BIRMINGHAM

WON 43%

LOST 39%

DRAWN 17%

Their Midlands' rivals tend to hate Villa more than Villa hate them, evidence that they are top of the pile. When in the Premiership, reasonably nearby Coventry were of absolutely no concern to Villa; if anything, Leicester City were treated as more of a threat. With West Brom and Wolves involved in their own bitter local dispute, the historical ferociousness between Villa and Wolves has lessened.

WOLVES

Villa's moment of history was slightly soured by the inexplicable decision of Ron Saunders to jump ship to Birmingham in 1982. Both sets of fans reacted with disbelief, but Birmingham inflicted a painful blow by beating the European Champions 3-0 in their first meeting after Villa's triumph.

'YOUR GROUND'S TOO BIG FOR YOU!'
RATING

LOVE/HATE

H A T E

Perhaps it is the case that *Doug Ellis* is a rational man in a thoroughly irrational world. Either way, the scale of the venom aimed at him is only slightly less incredible than his ability not to give a monkey's. Such is the size of the lettering of the stand named after him, it may be the most prominent feature of Birmingham from a satellite. A 'gift' to Ellis on his 70th birthday, many fans spurn the name change, preferring to stick to The Witton Lane Stand.

CHANTS

A weird example of weaving a player's name into an existing chant

'There's only Juan Pablo Angel'

100

80

60

40

ATTENDANCE AS A PERCENTAGE OF CAPACITY
85%

20

0

DOH!!

Investors in the beautiful game haven't been enriched with Aston Villa's shares; 1175p in 1997, trading around 280p in 2004.

BARNSLEY

Recommended website: **www.barnsleyfc.net**

WHO ARE YA?

It was the miners' strike that put Barnsley firmly on the map and the Iron lady who wanted it quickly wiped off. Rarely a popular tourist haunt, the town has adapted to the brave new world of the service sector. If you are trying to return your dud PC, bought online from a reputable company who have debited your visa card but failed to deliver, the call centre employee may be putting you on hold from Barnsley (or Bangalore). Although lacking in skilled jobs, it has commuting potential for the major northern cities, and the wilds of the Peak District on its doorstep.

CELEBRITY FANS
MICHAEL PARKINSON
Chat show host
DICKIE BIRD
Cricket Umpire
HARRY HAMER
Chumbawamba

With Barnsley bruised and battered over the 80s political spasms, the football club came to provide an outlet for passion and community feeling. In spite of Leeds only being 12 miles up the M1, and Sheffield on its southern boundary, Barnsley has pulled in the second best crowds in Division Two. The love for the underdog mentality saw more than just locals celebrating their debut in the Premiership in 1997. The (relatively) small town boys beating Manchester United and Liverpool were two of the increasingly few Premiership fairytales.

IN and AROUND

A study showed that on average only 115 people left the borough each year, making Barnsley's population amongst the most stable in Britain.

The drop from the Premiership nearly sunk Barnsley for good, prompting fans' action groups to bail out the club. None more so than Mr Save Barnsley FC. Courtesy of deed poll, Paul Stevenson explored all avenues to get publicity for the cause. With stability now returned under Peter Risdale (ex-Leeds), the artist formerly known as Save has reverted to his previous name.

Though not a town associated with asparagus appetizers and Hollywood previews, Barnsley residents thought things were about to go upmarket with the arrival of Liz Hurley, only to find she was buying (sorry, buying in) Barnsley, Gloucestershire. But the real culture is provided by Barnsley FC's first poet-in-residence, long-time fan Ian Macmillan. He was Danny Wilson's first Premiership signing and puts the club alongside such greats as Marks and Spencer who also have their very own scribe, presumably churning out ditties about good quality underwear.

1st

POST-1960 LEAGUE POSITION

YO-YO RATING 48%

AVERAGE POSITION

92nd

1961 1962 1963 1964 1965 1966 1967 1968 1969 1970 1971 1972 1973 1974 1975 1976 1977 1978 1979 1980 1981 1982 1983 1984 1985 1986 1987 1988 1989 1990 1991 1992 1993 1994 1995 1996 1997 1998 1999 2000 2001 2002 2003 2004

PROGRESS REPORT

110 years on, Barnsley finally made it to top-flight football in the 1997-1998 season, but it lasted only a season, finishing second to bottom. It was a terrible year generally for staying up, with all three newbies getting relegated immediately.

The recent dip into the Level Two puts Barnsley below their natural standing, having spent 16 consecutive years in the Level One since 1981, and 30 consecutive years in their early history. Not ones for excessive movement, they tend to take root wherever they end up – a habit they'd like to swiftly change.

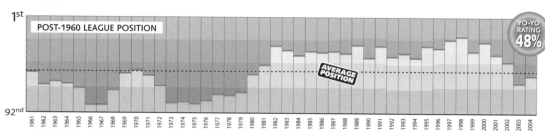

...In 1946 before an FA Cup replay, managers at a Barnsley colliery put up a notice asking how many miners would be attending a funeral on that day...
...Have been in Level One for more seasons than any other league club...

RIVALS

The (lack of) relationship between Barnsley and Sheffield Wednesday existed well before the career movements of Danny Wilson. An ex-Wednesday player, Wilson's first managerial post guided Barnsley to the heights of the Premiership, only to go back down the road when the dream was over. In some ways, he proved to be Barnsley's ultimate weapon, struggling for three seasons at Wednesday, before they too disappeared from the Premiership in 2000.

SHEFFIELD WEDNESDAY

Whilst a minority of Barnsley fans dislike The Blades with an equal intensity, Wednesday are far and away the number one loathing – the sort of bad feeling often aimed at previously great clubs whose fortunes take a turn for the worse. Slipping down the leagues, they cling on to the assumption that it is a temporary spell, looking down their noses at fans of 'smaller' teams, even when they are beaten by them.

PERFORMANCE AGAINST RIVALS
SHEFFIELD WEDNESDAY

WON 27%

LOST 55%

DRAWN 18%

Barnsley suffer multiple irritations with being close to a 'massive' club. The theory goes that Barnsley could easily rival 'Wendy' for support if all football fans in Barnsley actually went to watch Barnsley, leading to the general feeling that the big city clubs have only got that way at the expense of the surrounding towns' sides. As for their status, from Barnsley it looks like one huge delusion of grandeur "based on a rusting heap of metal they can't afford to live in". Wednesday's preciousness gives the impression that they "watch Brazil every Saturday".

SHEFFIELD UNITED

Interestingly for towns that are so close, there is a sense of a cultural split, with Barnsley characterising Sheffield as 'northern cockneys', i.e. geographically north but with the swagger of perceived prosperity. Sheffield folk's odd pronunciation of 'th's' (as if the word begins with a 'D') has led to the nickname dee-dahs. Needless to say, the "infernal tootling band" at Hillsborough are unlikely to get many bookings for Barnsley weddings.

SUPPORTERS' VFM 63%

LEEDS UNITED

Depending on divisional standing Leeds United, Huddersfield, Rotherham and Bradford can get up the Barnsley noses. Sheffield United, seen as having a more authentic South Yorkshire pedigree, largely let off the hook. They are "whinging, scrubby set of sore losers" to some, though unusually, there is a good word for Neil Warnock; "anyone who can wind up Phil Thompson that much can't be all bad".

LOVE/HATE

Although customary to blame the referee for losing a match, the 'Gary Willard' effect is held, by some fans, as responsible for much more. The sending-off of three Barnsley players in their 3-2 defeat by Liverpool in March 1998 saw incensed fans invade the pitch and the referee retreat to the dressing room. The game came after three consecutive league victories but was followed by just four points from 27 and relegation.

Overlooking his Wednesday connections, *Danny Wilson* is a hero to many Barnsley fans as the manager who achieved the fondly remembered temporary trip to the Premiership.

CHANTS

The unlikely

'It's just like watching Brazil'

can (occasionally) be heard at Oakwell. In a comfortable lead, Stockport replied

'It's just like playing Scotland'

(who had recently been held to a draw by the Faroe Islands).

'YOUR GROUND'S TOO BIG FOR YOU!'
R A T I N G

100

80

ATTENDANCE AS A PERCENTAGE OF CAPACITY 41%

60

40

20

0

DOH!!

The Wilson magic almost had immediate effect. In his first season at the club, Barnsley finished sixth in Level One – a position that in any other year would have earned a play-off place. But in 1995, the Premiership was shrunk with only two going up.

BIRMINGHAM CITY

Recommended website: **www.dspace.dial.pipex.com/town/park/yfh45/index.shtml**

WHO ARE YA?

The original Small Heath club were quite a progressive lot in their formative years but the combination of early ambition and a substantial number of fanatically loyal fans have not been sufficient to produce anything other than an average record. Younger footie followers might, until recently, have thought of Birmingham as ranking around third or fourth in the West Midlands' pecking order. Their unofficial nickname, the Bluenoses, is used both as a term of abuse by others (as in being left out in the cold), and by Blues' fans themselves. But after a couple of decades in the wilderness, they had little trouble in establishing themselves in the Premiership.

Having gone down to Level Two in 1989 for the first time in their history, Birmingham City's backroom dramas didn't hint at there being a new dawn. In 1992, the club was indirectly hit by the collapse of the BCCI bank, who had lent funds to the owners, the Kumar brothers, to rescue the club. Whilst in receivership, an unlikely white knight appeared in the shape of owner of the borderline newspaper, The Sunday Sport, David Sullivan. The team he introduced to the club was a heady mix of personalities, with Barry Fry as manager and Karen Brady as managing director. Brady was treated with great suspicion by supporters and derision by other fans as her media coverage was wildly out of proportion to her importance. Though seen at the time as a puerile attempt to increase the club's totty rating, Brady has largely answered her critics on account of her sheer longevity. The era has been characterised by a certain amount of commercial over-stretching. At one point, the club attempted to sell domestic gas supplies.

> **CELEBRITY FANS**
> **JEFF LYNE & BEV BEVAN**
> *ELO*
> **JASPER CARROT**
> Comedian

> **IN and AROUND**
> Birmingham has 35 miles of canals, beating Venice's 26 miles, though it has to be said that the Northern Italian city is tiny in comparison.

After the partial success of local hero Trevor Francis, Birmingham's next appointment was a bit of a shot in the dark. Current god, Steve Bruce was sacked by Crystal Palace for expressing a mild interest in the Blues job, having had a choppy managerial career with four jobs in three years.

St Andrews has gained a reputation for having the best atmosphere in the Premiership, helped by vociferous fans who ensure that the visit for away fans is particularly intimidating. In this league table, it is probably second only to Cardiff.

For a club that has become synonymous with misfortune, it was apt that the stadium fire they suffered in 1942 had comic overtones. Attempting to put out a small fire in the main stand, a volunteer fireman emptied a container of what he assumed was water onto the flames. It was actually petrol. The resulting inferno completely gutted the main stand.

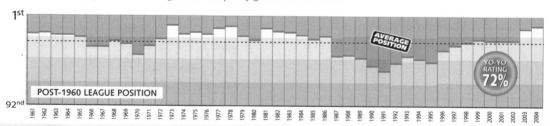

POST-1960 LEAGUE POSITION

1st ... 92nd

1961 1962 1963 1964 1965 1966 1967 1968 1969 1970 1971 1972 1973 1974 1975 1976 1977 1978 1979 1980 1981 1982 1983 1984 1985 1986 1987 1988 1989 1990 1991 1992 1993 1994 1995 1996 1997 1998 1999 2000 2001 2002 2003 2004

AVERAGE POSITION

YO-YO RATING 72%

PROGRESS REPORT

There is now a generation of fans to whom Birmingham's 70s' side means next to nothing. Although Trevor Francis was a bright spark, the club's 12 seasons in the top-flight up to 1986 never mustered better than their 10th, achieved in the first year they were there. The mid-80s' rot saw them hit a low of 12th in Level Two in 1991. It took four consecutive Level One play-offs before promotion to the Premiership in 2002.

```
         ...The first goalscorer at St Andrews was awarded a piano as a bonus...
...St Andrews was almost destroyed by 20 separate hits from German bombers during World War II...
          ...Didn't add the 'City' bit to their name until after World War II...
```

RIVALS

The Birmingham/Villa rivalry is a text book case of bad blood between teams from the moment of their formation. Aston Villa were not only original members of the Football League, it was virtually their idea to form a league in the first place. Small Heath, as Birmingham were then called, were up against it from day one. Birmingham FC historians would claim that it was their club that won the first meeting in 1879, though there is some dispute over whether it was 1-0 or 1-1.

ASTON VILLA

WEST BROM

In some ways, Birmingham were more forward thinking than Villa in the early days. They turned professional and in 1895, were the first club to form themselves into a Limited Company. This was all a bit too snazzy for the Victorian Football authorities who snubbed their application to join the new League, preferring Wolves and West Brom.

WOLVES

It's easy to forget that, for a period in the 60s and early 70s, the Blues were riding high over Villa, who had a spell playing second fiddle in Level One. The situation reversed itself in the 80s, with Birmingham on the slide while Villa were gaining European glory and establishing themselves as top-flight long-stayers.

SUPPORTERS' VFM 96%

PERFORMANCE AGAINST RIVALS
ASTON VILLA

WON 39% LOST 44% DRAWN 17%

There is some puzzlement over the differing reputations of West Midlands' fans. Birmingham and Wolves are often seen as having a hooligan problem, whereas Villa and West Brom are better behaved. Birmingham fans were seen as relatively blameless for the riot that erupted after their last-minute winner at Millwall in the play-offs of 2002, but there is clearly a small element who will seek out trouble in order to try and boost their club's bad-boy reputation. This tends to lead to problems with others, such as Cardiff and Stoke, who have a minority with similar intentions.

Villa had chalked up six straight wins before the two reacquainted themselves in 2002. Fear of trouble at the game led to an unprecedented poster campaign featuring pictures of fans as workmen united in their 'friendship'. The combination of this and the slogan 'working together, playing together' gave the campaign a distinctly Village People type feel. By 2003, the turnaround in the clubs' fortunes was seen to be complete with Birmingham's 13th place, beating Villa by three positions in the Premiership table.

LOVE/HATE

The transfer of *Dwight Yorke* ♡ to Birmingham in 2004 was risky to say the least seeing his previous links with Villa. He was held in very low esteem after taunting Blues' fans when scoring against them the previous year. Thirty goals in a season might win them round.

They're more certain about *Ron Atkinson*.

CHANTS

Andrew Lloyd Webber's tear-jerker has been transformed into

"Don't cry for me, Aston Villa... the truth is I cannot stand you".

DOH!!

In 2004 Birmingham chairman David Gold was 'stunned' that Karen Brady had been omitted from the guest list for 'Her Majesty's Women of Excellence' lunch. He earnestly complained that *"I'm afraid its yet another case of the Second City being left out"*.

Brady had received an invite months before, but hadn't bothered to tell Gold.

'YOUR GROUND'S TOO BIG FOR YOU!'
R A T I N G

100

80

60

40

20

0

ATTENDANCE AS A PERCENTAGE OF CAPACITY
97%

BLACKBURN ROVERS

Recommended website: **www.brfcs.biz**

WHO ARE YA?

With every year that goes by, Blackburn's feat of winning the Premiership in 1995 will look better and better. Since then the honours have been carved up by Manchester United and Arsenal. With a noticeable gap opening up between a handful of elite clubs and the rest, Blackburn look destined to go into history as the last non top-tier club (to put it diplomatically) that have got their hands on the Premiership. The jibe from opposing fans that they bought their success, although partially true, is probably unfair, since these days, success doesn't really come any other way. Where many have tried flashing the cash to grab the title, Blackburn are possibly the solitary example of an occasion when it actually worked.

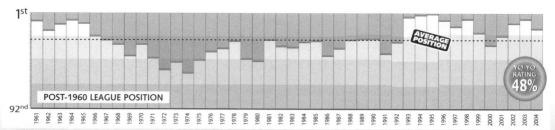

CELEBRITY FANS
JACK STRAW
Labour Cabinet member
JIM BOWEN
TV Presenter - *Bullseye*
DENIS TAYLOR
Ex-Snooker World Champion

The money was provided by local multi-millionaire Jack Walker, who held a majority stake in the club from 1991. The total bill was around £23 million - including a record £3.6 million for Alan Shearer from Southampton - and in 1994, splashing out £5 million for Chris Sutton. The club is used to the taunt 'plastics' (as in plastic credit card) to belittle their efforts. Despite a glorious early history (they were founders of the Football League), by as late as 1986 the club was reeling from debts, a major ground fire and average gates of 8,000. Relegated in 1999, amidst acrimony, with players and fans alike accused of a lack of commitment, it would have been easy for the club to sink back to relative obscurity. But with Graeme Souness returning them to the Premiership, Blackburn are one of the very few who can genuinely claim to have become a 'big' club from next to nowhere.

IN and AROUND
Blackburn is one of the three football towns to get a namecheck in a Beatles song. (Southampton and Liverpool are the others). Inspired by a report in the Daily Mail about the cost of employing someone to check road surfaces, John Lennon penned the line '4,000 holes in Blackburn, Lancashire' for 'Day in the Life' on Sgt.Pepper.

With a reputation for veering between the magnificent and the terrible under Souness, it's still not exciting enough to keep one loyal from dozing off. The George Hotel in Darwen helpfully provides a bus to the ground, but after over-enjoying a pre-match drink, one fan claims never to have actually stayed awake throughout an entire game. Frequently accompanied by his 5-year old nephew, it is rumoured that the lad has come to know him as 'Uncle Knobhead'.

1st — POST-1960 LEAGUE POSITION — 92nd

1961 1962 1963 1964 1965 1966 1967 1968 1969 1970 1971 1972 1973 1974 1975 1976 1977 1978 1979 1980 1981 1982 1983 1984 1985 1986 1987 1988 1989 1990 1991 1992 1993 1994 1995 1996 1997 1998 1999 2000 2001 2002 2003 2004

AVERAGE POSITION

YO-YO RATING 48%

PROGRESS REPORT

Blackburn will need to hang around in the Premiership for a few more seasons before their post-1960 average creeps out of Level One. With Souness gone this might be asking a lot. The Walker era effectively jumped them 24 places up the pecking order.

```
          ...Once beat Manchester United 18-0 in a friendly
        (though it was when The Reds were still at Newton Heath)...
               ...Margaret Thatcher was made an honorary director...
      ...A contender for best ground name - their first home was 'Oozehead'...
```

RIVALS

It probably takes something special to be hated by Burnley, because with so many clubs naming them as rivals, they must be exhausted with all their Derby games. In many ways the Blackburn/Burnley dislike is incredible. Of all Burnley's foes, it is Blackburn they name as their number one hate, but in recent history the teams have hardly met. Their paths crossed in 2000/01 in Level One, but you need to go back to 1982 to find them in the same league. Geographically, both Preston North End and Bolton are closer. The first significant 'incident' between the teams dates back to the turn of the century, when it is said, Blackburn were the first team to dabble in the 'international' transfer market (well, Scotland). Said to be paying some of its players (illegally, as clubs had a strict amateur status) the 'big money' team took on a decidedly rough and ready side of Burnley amateurs. Most of the Blackburn team stalked off at half-time, complaining of the opposition's dirty tactics. The goalie, however, decided to play on solo, but Burnley couldn't score as they were adjudged to be constantly offside!

BURNLEY

SUPPORTERS' VFM
65%

By the time the two met in 2000, bad feeling was rife with Burnley on the up and Blackburn seemingly going in the other direction, having rubbed their neighbours' noses in it with their recent successes. Described as 'worse than Celtic v Rangers', the atmosphere was hostile in the extreme, with police mounting a huge operation to keep the sets of supporters apart.

Towns that are sandwiched between the two suffer the intensity of the rivalry, notably Clitheroe, Darwen and Accrington. When Accrington Stanley went bust in 1962, many felt that the Burnley Chairman, Bob Lord, could have done more to help the ailing neighbours, as he was an influential figure in English football at the time. Nowadays, the rivalry is considered no laughing matter. When residents of the two towns cross each other's paths there is a tacit understanding that talking about football is liable to lead to trouble. Burnley think of themselves as Lancastrians through and through, but there is a perception in Blackburn that they are not as 'pure' as they claim, with an accent that has suspicious traces of the vowel pronunciation of West Yorkshire. They also make the accusation that a lot of Burnley fans seep across the border, from towns such as Skipton in Yorkshire.

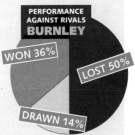

PERFORMANCE AGAINST RIVALS
BURNLEY

WON 36%
LOST 50%
DRAWN 14%

The now common nickname for opposing fans 'The Dingles', after the unfeasibly thick family in *Emmerdale*, is a favourite taunt used by Blackburn, made doubly delicious by the fact that the actor who plays Zak Dingle comes from Burnley.

LOVE/HATE

Only one contender, *Jack Walker*, who died in 2000 having dragged Blackburn from the doldrums to the Premiership title.

Roy Hodgson  is not fondly remembered for either his side's workaday performances or for his reputation for drawing a huge salary.

CHANTS

Blackburn have gained a slight notoriety for their lack of original chants - though they recently claim to have originated the

'You're just a small town in....'

craze, having used

'You're just a small town in Yorkshire'

against bitter (Lancashire) rivals Burnley. In turn, Manchester United have taunted Blackburn with

'You're just a small town in Burnley'.

YOUR GROUND'S TOO BIG FOR YOU!
RATING

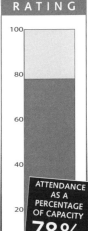

100
80
60
40
20
0

ATTENDANCE AS A PERCENTAGE OF CAPACITY
78%

DOH!!

Roy Hodgson paid a staggering £7.5 million for relatively unknown striker Kevin Davis in 1988, whilst letting go of John Hendry. The cash succeeded only in buying a side that plummeted down the Premiership table. Following the Premiership title, Dalglish made a hasty dash upstairs as Director of Football, in a move that is still talked about in conspiratorial terms. It started four years of consistent decline.

BLACKPOOL

A.K.A. DONKEY LASHERS

Recommended website: **www.seasiders.net**

WHO ARE YA?

The Blackpool coast has a deserved reputation of being battered with high winds and freezing rain – and out of season it's even worse. With the semi-renovated Bloomfield Road barely inland from the prom, it's hardly surprising that Blackpool has had its fair share of weather related incidents. It was certainly too much for the softies from Chelsea in October 1932. In a typical northwest blizzard, five of the team collapsed because of the cold, leaving the remaining six to battle on to a 0-4 defeat. Around the same time, Blackpool's full-back died when heading a heavy, wet ball.

Flamboyant socialist millionaire Owen Oyston kept the club alive during the dark times in the 80s promising to move the club from the increasingly dilapidated Bloomfield Road. But planning hassles and in-fighting were aggravated further by Oyston's conviction of rape in 1996. Refusing to accept his guilt (lengthening his time in jail), the case has a minor place in the annals of legal conspiracy as the law concerning admissibility of evidence in rape cases was changed six weeks before the trial. With the club flailing around in Level Three, the ground fell into such a state of disrepair that it was hard for the casual passer-by to imagine it could possibly stage football at all. With its creaking stands, peeling paint and 40-year-old billboards, Bloomfield Road became a spooky monument to a different age.

Indeed, the club has seen some particularly dark moments. In 1968, there was much media wringing of hands after an ammonia throwing incident. It saw the first murder of a supporter when, in 1974, a Blackpool fan was fatally stabbed at a league game with Bolton. It was largely in reaction to this incident that the segregation of rival supporters became standard practice. The club also holds the uncovetted record of being the scene of the first deployment of police in full riot gear, when in 1989, after a day of skirmishes in the town, Birmingham City fans rioted inside the ground, despite an attendance of only 5,737.

CELEBRITY FANS

LENNY BENNETT
Comedian
BILL BEAUMONT
Ex-England Rugby Captain – *Question of Sport*

IN and AROUND

If laid end to end, the number of hot dogs eaten in Blackpool every day would stretch for 47 miles.

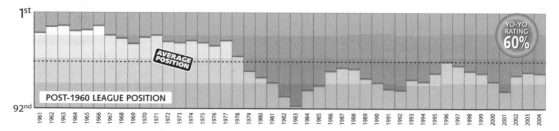

1st

YO-YO RATING 60%

AVERAGE POSITION

POST-1960 LEAGUE POSITION

92nd

1961 1962 1963 1964 1965 1966 1967 1968 1969 1970 1971 1972 1973 1974 1975 1976 1977 1978 1979 1980 1981 1982 1983 1984 1985 1986 1987 1988 1989 1990 1991 1992 1993 1994 1995 1996 1997 1998 1999 2000 2001 2002 2003 2004

PROGRESS REPORT

Although it is customary to use the word 'glorious' to describe Blackpool's history, they have never actually won the League Championship. After their triumph in the Matthews FA Cup final of 1953 and a Championship runners-up place in 1956, a very gradual slide took hold until a fixture backlog caused by the bad winter of 1978-79 was partly responsible in seeing them slip into the Level Two for the first time. Following a further drop, they have maintained an erratic record pivoted somewhere around the top of Level Two.

```
           ...Only league team with Tangerine strip...
    ...'Lost League because of Hitler' (Blackpool were top of the old First Division
           after three games before football was suspended for World War II)...
    ...The Bolton v Blackpool Cup final of 1953 was the first match to be televised live...
```

RIVALS

Fans of Blackpool and Preston North End endlessly argue over the virtues of each other's clubs, frequently having to hark back to near-ancient history to find much to get excited about. But the winning hand from the Matthews/Finney era can probably be played by Blackpool – not so much because of superiority on the pitch but the overall attractiveness of the town.

PRESTON NORTH END
☠☠☠☠☠

Until the early 60s, Blackpool was a haven for workers from the Lancashire towns, escaping from the pollution of the mills for their annual two-week break, constantly amazed at how fresh the seaside air was compared to the fug they'd been used to. The workers generally headed west to Blackpool, the better off to the more tranquil east coast resorts such as Bridlington.

In latter days, the clubs' records are startlingly similar. They kept each other company as they both plummeted down the divisions in the late 70s. But unlike The Seasiders, Preston managed to plot their escape to Level One the First in 2000 and haven't been in much danger of rejoining them – adding a tinge of jealousy into the mix. Worse still, Preston's long awaited promotion to Level One coincided with Blackpool diving into Level Three. Their self-esteem has been further dented by Wigan and traditional rivals, Burnley, reaching Level One as well.

BURNLEY
☠☠☠☠☠

With a slight over-reliance on the past, both clubs indulge in some aimless comparisons between their two best known stars. The Matthews versus Tom Finney debate doesn't get much further than Matthews was never really a goal scorer (according to Preston) and Finney was only a plumber (according to Blackpool). To give them some credit, Preston still tend to name now lower division Blackpool as their main rivals, though at only 10 miles away Blackburn would seem a more logical choice.

The date of the first derby game reveals a slight anomaly. Generally recorded as a meeting at Deepdale in 1895, Blackpool weren't even officially formed until 1897.

PERFORMANCE AGAINST RIVALS
PRESTON NORTH END

WON 36%
LOST 39%
DRAWN 25%

SUPPORTERS'
VFM
29%

LOVE/HATE

With Dad doing porridge, handing over the reins to son Karl Oyston ♡ 👊 (whose interest in football seemed questionable) seemed doomed to failure. With ex-Liverpool bruiser *Steve McMahon* 👊 as manager, the two soon clashed over the usual chairman/gaffer issues of lack of cash, ambition etc. etc. But a home crowd over-reliant on the chant 'Steve McMahon's Tangerine Army' fell silent in January 2004, as their former hero announced he was walking out, giving veiled hints that disagreements with Oyston were behind it. There then followed a 'should I stay or should I go?' saga with McMahon hanging on, reputedly annoying players in the process, until finally walking at the end of the season.

CHANTS

Clearly not at ease with the plans to turn the town into an international leisure resort:

'Get back on your bus and leave Blackpool to us, day trippers go home'

'YOUR GROUND'S TOO BIG FOR YOU!'
RATING

100

80

60

40

20

0

ATTENDANCE AS A PERCENTAGE OF CAPACITY
62%

DOH!!

Want to name part of your stadium after the greatest player in the club's history? It seems straightforward. But as Blackpool's contribution to unbelievably crass commercialisation, the West Stand of their partially developed new stadium was named 'The Pricebuster Sir Stanley Matthews Stand'.

BOLTON WANDERERS

Recommended website: **www.boltonwanderers-mad.co.uk**

WHO ARE YA?

The theory goes that the old established Lancashire clubs were unduly affected by the introduction of the maximum wage in the early 60s. Whatever the reason, by the 1980s, a clutch of the founding League clubs were facing ruin. As recently as 1988, Bolton were messing around in Level Three with average gates of just over 4,000. It was an act of semi-desperation that saw them drag their way out of the mire. Upon the closure of the Bury to Bolton line, they took the unusual step of flogging half the railway end of their old Burnden Park ground to make way for a supermarket. Having raised a bit of cash, a faltering assault was made on the top-flight.

CELEBRITY FANS
DAVE SPIKEY
Actor/Comedian, *Phoenix Nights*
VERNON KAY
Presenter, *TOTP*
KENNETH WOLSTENHOLM
Football Commentator

The springboard for this effort was the building of the nifty new Reebok Stadium, even if it was in Lostock rather than Bolton itself. Sensing that the place needed its atmosphere perking up, the club hired a band of drummers

IN and AROUND

Whilst an anagram of Bolton, Noblot is used as a term of mild abuse, it is its palindrome (backwards spelling), Notlob, that is better known following its mention in the full length version of Monty Python's parrot sketch.

and dancers, along with 2,000 inflatable bongos. Although constantly in the list of clubs that pundits favoured for the drop, Sam Allardyce defied his detractors by building a side that, by 2004-2005, were seen as amongst the Premiership's most attractive outfits, though the manager is a long way from the sophisticated breed of European managerial imports. But behind his 'I'll have that drain unblocked for you in a jiffy' exterior seems to lie a thoroughly modern boss – taking coaching techniques rather more high-tech than some fans welcomed when spending a fortune on software to monitor a player's performance. Bolton were the first to use the Teamcard system at the turnstiles – a season ticket/loyalty scheme that fans put through a swipe as they go in.

Bolton were forced to literally take the shirt from one supporter's back. Travelling to a match at Arsenal as a non-squad member, Djibril Diawara had an emergency call-up for Nick Southall, though the club didn't bring his kit. A search of supporters of a similar size found Lee Houghton, a 34-year-old postman, whose shirt was whisked away and hastily patched up with Diawara's name and squad number. But the Senegalese international's reputation for boozing the night before games soon earned him a plane ticket back to the Italian League and a nomination as the club's worst player in recent history.

The club's nickname The Trotters is one of those shrouded in obscurity. Some granddads reckon it used to be local slang for practical jokers.

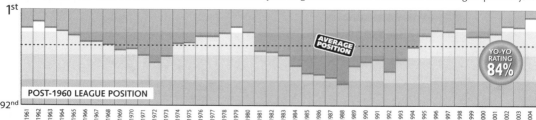

1st

POST-1960 LEAGUE POSITION

AVERAGE POSITION

YO-YO RATING 84%

92nd

1961 1962 1963 1964 1965 1966 1967 1968 1969 1970 1971 1972 1973 1974 1975 1976 1977 1978 1979 1980 1981 1982 1983 1984 1985 1986 1987 1988 1989 1990 1991 1992 1993 1994 1995 1996 1997 1998 1999 2000 2001 2002 2003 2004

PROGRESS REPORT

Bolton's relationship with the old First Division came to an end in 1964 and with the exception of two seasons in the top-flight in the late 70s, they didn't look like a serious longer term proposition until nearing the turn of the Millennium. Totally down and out when relegated from Level Two in 1987, it started a period where virtually every season promised/threatened a change of division. From 1986 to 2003, they only had three 'middling' seasons. In the other 14, they went up, down, were involved in play-offs or had a last ditch relegation struggle. A hyper-wobble of three separate spells in the Premiership gave way to the tranquillity of 8th in 2004, the club's highest finish since 1960.

```
          ...First goal nets to be used were at their ground...
     ...First club to use squad numbers (1995)...Reebok's head office is at stadium...
```

RIVALS

Half the population didn't always hate Manchester United. In the shadow of the Munich air crash, there was only one side neutrals wanted to support in the 1958 Cup final. They were disappointed, as Bolton won 2-0 to complete their fourth and last Cup triumph. Today, United are natural rivals with the geographical borders between the two becoming blurred, and debates raging locally as to whether Bolton is in Lancashire or if its official status as part of Greater Manchester is bearable. But at least one part of the 'small town in Manchester' jibe is untrue, because with the promotion of Sunderland to city status, Bolton is left as the largest town in England.

MANCHESTER UNITED

SUPPORTERS' VFM 94%

With local magistrates handing out a comparatively high number of banning orders, the club's zero-tolerance attitude to disorder at the Reebok has possibly caused the problems to be shifted elsewhere. In 2003, police clampdowns in the town centre led to the unorthodox tactic of an arrangement with Manchester United hooligans that anyone looking for a fight should head off to Chorley instead. Bolton's moans with United don't differ much from those expressed elsewhere; that their fans expect everything, that they can't accept responsibility, and that they are the club the expression 'sore losers' was invented for.

BLACKBURN

Further afield, Blackburn are perceived to be constantly looking down on them, and there is a slight feeling that Bolton fans very much favour Burnley of the two involved in the most notorious Lancashire derby. Now that John Aldridge has left Tranmere, there has been a slight calming of what was becoming a bitter feud between the two managers, though Tranmere's scuppering of Bolton's 100 points and 100 goals record in 1997 hasn't been forgiven.

PERFORMANCE AGAINST RIVALS
MANCHESTER UNITED

WON 27%

LOST 58%

DRAWN 15%

In one of the more unfathomable cases of organised football hooligan activity, a fervent Bolton Wanderers' supporter, Steven Openshaw, was jailed in 2004 for his part in organising what became known as the 'Battle of Maze Hill', at a south London railway station. The fight was 'orchestrated and organised' by an unlikely combination of Bolton, Tranmere, Liverpool and Port Vale fans with England connections, though the actual trouble was between supporters of Charlton and Southampton.

TRANMERE

WOLVES

With Wigan lingering on the brink of the Premiership, a new derby is potentially emerging, though Bolton remain lethargic about the possibility - "I can't see them being as much of a threat". Wigan have very different plans.

LOVE/HATE

Bolton born *Nat Lofthouse* clocked up the club record of 285 goals in 505 games. He has spent 50 years with the club in various capacities and even did his bit for the local economy by working a full shift down the mine on match days.

Barry Knight is not welcome at the Reebok following his decidedly heavy-handed refereeing of the Bolton v Ipswich play-off in 2000. The 5-3 extra-time defeat was punctuated with Bolton having two men sent off, nine booked and three penalties awarded against them. Allardyce and six players were charged with misconduct that left the boss spluttering "what happened that night was despicable".

CHANTS

A survey concluded that Bolton's fans were the most tuneless in the country. Living up to this reputation on being goaded

'You're not singing anymore',

the reply came

'We're tone deaf'.

'YOUR GROUND'S TOO BIG FOR YOU!'
RATING

100

80

60

40

ATTENDANCE AS A PERCENTAGE OF CAPACITY 95%

20

0

DOH!!

Sam Allardyce thought he'd bagged a free-kick specialist when taking Con Boutsianis on loan from Perth Glory in 2000. But his enthusiasm waned when he discovered Boutsianis had admitted to acting as a getaway driver in a robbery at a restaurant in 1998.

BOSTON UNITED

Recommended website: **www.bufc.drfox.org.uk**

WHO ARE YA?

Boston isn't the first name you'd think of when trying to recall great non-league exploits of the past, though they had their moment in 1955 when beating Derby County 6-1 in the second round of the FA Cup to notch up the widest victory against a League team. Ironically, in the months leading up to the tie, Boston had poached almost half the Derby side. The same opposition was not amused when held to a 0-0 draw at the Baseball Ground in 1974.

CELEBRITY FANS
JOHN MOTSON
BBC Football Commentator

Boston's winding trip through the non-league structure could have come to an illustrious conclusion much earlier. In 1978, the club were hopeful that they would replace Southport in the League, but their York Street ground was given the thumbs down and Wigan Athletic grabbed the place instead. Oddly, when relegated from the Conference in 1993, it was Southport who took their place.

IN and AROUND

Boston Stump at 272ft has frequently claimed the title 'Highest Parish Church in England', although Louth Parish Church, at 295ft is the purist's choice.

Of all the clubs to have benefited from automatic promotion to the League, it has to be said that Boston have failed to maintain an upward trajectory enjoyed by other newcomers. Part of the problem has undoubtedly been the boardroom squabbles that took hold shortly before their promotion. An ownership tussle involving the Mackinson family and Mansfield property developer Des Wood threatened to overshadow what should have been the most thrilling moment in the club's history. Wood's master plan was the same as every other developer's strategy who has become involved with football – namely to sell the ground on the vague promise of relocating the club elsewhere. Like virtually all such schemes, before and afterwards, the whole thing ended in tears.

Things have been fairly rocky with the manager as well. Steve Evans was in charge during their burst to the top of the Conference, but received a 20-month ban for 'financial irregularities before rejoining the club in 2004. Despite his track record, around half the fans loathe him for his gobby asides aimed at fellow staff, officials, fans and the media. When Boston had been confirmed as promoted, Evans was pleased to reveal the sources of congratulatory messages the club had received. These logically included ones from recent League newcomers Rushden and Diamonds and Cheltenham, as well as neighbours Lincoln, though inexplicably Celtic and West Brom also felt moved to offer a warm welcome.

Boston fans have gained a slight reputation for handing out plenty of stick to visitors and the club's siege mentality is reflected on the pitch as well. In an unusual move, whilst mired in a relegation battle in 2003, the entire squad travelled to upcoming opponents Shrewsbury in an attempt to glean some tactical advantage. The ruse may have paid off as the following Saturday Boston achieved a 2-1 win.

A rather more questionable form of male bonding happened when the players posed in the nude for a 2003 calendar – all in the name of charity you understand.

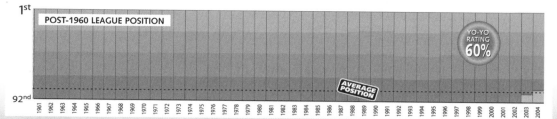

1st

POST-1960 LEAGUE POSITION

YO-YO RATING 60%

AVERAGE POSITION

92nd

1961 1962 1963 1964 1965 1966 1967 1968 1969 1970 1971 1972 1973 1974 1975 1976 1977 1978 1979 1980 1981 1982 1983 1984 1985 1986 1987 1988 1989 1990 1991 1992 1993 1994 1995 1996 1997 1998 1999 2000 2001 2002 2003 2004

PROGRESS REPORT

Boston came from next to nowhere to achieve League status. They had only regained their place in the Conference in 2000, where they bounced back from 12th in their first year to topping the table in 2002. But neither season in the League was a breeze. Their first degenerated into something of a dog-fight but they recovered to 15th. Things improved with a credible 12th in 2004, but they are some way from establishing a permanent home in the Football League.

```
        ...Their highest attendance was in a friendly against Corby Town in 1955...
  ...Share Pilgrims nickname with Plymouth...First club to start a season on minus points...
```

RIVALS

Boston's list of rivals varies according to the age of the fan. Those with really long grudges still name Peterborough as the club they would most like to pull one over. This dates back to the Midland League days of 1960 and a web of intrigue over who should replace Gateshead.

LINCOLN CITY

If history is anything to go by, Lincoln might be expected to allow Boston a decade or so of bedding in before they could be elevated to rival status. But they appear to have taken them to heart almost immediately and are now quite happy to name Boston as hate figures, making it one of the quickest animosities to develop between an established and newly promoted club. When Sleafordian coaches won the contract to provide transport for Lincoln City, the package included driver Keith Taylor whose credentials had one slight flaw, as he is a confirmed fanatic of Boston United.

SUPPORTERS' **VFM** **51%**

PERFORMANCE AGAINST RIVALS
LINCOLN

WON 20%
LOST 40%
DRAWN 40%

But Boston have at least half an eye on the past. They were involved in a nip and tuck struggle with Dagenham and Redbridge for the Conference title. Things heated up with some ill-judged comments from both managers as things came down to the wire. Garry Hill and Steve Evans became known as the Wenger and Fergie of the Conference "I don't like him at all and I certainly don't respect him" surmised Hill. At the root of the problems were the scenes following Boston's defeat in Essex in March 2002. What turned out to be an exceedingly premature lap of honour was embarked upon by the home players and there were allegations of comments along the lines of 'You're finished' echoing around the dressing room afterwards.

DAGENHAM & REDBRIDGE

In theory, Hull City shouldn't be too bothered about the League newbies either, though one of the worst violent incidents in the town occurred in 2003 when six coaches of Boston United fans were virtually destroyed in a hail of bricks lobbed by locals. Late in the game, Boston fans had unwisely attempted to storm the home end after their team lost a last minute goal, provoking the unpleasant retribution.

LOVE/HATE

Dagenham and Redbridge are perceived to have benefited from a distinct London media bias. The fact that Garry Hill had been 'robbed' of promotion to the League twice before in his career got a good airing, lending weight to the suspicion that there was a general preference for Boston to fail in their quest. Anger was particularly directed at *The Non-League Paper* who were seen to be particularly favouring D & R.

CHANTS

The web of disputed county boundaries and names on the East coast leads to some interesting geographical claims such as Boston fans' chants of

'We're the pride of Bostonshire',

an, as yet, unrecognised county.

'YOUR GROUND'S TOO BIG FOR YOU!'
RATING

100
80
60
40
20
0

ATTENDANCE AS A PERCENTAGE OF CAPACITY
45%

DOH!!

Contrary to their actual record, Boston seem to have taken on the character of a club with a glorious history that has descended into in-fighting as they have slipped down the divisions. In 2004, chairman Jon Sotnick had hardly been behind his desk five minutes before the moaners got their pencils sharpened – a typical example being a letter to the local paper complaining "it seems he is leading us down the garden path".

AFC BOURNEMOUTH

A.K.A. BOREMOUTH

Recommended website: **www.rednblack.net**

WHO ARE YA?

There are countless anecdotes from clubs who are caught in financial meltdown, but Bournemouth have more than their fair share. Said at one stage to be five minutes away from the Inland Revenue forcing the club's complete shutdown, one sponsor, Fitness First, had their name plastered all over Dean Court - not because they had paid for advertising - but for simply giving Bournemouth a loan. Rockbottom was hit in 1987, with the club going into receivership. Fans rallied round, providing funds and setting a blueprint for community involvement in football. With just 24 hours notice, 5,000 of them turned up at the Winter Gardens for a mass crisis meeting. On that day alone, £30,000 was raised.

Opinions differ as to how meaningful the fan's involvement really is. Trumpeted as the first club to form a supporter's trust, the 3,500 fan shareholders have a degree of clout, though there is no actual supporter representation on the Board. However, Bournemouth can still claim to be amongst the most fan-friendly clubs in the country, with a host of charitable concerns and links with local organisations.

CELEBRITY FANS

THIN ON THE GROUND.
Local resident
MAX BYGRAVES
was given a ticket by the club
but failed to show
KEN BAILEY
England Cheerleader

IN and AROUND

In 1995 Bournemouth opened Britain's first stretch of non-smoking beach.

In contrast to its well-heeled image, Bournemouth have one of the more unorthodox looking fans. Gordon, a tramp, and his faithful dog are regulars at Dean Court, where he is not charged for admission - though, unfathomably, he always goes in the away end. He even found his way to Dorchester, where the club played nine games while Dean Court had a face-lift.

When Bournemouth make the headlines, it tends not be for anything on the field. It is typical of a club that always seems to make life complicated for itself that arguably their greatest moment was a relegation dog-fight. With the reshuffling of the Premiership leading to five teams being relegated from Level Two, 1994 was not the year to lose all your seven opening games. At Christmas Bournemouth had collected only nine points and looked set to finish bottom. Manager Mel Machin was handed a hopeless task, but with a squad of young, cheap players, began to turn things around. In the second half of the season they amassed 41 more points - form that had it been maintained throughout the season would have seen them promoted. They managed to squeeze out of the bottom five with a win against Shrewsbury on the last day, crowning what is now universally known as 'The great escape'.

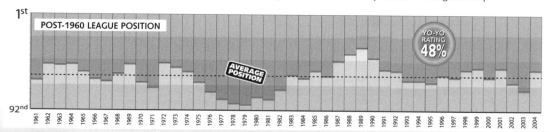

1st

POST-1960 LEAGUE POSITION

AVERAGE POSITION

YO-YO RATING **48%**

92nd

1961 1962 1963 1964 1965 1966 1967 1968 1969 1970 1971 1972 1973 1974 1975 1976 1977 1978 1979 1980 1981 1982 1983 1984 1985 1986 1987 1988 1989 1990 1991 1992 1993 1994 1995 1996 1997 1998 1999 2000 2001 2002 2003 2004

PROGRESS REPORT

Bournemouth are essentially a mid-Level Two outfit, whose only significant deviations has been a spell in the basement (1975-82), and a brief flirtation with Level One (1987-90).

...The fastest ever football league hat-trick was scored by Bournemouth's James Hayter in 2 minutes 20 seconds in 2004...Ryan Giggs and George Best had spells at the club... ...Their red and black kit, adopted in 1971, was based on Inter Milan...

RIVALS

LEEDS

Even nearby foes Bradford City can find it in their hearts to sympathise with the agonies of Leeds United, but they needn't bother crying in Bournemouth's direction, who are more likely to say 'stuff 'em'. On the 1990 May Bank Holiday, fans and residents watched in horror as Leeds supporters - needing a win to gain promotion - attempted to demolish most of Bournemouth. With over 100 arrests, overturned buses and assaults on women, Cherries' supporters did well to react with restraint, but long term the club probably came out worst. Banned from playing any Bank holiday fixtures for the next 12 years, the resultant loss of gate receipts hardly helped them at a time when they were teetering on the brink.

SOUTHAMPTON

It is not surprising that Bournemouth are amongst the least disliked clubs in the country. They have no sides within easy travelling distance in the same division, with only Southampton and Portsmouth vaguely nearby. A fairly low level rivalry exists with Reading (not a trip you'd want to make by bike), heating up following a 3-3 draw in 2001, a game

READING

Bournemouth needed to win to reach the Level Two play-offs. Older fans remember the glory days against the 'scummers' (Southampton). Their last meeting, in the 1987 League Cup, saw Bournemouth winning 3-2 and there were minor hooligan clashes between them in the 70s. But such has been their recent grip on Premiership status, they now feel fairly paternal towards their neighbours, to the extent that a half-time announcement at St.Mary's that Bournemouth are leading is greeted with a ripple of applause. It is admitted, through gritted teeth, that Southampton have provided various forms of assistance to the club over the years.

PERFORMANCE AGAINST RIVALS
SOUTHAMPTON

WON 50%

DRAWN 50%

There is a slight 'seaside thing' with Brighton and Torquay named as foes along with a ragbag of other sides where there have been contentious player/manager links: Bristol City, Gillingham and Norwich, but the chance of being physically threatened by a mob of Bournemouth hard cases remains remote.

That said, Bournemouth maintains a very small and very young hooligan contingent who swap half-baked ideas on an internet message board - a fairly rare type of forum for a comparatively small club.

SUPPORTERS'
VFM
69%

LOVE/HATE

HATE

The usually peaceable Bournemouth fans were so incensed by the performance of referee *Barry Knight* in a 0-4 defeat to Crewe in 1995, a mob decided to confront him in the carpark afterwards. A string of seemingly incredible decisions included sending off two Bournemouth players for apparently no reason and allowing more than one highly dubious looking Crewe goal.

Despite the moans about what supporter's representation really means, the current Chairman *Peter Phillips* ♡ has an 'all-round good bloke' image. In particular, his habit of hanging around in the bar with fans pushes all the right buttons.

CHANTS

Bournemouth interpreted Southampton's legendary

'When the Saints go marching in' as *'When the Saints go Nationwide'*.

'YOUR GROUND'S TOO BIG FOR YOU!'
R A T I N G

100

80

60

40

ATTENDANCE AS A PERCENTAGE OF CAPACITY
72%

20

0

DOH!!

...arre injuries have struck Bournemouth in recent seasons. In a freak playground accident Steve Fletcher was hit by a swing, sustaining a black eye, Gareth O'Conner dropped a bed on his foot, a fridge crushed Gareth Stewart's hand, and on-loan Graham Tomlinson improbably injured his back lying on a water bed.

BRADFORD CITY

USUALLY PRONOUNCED BRATFUD

Recommended website: **www.boyfrombrazil.co.uk**

WHO ARE YA?

Bradford's Valley Parade is situated in a mainly Asian area to the north of the city centre. Like those in other multi-ethnic cities, they have struggled to attract non-white supporters and, as the seventh largest British city, their attendances suggest a population with more on its mind than football. Today, most of its support comes from Bradford's northern and southern suburbs, but with not a great deal in between.

The club has a proud history of amiable plodders. In the early 80s the goals of Bobby Campbell, a man who looked the antipathy of a pro footballer, helped the club escape long-term obscurity in Level Three. The hefty Cecil Podd endeared himself to the City faithful with a sterling 14 years service between 1970 and 1984. One of the first regular black players in the football league, he was subject to appalling racist taunts throughout his career, but committed the ultimate footballer's sacrifice for his club, by refusing a transfer to Manchester United. Many fans recall the club's 'coming of age' moment as the tannoy announcement in 1997 that the club had signed Brazilian Edinho, hence the initially perplexing title of the fans' website www.boyfrombrazil.co.uk.

IN and AROUND

Bradford's transport Interchange is an odd affair. Until half of it was demolished, it contained Europe's largest bus station - but, for such a large place, it manages with a tiny railway terminus.

CELEBRITY FANS
JOHN HOLMES
'Gonch' in *Grange Hill*
SMOKIE
Pop Group
GEORGE LAYTON - Comedy actor
Doctor in the House, It Aint 'alf Hot Mum.

In 1998, one of the most plausible sounding league chairman, Geoffrey Richmond, eyed the Level One fixture list. Reckoning that his recently promoted City were up against relatively weak opposition, he decided to take a gamble to push for the Premiership. His chequebook helped Bradford back into the top division for the first time in 77 years. But, in a way, the 98/99 was the worst season in which to be promoted, coming at the height of the TV money bubble. They enjoyed a shotgun two-season stay in the Premiership, famously parading on an open top bus having dramatically escaped relegation in 2001.

The ground has been effectively redeveloped twice since the stadium fire of May 1985. The disaster not only changed sports ground design but also prompted a new culture of safety in public life.

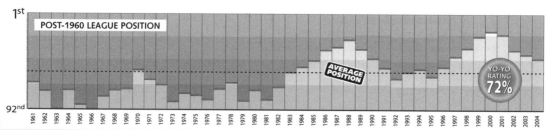

POST-1960 LEAGUE POSITION

1st

AVERAGE POSITION

YO-YO RATING 72%

92nd

1961 1962 1963 1964 1965 1966 1967 1968 1969 1970 1971 1972 1973 1974 1975 1976 1977 1978 1979 1980 1981 1982 1983 1984 1985 1986 1987 1988 1989 1990 1991 1992 1993 1994 1995 1996 1997 1998 1999 2000 2001 2002 2003 2004

PROGRESS REPORT

City have come full circle since the fire. Now back in the Level Two, they are utterly broke, and with a vastly expensive 25,000 capacity stadium that may only attract average crowds of a third of this.

Although there are suspicions that Bradford's spells in administration have been somewhat 'tactical', City's chances of long term survival are questionable.

...Harry Potter appears to wear City scarf...Escaped relegation from Premiership with smallest points total (36 in 1999/00)...Were elected to football league before they had a team...

RIVALS

Leeds and Bradford virtually merge into one giant West Yorkshire conurbation, but even with only a ring road and large Asda between them, the cities have a completely different feel. Fleetingly in their recent histories they have reached league parity with a small number of notorious derby games resulting in almost unbelievable scenes at Bradford's temporary home at Odsall Stadium in 1986. What seemed like the entire section of away supporters rushed the Bradford stand, setting a chip van on fire in the process. Held up for half and hour, the game resumed to play the final two minutes in front of around a dozen supporters.

LEEDS UNITED ☠️ ☠️ ☠️ ☠️

In later days, with both clubs in dire trouble at the time of writing, they have more pressing matters than inter-county rivalry. If anything, the recent woes of both have shown supporters that there is more that unites them than divides them. The general feeling is that hostilities will be resumed when (or if) financial order is restored.

HULL CITY ☠️ ☠️ ☠️ ☠️

SUPPORTERS' VFM 53%

A familiar theme throughout the pattern of British football rivalries is that there are ones which are recognised by everyone associated with the club, but others that are what could best be described as 'firms' animosities: combinations of clubs where the nutters like to wade in to each other, but that the everyday fans are largely unconcerned about. To the hard-core of both clubs, the Bradford - Hull City rivalry is the usual tale of pre-planning, semi-organised fights and legendary confrontations. But to the 'normal' City supporters there is little going on between the clubs at all.

HUDDERSFIELD TOWN ☠️ ☠️ ☠️ ☠️

Currently the greatest animosity is towards Huddersfield Town to the south. Although bubbling below the surface for many years, the atmosphere between the two clubs became particularly sour, not just between fans, but amongst players and the respective Boards as well. In February 1997 during the derby game at Valley Parade, a lunge by Huddersfield's defender Kevin Gray at recently signed Gordon Watson left the striker with a multiple fracture, a seven inch pin in his leg, and little prospect of returning to professional football. His QC described the incident as a 'jump from a significant distance with both feet'. Bradford sued both the player and Huddersfield Town (a case that was lost) though Gray was found legally liable for the injury, paving the way for a compensation award of £900,000.

PERFORMANCE AGAINST RIVALS
HUDDERSFIELD
WON 26% — LOST 34% — DRAWN 40%

City fans allege instances of Huddersfield 'fire' chants and characterise their supporters as dour, humourless and mean-spirited, in a ridiculous 'legoland' stadium. The clubs have bounced around the leagues in relative tandem.

LOVE/HATE

Stuart McCall ♡ is seen as long-term ambassador for the club and, when playing for Leeds prior to a Champions League clash with Glasgow, said that he was sure Bradford supporters would be rooting for their Yorkshire rivals.

There is considerable resentment to ex-player *Ashley Ward*, who, when the club were making staff redundant, was on £18,000 per week for some extremely average performances.

CHANTS

Directed at Huddersfield, to the Adams family theme:

'They think their ground's fantastic, but it's just made of plastic'...

DOH!!

A personnel crisis in March 2000, led to Neville Southall - aged 41 years and 178 days - turning out in goal for City in a vital live TV match against Leeds. First choice goalie, Matt Clarke, had managed to fall down the stairs and the club were unable to secure the services of the Leeds' reserve, as the two teams were about to play each other. Southall, even at the peak of his career, was not known for his agile sleekness. Barracked by Leeds fans who could hardly believe his bulk, Southall had a 'what the hell am I doing here?' look on his face for much of the game. Thankfully not called into action much, he arguably was at fault for Leeds winning goal - and hung up his gloves for good.

'YOUR GROUND'S TOO BIG FOR YOU!'
RATING

100
80
60
40
20
0

ATTENDANCE AS A PERCENTAGE OF CAPACITY
45%

BRENTFORD

Recommended website: **www.beesotted.com**

WHO ARE YA?

Welcome to the twilight zone. Brentford are rarely good enough to cause much excitement, but nor are they sufficiently awful to attract much attention either. They have virtually taken root in Level Two, with only two seasons outside it in 25 years. Even when finishing second in 1995, their timing ensured that they'd remain in their comfort zone, as it was the one season when the runners-up weren't automatically promoted.

But Brentford FC isn't quite one long snoozefest, thanks largely to the appearance of Ron Noades in 1998. The original 'sell it off, build the flats, and hope for the best' merchant, Noades has his fingerprints on just about every major off-field story involving a south/west London club. Fans of his former teams, Wimbledon and Crystal Palace, didn't exactly give him a glowing reference. Upon his take over, Brentford were having one of their rare flirtations with the basement. Having jettisoned Mickey Adams, Noades took the decision feared by fans the length and breadth of the country…he took over as manager. But the tale has an unexpected twist. Under his tutelage, the team secured promotion back to the Second (and he didn't make a song and dance about it).

CELEBRITY FANS

DEAN GAFFNEY
Eastenders Actor, 'Robbie'
ROD STEWART
was an apprentice
SARAH CRACKNELL
St. Etienne

IN and AROUND

Brentford falls within the historic county of Middlesex, politically disestablished in 1965. There was a further blow for Middlesex devotees when in 1996 the Post Office no longer required any county name for a postal address to be valid.

But his role as chairman was more predictable. Desperate to up and go, plans were hatched to relocate so new houses could be plonked onto Griffin Park. Somewhere in the plot, Kingstonian FC would have to be wound up. The Bees supporters' group could foresee the club 'doing a Brighton' and ending up as vagrants. After buckets of energy and cash were burnt up on the proposals, Noades did the honourable thing and took the ball home with him, resigning in 2003, stating that his time at Brentford had been 'a mistake'. By 2004, he was said to be having cosy chats with Ken Bates over a possible bid for Crystal Palace, which could potentially put them on a collision course with Libyan president Colonel Gaddaffi – an occasion worth booking tickets for.

A TV crew in the 80s felt the story of Brentford needed some sexing up. Disappointed to learn that the name Griffin Park had no more exiting roots than being named after some bloke called Griffin, the producer of the Six O'Clock Show weaved a tale of a giant griffin-like bird that had been seen swooping down around the rooftops of the area. Viewers watched residents pointing to the west London sky, identifying where Griff had been spotted. In fact, the finger pointing was just a response to the reporter asking them where the flight path to Heathrow was. The footage could be crudely dubbed with a lot of cobblers about a mystery bird.

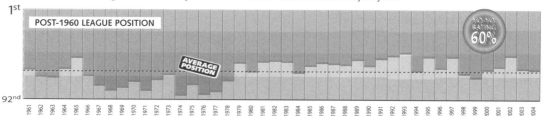

1st
POST-1960 LEAGUE POSITION

YO-YO RATING **60%**

AVERAGE POSITION

92nd

1961 1962 1963 1964 1965 1966 1967 1968 1969 1970 1971 1972 1973 1974 1975 1976 1977 1978 1979 1980 1981 1982 1983 1984 1985 1986 1987 1988 1989 1990 1991 1992 1993 1994 1995 1996 1997 1998 1999 2000 2001 2002 2003 2004

PROGRESS REPORT

Although Brentford enjoyed a spell in the old First either side of the Second World War, their post-1960 record reveals nothing more thrilling than one significant step from Level Three to Level Two in 1978. Stuck in their little world, they have managed to finish in every position, bar five, in Level Two.

```
          ...In 1962, the first team to play all other League clubs...
...Ref walked out on friendly with Tottenham because managers wouldn't let him use yellow card...
      ...Ex-player Chic Brodie had his career ended with a tackle by a sheepdog...
```

RIVALS

Rivalries don't really 'work' in this part of the world. There are no significant reciprocated animosities because everyone seems to spend their time telling each other how unconcerned they are. Chelsea would like to point out that they couldn't care less about Fulham, and Fulham want the world to know that they are practically and spiritually a league apart from QPR, (forgetting the fact they were the worst of the quartet for a spell). All three of them look down on Brentford – though a significant number of QPR fans have what might be best described as 'sympathy' for The Bees. Brentford would request they just all shut up going on about how much they're not bothered.

QPR

One of the original mad merger plans was to splice Brentford and QPR in 1967. With the then Brentford chairman looking to bail out, Griffin Park would have become the home for both, though there was an implication that QPR would be by far the dominant partner. This laid the foundations for the dislike of the Shepherd's Bush lot, which were evident as QPR organised a parade for their promotion to Level One in 2004. The fact that they felt they deserved a parade for finishing second and 'bought a cup to present themselves with' caused some hilarity with the Brentford faithful. (Actually it was presented by the Football League – an odd innovation for non-winners). One 15-year-old fan risked needing an emergency boarding up service by flying a Bees' flag from his bedroom throughout the festivities, before a hail of eggs and a request from the police changed his mind.

BIRMINGHAM

There is some disagreement within the ranks as to who should have the honour of being named number one hate. Fulham's exploits in breezing past Brentford with the bottomless pit of Al Fayed's bank accounts have hardly helped, though proof that there was a problem before is provided by the fact that most Bees' fans will point to the 4-0 thrashing of Fulham in 1992 as perhaps the best moment of their lives. Though Fulham's reputation for trouble is now non-existent, even these two managed to create some havoc when hooliganism was at its peak in the 80s.

The Brentford fanzine, Beesotted, ran a competition to suggest the wording on the top of a stand. Most popular was the simple directive to aircraft passengers on the Heathrow flight path 'Flush over Fulham', though according to black and white clad meteorologists, the prevailing wind would ensure that a deposit timed to land on Craven Cottage would actually end up as a poopy pile very close to Griffin Park.

FULHAM

SUPPORTERS' VFM 71%

PERFORMANCE AGAINST RIVALS
FULHAM

WON 40%
LOST 32%
DRAWN 28%

LOVE/HATE

Dislike of *Mark Rowlands*, who defected from Brentford to QPR, was already strong before the two met in November 2003. Following Rangers' 1-0 victory, four players were labelled 'mindless idiots' by Brentford's communications officer after provocative celebrations in which Rowlands kissed his new club badge directly in front of the Brentford end.

CHANTS

Visitors to Griffin Park may be treated to a full, word perfect, version of The Beatles 'Hey Jude'.

DOH!!

To try and recover from the heartbreak of losing the 1987 play-off final, the club booked a trip to Magaluf for some rest and recuperation. On arriving at the resort, they were further deflated to learn that the side that had beaten them, Crewe, had booked the same hotel for their celebration bash.

'YOUR GROUND'S TOO BIG FOR YOU!'
RATING

100

80

60

40

20

0

ATTENDANCE AS A PERCENTAGE OF CAPACITY 43%

33

BRIGHTON & HOVE ALBION

A.K.A. SEAWEEDS

Recommended website: **www.bhafc.net**

WHO ARE YA?

The fact that he'd actually scored to give Brighton the lead against Manchester United in the 1983 FA Cup final is now overlooked, but Alan Smith's contribution to football history was assured with a shot against Gary Bailey's legs. The BHA fanzine that named itself after John Motson's commentary 'And Smith must score' no longer exists. But the moment was more than a piece of inconsequential Wembley trivia. Losing the replay 0-4, it was the start of a staggering decline in which the club went from mid-table in the old First Division to, in December 1996, six points adrift in Level Three and looking down the gun barrel of The Conference. It says something about the state of lower league football that Brighton's six-year homelessness is not the worst ground cock-up in the English league – that dubious honour surely going to Wimbledon.

CELEBRITY FANS
DES LYNAM
Football Presenter
RALPH BROWN
Actor – *With Nail and I*

IN and AROUND

Closed to the public since 1975, the town's derelict West Pier has been home to 10,000 starlings. It was finished off by fire in 2003 courtesy of men firing rockets into it from a rubber dinghy, raising suspicions that the motive might have been more than petty vandalism.

The peak of the early 80s was by far the best period in the club's history. Stuck in the Third Division South for 30 years without a break, the four seasons Brighton enjoyed in the old First Division under Alan Mullery were a surprisingly short peak for a club that managed to achieve huge attendances even when it was struggling. In 1959-60 the average attendance was 3,469…for its reserve games. In many ways, the eventual near-ruination of the club was brought about by its location – handy for assorted nutcases supporting London teams to descend on the town looking for a weekend break centred around beer, ice-cream and aggro (in no particular order). Meetings with Crystal Palace were ritually scheduled for Easter and Boxing Day, turning the town and beach into a virtual no-go area on public holidays. The old Goldstone ground had a 35,000 capacity in the 1970s and saw more than its fair share of crowd trouble. The moment the ground became seen as unsuitable for large attendances, the rot started. Villains on the Board, ex-Lib Dem politician David Belloti and Bill Archer, sold the site with no plans for relocation. Frequently run out of the ground by irate fans, the protests coincided with the club's worst performances as they stumbled around the foot of Level Three.

With the club sharing with Gillingham, 70 miles to the east in Kent, Brighton supporters could at least claim to be the furthest travelling in the country. Whilst at the Priestfield from 1997-1999, it was calculated that anyone seeing all the 'home' games would have travelled 7,200 miles, close to the diameter of the earth. Now in the hopelessly inadequate 7,000 capacity Withdean Athletics Stadium, plans to build a new stadium at Falmer grind their way through a torturous planning process. The way things are looking at present, BHA may clock up 10 years without a proper ground.

Appropriately, in 2004, BHA signed a sponsorship deal with Skint Records.

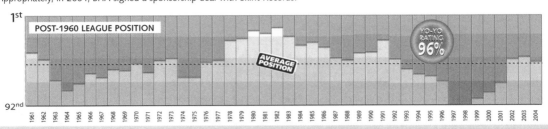

1st

POST-1960 LEAGUE POSITION

AVERAGE POSITION

YO-YO RATING **96%**

92nd

1961 1962 1963 1964 1965 1966 1967 1968 1969 1970 1971 1972 1973 1974 1975 1976 1977 1978 1979 1980 1981 1982 1983 1984 1985 1986 1987 1988 1989 1990 1991 1992 1993 1994 1995 1996 1997 1998 1999 2000 2001 2002 2003 2004

PROGRESS REPORT

Considering its unsuitability, Brighton have a remarkable record at Withdean. Helped by the goals of Bobby Zamora, Brighton's return from Gillingham was followed by a mad dash to Level One for a solitary season in 2002-03. Their post-1960 average has settled precariously in the top half of Level Two.

...Only league club with four words in title...
...Only league team to have played in every round (including qualifying) of FA Cup...
...Brighton's Darren Freeman scored the first league goal of the 21st century...

RIVALS

Brighton's hatred of Crystal Palace has many components of everything that is likely to spark off bad feeling, except, strangely, that the clubs are 40 miles apart. The two consistently met each other in the Third Division South, with honours roughly shared, though during the wartime games (not officially recognised), Palace enjoyed a string of wins by large margins.

CRYSTAL PALACE ☠☠☠☠☠

PORTSMOUTH ☠☠☠☠☠

It is whispered that Allan Mullery, who joined Brighton in 1976, was peeved that Terry Venables had landed the Palace job over him. Whatever its origins, the two loathed each other. Five meetings between their sides in 1976-77 led up to the real flashpoint. A pre-Christmas second replay in the FA Cup was an ill-tempered match in which referee Ron Challis ordered Brighton's Brian Horton to retake a successful penalty. On missing his second attempt, a scene from hell descended on the Goldstone, with Mullery openly protesting in front of areas of Palace supporters, who naturally hurled abuse. Reaching into his pocket, he flung some notes and change in a puddle yelling 'You're not worth that, Palace'. Mullery was thought to be a driving force behind Brighton's change of nickname to 'The Seagulls' – itself an ironic answer to Palace's constant cries of Eagles.

SUPPORTERS'
VFM
43%

PERFORMANCE AGAINST RIVALS
CRYSTAL PALACE

WON 39% LOST 29% DRAWN 32%

The clubs' league placings seemed to have developed a magnetic attraction. In a run of seven seasons bridging the 70s and 80s, they conspired to stay in the same division, each rising from Level Two to old Division One, with Palace stealing the 1979 Level One Championship on the last day from a fuming Brighton.

With much of the focus between the clubs on what is happening off the field, their meeting at Easter of 1989 provided the record of the most penalties awarded in a single league match. Palace's 2-1 victory consisted of one converted penalty and three misses to Brighton's one scored.

LOVE/HATE

Brighton's plans for a new stadium have been frustrated by *Falmer Nimbys*. To supporters of the development, the site is little more than disused scrubland adjacent to The University of Sussex. To opponents, it seems to have acquired the status of an area of outstanding natural beauty whose destruction may lead to the end of human civilisation.

CHANTS

Brighton's recollection of their 'nearly' moment:

*'Robbo was through, but he passed it to Smith
The stupid Scotch bastard was p*ssed
and he missed'*

'YOUR GROUND'S TOO BIG FOR YOU!'
RATING

100
80
60
40
20
0

ATTENDANCE AS A PERCENTAGE OF CAPACITY
90%

DOH!!

Even in their heyday at the Goldstone, BHA were known for their high ticket admission prices; charging 70p in 1977 was considered top whack. With the club charged £30,000 per game for their temporary home in posh Withdean, fans have to stump up £21 to get into what most visitors consider to be the worst ground in England, easily offering the poorest supporters' value for money.

BRISTOL CITY

Recommended website: **www.theincider.com**

WHO ARE YA?

There is a traditional excuse for towns and cities whose football clubs seem to have underperformed through history. Places like Hull can genuinely point to the dominance of rugby. The same argument has been put forward to defend the record of the two Bristol sides, but it is looking increasingly thin, particularly as Rovers managed to buy their stadium back after the rugby club they were sharing with went bust.

Bristol, Britain's eighth largest city, is relatively isolated when it comes to competition from other League clubs. This fact may have contributed to the fanatical absorption that City and Rovers fans have with each other, a situation that some suspect has contributed to both sustaining markedly awful League records. City's chief claim to fame is that they spent four years in the top-flight between 1976 and 1980. But it was the manner of their decline that sticks in the memory, a staggering fall all the way down to 14th in the Fourth in consecutive seasons, the first time any club had experienced the indignity. The consensus nowadays is that in order to stay afloat in such circumstances, the trick is to off-load wage-draining players in double-quick time. But City's difficulties were made even worse by their policy of maintaining a top-flight wage bill when they were slipping through the divisions and haemorrhaging fans. The result was the first in the modern age of footballing financial crises, as well as one of the infrequent displays of player loyalty and self-sacrifice. A group of players, immortalised as the 'Ashton Gate Eight', allowed the club to complete fixtures during the darkest days of bankruptcy even though they couldn't draw any pay cheques. Seen by many as a loophole in company law, a new group of directors took over following the liquidation of the old club. Writing off debts, to the annoyance of those who were owed money, the club reformed as the catchy Bristol City (1982) plc. Manager of the time, Terry Cooper, had little more than a collection of apprentices, plus himself, aged 40, who could be afforded to take the field of play.

An innovative long-term solution was arrived at, with City founding the first footballing academy outside the Premiership.

'Nelson Mandela House' in *Only Fools and Horses* is really the exterior of a block of council flats, Whitemead House, which overlooks Ashton Gate.

Bristol City's association with drinking cider is largely self-promoted, mostly through chants, and they have the pleasure of being supported by the group that epitomises West Country stereotypes, The Wurzels, who wrote the lyrically challenged *'One for the Bristol City'* in their honour.

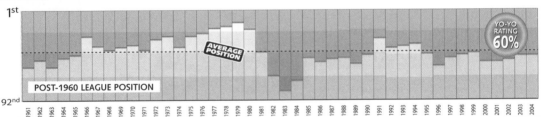

1st

YO-YO RATING 60%

AVERAGE POSITION

POST-1960 LEAGUE POSITION

92nd

1961 1962 1963 1964 1965 1966 1967 1968 1969 1970 1971 1972 1973 1974 1975 1976 1977 1978 1979 1980 1981 1982 1983 1984 1985 1986 1987 1988 1989 1990 1991 1992 1993 1994 1995 1996 1997 1998 1999 2000 2001 2002 2003 2004

PROGRESS REPORT

City recovered from their calamitous drop to a life pivoting around the top half of Level Two and bottom half of Level One. They probably should have spent more time in Level One. Their recent seasons in Level Two have all been knocking at the door of promotion and they have had the despair of finishing third for two seasons in a row without experiencing play-off success. Despite this, their post-1960 record just edges into the top half of the league structure.

```
...Goalkeeper Stephen Cashley scored from clearance (1973), one of only four times
     this has happened in League...Formed as 'Bristol South End'...
        ...Red shirts inspired by Italian revolutionaries, The Garribaldis...
```

RIVALS

England's most poisonous rivalry isn't one that stretches back into ancient history. In the 1960s, City and Rovers were on reasonably good terms. But what Rovers saw as their expulsion from the City in 1986 brewed up to a mutual hatred that probably can only be equalled by the Swansea/Cardiff derby. City have a much larger fan-base and tend to see Rover's very existence as a bar to the 'real' Bristol club doing something meaningful.

BRISTOL ROVERS

SWINDON

Following the fire at Rover's 'temporary' home at Twerton Park, Bath, in 1990, (the responsibility of rogue City supporters) the atmosphere between the clubs has, understandably, been one of pure loathing. To the relief of the police, the two parted company in 1993 after being in the same division for nine consecutive seasons. When they were thrown together again in 1995-96, there was every expectation of serious disorder at derby games. Remarkably, the match at Ashton Gate in January was not made all-ticket and the 20,000 all-seater ground was swelled with anywhere between 2-4,000 fans standing in aisles, with another 3,000 left outside. It was possibly the threat of a Hillsborough-like crush that kept tempers on an even keel. But by the time of the return match at City, the game had become hugely over-hyped by the local press, keen to play up the fact that it signified the return of Rovers to the city of Bristol after their decade in the wilderness. Probably unwisely in retrospect, Sky TV chose to transmit the game live, on 15 December. They got what they were looking for. With Rovers losing 1-0, and a man down, they launched a final assault on the City goal, equalising in the last minute. This triggered a pitch invasion from the City end involving at least 300 individuals, preventing the final whistle being blown. After six minutes of pitch clearing, the players returned only for another invasion to take place at the end of the game, which saw Rovers' players targeted.

CARDIFF

Unusually, City are involved in two seriously bad-tempered derbies simultaneously. Their visits to Cardiff are extremely tense affairs, to put it mildly. Their meetings in the play-off semi-final of 2003 triggered a massive police campaign of contain and control in an effort to avert what had become almost routine violence between the two in the past, most worryingly when a chance encounter on Cheltenham Spa railway station saw steel benches torn from their fittings and hurled at a carriage carrying 30 Cardiff fans travelling from Crewe. The barrage of anti-English/Welsh chants that are swapped when the two meet provides a constant aggravation.

When Christian Roberts scored a last gasp winner for City against his old club Cardiff, at Ninian Park in 2002, he revealed that he did not celebrate the goal so as to try and ward off attacks on his own family who were living in the Welsh capital.

SUPPORTERS' VFM 53%

PERFORMANCE AGAINST RIVALS
BRISTOL ROVERS

WON 40%

LOST 29%

DRAWN 31%

LOVE/HATE

Hero of the club's first match in the top-flight, when scoring against Arsenal in 1976, *Paul Cheesley* is usually named as the fans' all-time number one.

Everyone was glad to see the back of manager *Tony Pulis* when he went to Stoke in 2000 after six months with the club. Something of a long-ball aficionado, his spell was characterised by a procession of 0-0 draws carried out with yawn-inducing efficiency by journeyman pros.

CHANTS

A not entirely accurate prediction in the basement days under Terry Cooper:

'We're on the march with Cooper's army We'll never get to Wembley'

Before the demolition ball went in, Bristol City made three appearances under the twin towers.

'YOUR GROUND'S TOO BIG FOR YOU!'
RATING

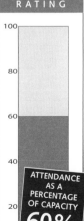

ATTENDANCE AS A PERCENTAGE OF CAPACITY
60%

DOH!!

A West Midlands Police initiative to implement 'police-free fixtures' backfired in February 1999 when Bristol City visited West Brom. Fighting broke out between rival fans inside the ground and the club was forced to dial 999 for assistance. It took 10 minutes for officers to respond to the call before order was restored.

BRISTOL ROVERS

Recommended website: **www.brfcreturn.com**

WHO ARE YA?

Bristol Rovers vie for the title of England's most disaster prone club...and they're up against some fairly stiff competition. The saga of their homelessness is bordering on the pitiful. In 1980 following a fire at their Eastville Stadium (caused by dodgy wiring), the owners decided that greyhound racing was a better long-term bet and effectively kicked them out by asking for an exorbitant rent. Bristol City then stuck the knife in deeper still. Plans to share Ashton Gate were drawn up just as City fell into administration. When they re-emerged with a new board, they were not so keen to play ball, forcing Rovers back into the hands of the greedy greyhound mob at Eastville. Unable to cope with the inflated price, they fled out of Bristol entirely to share with non-league Bath City at the grotty Twerton Park. It became grottier still when a group of Bristol City fans travelling back from an away game set fire to the main stand. If anything, their next move was even more downmarket, sharing the two-sided Memorial Stadium with Bristol RFC in 1996. A stroke of good fortune saw the rugby club go bust, allowing Rovers to buy them out at a knockdown price, leaving the bewildered supporters in a ground that they have little affection for, but at least it belongs to the club and is actually in Bristol.

On the field, the team has only sporadically got out of second gear. Whilst at Twerton Park, they managed a brief surge under Gerry Francis, winning the Level Two title in 1990 and making it to the Leyland Daf final (losing to Tranmere), which at least gave them a solitary bite at a Wembley game. But realistically, avoidance of the Conference has to be the prime medium-term goal.

> **CELEBRITY FANS**
> **GEOFFREY ARCHER**
> Author and occasional Perjurer
> **RONNI SIZE**
> Dance Music Impresario

> **IN and AROUND**
> The house in which movie matinee idol Cary Grant was raised is a five-minute walk away from the Memorial Ground.

Rovers' nickname, The Gasheads, began as a derogatory term used by supporters of Bristol City, based on the supposedly noxious odour which emanated from the Eastville Gas Works and permeated the air around Rovers' original ground. The moniker stuck and now Rovers' fans are actually quite fond of their nickname.

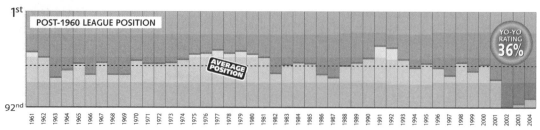

POST-1960 LEAGUE POSITION — 1st ... 92nd — AVERAGE POSITION — YO-YO RATING 36%

1961 1962 1963 1964 1965 1966 1967 1968 1969 1970 1971 1972 1973 1974 1975 1976 1977 1978 1979 1980 1981 1982 1983 1984 1985 1986 1987 1988 1989 1990 1991 1992 1993 1994 1995 1996 1997 1998 1999 2000 2001 2002 2003 2004

PROGRESS REPORT

Consistently unspectacular is the best way to describe Bristol Rovers' performance since their formation in 1883. For the first 120 years of their existence, they troubled neither the top or bottom flight, preferring to spend their time alternating between the middle two divisions. The spell was finally broken in 2001 with a poor season culminating in a disastrous run of form which saw them win only one of their last 16 games. Their first experience in Level Three was nearly their last, slumping to 23rd. Subsequent campaigns have been only marginally better.

```
...Had four players sent off against Wigan in 1997...
        ...Originally called the Black Arabs...
...Wore quartered shirts in an effort to make players look 'larger than life'...
```

RIVALS

The Bristol derby is one of the only inter-town rivalries to be fuelled by a real sense of a social division, cutting roughly along a north/south boundary. The south and west, with the posh, arty Clifton area, are considered to be the wealthier regions of the city, and generally are allied to City, whereas Rovers predominantly draw their fan base from the less salubrious north and east.

BRISTOL CITY

Rovers see City biases everywhere. The local media are said to be particularly 'sycophantic' towards City and the arrogance of imagining that they are any form of sleeping giant is a permanent irritant. Rovers are constantly portrayed to be the poor neighbours and only owe their existence to the fact that a city the size of Bristol warrants two League football teams. It is this, as one fan told us, 'over inflated opinion of themselves' that

CARDIFF CITY

really drives the hatred from the Rovers' side of the city.

SUPPORTERS' VFM 27%

Rovers are deeply suspicious of the City Council. Indeed there are solid grounds for thinking that, during the critical period, the chamber was packed with members with a decidedly pro-City stance, to the point that they positively discouraged Rovers from re-entering the city at all during their long spell in the wilderness. When searching for a site for a new stadium in the 90s, the Council recommended Hallen Marsh, but failed to inform Rovers that it was so close to a local chemical works that it would be unsafe for fans and players alike. Unfortunately for the club, they had already invested £300,000 in the project before discovering this minor fact.

Whilst many fans point to a 'history' between themselves and their nearest rivals, the problems in Bristol are real and relatively current. When seven City fans were convicted of starting the fire

SWINDON

at Twerton Park, it ratcheted up the hatred to a level that puts the rivalry in the premier league.

PERFORMANCE AGAINST RIVALS
BRISTOL CITY

WON 29%
LOST 40%
DRAWN 31%

LOVE/HATE

In the words of one Rovers' fan, 'we hate anything or anybody associated with City'. No surprises there then, but The Gasheads always managed to save their strongest vitriol for *Scott Davidson*. This special treatment was down to the fact that he was chairman of Bristol City, though neutrals may like to take into account his more heinous crime of playing keyboards for 80s pop band, Bros.

CHANTS

A decent riposte at Colchester who were claiming

'You're Welsh and you know you are', *'You're Dutch and you know you are'*

'YOUR GROUND'S TOO BIG FOR YOU!'
R A T I N G

100
80
60
40
20
0

ATTENDANCE AS A PERCENTAGE OF CAPACITY 61%

DOH!!

Posing as feng shui experts, comedians Guy de Beaujeu and Patrick Stockhausen convinced Bristol Rovers that they could improve results, along with the balance and harmony within the club, by making a few small alterations to the layout of the Memorial Ground. Following their advice, the club duly installed a tank of plastic fish behind the goal, an ornamental ceramic frog above the entrance to the stadium, house plants in all four corners of the dressing room and hanging wind chimes at strategic points around the ground. For added good fortune, club officials were also instructed to keep all toilet seats down.

Beaujeu and Stockhausen finally revealed that the whole escapade was merely a stunt for their forthcoming television series, Gatecrashers.

BURNLEY

Recommended website: **www.park-road.u-net.com**

WHO ARE YA?

For at least a short period in their lives, most teams' supporters will have witnessed a period when their side has performed at or above their expectations. But there is a generation of Burnley fans who have struggled through such prolonged lean times that the phrase 'shadow of their former selves' could have been invented especially for the club. Burnley supporters' fanaticism and numerical strength provides for some eye-opening facts. The Level Two play-off final of 1994 against Stockport was swamped by around 35,000 fans – equivalent to virtually the entire male population of the town. Whatever has gone on since the mid 70s, Burnley's football prominence is completely out of proportion to the town's insubstantial size. As the smallest town to have enjoyed more than a single season at the highest level, there is probably a convoluted calculation, involving a ratio of its fan base to trophies won, that would conclude that Burnley FC is the most successful club in English League history.

Not that this is of huge comfort for fans who are much under the age of

IN and AROUND

3,000 of the town's houses have been abandoned, with Daneshouse having the cheapest properties in the country. Someone selling an average house in Windsor could afford 22 in the most deprived area of Burnley.

50. Football League Champions in 1960 and FA Cup runners up two years later, their 70s' and 80s' collapse was not even a short, sharp shock followed by a spirited bounce back, more like slow torture and a protracted convalesce. By the early 80s, the failure of the team coincided with the failure of the local economy. By 1987, the club was at one stage in a stable fifth in the basement before a tailspin set in. It was the first season in which automatic relegation to the Conference was introduced so all eyes were on the strugglers. Salvation was only achieved in the last game with a 2-1 win over Orient, sending Lincoln down instead. During its collapse, the club became a focus for the London-based press syndicating pieces along the lines of 'this once proud club…formerly contented whippet-breeding population…mills standing empty…" as the town became a focus of endless north/south divide comparisons. In fact, such apparently sympathetic coverage has probably not helped its cause as it has attracted the accusation of continually moaning about its plight and harping on about its long-term potential, when it is often the national media doing it on its behalf.

Burnley's final ascent back to the respectability of Level One in 2000 was helped with one of the more audacious transfers. Having become almost welded into fifth spot, the board splashed out on Ian Wright who was persuaded to join them for three months at the end of the season. Though he didn't actually do much on the field, his appearances gave Burnley a feel-good factor that many followers had never witnessed. They squeezed into an automatic promotion place at the death.

Downing Street officials knew it wasn't worth attempting to contact Alistair Campbell when Burnley were playing, as it was the only time he ever turned his pager off.

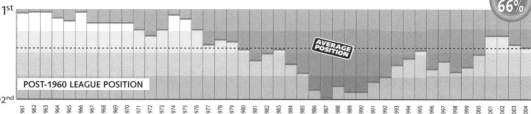

YO-YO RATING **66%**

1st

AVERAGE POSITION

POST-1960 LEAGUE POSITION

92nd

1961 1962 1963 1964 1965 1966 1967 1968 1969 1970 1971 1972 1973 1974 1975 1976 1977 1978 1979 1980 1981 1982 1983 1984 1985 1986 1987 1988 1989 1990 1991 1992 1993 1994 1995 1996 1997 1998 1999 2000 2001 2002 2003 2004

PROGRESS REPORT

Everything seems to take that bit longer at Burnley. Their post-1960 graph shows only two trends, a 25-year slide that got steeper towards its end, followed by a steady but unspectacular recovery, leading them to the pinnacle of 7th in Level One in 2001 and 2002.

...Have won the Championship of all four of the old divisions...Were the last champions of the defunct Fourth Division...Manager died when he fell out of a train (Spen Whittaker 1920)...

RIVALS

Burnley still pursue a dream that Blackburn will go back to where they came from after their heyday of the Jack Walker period. The change in the balance of power between the two clubs has been a gradual affair. In the early 60s, both were riding high in the old First with Burnley's status a couple of notches above their neighbours. The derbies were major affairs, with attendances accounting for at least a quarter of the combined towns' populations. Blackburn's demise started before Burnley, who won many plaudits in the Leighton James/Martin Dobson era, much to Blackburn's annoyance who were muddling around in Level Two. The last fixture for nearly 20 years occurred in 1983 in the old First before the clubs went on very different journeys – in Blackburn's case to the Premiership title in 1995. Blackburn then feigned indifference towards them and 'pretended' that Manchester United were their real rivals – a fact that ensures that The Reds get an unusually positive billing in Burnley.

BLACKBURN

Burnley's revival and Rover's exit from the Premiership set up the nightmare of all grudge matches at Turf Moor in December 2000. The 4pm kick-off resulted in a 2-0 defeat that sparked the partial destruction of Burnley town centre, primarily caused by Burnley fans – an unusual occurrence in the history of football-related violence. An appalling atmosphere hung over the return match, with the police stating that they'd planned for the game 'for months'. Overall, there were only 36 arrests in the most heavily policed game Lancashire had ever witnessed, which, seeing the result, a 5-0 win for Rovers, was a minor miracle, though trouble broke out in the 'grey zone' towns between the two clubs, with problems in Accrington and Oswaldtwistle.

SUPPORTERS'
VFM
65%

PERFORMANCE
AGAINST RIVALS
BLACKBURN

WON 50%

LOST 36%

DRAWN 14%

PRESTON NORTH END

Millwall's 'No one likes us..we don't care' would be even more appropriate for Burnley. With the exception of Manchester United, Burnley feature more prominently in others' list of rivals than any other club. Away supporters (especially of a timid disposition) name Turf Moor as one of the most intimidating atmospheres in the League, with only Cardiff topping it on aggression rating.

LOVE/HATE

The performance of *Barry Knight* (aka *Shite*) in a crunch home match against Wolves in 2002 did him no favours in this neck of the woods, to the extent that Bournemouth and Burnley fans started a campaign to get him removed from the referees' list.

CHANTS

Feigning indifference to fans of other clubs who see Burnley as rivals, the faithful sometimes like to remind them that

'We only hate Bastard Rovers' (Blackburn).

'YOUR GROUND'S
TOO BIG FOR YOU!'
RATING

100

80

60

40

20

0

ATTENDANCE
AS A
PERCENTAGE
OF CAPACITY
55%

DOH!!

To enliven the atmosphere in 1999, the club invited The Swanky Pants Performing Dog Troupe to strut their stuff at half-time. This japery consisted of some tarted up handlers accompanying a bunch of wretched Afghan hounds dressed variously in Burnley shirts, military combat fatigues and duck costumes. On their third appearance, the number of missiles lobbed in their direction suggested that they were less than welcome.

BURY

Recommended website: **www.y3kshakers.co.uk**

WHO ARE YA?

There was a time, even though it was around 110 years ago, that Bury FC could claim to be a bigger outfit than Newton Heath (aka Manchester United). Somewhere around the turn of the 20th century, Bury were comfortably ahead of them in the League and in 1903, strolled to a record-breaking 6-0 FA Cup final victory against Derby, with the added spice that they didn't concede a single goal in their progress to the Cup. By 1986, they could at least point to the fact that they managed to take the lead at Old Trafford, but otherwise there had been an ever-so-slight reversal in the respective clubs' fortunes.

A diminishing number of green(ish) fields separate Bury from the bulk of north Manchester. In 2002, then joint chairman John Smith moaned that the people of Bury were too inclined to go and watch "Manchester United, Bolton, Blackburn…and even Burnley" (suggesting they must have been fairly desperate). Bury have been in a stately decline virtually since their inception. About halfway through their history, in 1957, they slipped into the lower half of the League structure for the first time. With pre-war crowds easily topping 20,000, the name of their "y3k" website makes an obtuse reference to the extent of support more recently.

CELEBRITY FANS
MARK E SMITH
Vocalist - *The Fall*
MIKE REID
DJ

IN and AROUND

Founder of the modern Police Force, a statue of Robert Peel stands in the Market Square. Handily, his finger points in the direction of the men's loo.

In 1997, major shareholder Hugh Eaves was the toast of the town, if not the bookies, from whom he took £25,000 in a bet that the team would be promoted. He loaned the club in the region of £4 million to keep it afloat, until an altercation on Stoke railway station with travelling fans (who gave him some curt advice about what he should be spending his cash on) persuaded him Bury FC was not really his cup of tea anymore. Another series of big bets in 1998 didn't go his way. Losing £15 million on the derivatives market, his misfortune had the knock-on effect of sending the club into meltdown, as it was flogged in an attempt to pay creditors, who, by 2001, included a company claiming £700 a day for interest on a mortgage that had been taken out on the ground.

In stepped the 'so good they named him twice' father of the Neville brothers, Neville Neville, who spearheaded a 'Save our Shakers' campaign, involving ceaseless bucket-rattling, including the first use of the 'auction for a place in the squad' tactic – won by brothers, one of whom was only 12. Even this didn't go according to plan as the auction was plagued with bogus bids, including one of £7,000, before settling on a winning price of £2,850.

Bury's Gigg Lane was often considered amongst the best playing surfaces in the land, although Swinton Rugby Club did their best to ruin it when they shared the ground.

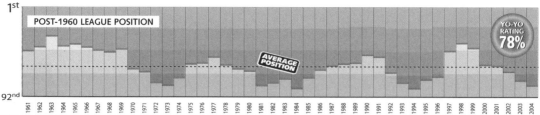

1st

POST-1960 LEAGUE POSITION

AVERAGE POSITION

YO-YO RATING 78%

92nd

1961 1962 1963 1964 1965 1966 1967 1968 1969 1970 1971 1972 1973 1974 1975 1976 1977 1978 1979 1980 1981 1982 1983 1984 1985 1986 1987 1988 1989 1990 1991 1992 1993 1994 1995 1996 1997 1998 1999 2000 2001 2002 2003 2004

PROGRESS REPORT

Despite not hitting the heights in living memory, Bury have had quite a fun time zipping around the lower leagues. Their highpoint, under Stan Ternant, came with successive promotions from Level Three in 1996 to Level Two champions in 1997. Currently on one of their customary slides, up to 2004, they have had progressively worse finishes for six consecutive seasons.

```
...Shortest name in football league...Fielded Indian International Baichung Bhutia...
        ...Neville brothers would 'like to finish career at Bury'...
```

RIVALS

North Manchester has some odd footballing geography. The teams form a (very) rough semi-circle around the city, in clockwise order: Wigan, Bolton, Bury, Rochdale and Oldham. Bury's main hates are Bolton, but they are reasonably indifferent to Oldham, and the feeling is just as weak in the other direction. The two 'on the edges', Wigan and Oldham, have their own private feud.

BOLTON

MANCHESTER UNITED

With few friends in the locality, Manchester United don't quite come in for as much stick as might be expected. During their darkest spell, Bury had a couple of coffer-boosting Cup ties at Old Trafford that, although lost, helped stabilise a sinking ship. United hosted a fundraising event and the Neville brothers' connection (they were born in Bury) gives some grounds for, if not friendliness, grudging acceptance. There was, however, a perception that after their poor performances in Euro 2000, the fact that they came from the town was suddenly more prominently mentioned in the media.

It's easy to forget that, for a period in the 80s, Bolton were well behind Bury in the pecking order. There was unrestrained joy when Bolton sunk into Level Three. But as their fortunes turned around, an increasing number of Bury residents were suspected of drifting off to the Reebok. Bury's record against them is not bad, reinforcing the impression that Bolton's league supremacy is a bit of a mirage. The defection of John McGinlay caused plenty of rancour, particularly as he'd been Bury's hat trick hero in a derby clash at Burnden Park.

ROCHDALE

Bury supporters were responsible for a well-circulated April fool about the Reebok Stadium sinking.

Although spending an increasing amount of time with them in Level Three, Rochdale aren't treated with much seriousness – so long as there's no more talk of mergers.

PERFORMANCE AGAINST RIVALS
BOLTON

WON 48%

LOST 28%

DRAWN 24%

SUPPORTERS' VFM
39%

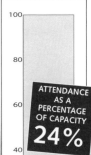

'YOUR GROUND'S TOO BIG FOR YOU!'
RATING

100

80

ATTENDANCE AS A PERCENTAGE OF CAPACITY
24%

60

40

20

0

LOVE/HATE

When under the control of Jonathan Pollard, *Robby the Bobby* ♡ was one of the better liked mascots. The policeman-shaped character was utterly lawless, mooning at will, ripping the ears off other mascots and breaking the nose of poor Bartley the Bluebird (Cardiff). Before joining his beloved Sheffield United in 1999, *Neil Warnock* had a poor spell at Bury, where he got the side relegated from Division One, thanks largely to a dire away record. Known to Bury fans as Colin, they claim to have discovered the two-word anagram of his name, of which 'Colin' forms the polite part.

CHANTS

'3-0 in your Cup Final'

At poor Rochdale, whose 'big day' (a league game v Bury) was ruined.

DOH!!

Just the sort of thing to warm the hearts of supporters being asked to put their hands in their pockets to save the club – Bury's shop decided to stock Manchester United merchandise.

CAMBRIDGE UNITED

Recommended website: **www.amberarmy.co.uk**

WHO ARE YA?

For a not especially massive place, it's a bit of an oddity that Cambridge has to sustain both a 'United' and a 'City'. Cambridge City were historically the bigger club. United's early history saw them drawing much of their support from the outlying villages, leaving City to mop up the central areas. During their non-league days, they had a ground to match their semi-rural status. The pitch at Station Farm was so ridiculously undulating that it became dubbed 'Celery Fields'. It was not until after the war that they ditched the name Abbey United, which gave visitors the impression they were up against a bunch of monks. Their entry to the League was as recent as 1970, to replace Bradford Park Avenue.

Whether they like it or not (and generally they don't), Cambridge are best remembered for the eccentric but highly successful management of John Beck. Steering them from the bottom half of the basement to a play-off place for the Premiership in 1992, Beck himself admitted that 'Dracula' was an apt nickname, in recognition of the perception that he was draining the life-blood out of football. His was a master of the

CELEBRITY FANS
JAMIE OLIVER
TV Chef
GODRIC SMITH
Prime Minister's Press Secretary

game's black arts, single-handedly introducing an element of gamesmanship that had not been seen before. The visitors' dressing rooms would either be too hot or too cold, they might be given soggy, under-inflated, practice balls and, if they were really unlucky, a large dose of salt deposited in their tea. Cambridge's tactics under Beck were unashamedly long-ball, a method given a helping hand by his instructions to keep the grass in the corners long and to smother the pitch in sand, so as to hold the ball up, allowing the forwards to muscle in on hapless defenders. Demanding unswerving commitment to the 'hoof and run' cause, Beck would have no qualms about taking a player off before half-time if he wasn't throwing himself around with the necessary oomph.

IN and AROUND

The roll call of Cambridge University Footlights reads like a Who's Who of British comedy, though the rising stars weren't always evident at the time. One 60s' reviewer, bemoaning that the quality of the revue was going downhill, commented that John Cleese and Graham Chapman were "responsible for the poorer material".

The club has a long list of illustrious ex-players and, in Ron Atkinson, one moderately illustrious ex-manager. Dion Dublin and John Taylor became firm favourites at the Abbey, despite the 'revelation' in The Sun that their Dads were both members of Showaddywaddy (it's not true). Though the population consists of a drifting and largely apathetic rump of posh students, Cambridge United haven't been under the financial cosh anything like as badly as their scholarly counterparts, Oxford United. The U's had a fright when faced with a £500,000 bill following the ITV Digital debacle, but a fan's whip-round helped them escape intact. One of their commercial ruses was to auction a place in the squad, offering the chance of a number 51 shirt, a training session with the pros and a season ticket, though it would have taken a gigantic injury crisis for them to get a game.

Their place in the history books is confined to being the first club to play a fixture on a Sunday. Their FA Cup tie on 6 January 1974 kicked off at 11.30am, three and a half hours before other fixtures. Prevented from charging for admission due to Sunday trading laws, the club neatly sidestepped the difficulty by asking for 50p for the 'compulsory' programme.

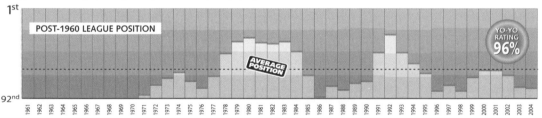

1st · POST-1960 LEAGUE POSITION · AVERAGE POSITION · YO-YO RATING 96% · 92nd

1961 1962 1963 1964 1965 1966 1967 1968 1969 1970 1971 1972 1973 1974 1975 1976 1977 1978 1979 1980 1981 1982 1983 1984 1985 1986 1987 1988 1989 1990 1991 1992 1993 1994 1995 1996 1997 1998 1999 2000 2001 2002 2003 2004

PROGRESS REPORT

Cambridge have performed two 'there and back' acts, before settling back to life in Level Three. Both the rises were spectacular; consecutive promotions in 1977 and 1978, and then repeating the feat in 1990 and 1991.

```
...Completed record 34 games without a win before beating Newcastle who were then
    top of the League (1983-84)...Have first five letters of alphabet in their name...
        ...Competed in the first play-off to be held at Wembley (1990)...
```

RIVALS

PETERBOROUGH UNITED

The fens' rivalry features fairly highly on an animosity rating, though is simultaneously one that fans of other clubs are rarely aware of. The private battle has been maintained from shortly after Cambridge's entrance to the League. As relatively recent League entrants, Cambridge have largely failed to attract the hostile interest of other clubs. So when Peterborough took up the bait, United were quite happy to cling onto the animosity to the extent of letting other clubs know that they have eyes for only one team. This leads to the intriguing claim of 'We hate 'Boro more than you' – a chant aimed at anyone who has the audacity to muscle in on their private world. The two have a slight habit of following each other up and down the leagues, though as far as Cambridge are concerned, Peterborough seem to "do whatever we do a season later". They are accused of being hopelessly fickle and benefiting from a substandard pitch.

Cambridge are happy to point out that there must be something inherently horrible about Peterborough as they have a Burnley-like tendency to annoy everyone, a statement that has a ring of truth if you count up the number of clubs where Boro are named as rivals. The 'problem', you'd suspect, might be down to the presence of Barry Fry, aka Barry Fry-up, whose image, it is claimed, isn't entirely in keeping with a club whose nickname is 'Posh'. Not that Fry could probably give a monkey's, as he's got his work cut out just keeping his own fans and press on-side. The fixture is rarely trouble-free, and generally accounts for most, if not all, of Cambridge's tally of arrests for each season. In one of the more unlikely hooligan incidents, a Posh fan was jailed for three months after hurling a bike at a Cambridge pub door. Such is the lack of trouble at The Abbey generally, one estimate of Cambridge's hardcore troublemakers put their numbers at around five, a significant decrease from the late 70s when there were said to be around 25, whose exploits were brought to a swift end when, in 1979, 22 of them were jailed.

Peterborough United's Ladies team weren't exactly thrilled when their new kit was unveiled – as it was identical to that worn by the men from Cambridge United.

PERFORMANCE AGAINST RIVALS

PETERBOROUGH

SUPPORTERS' VFM 29%

WON 34%
LOST 38%
DRAWN 28%

NORTHAMPTON TOWN

LOVE/HATE

Here's gratitude for you. Though ex-manager *Ian Atkins* gets a mention, plenty of bile was directed at *John Beck* ♡ 🔨, who should, in theory, be an undisputed long term hero. When he returned to the club for a spell in 2001, fans were split around 50/50, though his support dwindled during his brief return, as he managed just nine wins in 36 matches. His departure to Preston in 1992 was aggravated by the fact hat he took no less than nine Cambridge players with him. He clearly didn't always inspire such loyalty, as Steve Claridge, when a player, was so incensed with his half-time rantings that he delivered a firm head-butt to his boss.

CHANTS

Realising *'It's just like watching Brazil'* isn't always appropriate when things on the pitch are not going their way, the variation

'It's just like watching Barhill' goes up.

Barhill is a village just outside Cambridge.

DOH!!

A low moment in their 1999-2000 campaign, whilst searching for their first away victory, occurred when they failed to score against Cardiff, despite the advantage of playing against 10 men for 45 minutes, nine men for 27 minutes and eight men for 15 minutes. They did get awarded a penalty, but missed.

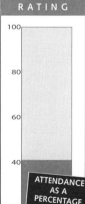

'YOUR GROUND'S TOO BIG FOR YOU!'

R A T I N G

100

80

60

40

20

0

ATTENDANCE AS A PERCENTAGE OF CAPACITY 41%

CARDIFF CITY

Recommended website: **www.bluebirdsonline.com**

WHO ARE YA?

There are not many around who remember Cardiff City's diminutive striker Len Davis, but in 1924, he fluffed a penalty that would have crowned his side as League Champions for 1924 - as it was they lost the title by 0.024 of a goal. Their solitary FA Cup success in 1927 (the only time the trophy has left England) was the last thing to get really excited about until the arrival of Lebanese businessman, Sam Hammam, who in 2000 had just managed to off-load Wimbledon before things turned exceptionally nasty.

Hammam reasoned that if the Welsh national rugby side could pull in 70,000 down the road at The Millennium Stadium, then it wasn't unreasonable to hope that a similar number would flock to Ninian Park as well. The technique he chose was an overt case of 'wrapping oneself in the flag'. The strategy paid dividends off the field whilst an array of comparatively expensive talent started to do the business on it, resulting in a rapid rise from Level Three to genuine promotion prospects from Level One in 2004.

Cardiff has a greater proportion of parks and open spaces than any other British city.

Hammam's vision saw Cardiff City as the natural club for the whole of the Welsh nation. Welsh language songs were subtly introduced into the PA play list, along with some official encouragement to adopt 'Men of Harlech' as the club's unofficial anthem. In practice, the renditions tend to descend into a cacophony of 'la-las', as hardly anyone knows the full words.

The case for the City of Cardiff being home to a Premiership club is strong. You have to travel over 100 miles to the West Midlands to find a top-flight team, and with the valleys of Glamorgan all 'pointing' in the direction of the Welsh capital, there are one million people within half an hour's drive of Ninian Park.

For some, Hammam's enthusiasm to immerse himself in the partisan fans' culture is likely to blow up in his face. He has made no secret of the fact that he enjoys the 'fortress Ninian' reputation of the ground and it is sometimes said that the distinctly prone position of visiting fans, sandwiched tightly between sections of vociferous home support, is no accident. It is not just the supporters of away sides that can find the trip unnerving. In 2003, QPR were staying in the Castle Manor Resort in Newport, when, at 3am, just 12 hours before their play-off match against Cardiff, a man set off the fire alarm. With commendable naivety, a spokeswoman for QPR commented, "I can't believe someone would do that".

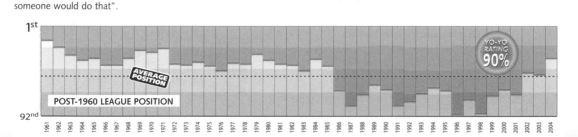

1st

YO-YO RATING 90%

AVERAGE POSITION

POST-1960 LEAGUE POSITION

92nd

1961 1962 1963 1964 1965 1966 1967 1968 1969 1970 1971 1972 1973 1974 1975 1976 1977 1978 1979 1980 1981 1982 1983 1984 1985 1986 1987 1988 1989 1990 1991 1992 1993 1994 1995 1996 1997 1998 1999 2000 2001 2002 2003 2004

PROGRESS REPORT

Cardiff's last spell in the highest division came to an end in 1962, after which they spent an almost unbroken spell in Level One for 20 years, only threatening the promotion places in 1971. By 1998, they reached their low of 21st in the basement, after which a climb set in, accelerating to a rapid ascent under Hammam, which took them to their recent best of 13th in Level One in 2004.

```
...One of many grounds to be built on a rubbish dump, a bedstead once rose to the surface
   of a Ninian Park goalmouth...Hammam mooted idea of changing name to Cardiff Celts...
              ...Hammam's misspelling of Hamman is almost universal...
```

RIVALS

Roughly equidistant from Cardiff and Swansea lies the town of Bridgend, torn in two by the factions that make up the rivalry with the most bitter history in the League. Some have argued that the intensity of the derby has had the effect of holding back Welsh football generally. Whatever the result, the claim to be the country's premier club grips both sets of supporters and at present, Cardiff are having things all their own way – a fact that incenses 'The Jacks', whose feelings of being treated as second class citizens within the province have only been heightened by Hammam's attempts to 'nationalise' Cardiff's support.

SWANSEA CITY

Trouble brewed between the two back in the 1960s with a well publicised spat when the two teams refused to socialise together after a game. The fixture has become legendary not so much for its results, but for the 'conquests' that have come through hooligan activity. Those who incline to the latter way of determining supremacy like to recall an incident in the late 80s when retreating Swansea fans were forced to dive into the sea to find safety. Although they have missed each other in the League since 1999, they have an 'alternative' fixture history in the Welsh Cup. The concern over their meeting in the final in 2002 caused such a headache that Swansea fans were only permitted to travel on official coaches having bought a voucher that could be exchanged for a ticket once they were on the road. Police had planned to turn away everyone else and became suspicious when they spotted six stretch limousines cruising into the Cardiff city centre. The occupants, all Swansea supporters, were escorted straight to the railway station.

PERFORMANCE AGAINST RIVALS
SWANSEA

SUPPORTERS'
VFM
71%

WON 30%
LOST 46%
DRAWN 24%

Cardiff's view of their frankly terrible reputation amongst away fans is a dismissive shrug of the shoulders, particularly when it comes to the oft repeated complaints about anti-English chanting. They have a reasonable point when they say that English fans are all too ready to dish out ridiculous regional insults and stereotypes, but are scared to death when they are on the receiving end.

BRISTOL CITY

STOKE CITY

With Swansea out of reach in a lower division, attention has turned to Stoke City, though this is often seen as a hooligans' private battle field that has little to do with feelings of 'real' fans. Sam Hammam didn't take the necessary precautions when leaving his car in the directors' car park at the Britannia Stadium, as it was vandalised by opposition supporters, though they had plenty of clues that it was his as it has registration that bears a distinct resemblance to the word CARDIFF.

Cardiff don't really consider Wrexham to be a Welsh club at all, hence the nickname 'Scousers'.

CHANTS

All-seater status put pay to one of the more unusual terrace rituals, the '*Ayatollah*', derived from the actions of funeral-goers in Iran. This involved crouching down and slowly rising to the feet whilst vigorously slapping one's own head – a symbol of Cardiff's malaise in the 80s, now performed with a more celebratory tinge.

LOVE/HATE

A common pre-match diversion is to scour the programme notes for the away players' biographies. *Anyone discovered to have any connection with Swansea whatsoever* is guaranteed to face 90 minutes of hell.

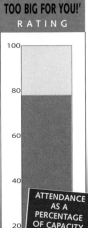

'YOUR GROUND'S TOO BIG FOR YOU!'
RATING

100
80
60
40
20
0

ATTENDANCE AS A PERCENTAGE OF CAPACITY
78%

DOH!!

During the cash-strapped days of 1989, the club found itself unable to afford a security van to transport the gate takings from its Cup meeting with QPR. Having left them at the ground overnight, staff returned to find every penny had disappeared. Fortunately, the bounty was later found on a mountain in Caerphilly.

CHARLTON ATHLETIC

Recommended website: **www.addicksonline.co.uk**

WHO ARE YA?

Difficult for outsiders to place without a London A-Z, Charlton Village is just south of the Thames Flood Barrier, with The Valley, surprisingly, slightly further north than Millwall, Fulham and Chelsea's grounds. The club's catchment area is a bit sausage shaped. Squeezed by its London neighbours in all directions but east, it attracts significant support from the leafy Kent suburbs. A proportion must be new fans or defectors from other clubs as The Valley has tripled its capacity since re-opening in 1992 and is routinely packed out for their Premiership campaigns. This leads to the inconsequential moan that the ground's atmosphere has taken a noticeable dip, particularly with the addition of a second tier on the North stand, which has increased the quota of placid families.

CELEBRITY FANS
JIM DAVIDSON
Comedian
GARY BUSHELL
Columnist
STEVE RYDER
BBC Sports Presenter

Charlton's entrance to the Premiership was thanks to what many consider the best Wembley game in the stadium's entire history, an exhilarating 4-4 draw in which Charlton needed three equalisers and seven penalties to finally dispense with play-off favourites Sunderland. Very strong on home-grown talent, perhaps the greatest symbol of how far the club has come is that manager Alan Curbishley has become a serious candidate for the England job.

IN and AROUND

Charlton House is a favourite of ghost hunters who claim the spooky Jacobean property is subject to inexplicable explosions and mysterious balls of orb-like light.

Charlton endured a carbon-copy of Wimbledon's plight; no ground to call their own, forced to play at Crystal Palace, about 40 minutes drive away, and at risk of losing their fan base entirely. But whereas The Dons disintegrated, Charlton prospered, thanks largely to a massive, good spirited fans' campaign that saw them organise their own political party, winning 15 percent of the vote for Greenwich Council in 1990. Raising £1 million for the scheme, The Valley was virtually built with the fans' bare hands.

In 2003, the club showed their displeasure at having to play at Stamford Bridge on a pitch that consisted mostly of sand. At the next game at The Valley, the PA played 'The green, green grass of home'.

Coded shopping advice came from a squad list of 2002, featuring; Young, Fish, Costa, Fortune.

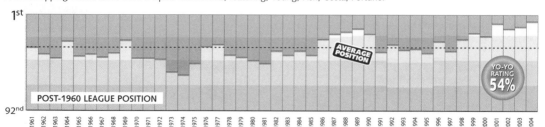

1st

AVERAGE POSITION

YO-YO RATING 54%

POST-1960 LEAGUE POSITION

92nd

1961 1962 1963 1964 1965 1966 1967 1968 1969 1970 1971 1972 1973 1974 1975 1976 1977 1978 1979 1980 1981 1982 1983 1984 1985 1986 1987 1988 1989 1990 1991 1992 1993 1994 1995 1996 1997 1998 1999 2000 2001 2002 2003 2004

PROGRESS REPORT

Charlton have a post-1960 record of a club comfortably lodged in Level One - with only occasional forays into anything higher or lower. A spell in receivership preceded a four-year trip into the top-flight that, oddly, coincided with their homelessness. But the next time the opportunity came along, they grabbed it with both hands. Though the late 90s were not the best time to try and establish a long term Premiership place, Charlton strengthened their position in consecutive years to start being mentioned as Champions' League contenders. Their Achilles heel is a pattern of going flat in the last quarter of the season.

```
       ...Pulled back from 5-1 down to win league match 7-6 (v Huddersfield in 1957)...
...Only FA Cup semi-finalist to lose a match on the way (1946, when there were two legged ties)...
  ...Had two players sent off for fighting each other (Mike Flanagan and Derek Hales, 1979)...
```

RIVALS

Not surprisingly, considering the club's rather different outlook towards the football business, Charlton have an antipathy towards Manchester United that is (even) greater than the average set of fans, not helped when virtually all their away following at The Valley in 2003 refused to sit down, leading Greenwich Council to order that 600 seats remain empty for their next visit, thus punishing the innocent party.

MANCHESTER UNITED

The usual landlord/tenant niggles are amplified between Palace and Charlton. The timing of the move was unfortunate. The sides were playing in the same division, and news came by way of an anonymous leaflet…during Charlton's home game with Crystal Palace. The row between the two tends to revolve around the endlessly fascinating question of which is the most successful South London club – but both have to draw on very long memories to gather evidence.

CRYSTAL PALACE

Palace have been slightly caught on the hop by the changes in local fortunes. Obsessed with Brighton, they have tended to historically ignore Charlton as minor players, preferring Millwall as their second-string dislike. But suddenly the two have been thrust together in The Premiership.

There is obviously a major cultural gulf between Charlton and Millwall. Interestingly, Charlton reject any claim that Millwall are a 'true' South London club and sneer that the self-styled true cockneys are swelled by wannabes from rural Kent.

MILLWALL

Although very low for violent incidents, Charlton have a tiny number of the completely ludicrous fringe. Even more unlikely than the fact that a married history teacher living in Brimingham was jailed for organising a fight at a London railway station in 2002 – was his allegiance to Charlton Athletic. Their foe at the pitched battle was Southampton, a club for whom Charlton have no particular antipathy. The pattern of organised fights between seemingly random clubs gives some weight to the argument that the phenomenon is only loosely linked with football.

For reasons best known to themselves, a few from Charlton imagine they have a natural kinship with Glasgow Rangers, a depressing sign of 'protestant solidarity' that has all the usual half-witted supremacist overtones. Otherwise, Charlton has probably the strongest anti-racist policies in the Premiership.

PERFORMANCE AGAINST RIVALS
MILLWALL

WON 16%
LOST 45%
DRAWN 39%

SUPPORTERS' VFM 84%

LOVE/HATE

The only trouble with having a booming youth academy is that it causes a lot of resentment when those who benefit jump ship for loads of dosh. Just as he had become a solid favourite at The Valley, *Scott Parker* was lured away to Chelsea. Having signed a five-year contract, Parker left the Addicks when placed fourth in the league and pushing for a European spot. He got into a strop, forcing Curbishley's hand and left Stamford Bridge to enjoy only intermittent first team action.

CHANTS

Sung at home to Manchester United,

'You only live round the corner'.

'YOUR GROUND'S TOO BIG FOR YOU!'
RATING

100
80
60
40
20
0

ATTENDANCE AS A PERCENTAGE OF CAPACITY 100%

Commentating at Euro 2004, Alan Curbishley lurched into uncharacteristic lads-speak when admiring the performance of a Latvian defender; "He's working his nuts.. er, socks off".

CHELSEA

Recommended website: **www.cfc-net.co.uk**

WHO ARE YA?

It says something about the change in the world economy that west London estate agents report that the only individuals rich enough to buy the swankiest Fulham and Chelsea houses are Russians. Every financial journalist with instincts for a good splash has tried to trace exactly where the money that is currently supporting Chelsea has come from. What is vaguely known is that Russian State oil assets were flogged to a variety of characters, including one Roman Abramovich, a man once questioned in connection with the disappearance of a train load of diesel. A clever series of ruses involving the flogging of the black syrupy stuff through a network of companies at knockdown prices somehow led to a football club who play in blue having the financial clout to buy absolutely anything it wants, though Jose Mourinho has hinted that the mega-spending days have reached their peak.

CELEBRITY FANS
DEREK FOWLDS
Comedy Actor – Yes Minister
JEREMY VINE
Broadcaster
LAWRENCE DALLAGLIO
England Rugby Union ace

IN and AROUND

The Borough of Kensington and Chelsea has always been chock full of the famous, influential and talented. Kylie and Dannie Minogue also have homes there. There is an impressive list of ex-residents in one road alone, Cheyne Walk. They include David Lloyd George (ex-PM), Sylvia Pankhurst (suffragette), Isambard Kingdom Brunel (Engineer), George Eliot (novelist) and American painter, James Whistler (as in 'Whistler's mother' which was defaced by Mr Bean).

Chelsea are simply the richest club in the world, having splashed out a cool £110 million on the squad in two years. Remarkably, they only just squeaked into the original line-up for the Premier League, when in 1989-90 all three promoted teams held on to their status, the last season this occurred. Two years later, the top clubs broke away from the Football League to form the Premiership.

Chelsea have long had one of the widest geographical distributions of fans, with regulars at the Bridge flocking in from Herts and Bucks to the north and west, and as far south as the Sussex towns. Their hardcore of supporters used to be the most feared in the Football League. Their fans have fought countless battles up and down the country, including a particularly notorious riot at Derby in 1973 when as many as 3,000 held a pitch battle on the Baseball Ground pitch. The long since demolished 'Shed' was the hangout for arguably the worst species of hooligans ever seen in British football, a far cry from the club's totally reformed glitzy image.

Under the affable Claudio Ranieri, it was difficult for outsiders to dislike Chelsea. Now the substantially less amusing Mourinho is in place, it will be interesting to see whether the club can retain the relative goodwill they've built up or if their high-rolling, free spending lifestyle will attract new enemies.

Chelsea have the distinction of being the first English League side to field a team consisting of entirely foreign players. This unique feat was achieved when Chelsea visited Southampton on Boxing Day 1999. The 11 sent on to the field that day by Gianluca Vialli (Italy) were:

De Goey (Holland), Ferrer (Spain), Thome (Brazil), Leboeuf (France), Babayaro (Nigeria), Petrescu (Romania), Deschamps (France), di Matteo (Italy), Ambrosetti (Italy), Poyet (Uruguay), Flo (Norway).

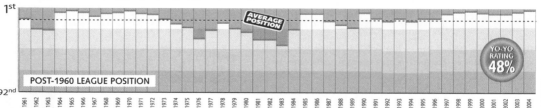

1st

AVERAGE POSITION

YO-YO RATING 48%

POST-1960 LEAGUE POSITION

92nd

1961 1962 1963 1964 1965 1966 1967 1968 1969 1970 1971 1972 1973 1974 1975 1976 1977 1978 1979 1980 1981 1982 1983 1984 1985 1986 1987 1988 1989 1990 1991 1992 1993 1994 1995 1996 1997 1998 1999 2000 2001 2002 2003 2004

PROGRESS REPORT

What has gone before hardly seems relevant to current-day Chelsea. A general improvement from their mid-table record is hardly likely to be enough for either Abromovich or the fans, for whom it's basically Championship or bust. Chelsea are actually bordering on bobbler status, with eight changes of division since 1960. They've now gone eight seasons in the Premiership in 8th position or better.

...Ken Bates bought the club for £1 in 1982...Pitch is above an underground car park...
...Stamford Bridge was built before their was a team to play there...

RIVALS

A glance at a map of the capital would suggest that, purely on a geographical basis, Chelsea's main rivals should be fellow west Londoners Fulham and Queens Park Rangers. Indeed, Chelsea are considered as rivals by both of these clubs, but the Stamford Bridge faithful are reluctant to return the 'compliment'. One Chelsea fan told us: "I have not heard an anti-Fulham or anti-QPR song at Stamford Bridge since 1968."

TOTTENHAM HOTSPUR

Chelsea supporters tend to direct what little anger they have more towards north London. Arsenal are obvious targets as the most successful London club in recent years, and whose crown the Chelsea faithful desire. However, Spurs are historically on the receiving end and, as with many not so obvious hostilities, the rivalry has its roots in the past and involves substantial amounts of aggro.

ARSENAL

The 1967 FA Cup final between Chelsea and Spurs was, by all accounts, a drab affair with Spurs emerging as the 2-1 victors. To add insult to injury, one of the Spurs' players stood in front of the Chelsea fans, pointed and started laughing. Outside the ground afterwards, street battles blew up. Subsequently, when Chelsea went to Tottenham in November of that year, there were more scenes and a large number of arrests. The rivalry was born, and to this day it remains reasonably strong, though Spurs are hardly seen as on-the-pitch equivalents. Unfortunately, even in this enlightened age, anti-Semitic songs can still be heard echoing around Stamford Bridge when Spurs are in town.

SUPPORTERS' VFM 88%

PERFORMANCE AGAINST RIVALS
ARSENAL

WON 31% LOST 41% DRAWN 28%

MANCHESTER UNITED

Plenty of older fans harbour bad feelings towards Leeds United. In the late 1960s, the two were involved in a series of high-stake games culminating in the 1970 FA Cup final when, after a Wembley draw, the match went to a replay at Old Trafford, played on a heavy pitch and featuring men on both sides carved out of granite: Ron 'Chopper' Harris, David Webb, Billy Bremner, Norman Hunter and Jack Charlton could all dish it out...and take it. This resulted in the ultimate rivals' match between teams that represented the north/south divide. Years later, top referee David Ellery watched a recording and reckoned that he would have sent fifteen players off.

LOVE/HATE

"Sit down Sir, you're a w**ker" was the response of Chelsea's ex-chairman *Ken Bates* when challenged by a fan at the club's AGM. This outburst reinforced the belief amongst the Chelsea faithful that the punters at Stamford Bridge were not exactly number one on Mr Bates's list of priorities, a feeling reinforced by the chairman's astonishing call for electric fences to be fitted in football grounds.

CHANTS

*'He's here, he's there, he's every-f***king-where, Frank Leboeuf...'*

After hearing this, Leboeuf said he was flattered, but also embarrassed as he did not want his young son to witness such bad language, hence the revision at the next Chelsea home game:

'He's here, he's there, we're not allowed to swear, Frank Leboeuf...'

'YOUR GROUND'S TOO BIG FOR YOU!'
RATING

100
80
60
40
20
0

ATTENDANCE AS A PERCENTAGE OF CAPACITY
97%

DOH!!

Though Stamford Bridge has managed to shed its reputation for outright violence towards visiting supporters, it is generally considered 'away fan' unfriendly. Many visitors to Stamford Bridge gripe about the high ticket prices (up to £49 each), the poor visibility from parts of the East Stand, cramped leg room and unmanageable queues for half-time refreshments.

CHELTENHAM TOWN

Recommended website: **www.electricrobin.com**

WHO ARE YA?

In some ways, Cheltenham's League status is a bit of a mystery. They didn't cut their teeth by way of FA Cup giant-killings or a long illustrious non-league history. Their promotion to the Conference was decidedly jammy. In 1997, having finished behind Gresley Rovers in the Dr Martens League, they were unexpectedly given the nod when Gresley's ground wasn't deemed to be up to scratch. They haven't had the luxury of being bankrolled by a loaded chairman, and they hail from a town that is usually only associated with the gee-gees.

Cheltenham's League exploits follow the same pattern as recent newbies Macclesfield Town. After the champagne has gone flat, League life for both has become a struggle. The exit of Bobby Gould in 2003 followed some fairly high pressure tactics from the local media, who were more than happy to continue to publish a stream of anti-Gould material. Unusually, when they finally parted company, the club issued a statement with the words "we feel that Bobby Gould was treated in an appalling manner". There was a dearth of high quality candidates for the position he vacated. The chairman received applications from a housewife, a prison officer and someone whose management qualities were demonstrated, they thought, by expertise on the computer game 'Championship manager'.

IN and AROUND

The walls have ears, in Cheltenham's case 9,000 of them, as the town's largest employer is the Government's communications monitoring centre GCHQ, which employs 4,500 people.

They couldn't complain about lack of media exposure during their formative League period as the regional football programme, Soccer AM, developed a cult-like fascination with Cheltenham Town, dedicating a slot to them every single week. The 'deal' to give them blanket publicity emerged when Robins' players explained that a goal celebration against Leyton Orient was an impression of the presenter, Tim Lovejoy, clapping his hands in his own penguin-like fashion. Impressed by their mimicry, the programme contacted the club and offered to give them loads of coverage if they'd perform a celebration of the presenter's choice. Dutifully, Cheltenham's opening goal against Exeter was met with the players waving their arms in the prescribed way.

When Cheltenham made it into the League in 1999, their Whaddon Road ground was possibly the most basic to host League football in recent years, but after the bulldozers went in, things improved hugely. However, the forces of commercial sponsorship have seen two sides jarringly branded the In2Print Stand and the UCAS Main Stand.

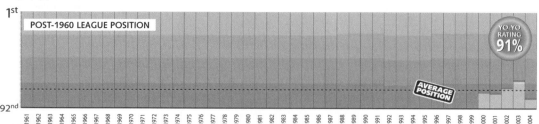

1st

POST-1960 LEAGUE POSITION

YO-YO RATING 91%

AVERAGE POSITION

92nd

1961 1962 1963 1964 1965 1966 1967 1968 1969 1970 1971 1972 1973 1974 1975 1976 1977 1978 1979 1980 1981 1982 1983 1984 1985 1986 1987 1988 1989 1990 1991 1992 1993 1994 1995 1996 1997 1998 1999 2000 2001 2002 2003 2004

PROGRESS REPORT

An uninspiring spell in the Conference ended with relegation in 1992. But once back up, it only took a couple of seasons to hit the big-time, winning promotion to the League in 1999. Following the pattern of the promoted side doing well in Level Three, good top-half finishes saw them go up again through the play-offs three years later. But they were relegated immediately, and fell back to their worst League position, 14th in Level Three, in 2004.

```
                    ...Sacked manager for swearing too much (1961)...
...League status was achieved by a goal in the 7th minute of stoppage time...First recorded
   match was against Dean Close School (couldn't they pick on someone their own size)...
```

RIVALS

GLOUCESTER CITY
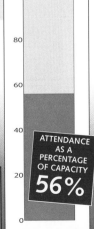

Gloucester City are the targets of the almost universally sung 'In your............slums', though in fairness to them, it is probably the most up-market town in Britain to have ever had to withstand the taunt. But there is a strong perception that Cheltenham is a classier place altogether, a fact that triggers general bad feeling between the major towns that have ended up with only a wafer of countryside between them. Now languishing two promotions away from Cheltenham, the gulf is so wide as to have put the rivalry to bed (as far as Cheltenham are concerned). But it is a symbol of the rapidity of their rise that the two were playing League fixtures against each other in 1996-97, when they engaged in a tit-for-tat battle at the top of the Southern League.

The problem of ditching your old foe is that life can seem a bit bland without any new enemies. Swindon aren't really interested in playing ball at the moment as they have their work cut out with Oxford and are unlikely to lower themselves unless the two's League standings take a long term twist. There's another problem as well – they've never actually met. Looking in the other direction, there's not much chance of exciting the interest of Cardiff – not that you'd really want to. So it was with some relief that an 'off the peg' rivalry was created with the promotion of Kidderminster Harriers in 2000. However, there is little sign of it turning into the new Celtic v Rangers as Town fans are generally quite appreciative of Kidderminster's efforts at securing League status and are more likely to point to a common bond between the clubs rather than emerging animosity.

KIDDERMINSTER HARRIERS

PERFORMANCE AGAINST RIVALS
GLOUCESTER CITY

WON 50%
LOST 20%
DRAWN 30%

SUPPORTERS' VFM 39%

Such is the total lack of interest in Cheltenham as a possible rival, the worst thing opposing fans say about them is that there are a 'few kids' attached to the club who like to try and stir things up. They'll find it hard, as The Robins seem to be well liked throughout much of the region. Even Cardiff City didn't have much luck causing trouble. In 1997, it is said that a group of their infamous Soul Crew paid a visit to Cheltenham with the intention of causing some serious grief, but was dismayed at the complete lack of anyone willing to engage with it. Cheltenham's Safety Officer was quoted as saying 'we ran into them a few months later at a motorway service station and they seemed very friendly'.

Everything points to Cheltenham being utterly peace-loving folk, with just one of them picking up a banning order from the 2002 World Cup. A streaker was arrested at their first League feature at Rochdale, but he turned out to be a local.

LOVE/HATE

Residents of Cheltenham have to put up with the GL postcode of Gloucester and *a tendency for everything to rise in price* when the gee-gees are in town for the Cheltenham Festival.

CHANTS

Seriously lacking in any sort of repertoire, Cheltenham's version of *'Blue Moon'* goes,

*'One song…
we haven't got one song.'*

'YOUR GROUND'S TOO BIG FOR YOU!'
RATING

100
80
60
40
20
0

ATTENDANCE AS A PERCENTAGE OF CAPACITY
56%

DOH!!

Playing at Rochdale in 2000, on-loan Jason Brissett had possession of the ball in his own area when he thought he'd heard the final whistle. Naturally, picking the ball up, he was mortified to discover the ref pointing to the penalty spot, as the sound had come from the crowd. 0-0 at the time, he was let off when the spot-kick was missed.

CHESTER CITY

Recommended website: **www.chester-city.co.uk**

WHO ARE YA?

For a long time, the only worthwhile Chester City factoid was that Ian Rush started and ended his playing career here. But the club's history has been considerably enlivened by 10 years of boom and bust (though leaning more heavily towards the bust). The only possible complaint Chester supporters can have over their resurrection from the dead is that Doncaster managed to pull off a remarkably similar escape act from the Conference just the year before, slightly taking the shine off what would have been the most incredible turnaround.

The club's meltdown effectively started with the takeover by property developer Mark Guterman in 1994. Guterman fled to Wrexham leaving the place with creditors lining up outside. But what followed was a tragi-comedy that only could occur in lower league English football. The attraction of the club to new owner, American Terry Smith, was largely based on visits to the zoo when he was younger. Immediately he could see what was needed, sacking manager Kevin Radcliffe and installing himself as boss, determined to bring his extensive football knowledge to bear. This might have been OK, though in his case the ball was the wrong shape, since his only experience was with a NFL side back in his native United States. Radcliffe was probably best out of it since at one point he had to fork out to pay Chester City's water rates of £5,000 out of his own pocket. Chester's tales of destitution are up with the best of them – a whip round by Southend supporters raised cash for the groundsman to buy some fertiliser for the pitch.

Chester's city centre branch of Macdonald's has no external signage – a position forced on the usually highly visible burger chain by stringent planning restrictions in the historic shopping quarter.

Amidst the chaos, Chester dropped in to the Conference, managing to attract risible crowds that only just struggled past the 500 mark. Smith was given fairly broad hints that the supporters would like him out, including an attempted all-hours picket of the new Deva Stadium. Some semblance of order was restored when Smith chucked in the towel, handing over the reins to Stephen Vaughan in 2001. Initially Chester thought they had completed a hat-trick of duff chairmen, as Vaughan's record at Barrow was suspiciously undistinguished. But helped by the appointment of manager Mark Wright, the team made a concerted effort to return to the League. Four years after losing their place in Level Three, they made mincemeat of the Conference in 2003-2004, in doing so clocking up a performance record that was only beaten by Arsenal's stroll to the Premiership trophy.

For a club embroiled in one of the only derbies where English/Welsh nationalism is a significant factor, Chester's newish Deva Stadium is in an odd geographical black hole. The legend has grown up that it is possible to take a corner in Wales towards a goal-mouth in England. In reality, the pitch is entirely on Welsh soil but the offices are solidly the other side of the border, allowing the club to officially register as English.

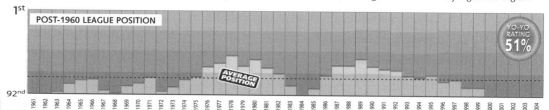

POST-1960 LEAGUE POSITION

1st

92nd

1961 1962 1963 1964 1965 1966 1967 1968 1969 1970 1971 1972 1973 1974 1975 1976 1977 1978 1979 1980 1981 1982 1983 1984 1985 1986 1987 1988 1989 1990 1991 1992 1993 1994 1995 1996 1997 1998 1999 2000 2001 2002 2003 2004

AVERAGE POSITION

YO-YO RATING 51%

PROGRESS REPORT

Chester have had a couple of reasonable spikes since 1960, but action outside the bottom two divisions has eluded them. The closest they have got was fifth in the Level Two in 1978. The drop to the Conference was not entirely predictable from the graphs. In the seasons immediately prior to the drop, they had maintained reasonable mid-table finishes The woes deepened even further with relegation to the Conference in 2000. By 2002, they were in deep trouble, finishing in a woeful 14th, making their effort in 2003-04 in securing automatic promotion back to the League look even better.

```
...Have won Welsh Cup three times...Played home games at Macclesfield for two years...
...Visiting player was cautioned for blowing a trumpet that had been thrown on to the pitch...
```

RIVALS

Chester can't get too shirty about the presence of the two Merseyside clubs. Both have done their bit to ease the financial burdens of the relative minnows, Chester and Wrexham, with coffer-swelling friendlies, indeed Chester's biggest attendance at the new Deva Stadium was for a pre-season match with Everton. Liverpool are currently not in their good books having taken their warm-up patronage to Wrexham.

WREXHAM

Being as isolated as they are, it is said that Wrexham were quietly pleased when Chester got back into the League, though the police might have hoped that the two stay put. The local constabulary certainly threw their hands up in horror when the two did a deal to ground-share after Chester sold their old home. This demonstrates the intensity of one of the most ferocious lower league rivalries, if anything aggravated by the fact that their meetings have been relatively few recently. In times past, the two enjoyed frequent clashes in the Welsh Cup. The city of Chester attracts serious night-time boozers from across the region, including many revellers from over the border, meaning that football related animosities tend to come to a head in 2am taxi queues, not really the best circumstances for good-natured banter.

Another particular difficulty in this part of the world is the strain of English/Welsh relations, which were never too good to start with on the northern border. There is a significant minority on both sides willing to get involved in trouble. A running battle in Chester city centre in 1997 was fought between at least 100 on each side. Otherwise, in the absence of fixtures, there is a suspicion of a degree of pre-organisation. In 2004, sets of fans had a less than friendly 'get-together' at a Chester social club.

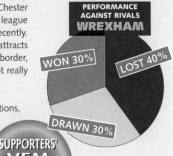

PERFORMANCE AGAINST RIVALS
WREXHAM

WON 30%
LOST 40%
DRAWN 30%

SUPPORTERS' VFM 51%

LOVE/HATE

The list of objections to ex-chairman *Terry Smith* is virtually endless. Some were somewhat trivial i.e. that his office was a mess and his car was unroadworthy. More critically, his management of the playing side was characterised with some of the most extraordinary tactical decisions, including the use of three captains – one for the defence, another for the midfield and one up front.

Their domination of the Conference was helped by the phenomenal strike partnership of *Daryl Clare* and a player formally known, unflatteringly, as Bungle, *Darryn Stamp*. Between them they conjured up an incredible 50 goals in the promotion season.

CHANTS

Considering the Deva's partly Welsh location, it seems a bit rich that Chester fans are so keen to indulge in anti-rural chanting accusing Wrexham of participating in ovine relations.

'YOUR GROUND'S TOO BIG FOR YOU!'
RATING

100
80
60
40
20
0

ATTENDANCE AS A PERCENTAGE OF CAPACITY 44%

DOH!!

Chester's departure from the League in 2000 was less than glorious. Two victories on the trot made Chester favourites to pull away from the dreaded last place. As it turned out, a home draw against Carlisle would have ensured safety. A dour goal-less struggle had reached the 80th minute with the visitors reduced to nothing more than a couple of half chances. Things swung even more Chester's way when Carlisle had two men sent off. The last 10 minutes saw the Carlisle goal under siege, until, in the last minute, Scott Dobie sprung an unexpected killer-blow by netting the winner for Carlisle.

CHESTERFIELD

Recommended website: **www.chesterfield-mad.co.uk**

WHO ARE YA?

In their early history, Chesterfield's claim to fame was that of signing the goalkeeper with the worst CV in English footballing history. At the end of the nineteenth century, Charlie Bunyan joined the club from Hyde, Lancashire, a club whose very mention tends to lead the mind naturally to the victims of the biggest ever English League drubbing, 26-0 to Preston in 1887. Despite this slight block on his copybook, he enjoyed a successful career with Chesterfield. Visitors to their Saltergate Ground over a century later might cynically point out that it looks like the last time any work was done on it it may have been during his era. To say it is showing its age is an understatement. Generally, football fans have conservative views on relocation, but a vote determined that the majority favoured to up sticks to a new site at Wheeldon Mill.

CELEBRITY FANS
JO GUEST
Model
JOHN LUKIC
Former Leeds and Arsenal goalkeeper

The on-field history of the club can be summed up rather more concisely than that off it. They won something called the Anglo-Scottish Cup in 1981, though its prestige can be gauged by the fact that the following season, the Scottish clubs withdrew. Otherwise, their main claim to semi-fame is that they would have been the only team outside the top two divisions to have played in a FA Cup semi-final, had they managed to overcome Middlesbrough in 1997.

IN and AROUND

Whilst playing at Chesterfield's ABC theatre in the summer of 1967, Jimi Hendrix broke his foot by dropping his guitar on it.

Behind the scenes, the club's fortunes are depressingly familiar, the low-light being a nine-point deduction for transfer irregularities and fiddling gate receipts. Supporters stepped in to buy the club out of administration in 2001. Now effectively in the hands of Chesterfield Supporters Football Society, it is perhaps the foremost example of true fan power. Mascot Chester the Fieldmouse gets stuck into a variety of community projects, including an engagement at the library where he is reported to have frightened staff in the 'downstairs snack bar'. Sounds nasty.

Though Southerners might see Chesterfield as a whippet-breeding, brass band oompahing type place, it is actually situated in a relatively rural area, as near to Sheffield as it is to the idyllic pudding country of Bakewell. With Derby and Nottingham nearby, the club's fan base is somewhat limited. Saltergate has a capacity of just over 8,000, but with average attendances only just topping 4,000, it is unlikely that the groundsman has to dust down the 'Sold Out' signs on too regular a basis.

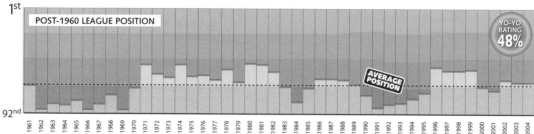

1st

POST-1960 LEAGUE POSITION

YO-YO RATING 48%

AVERAGE POSITION

92nd

1961 1962 1963 1964 1965 1966 1967 1968 1969 1970 1971 1972 1973 1974 1975 1976 1977 1978 1979 1980 1981 1982 1983 1984 1985 1986 1987 1988 1989 1990 1991 1992 1993 1994 1995 1996 1997 1998 1999 2000 2001 2002 2003 2004

PROGRESS REPORT

Their grip on Level Two is less than convincing, two 20ths and one 18th in the last three seasons. The last time Chesterfield were outside the bottom two leagues, the British populace were still emerging from the air-raid shelters. Their post-1960 average just manages to keep its head above the depths of Level Three.

```
...Once played in a Union Jack design strip (1892)...
...Gordon Banks made his league debut for the club...
```

RIVALS

The skeletons of the miners' strike still get dug up, often inappropriately between teams from regions with little direct involvement. But the Mansfield/Chesterfield derby is the real thing. 1984 was the beginning of the end of the industry on any significant scale in the UK. The industrial dispute managed to divide communities, and even families, in the Derbyshire, Nottinghamshire and Yorkshire areas. When the Nottinghamshire miners took the decision to return to work and effectively removed any last semblance of solidarity, the seeds were sown for the intense rivalry and hatred felt between the two clubs. The chant of 'scabs' is still, to this day, directed at the visiting fans whenever Mansfield Town visit Chesterfield, although when the Mansfield fans retort with their club's nickname, 'Stags', it can sound as if everyone within the Recreation Ground is singing from the same hymn sheet.

MANSFIELD TOWN

The rivalry is far from good-natured, and it is rare that encounters between the two end up trouble-free; hardly surprising as both clubs appear to have a disproportionate number of troublemakers within their core following. However, the official stats may mask the fact that both attract a number of floating nutters, with significant numbers of Derby fans temporarily switching their allegiance to Chesterfield whenever there's a chance of some Derbyshire/Nottinghamshire antagonism.

The Saltergate firm affectionately call themselves the 'Chesterfield Bastard Squad', a name that alludes to an uncertain parentage. But consideration has been given to its lineage. The ongoing future of the firm is guaranteed by the regular recruitment of new members, usually from a charming bunch known as the 'Newbould Young Offenders', a sort of Bastard Squad feeder organisation. It should not be assumed, however, that all within their number are hellbent on causing trouble. One Chesterfield fan had an original view on personal security "I'm not a hooligan, but I often travelled to away games with them. You knew that if anything started there were plenty around you who would sort things out!"

SHEFFIELD UNITED

Unlike Barnsley, who dislike Wednesday more, Chesterfield fans are also less than enamoured with Sheffield United, for the same reasons as half the country. Cue anti-Neil quote: "that w**ker just winds me up every time he opens his mouth".

PERFORMANCE AGAINST RIVALS
MANSFIELD

WON 33%
LOST 41%
DRAWN 26%

SUPPORTERS' VFM 65%

LOVE/HATE

The Spireites were at risk of a nosebleed when, in 1997, they reached a FA Cup semi-final against Middlesbrough. When a shot bounced down off the crossbar and clearly over the goal line, there wasn't a Russian linesman in sight. Chesterfield were enraged as referee *David Ellaray* casually waved play on. The match ended in a 3-3 draw with Middlesbrough going on to win the replay and meet Chelsea in the final.

CHANTS

'Carefree, wherever we may be We are the famous CFC'

Chesterfield would like to point out that the other CFC, Chelsea, aren't remotely as famous.

'YOUR GROUND'S TOO BIG FOR YOU!'
RATING

100
80
60
40
20
0

ATTENDANCE AS A PERCENTAGE OF CAPACITY
51%

DOH!!

The seemingly innocuous transfer of Luke Beckett from Chester to Chesterfield in 2000 was the catalyst for a chain of events which nearly forced the club out of existence. Suggestions of impropriety caused the FA to investigate the then chairman, Darren Brown, on charges of financial irregularities. Brown had taken out a number of loans secured against the Recreation Ground, and then used the funds to finance his other business and sporting activities. The resulting punishment, consisting of a £20,000 fine and nine-point deduction, robbed Chesterfield of the Level Three Championship that season. However, they were still promoted, albeit in third place, leading to some gripes that they 'got away with it'.

COLCHESTER UNITED

Recommended website: **www.colchesterutd-mad.co.uk**

WHO ARE YA?

No matter how poor a lower League club's record, one decent giant-killing act can live on in the public's memory years after people have forgotten who went on to win the major honours. In 1971, Leeds were gaining a reputation for being the strong-arm bullies of the English game. In terms of the gulf in class, Colchester's 3-2 victory in the Fifth Round of the FA Cup can probably only be beaten by Walsall knocking out Arsenal in 1933, but for causing delight for neutrals, the humbling of Leeds was a class above. The U's are less keen to remember the feat of tiny Northern League outfit, Bedlington Terriers, who dumped Colchester out of the FA cup in 1999.

CELEBRITY FANS
STEVE LAMACQ
DJ
BOB RUSSELL
Local MP

England's oldest established town lost its League representation in 1990. The funds had all but run out, not helped by the fact that following the Bradford Fire, sections of the decrepit wooden bits of Layer Road couldn't be used. A ban on away fans caused income to plummet. Nor did one of the more extraordinary sackings in lower League history help their cause. Whilst riding high in second spot of Level One in 1987, ex-goalkeeper Mike Walker was unexpectedly given his marching orders, as, in his words, the chairman wanted to 'kick their way out' of the division. By late 1993, Walker was leading Premiership Norwich to one of the great British triumphs in Europe, beating Bayern Munich. The same night, Colchester conceded seven against Darlington. Drifting into the Conference in 1989, there seemed no reason as to why the club shouldn't disappear without trace. But just two seasons later, they won a titanic battle with Wycombe Wanderers to regain their League place, with much credit going to player/manager Roy McDonough, whose standout non-footballing characteristic was an uncanny resemblance to Basil Fawlty.

A trainspotters' heaven - Colchester has Britain's longest railway platform.

In one of the more daring moves to boost attendances, the club let everyone in for free to a League game with Doncaster in 1995, the first time this had been done by a British League club. They even threw in free transport and a cup of coffee. The service got even better for the eight fans that travelled with the club to Wycombe in the Bob Lord Trophy, an exceedingly minor non-league competition. With it not commercially viable to open the snack bar just for them, they moaned at their goalkeeper, Scott Thompson. At half-time, they were escorted to the other end by the police to pick up eight cups of tea, purchased for them by the Colchester goalkeeper, who couldn't bear to see them go thirsty.

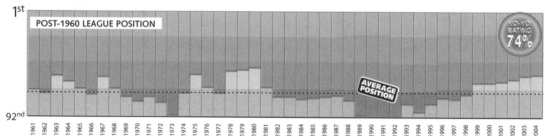

POST-1960 LEAGUE POSITION

YO-YO RATING 74%

AVERAGE POSITION

1st ... 92nd

1961 1962 1963 1964 1965 1966 1967 1968 1969 1970 1971 1972 1973 1974 1975 1976 1977 1978 1979 1980 1981 1982 1983 1984 1985 1986 1987 1988 1989 1990 1991 1992 1993 1994 1995 1996 1997 1998 1999 2000 2001 2002 2003 2004

PROGRESS REPORT

A flying start to the 2004-2005 season saw Colchester scaling the heights of Level Two – a record that if maintained would give them their best finish since 1960. Up to 1980, they flitted between the bottom two divisions, before bedding into the basement for nine years, followed by two seasons in the Conference. Having reached Level Two in 1998, they have been on a very gradual upward path.

```
...Had to use three goalies in one match after two were sent off (1993)...
      ...Won the double (Conference and FA Trophy)...
   ...Took the idea for club kit colours from Huddersfield Town...
```

RIVALS

Considering their Essex location and long-term status, Colchester should primarily have eyes only for Southend, but their hatred of Ipswich in Suffolk, which is closer, is based on something more than just the usual little club/big club jealousies.

IPSWICH

With a distinct lack of Christmas spirit, the then manager of Colchester, George Burley, resigned from the club on 24th December 1994. The U's' board was spitting blood, claiming that neither Ipswich nor anyone else had any right to be talking to him. Caretaker boss Dale Roberts took charge, only to run off to Ipswich as well shortly afterwards. The row over compensation payments led to Colchester sending in the lawyers. Burley's nervousness at the episode may well have got to his new club, as with the writs flying, Ipswich suffered a record Premiership mauling leading to unrestrained joy at Layer Road when the tannoy announced a final score of Manchester United 9, Ipswich 0. If anything, the bad feeling was made worse by the clubs when Ipswich only settled as the judge was getting wigged up, leading to the impression that despite months of protesting their innocence, they were simply hoping Colchester would run out of money to contest the case.

SOUTHEND

Colchester maintain a handful of rivalries with clubs, most of whom dislike Colchester somewhat more than Colchester hate them. Southend United are seen as a blot on the Essex landscape; a bit of the East End transplanted onto an otherwise fine county. Having dodged each other in the Leagues, it was a pre-season friendly between the two that sparked the worst recent trouble, when 15 were arrested at Roots Hall in 2003, following an assault on a steward.

WYCOMBE

Wycombe Wanderers feel utterly cursed by Colchester having had a dismal record against them in crucial games, aggravated by what they see as a hardcore of distinctly unpleasant Colchester fans. Colchester is firmly a garrison town with over 4,000 troops stationed there, and it is generally accepted that a number of them use the football team to let off steam.

PERFORMANCE AGAINST RIVALS
SOUTHEND

WON 39%

LOST 29%

DRAWN 32%

SUPPORTERS' VFM
86%

LOVE/HATE

HATE

Former player *Steve Wignall* was the master-mind of their promotion to Division Two. His resignation as manager in 1999 was relayed to ardent DJ follower Steve Lamarcq who was doing his BBC 1 radio show at the time. He took the news badly, being 'barely able to speak for four records'. Much maligned towards the end of his spell in charge, after a hybernation Wignall turned up managing rivals Southend.

CHANTS

♪**♪*!

'He's fat, he's round…he bounces on the ground'

Aimed at the slightly rotund Barry Fry

DOH!!

In 1987, manager Roger Brown came to the club with the promise of taking them to the top-flight via successive promotions. Neither his track record of managing a small factory nor an unsuccessful minor team suggested his dream was entirely realistic. The central plank of his strategy was a cunning tactical innovation whereby on winning a corner, most of the team would huddle together by the flag and burst out in all directions as soon as the kick was taken, so disorientating the opposition.

The ploy failed to result in a single goal.

'YOUR GROUND'S TOO BIG FOR YOU!'
R A T I N G

100

80

60

40

20

0

ATTENDANCE AS A PERCENTAGE OF CAPACITY
47%

COVENTRY CITY

A.K.A. THE LADY GODIVAS

Recommended website: **www.gmkonline.co.uk**

WHO ARE YA?

CELEBRITY FANS
RICHARD KEYS
Sky Sports Presenter
EDDY JORDAN
F1 Boss

Much of Coventry's strategy was well ahead of its time. The club underwent 'rebranding' 20 years before anyone had heard of the term, changing their nickname The Bantams to the more upbeat Sky Blues in 1967.

Best known by modern day fans for hanging on by their fingernails to Premiership status, logically Coventry probably shouldn't have stayed in the top-flight as long as they did. Considering their average position whilst there was only 16th, it is a bit of a statistical freak that they performed so many last minute escapes. On ten occasions, they could have been relegated on the final afternoon, but survived. The whispers about the circumstances of these results continues – in particular their habit of being able to know other important results whilst still playing their final matches. This was thanks to a number of helpful 'incidents', most notably in 1977 when both Coventry and visitors Bristol City could have been relegated depending on results elsewhere. Traffic jams helpfully prevented the Bristol contingent from getting to the ground on time, so a delay to the kick-off meant that both teams knew exactly what they had to do in the last five minutes – precisely nothing. With the game at 2-2 they only needed to play out a draw to ensure that Sunderland would go down. Predictably, the game suddenly slowed to a good-natured kickabout.

IN and AROUND

Highfield Road could best be described as an example of an old new stadium – the first ground, in 1981, to experiment with an all-seater format. Optimistically, when plans were formulated in the late 90s, a new stadium was planned for a former gas works site, codenamed 'Arena 2000'. As 2000 came to an end without the bulldozers going in, it became 'Arena 2001'. At the end of 2001, following relegation from the Premiership, the reference to the year of completion was quietly dropped.

Being shunned by friends is widely known as being 'sent to Coventry', but there is no consensus over the origins of the phrase. It may relate to St. John's Church, Coventry, used as a prison in the English Civil War where prisoners were ignored, though this interpretation doesn't really explain the current meaning.

Since the change to a sky blue kit was so deliberate, it's strange that the club has frequently annoyed fans by indulging in endless revisions. Considered by some to be the most stunningly awful football kit of all time – in 1978, Coventry's away strip was chocolate brown.

The club has a history of dubious signings. In particular, Craig Bellamy was loathed by the fans. Bought from Norwich for £6 million to replace Robbie Keane, his efforts up front failed to prevent relegation. Then manager Gordon Strachan made a veiled reference to the fact that his poor finishing had been partly responsible. Bellamy didn't hang around once they went down and then sealed his notoriety with a few parting shots in the press.

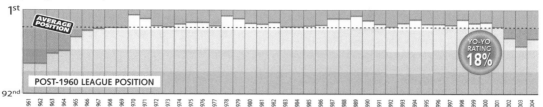

1st

AVERAGE POSITION

POST-1960 LEAGUE POSITION

YO-YO RATING 18%

92nd

1961 1962 1963 1964 1965 1966 1967 1968 1969 1970 1971 1972 1973 1974 1975 1976 1977 1978 1979 1980 1981 1982 1983 1984 1985 1986 1987 1988 1989 1990 1991 1992 1993 1994 1995 1996 1997 1998 1999 2000 2001 2002 2003 2004

PROGRESS REPORT

Anyone under the age of 50 will tend to perceive Coventry as basically a Premiership side who have had a recent turn for the worst. Their historical pattern is unique. For such a large city, they were surprisingly minor players in the lower leagues until promotion to the old First Division in 1967. Having made it, they put up a ferocious fight to stay there, resulting in a run of 34 consecutive years in the top-flight, though their best finishing position was only sixth during the entire period. Their post-1960 average rests between the Premiership and Level One. But having finally gone down in 2001, they have failed to put together a concerted challenge to return.

```
    ...Highfield Road's conversion to all-seats caused attendances to collapse by 8,000...
    ...Made cameo appearance as answer to a quiz question in Monty Python at the Hollywood Bowl'...
```

RIVALS

For it size and prominence, Coventry are possibly the best liked (or more realistically, least hated) club in the football league. It is a quirk of geography and heroic on-the-field exploits that have ensured that Coventry are effectively frozen out of any volatile derby situations. Situated between the Birmingham/West Midlands sprawl and the distinct cities to the east, nobody is that bothered with Coventry in the middle. To their east, Leicester are named as number one rivals, though Leicester themselves primarily have eyes for Nottingham Forest and Derby. Walker's crisps, manufactured in Thurmaston, Leicester, are boycotted by many Coventry fans. One supporter, commenting on the features of the town and club said, 'different county, different accent, the way members of the club have behaved in the last few years and the low intellect of their supporters'. The

LEICESTER

saga of Leicester City's break in La Manga in 2004 put the club well down the list of sides that neutrals tend to like – the reverse of the Sky Blues who still attract neutral support off the back of beating Spurs in the FA Cup final of 1987. Villa are naturally disliked as they were Birmingham's top side during Coventry's Premiership stay. Britain's second city is seen as 'getting everything, whilst Coventry misses out'.

SUPPORTERS' VFM 47%

ASTON VILLA

With the larger Birmingham and East Midlands clubs' tendency to bob around between the Premiership and First Division, rivalries are constantly being revised according to who is seen as the biggest on-the-field threat. Traditionally, in the lower league days, Northampton were named as Coventry's rivals, with Wolves taking over during their heyday.

PERFORMANCE AGAINST RIVALS
ASTON VILLA

WON 15%
DRAWN 29%
LOST 56%

Jimmy Hill was one of the first to actively campaign against hooliganism in the 1970s. With a strong anti-violence culture, the club has an admirable record of not being involved in serious incidents – a good record considering its low to middling social conditions.

LOVE/HATE

Ex-chairman *Bryan Richardson*  is a member of the ever-increasing number of the football league's despised ex-board members. The pattern is familiar. Richardson was the saviour, particularly for bringing Strachan to the club. But soon he developed a reputation for endless promises but no delivery, with relegation in 2001 breaking the spell decisively. The revelation that the club had mounted up a £10 million debt didn't help either. Jimmy Hill, despite his long-term association with the club, is frequently named as a dislike as well.

The 'people's pro', *Stuart Pearce*, guaranteed himself a good reception at Highfield Road.

CHANTS

'In our Coventry homes
We speak with an accent
exceedingly rare
If you want a cathedral
we've got one to spare'

They could even do you a BOGOF offer, as they've got three of them.

'YOUR GROUND'S TOO BIG FOR YOU!'
RATING

100

80

60

40

ATTENDANCE AS A PERCENTAGE OF CAPACITY
64%

20

0

DOH!!

Coventry's Premiership escape acts left them with little energy to fight prolonged FA Cup campaigns, which makes their win of 1987 even more remarkable. Famed for going out to lower league opposition, they surpassed themselves by managing to lose to non-league Sutton United the following season.

CREWE ALEXANDRA

Recommended website: **www.crewealex.com**

WHO ARE YA?

If you'd crash-landed from another galaxy and felt one of your first priorities was to choose which football team to support, unaffected by the bias of an earthly upbringing, Crewe would be a logical choice. On many fronts, they could justifiably think of themselves as the 'best' team in the country for fans. To the disinterested, they have an almost frustratingly long list of virtues – stability on and off the field, a highly popular long-serving manager, a decent chairman, a genuine history of listening to supporters, no violence or bigotry and a ground that has grown with the club.

CELEBRITY FANS
ELAINE LORDAN
Lynn Slater in *Eastenders*
MICHAEL CRAWFORD
Actor - *Some Mothers Do 'ave 'em*
DARIO G
Pop group named after Crewe manager

Though not a problem for train enthusiasts, Southerners have difficulty placing Crewe on a map. To them it sounds rather more north than it actually is. Sandwiched uncomfortably south of Liverpool and Manchester and to the north of Stoke, Crewe has a fairly small catchment area surrounding a less than massive town. The fans' keenness on the association with the railway is questionable. The official nickname of the 'Railwaymen' is spurned in favour of simply 'Alex', though a decision to drop the railway emblem from the shirts caused a stink with many. Gresty Road has a lopsided feel, with the stand on the south touchline huge compared to the other three. It is sited so close to the west coast mainline that steam locos used to belch white smoke over the pitch in play – leading on one occasion in the late 50s to Crewe controversially sneaking the ball into their opponents' net through the haze.

IN and AROUND

Until 2002, Crewe was the home of the world's most prestigious motor, the Rolls Royce.

Despite their reputation for keeping a large ear out for fans' views, there have been constant gripes about the kit design. The supposedly red shirt has undergone endless mutations where bits of white and blue have found their way in – including a notorious version in 1992-93 with small red and white squares; from a distance, a sickly pink.

Continuity and good management have bred unusual loyalty amongst players. In 1999, fighting relegation, midfielder Seth Johnson delayed a £3 million transfer to Derby to try and keep Crewe in the First Division. Danny Murphy unexpectedly came back to Crewe on loan from Liverpool to boost the cause as well, allowing them to avoid the drop.

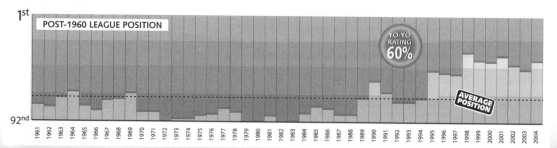

POST-1960 LEAGUE POSITION — 1st ... 92nd — YO-YO RATING 60% — AVERAGE POSITION

1961 1962 1963 1964 1965 1966 1967 1968 1969 1970 1971 1972 1973 1974 1975 1976 1977 1978 1979 1980 1981 1982 1983 1984 1985 1986 1987 1988 1989 1990 1991 1992 1993 1994 1995 1996 1997 1998 1999 2000 2001 2002 2003 2004

PROGRESS REPORT

Historically, Crewe could lay claim to the title of England's most obscure league club. In the 50s, they managed to finish bottom of Level Three on three consecutive occasions, and had an undistinguished history of being dumped out of the FA Cup by non-league opposition. Still hanging on to Level One status, they are amongst a handful of clubs who are currently well over a whole league higher than their average. Decades of bumping along in the basement leaves them with an average league position in Level Three.

```
...Once fielded four 'Jones' in the same team...Ball kicked from ground ended up in Scotland
(via train carriage)...Have won Welsh Cup twice - an achievement for an English club...
```

RIVALS

Stoke City may like to think of themselves as bigger and better, but, unlikely as it seems, Crewe have maintained a better league position over the last decade. In their heyday, Stoke had bigger fish to fry with a clutch of venomous rivalries with every mad mob in the country. But the unmissable fact that their neighbours to the northwest were doing better than them started to put Crewe on the radar. Although the mock Icelandic 'Sjoke City' is a popular term of abuse from others, Crewe (and Port Vale) prefer to call them Clayheads.

STOKE CITY ☠☠☠☠☠☠

STOCKPORT COUNTY ☠☠☠☠☠☠

Stockport, though by no means neighbours, are often named – mostly because the two have a bit of a divisional magnet to each other. There's a minor antagonism between Wrexham and Crewe that boils down to a bit of cross-border nationalistic abuse, but if anything it is the fact that Alex are well regarded by other clubs' fans that is most noteworthy. Having been beaten by Crewe in the play-off semi-final in 1997, Luton fans trooped onto the pitch and applauded the Alex faithful.

Crewe have no known record of any violent activity and their reputation as all round good eggs is bolstered by their good-natured musical accompaniment, in latter days provided by a bass drummer. In fairness, the ground needs it. Gresty Road is one of the quieter atmospheres you'll come across and a few hundred away fans can find it quite easy to steal the day.

Crewe's lack of aggressive intent is demonstrated by their fans' habit of breaking into rounds of stately applause in their appreciation of skilful play from either side. This phenomenon has become known as the 'Gresty Clap' – an unfortunate term that conjures up images of a condition that can be caught from a toilet seat.

PERFORMANCE AGAINST RIVALS
STOKE CITY

WON 50%
LOST 33%
DRAWN 17%

SUPPORTERS' VFM **61%**

LOVE/HATE

Possibly the best known piece of football trivia in every playground is that *Dario Gradi* ♡ is the longest serving manager in the football league, having joined Crewe in 1983. (Sir Alex Ferguson is second in the table – at Manchester United since 1986). Fans marvel at his ability to regenerate the team with young talent. They also like the chairman, the pies, the girls who sell programmes...just about anything and everything associated with Alex in fact.

Of seven respondents to the author's questionnaire, Crewe fans were unable to summon up a single hate! When severely pressed, ex-player *Colin Cramb* 🖐 is not well-regarded for managing to fall out with virtually everyone at the club and Wrexham old-boy *Gary Bennet* 🖐 is unpopular.

CHANTS

Crewe almost certainly originated 'Blue Moon' as a football song before it was adopted by Manchester City. A slight antipathy towards Stockport masks the fact that both have a reputation for chants highlighting how rubbish they are (when appropriate) – hence Crewe singing

'We're even worse than Stockport'

whilst suffering a 0-6 trouncing by Coventry.

'YOUR GROUND'S TOO BIG FOR YOU!'
R A T I N G

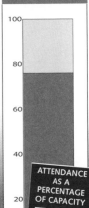

100
80
60
40
20
0

ATTENDANCE AS A PERCENTAGE OF CAPACITY **76%**

DOH!!

A pre-Christmas league match against Leyton Orient was joined by some late arriving Crewe fans in seasonal fancy dress. The assorted Father Christmas's exuberant goal celebrations turned to embarrassment when it was pointed out they were cheering an Orient goal...Crewe were not playing in red that day.

CRYSTAL PALACE

Recommended website: **www.c-palace.org**

WHO ARE YA?

Crystal Palace had been in serious danger of slipping into semi-permanent obscurity, when at Christmas 2003, they engineered one of the great mid-season turnarounds. On 22nd December, new boss Ian Dowie inherited a side sixth from bottom in Level One. Five months later, they had scraped into a play-off place, beating West Ham in the final to secure an unlikely Premiership place.

CELEBRITY FANS
JO BRAND
Comedian
EDDIE IZZARD
Comedian
NEIL MORRISEY
Actor – *Men Behaving Badly*

Things had come full circle from 1998 when Ron Noades, who many felt was holding the club back, sold out to dewy-eyed lifelong supporter Mark Goldberg, whose five-year plan to get Palace into Europe involved hiring Terry Venables at £750,000 per year plus a £10 million budget for players. During negotiations, Palace got relegated from the top-flight. The price tag of £23 million was steep to start with; it now seemed ludicrous. Goldberg took a hit on his other business interests with a plunge in the stockmarket, and the scene was set for some near-farcical financial struggles which culminated in a 'farewell' game at Tranmere at the end of the 1999-00 season that many thought would be the last time a Palace team took the field of play.

IN and AROUND

The name 'Crystal Palace' was not the official name of the showpiece glass structure at Sydenham. Rather it was an invention of Punch Magazine in 1850. It contained 293,655 panes of glass.

Stabilisation under new chairman Simon Jordan was, until 2004, at the cost of the club's relative anonymity, broken only by a major contribution to martial arts culture with the goading of Eric Cantona resulting in his donkey kick against Palace fan Matthew Simmons in 1995. To away fans, Selhurst Park seems to exist within its own version of the Bermuda triangle. Buried somewhere in the suburbs of Norwood/Selhurst, it is notoriously difficult to find. When approaching either by car or by foot, visiting fans get the impression that the direct route to the ground actually involves walking in a series of ever-decreasing circles. There is a pseudo-scientific explanation of all this, something to do with the convergence of true and magnetic north.

Palace were harsh landlords of hapless Wimbledon. The contract for the use of Selhurst Park included a clause that prohibited the discounting of tickets. The tenants weren't allowed any branding or advertising revenue, and Palace picked up the loot from food sales.

Ron Noades has appointed Steve Coppell to management on four separate occasions.

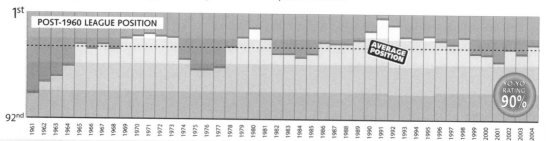

POST-1960 LEAGUE POSITION

1st ... 92nd

AVERAGE POSITION

YO-YO RATING **90%**

1961 1962 1963 1964 1965 1966 1967 1968 1969 1970 1971 1972 1973 1974 1975 1976 1977 1978 1979 1980 1981 1982 1983 1984 1985 1986 1987 1988 1989 1990 1991 1992 1993 1994 1995 1996 1997 1998 1999 2000 2001 2002 2003 2004

PROGRESS REPORT

A case of 'you don't know what you've got until you lose it', Palace had maintained an unstable but noticeably upward trajectory until major backroom shenanigans hit the club in 1998. Relegation that year was followed by successive mediocre/poor finishes in Level One, until the heroic push of 2004.

```
...Only league team with a name with no vowels in the first five letters...
    ...Were hosts of the first official ground-share, with Charlton in 1985...
...Provided an England centre forward, Johnny Byrne, whilst in Level Two (1961)...
```

RIVALS

Palace have been slightly out of the loop of South London rivalries, which partially explains their obsession with Brighton and Hove Albion. One of a host of clubs to mention Millwall in their hate list, the feeling isn't strongly reciprocated, though a public bust-up between the respective chairmen is just the sort of incident that could spark things off long-term. The ground-shares with Charlton and Wimbledon slightly increased what was only a lukewarm rivalry anyway, though back in the Premiership, Charlton now look obvious targets. The 40 miles between Palace's home turf in South London and coastal Brighton is not hotly fought over between the two clubs. Stuck in the middle is Crawley, with a population of 100,000, conspicuous by its lack of league team (though Crawley Town are doing their best to remedy this), but otherwise too far north to attract much Brighton support, and too far south to be associated with Palace.

BRIGHTON & HOVE ALBION
💀💀💀💀💀

MILLWALL
💀💀💀💀

CHARLTON
💀💀💀💀

With its quirky geographical basis, the rivalry is a rare example of one where animosity between the mid-70s' managers was key to stoking the flames. Alan Mullery's unbridled passion was his best and worst asset and frequently demonstrated with his less than diplomatic comments to the press, many aimed at Palace.

In other respects, the rivalry was more typical. The pattern of sides being promoted together always tends to heat things up between clubs. Unusually the two sides stuck like glue to each other between 1974 and 1984, simultaneously progressing from Level Two up to the Old First. Steve Coppell, caught up in the maelstrom of boardroom antics of the 1990s, had four different spells managing Crystal Palace between 1984 and 2000. His decision to move to the hated Brighton in 2002 should perhaps have instantly turned him into an arch hate-figure. Instead, Brighton fans were bemused to hear strains of 'There's only one Steve Coppell' wafting from the Palace end during their meeting that year.

But the faithful weren't so tolerant of a move in the other direction. Attendances dipped when Alan Mullery joined Palace in a shock move in 1982. It is rumoured that the majority of the lost fans swapped allegiance to Chelsea.

When, after 13 years, the two enemies finally met again in 2002, a lot of water had passed under the bridge. 6,000 Brighton fans made the trip with riot police at the ready in numbers. Though the same animosity was still there, the furry mascots, the blaring music from the tannoy and the 'family entertainment' were a long way from the pitched battles at Brighton station of the 70s.

SUPPORTERS' VFM
63%

PERFORMANCE AGAINST RIVALS BRIGHTON

WON 29%
LOST 39%
DRAWN 32%

LOVE/HATE

Millwall Chairman *Theo Paphitis* had a memorable altercation with his Palace counterpart, Simon Jordan, who questioned the sacking of Mark McGhee as a 'knee-jerk' reaction. Dubbing Palace's ground as 'Smellhurst Park', Paphitis opined that the words 'knee' and 'jerk' should be part of the Palace crest – though the negative connotations of the knee aren't immediately obvious.

CHANTS

Brighton's horror moment, losing 5-0 at Selhurst in 2002, was made worse by the fact that the visiting fans weren't even allowed to make an early escape from the ground, as gates were locked (rather at odds with the Taylor Report). Palace gloated with the chant

'5-0, and you can't go home...'

'YOUR GROUND'S TOO BIG FOR YOU!'
RATING

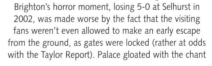

ATTENDANCE AS A PERCENTAGE OF CAPACITY
66%

DOH!!

Ex-chairman Ron Noades put his foot in it, to the horror of Palace fans, when in 1991, he declared that 'the black players at this club lend the side a lot of skill and flair, but you also need white players in there to balance things up and give the team some brains and skill'. It was too much for then star player Ian Wright to stomach, and he requested an immediate transfer. Within 18 months, then at Arsenal, he scored one of the goals that got Palace relegated.

DARLINGTON

Recommended website: **www.the-tinshed.co.uk**

WHO ARE YA?

For a Level Three club with little headline-grabbing potential, it was going to take something rather special to elevate the tale of Darlington FC to legendary status. In 1999, enter George Reynolds, (estimated worth £260 million). At a pensionable age, and with a colourful past, i.e. criminal, Reynolds set about transforming the outfit in preparation for Premiership action. The clearing of £5 million of debt received his immediate attention, but more controversially he set about constructing a new 25,000 capacity stadium that was opposed by residents and thought to be extravagant by others, since Darlington's average crowd was around 3,000. Though George's plans were standard fare for a new chairman, his techniques for dealing with any dissenters fell back rather heavily on his shady, safe-cracking past. So keen was he to engage in dialogue, he adopted the habit of turning up on people's doorsteps at 2am. One recipient of these bully-boy tactics was website editor Scott Thornbury, who was visited six times and treated to dozens of phone calls.

To his credit, Reynolds reduced admission prices to the lowest in the League, and had no qualms about confronting player wage inflation, albeit by the unorthodox tactic of handing over details of all salaries to the press. Readers were equally surprised that one player was paid as much as £123,000 a year as they were that the security guard was paid as little as £4 per hour. As things on the field remained flat, Mrs Reynolds unhelpfully made an impassioned speech in which she appeared to hint that players might be throwing games, on hearing which they stormed out.

IN and AROUND

Darlington's unique place in locomotive history is commemorated with David Mach's brick train sculpture at the Morrison's shopping complex at Morton Palms. Locomotion No 1 has been recreated to straddle the Gents toilets. Unusually, in this case it is permissible to use the facilities whilst the train is stationary.

The lavish stadium, inevitably called the Reynolds Arena, was opened in 2003, complete with escalators, Axminster carpets and marble adornments. A 2-0 defeat did nothing to lift the spirits, and after the initial enthusiasm, crowds slipped back to risible levels. Ironically, considering home games then and since had 22,000 spare seats, the small band of followers were exceedingly uncomfortable. The stadium is renowned for having perhaps the worst legroom in the country.

With Premiership status even less achievable than when he arrived, Reynolds bowed out in early 2004 leaving the club in administration. The letters of the 'Reynolds Arena' (costing £1,000 per letter) were removed and the ground's postcode was returned to its normal form, rather than the GR ending it had gained under the ex-chairman.

Shortly after leaving the club, George Reynolds was arrested after police discovered £500,000 cash in his car.

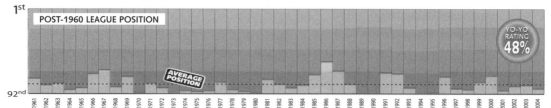

1st / 92nd — **POST-1960 LEAGUE POSITION** — AVERAGE POSITION — YO-YO RATING 48%
1961 1962 1963 1964 1965 1966 1967 1968 1969 1970 1971 1972 1973 1974 1975 1976 1977 1978 1979 1980 1981 1982 1983 1984 1985 1986 1987 1988 1989 1990 1991 1992 1993 1994 1995 1996 1997 1998 1999 2000 2001 2002 2003 2004

PROGRESS REPORT

Darlington's only recent highlight was a Level Three play-off final against Peterborough in 2000. The club experienced an exceptionally topsy-turvy spell beginning in 1985 when they earned a rare promotion to the Level Two. In the following seven seasons, they changed Leagues five times, including four consecutive swaps between 1989 and 1992. This included a solitary season in the Conference, from which they escaped to continue their tradition of low basement placings.

...Once managed by Cyril Knowles, subject of the song 'Nice One Cyril'...Were eliminated from the FA Cup twice in 1999-00 (following Manchester United's entry to the World Club Championship)... ...Installed floodlights in 1960, but an electrical fault caused the stand to burn down...

HARTLEPOOL ☠☠☠☠☠

RIVALS

It is sometimes commented that Darlington and Hartlepool have settled for each other as rivals, rather than trying to turn on someone bigger than them – a move that would at least show some ambition. The symmetry of this long-lasting feud has been broken somewhat by Hartlepool's escape to Level Two, a factor which has started the rumour among Hartlepool fans that they might be getting too successful to worry about Darlo any more. Darlington's nickname, The Quakers, hints strongly at a religious origin. Some have pointed to a vague sectarian divide between the two clubs.

The rivalry between the towns is fuelled by one of the less appetising local legends. The endless chants of 'Monkey hangers' aimed at Hartlepool have their origin in a tale that dates back to the Napoleonic wars. Having sighted a ship off shore, a group of Hartlepool fishermen feared an invasion by the French. They followed the course of the ship only to watch it get sunk during a storm. Amongst the wreckage that washed ashore was the ship's monkey. No one spoke French, which was considered a major drawback since they wanted to conduct a detailed interrogation (!?). A short trial was conducted on the beach with the monkey resplendent in its full military uniform (it came off the ship like that, they didn't dress it specially). The fishermen reached the staggering conclusion that it was probably a French spy. This sealed the creature's fate, and the monkey was condemned to death. The sentence is said to have been carried out using gallows made from the ship's mast.

Quite how this rubbish relates to social divisions in the Northeast is lost on the good folk of Hartlepool, though detractors, such as Darlington fans, claim some sort of spiritual affinity with the ape.

Matches between the two routinely throw up a handful of arrests on either side, with a liberal amount of CS gas being sprayed around by police when the two met in 2001. In 2000, star Darlington striker, Marco Gabbiadini, was struck by a Hartlepool supporter as he made his way down the tunnel, a fact that made his later signing for Hartlepool even more ghastly.

Carlisle United were generally named as lukewarm second hates but with their relegation to the Conference in 2004, Darlington can now give their undivided attention to Hartlepool.

SUPPORTERS'
VFM
61%

PERFORMANCE
AGAINST RIVALS
HARTLEPOOL

WON 37%

LOST 41%

DRAWN 22%

'YOUR GROUND'S
TOO BIG FOR YOU!'
RATING

LOVE/HATE

The former Newcastle United player, *Faustino Asprilla*, sensationally agreed to sign for Darlington in the summer of 2002. He was paraded before a packed home crowd after securing a deal allegedly worth £17,000 per week, a car and a bungalow (he obviously doesn't 'do' stairs). The whole thing came to a shuddering halt when Asprilla, without any hint of an explanation, left the country.

CHANTS

'Give me a D...deeeeee,
Give me an A...'

It goes on a bit.

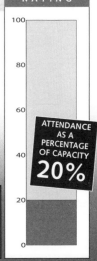

100

80

60

ATTENDANCE
AS A
PERCENTAGE
OF CAPACITY
20%

40

20

0

DOH!!

Turnstile operator Jennie Brown (5ft 3 inches, and 18 years old) was threatened by five Hartlepool fans that if she didn't let them in for free they would 'kick her head in'. Having let them pass, she immediately alerted the police, saying 'I'm only small and couldn't put up much of a fight'. Showing a distinct lack of sympathy, the club sacked her on the spot. A spokesman reasoned that her complaint to the FA was a case of 'sour grapes'.

DERBY COUNTY

Recommended website: **www.therams.co.uk**

WHO ARE YA?

Derby County were subject to the first well publicised piece of footballing hokum. Having evicted gypsies to enable the building of the Baseball Ground, folklore decreed that a curse had been placed on the club that would prevent them from winning the FA Cup. Having been on the losing end three times prior to the 1946 final, the captain crossed a gypsy's palm with silver to lift the spell. Perhaps it worked, as Derby won, though it's not known whether he managed to hang on to his wristwatch. They haven't appeared in a final since.

During the early 70s, the Baseball Ground was infamous for its atrociously boggy pitch. Brian Clough ordered the groundsman to ensure it was kept that way with plenty of unnecessary watering. This culminated in the much replayed incident of a penalty spot having to be repainted midway through a cup-tie against Manchester City in 1977, notable for John Motson's incredulous commentary and the man with the pot needlessly adopting a silly walk.

The arrival of Robert Maxwell in 1984 coincided with the club's historical low. Celebrating their anniversary,

Developed by local company Core Design, it's possible to (loosely) claim that Lara Croft was born in Derby

the state of Derby's finances meant that it could easily have been their last year of existence. Maxwell [sort of] kept his promise to save the club, though after his departure, a gaping black hole was discovered in the balance sheet - a similar theme to most things he got his flabby paws on. The suspicion that he'd been fishing for any old club to get his teeth into was prevalent at the time, since he had already caused a storm by proposing a Reading/Oxford merger. He did at least have a house near Oxford; his links with Derby County were non-existent. TV crews soon caught onto the fact that his regular seat became empty towards the end of a game – hardly surprising considering his renowned flightiness and only partial interest in football. His non-attendance led to arguably the most famous football chant in history 'He's fat, he's round...he's never at the ground'. His death in 1991 coincided with relegation. Upon their return in 1996, new chairman Lionel Pickering splashed out on a diverse bunch of foreign signings to keep them there, but since sinking back down in 2002, an almighty Premiership hangover has taken hold.

Pride Park, opened in 1997, is generally considered as one of the better breed of new stadia. They are generous with their allocation of away fans' seats, but not tolerant of smoking, which is banned throughout the ground.

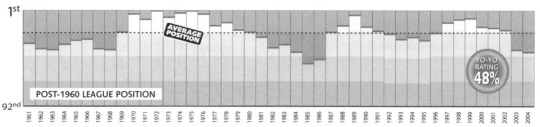

1st — 92nd

AVERAGE POSITION

POST-1960 LEAGUE POSITION

YO-YO RATING 48%

1961 1962 1963 1964 1965 1966 1967 1968 1969 1970 1971 1972 1973 1974 1975 1976 1977 1978 1979 1980 1981 1982 1983 1984 1985 1986 1987 1988 1989 1990 1991 1992 1993 1994 1995 1996 1997 1998 1999 2000 2001 2002 2003 2004

PROGRESS REPORT

Two Championship wins under Clough and Dave Mackay in the 70s gave way to the nadir of a spell in Level Two in the early 80s. Jim Smith was hardly strapped for cash in the Premiership, but in The Rams' case the 'success or bust' strategy has ended fairly resoundingly in 'bust'. Their Level One record since falling from the Premiership is diabolical. The 18th in 2003 looks almost respectable compared to finishing one point above relegated Walsall in 2004.

```
        ...The old Baseball Ground did host baseball for a few years after 1895...
...Clocked up record FA Cup loss to non-league opposition (6-1 against Boston United in 1955)...
        ...Replaced black shorts with navy blue in order to 'look like England'...
```

RIVALS

Having taken Derby to the Championship in 1972, the abrupt departure of Brian Clough and Peter Taylor to Nottingham Forest 18 months later was almost one of those 'where were you when you heard...?' moments, such was its shock value at the time. He had fallen out with the board as they had become jittery that he was launching a full takeover of the club.

NOTTINGHAM FOREST ☠☠☠☠☠

The fact that he went on to even greater heights with Forest is a huge bone of contention - a slight case of 'what might have been' at Derby. Adding some credence to this argument is the fact that, by his own admission, Clough is, at heart, a Derby person and bitterly regrets his hasty resignation.

Considering the two are not far from physically merging into one another, the perceived cultural gap is pronounced. Derby is lumbered with something of

LEICESTER CITY ☠☠☠☠☠

a rural image by Forest fans, an impression hardly borne out from looking at a map of the East Midlands. The use of this term is now highly problematic. Deemed to be too abstract for foreigners to grasp, East Midlands Airport is now renamed Nottingham East Midlands Airport, though it is actually in Leicestershire and has a Derby address. Derby has the ammunition that its 'city' neighbour has the reputation of one of Britain's binge drinking capitals, with central Nottingham descending each weekend into a vodka shot induced battleground.

SUPPORTERS' VFM 65%

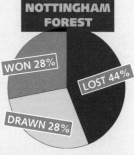

PERFORMANCE AGAINST RIVALS NOTTINGHAM FOREST

WON 28%
LOST 44%
DRAWN 28%

Derby had the unusual experience of having to 'withdraw' from their main rivals rather swiftly. Competing in Level Two in 1984-85, Bradford City had become the main focus of hate following Roy McFarland's jump between the clubs. Shortly before it was engulfed in the end-of-season fire, serious disorder had broken out in the main stand at Valley Parade as Derby supporters launched a surprise attack, aided by a gentleman wielding an attaché case. Derby quickly left City behind, but it seems unlikely they would have had much stomach for continuing the feud.

LOVE/HATE

Derby's superhero of the 70s *Kevin Hector* ♡ was wedded to the town as a footballer. Although he effectively ended the glory days by moving to Canada in 1978, he returned to the club in the 80s to break its appearance record. To prove his loyalty, he has been a postman in Derby since his retirement from the game.

Considering his feeble to moderate impact on the clubs he played for, Forest's *Stan Collymore* was seen as gaining a disproportionate amount of column inches.

CHANTS

'You're not famous anymore'

is a common taunt against Nottingham Forest.

'YOUR GROUND'S TOO BIG FOR YOU!' RATING

100
80
60
40
20
0

ATTENDANCE AS A PERCENTAGE OF CAPACITY 66%

DOH!!

Derby's present predicament is largely blamed on the club's naïve transfer policy. Their habit of bringing in clapped out foreign signings on lucrative and over-long contracts has done irreparable damage to their finances. Mikkel Beck is generally named as donkey number one, though in terms of haemorrhaging the bank account, 40k per week Fabrizio Ravenelli was the worst of the bunch.

DONCASTER ROVERS

A.K.A. DOWNCASTER

Recommended website: **www.doncasterrovers.co.uk**

WHO ARE YA?

If a Hollywood producer were scouting around for the subject of a football blockbuster, it would probably boil down to a choice between Darlington and Doncaster Rovers. But *Raise the Donny* might strain the credulity of any movie goer.

Doncaster's history prior to 1997-98 doesn't really need to detain us, apart from a reasonable spell in the Level Two in the 80s. Then, enter Ken Richardson whose main claim to fame was a nine-month suspended prison sentence for his role in 1982 Flockton Grey horse ringing saga. Initially Richardson's role as 'benefactor', *not* chairman (he threatened the Yorkshire Post with legal action if they used the term), was the usual mix of splashing out on players and praying for a redevelopment opportunity for the grizzled Belle Vue ground. When the Labour council wouldn't play ball, he reacted with something less than gentlemanly good grace, paying, in 1995, to have it burnt down. But his attempts at concealment were undone when the ex-soldier hired for the task left his mobile phone at the scene. Police found their investigation fairly undemanding since the attackers had been caught on CCTV buying cans of petrol and had let Richardson know of the operation's success by leaving a message on his answerphone, 'It's been done'.

IN and AROUND

Doncaster hosts the oldest classic horse race in the world, the St Leger.

But with the case winding its way to court, Richardson was, incredibly, still in charge. By 1997, he pronounced that he wanted 'nothing more to do with them' (the players) and, surprise, surprise, the death threats began to mount. With morale already bad, the threadbare Level Three squad launched a bid to sustain the worst season's record in British history. With up to six non-league players on the pitch at a time, and barely 100 season ticket holders, Rovers managed just four wins all year. The farce plumbed new depths with Richardson and his accomplice, Mark Weaver, picking the side and giving stirring team talks by way of a mobile phone passed round the dressing room. At one point, official manager Danny Bergara (who lasted all of November 1997) announced he would not be attending matches. In an episode typical of the time, a suspiciously fat goalkeeper, David Smith, was drafted in from Sunday League side Bramhall in Cheshire. He declined to come back out for a second half when supporters rumbled that he was a neighbour of Richardson.

A five-year spell in the Conference followed. But with Richardson jailed for conspiracy to cause the fire, Doncaster rose from the ashes to become champions in 2003, adding another chapter to the fairy tale by running away with Level Three in 2004, completing what must be the most staggering 10-year period in any British club's history.

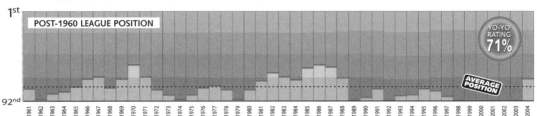

1st

POST-1960 LEAGUE POSITION

YO-YO RATING **71%**

AVERAGE POSITION

92nd

1961 1962 1963 1964 1965 1966 1967 1968 1969 1970 1971 1972 1973 1974 1975 1976 1977 1978 1979 1980 1981 1982 1983 1984 1985 1986 1987 1988 1989 1990 1991 1992 1993 1994 1995 1996 1997 1998 1999 2000 2001 2002 2003 2004

PROGRESS REPORT

After falling into the Conference in 1998, Doncaster were close to the indignity of a further relegation. Reeling from the chaos of the Richardson years, salvation was at hand in the form of new owner John Ryan. Finishing 16th in their first season, they made almost linear progress, improving to 10th, 9th, 4th and 3rd in successive seasons. They attracted nearly 7,000 to Belle Vue to see their first leg of the Conference play-off versus Chester, 10 times their low of 1997-98.

```
...Fanzine was called 'Stand up if your seat's on fire'...
...Club physio in the season they went out of the league was also at Halifax
            when they were relegated to the Conference...
```

RIVALS

The competitiveness between Doncaster and Hull is mostly a case of seeing who could get out of the mire the fastest. Both have made a good fist of it and have a habit of meeting one another for crunch matches. Before Hull get too many fantasies of Champions League action, it's worth taking a look back at Level Three table at the end of the 1997-98 season. With Doncaster miles adrift on 20 points, they were joined in the bottom four by Brighton, Cardiff and Hull, a quartet who, six years later, are all looking in good shape. Donny's fourth and last win of that season, against Hull, prevented them from doing even worse than Workington's miserable 19 points in 1976-77, just prior to them being chucked out of the league.

HULL

ROTHERHAM

A mild allegiance exists with Brighton whose story has a similar ring to Doncaster's. Seagulls' fans were happy to respond to chants of 'Sit down if you hate Richardson'. Traditionally, Doncaster have tended to name Rotherham and Scunthorpe, but the main battle is now very much with Hull, particularly as they spent much of 2003-04 in the top two spots of Level Three. Once mathematical supremacy had been established, two Doncaster supporters scraped together close to £1,000 to hire a Cessna light aircraft to do a few circuits round the KC stadium with a banner 'Doncaster Champions 2004' during their rival's match with Bristol City. The local police were consulted but couldn't find anything in the statutes to prevent it. Intended as a 'light-hearted' gesture, those below cursed their lack of surface-to-air missiles, and the stunt brought a dismissive response from Hull's fans' liaison officer who said: "We still see teams like Sheffield United, Sheffield Wednesday and Leeds as rivals, and we don't really think about Donny'.

It's fair to say that there is a slight disparity in the standard of their grounds, though when shot of the old Belle Vue, Doncaster hope to have something to match the KC that has been privately funded rather than Hull's effort which saw them 'bailed out by the council'. Doncaster would also like to know why, if they are not bothered with them, Hull fans are constantly infiltrating their internet message boards and posting snide comments.

As a symbol of their re-birth, Doncaster are in the unlikely position of being able to gain an acquaintance with Barnsley and Sheffield Wednesday in Level Two, the latter of which were enjoying Premiership action when Donny were in the Conference.

SUPPORTERS' VFM
82%

PERFORMANCE AGAINST RIVALS
HULL

WON 20%
DRAWN 20%
LOST 60%

LOVE/HATE

HATE

It is safe to say that *Mark Weaver* and *Ken Richardson* would want to avoid Doncaster as a destination for a weekend break.

CHANTS

♪**♪*!

Doncaster fans are getting ready to put the past behind them, but riding high in 2004,

'Are you watching Richardson?'

was aired at every opportunity.

DOH!!

Fans have professed to be 'not the slightest bit interested' in what chairman John Ryan does in his garden. But the 'vulgar additions' to his Cheshire home caused sufficient fury from locals to feature in BBC's Neighbours at War.

'YOUR GROUND'S TOO BIG FOR YOU!'
RATING

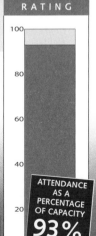

100
80
60
40
20
0

ATTENDANCE AS A PERCENTAGE OF CAPACITY
93%

EVERTON

Recommended website: **www.toffeeweb.com**

WHO ARE YA?

It comes as a slight surprise that Everton were the third best team of the 20th century, when taking only league finishing positions into account. Fans prayed that the windfall from the sale of Wayne Rooney would be sent wisely as the club's slight 'stuck in the mud' tendency didn't hold them in good stead for plundering overseas talent - the club have a fairly dire record of foreign imports. Daniel Amokachi was the club's first black player - signed as late as 1994, but only partially shone, along with equally out-of-place Anders Limpar. Walter Smith took a risk taking Alessandro Pistone from Newcastle, where he was notorious for his lack of commitment - a situation that hardly changed at Everton.

CELEBRITY FANS
CLIVE TYLDSLEY
Football Commentator
DERMOT MURNAGHAN
Newsreader
MICHAEL OWEN
eh...Ex-Liverpool footballer

The fact that Duncan Ferguson didn't get the bird from Everton fans when he flitted off to Newcastle must have helped him make the decision to come back for another spell. But brutal treatment has been meted out to another who flew the nest for Newcastle, then captain, Gary Speed. His real sin was to fail to turn up for the Everton coach for the trip to West Ham in 1998. The whispers are that Howard Kendall actually requested he did not make the trip and then, hours later, attacked Speed in interviews saying he wanted to be rid of the trouble-maker - an excuse that would play better with the Goodison faithful than the true fact that the club needed the cash.

IN and AROUND

There is scant evidence that the Beatles had any interest in football, though Paul McCartney is sometimes claimed to be an Everton fan. He did go to Goodison with his uncle, but there is no suggestion that he's kept up with developments. George Harrison helpfully once said 'there're three teams in Liverpool and I support the other one'.

Everton are clearly badly squeezed for support by their neighbours, with all but a small enclave of Merseyside. Legend has it that the average travelling distance per supporter to Goodison is the lowest in the Premiership.

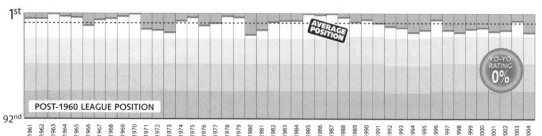

1st
AVERAGE POSITION
YO-YO RATING 0%
POST-1960 LEAGUE POSITION
92nd

1961 1962 1963 1964 1965 1966 1967 1968 1969 1970 1971 1972 1973 1974 1975 1976 1977 1978 1979 1980 1981 1982 1983 1984 1985 1986 1987 1988 1989 1990 1991 1992 1993 1994 1995 1996 1997 1998 1999 2000 2001 2002 2003 2004

PROGRESS REPORT

Such is the effect of their 102 years in the top division, Everton have a better average league position than Manchester United, putting them behind only Arsenal and Liverpool in the rollcall of all-time greats. Although sneered at by Liverpool for their 'lack of Championships', their tally of nine is still better than what could be reasonably expected statistically, including the two immediately before the outbreak of the World Wars. Although neither would want to, putting the records of the two Merseyside clubs together reveals Liverpool as being easily the most successful footballing city per head of population in the English League.

...Everton take to the field to the theme from the 1960s police drama 'Z cars'...
...Share their name with Corparacion Deportivo Everton in the Chilean League...
...Everton won their first Championship in 1891 - playing at Anfield...

NUTTER RATING
RANKED 61st

RIVALS

Although Everton are involved in one of the most intense and well documented football rivalries, their overall lack of enemies makes them the least hated Premiership club. Indeed the relationship with Liverpool is tinged with both bitterness and a degree of friendliness. On the one hand, Everton can reel off a list of the Reds' failings. For instance, that they were only born because of the greediness of local businessmen in the late 19th century, to the up to date moan that Graham Souness sold his story to the hated Sun newspaper. (Though note that Everton fans supported the boycott following the negative coverage after Hillsborough). In terms of single-minded fanaticism, Everton are towards the very top of the table. Interestingly their supporters share many attributes of those of Manchester City, with both having to endure close neighbours getting most of the attention. Everton fans' energies in getting Peter Johnson to take over the club were only matched by their efforts to get rid

LIVERPOOL

of him later - a tale that is reminiscent of Manchester City's love/hate relationship with Francis Lee.

Countering the obsessive dislike is an unusual willingness to, if not co-operate, cohabit in relative harmony. The plan to ground-share with Liverpool at an entirely new stadium, whilst not exactly a cause for celebrating in the streets, is accepted by many as a reasonably sane proposition. However, the image of the Everton/Liverpool rivalry as being 'good-natured' may be pushing the point too far. Both clubs have their own shrines, Everton's to Dixie Dean, the top division's record goalscorer, and Liverpool's to the victims of the Hillsborough tragedy. Both have been subject to frequent vandalism where opposition supporters have been blamed, understandably raising the temperature locally.

Everton now see themselves as the only genuine Merseyside team, with Liverpool's support perceived as drifting in from all parts of Europe (along with their current players). This leads to the somewhat far-fetched claim that the majority of current Liverpool fans would support Manchester United - if only they could get tickets.

In a sign of solidarity following the Hillsborough disaster, blue flags were intertwined with red at the temporary memorial that developed at Anfield. However, fans are quick to point the finger at Liverpool for effectively scuppering Everton's hopes of a golden European age following their victory in the Cup-Winners' Cup in 1985. With events at the Heysel keeping British clubs out of Europe, the Blues' ambitions were thwarted.

Everton fans have a natural aversion to all things red - to the extent of buying their own specially manufactured blue Santa Clauses.

PERFORMANCE AGAINST RIVALS
LIVERPOOL

WON 23%
LOST 41%
DRAWN 36%

SUPPORTERS' VFM 73%

LOVE/HATE

In June 2000, *Nick Barmby* decided he was worth more than the £25,000 per week offered by Everton to renew his contract. Up to this point there was absolutely no history of any Everton players going to the other side of Stanley Park, but in an infamous moment he announced that he would like to play for Liverpool. The resulting uproar filled the columns, and on one occasion the front page, of the Liverpool Echo, guaranteeing Barmby the roughest of receptions when he returned playing in red. Evertonians recall him stating that his boyhood team had been Hull. When he jumped ship his memory returned, claiming he had always been a Liverpool supporter.

DOH!!

In the 1966 FA Cup final the BBC were so embarrassed by the name of Everton's Mike Trebilcock, they instructed that it should be pronounced 'Trebilco'.

CHANTS

On the same day as the Grand National, and winning 3-1, Chelsea fans gave some advice to the Everton contingent:

'You should have stayed at the races'.

'YOUR GROUND'S TOO BIG FOR YOU!'
RATING

100
80
60
40
20
0

ATTENDANCE AS A PERCENTAGE OF CAPACITY 97%

FULHAM

A.K.A.
THE COTTAGERS – BAD ENOUGH AS IT IS

Recommended website: **www.fulhamfocus.co.uk**

WHO ARE YA?

It's not clear whether Mohammed Al Fayed's statement that he intended to turn Fulham into the 'Manchester United of the South' was a threat or a promise. The greatest compliment to the club is that it's difficult to remember just how awful they were. In 1996, ex-chairman David Balstode was eyeing a merger with QPR to form Fulham Park Rangers. This would enable Craven Cottage to be flogged for the development of luxury apartments. But a knockback from the council saw him retreat back to the bedroom, where he joined the small club of men to have expired while on the job. His death paved the way for a fans' consortium to concoct a cunning plan that centred around building a large pub – something that would have come in handy to dull the pain of what was happening on the field.

Around the time Tony Blair was stepping into Number 10 for the first time in 1997, Fulham were escaping Level Three - a spell that had seen them wallow in 91st place in the League. One general election later, having generously donated manager Kevin Keegan to the nation, Fulham motored into the Premiership one year ahead of schedule. (On taking over in May 1997, Al Fayed promised Premiership action within five years). It cost around £60 million to complete the most dramatic rags to riches tale of the recent footballing era.

Fulham residents supposedly endure the worst quality sleep in the country – probably caused by all the worry over whether their house values are about to collapse.

The trip up the League required four managers and a bewildering range of styles of play, but throughout the rise the fans didn't object to entertaining their Egyptian owner's eccentricities, including handing Kevin Keegan the pseudo-medical job title of Chief Operating Officer. Al Fayed indulged himself with possibly the worst football record of all time (and there's some tough competition) with a stumbling rap featuring the improbable rhyme 'We're not Real Madrid, we're not Barcelona. We are Fulham FC, Al Fayed is our owner'.

Singer, Michael Jackson paid a flying visit for a match in 1999 clasping an umbrella to shield his disintegrating features from the glare of the west London sun. But an even more incredible celebrity endorsement was extracted when rumours surfaced that Pope John Paul II was a Fulham supporter. It transpired that the pontiff used to be a regular at the Cottage when studying to be a priest in Roehampton. The claim of papal backing led Ken Myers of Independent Fulham Fanline to phone the Vatican to check the veracity of the story. A spokesman confirmed the Pope's support and wished them luck for their next fixture against Wigan.

The appointment of inexperienced Chris Coleman and an uncharacteristic lack of spending in 2003 saw Fulham installed as near certainties to wave goodbye to the Premiership. A fuming Al Fayed threatened to make journalists 'eat their words'. Ensuring their survival easily in 2003, small packages from Harrods were soon winging their way to assorted hacks containing copies of their articles, along with knives and forks.

In 2004 Fulham finally made it back to Craven Cottage.

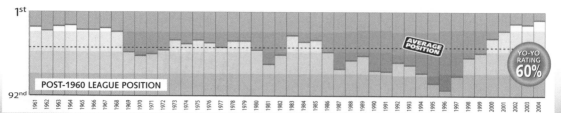

1st

POST-1960 LEAGUE POSITION

AVERAGE POSITION

YO-YO RATING 60%

92nd

1961 1962 1963 1964 1965 1966 1967 1968 1969 1970 1971 1972 1973 1974 1975 1976 1977 1978 1979 1980 1981 1982 1983 1984 1985 1986 1987 1988 1989 1990 1991 1992 1993 1994 1995 1996 1997 1998 1999 2000 2001 2002 2003 2004

PROGRESS REPORT

Not a lot to Fulham's graph but a slow strangulation from 1960 until 1997. It then took just two seasons in each of Level Two and Level One before securing a place in the top-flight for the first time since 1968.

```
...The original Craven Cottage was built in 1780 and had been home to an exiled French Emperor...
            ...The only League team ever to begin with the letter 'F'...
    ...Paid a record £750,000 for a 15-year-old, Matthew Collins, from Swindon Town...
```

NUTTER RATING

RANKED 83rd

RIVALS

If there was really any evidence that football violence had somehow become the preserve of the professional middle classes, then most Fulham supporters would be locked up by now. The club has the highest socio-economic profile of any of the 92 sides, and, not surprisingly, a correspondingly low to non-existent number of violent incidents. Fulham and Charlton comfortably head the table of Premiership good boys. The club draws its support from the well-heeled Middlesex and Surrey suburbs, stretching as far south as Guildford.

CHELSEA

Their early history was intertwined with Chelsea, in theory with the potential to give the derby an edge to rival that between Everton and Liverpool, whose development was on similar lines. But with Fulham out of the limelight for much of their history, The Blues have hardly given them a second thought, even on the occasions they have found themselves in the same League – a factor that makes Fulham hate them even more. It has gone down in the annals of footie trivia that Fulham 'could have been Chelsea' – highlighted by the fact that Fulham are the oldest currently established London club. In 1905, property developer Gus Mears invited Fulham to inhabit the new arena he had built at Stamford Bridge. It was only their refusal that led him to form Chelsea. It is clear from the area's footballing geography that a historical hiccup has taken place – as Stamford Bridge is closer to Fulham Broadway than Craven Cottage.

SUPPORTERS' VFM 84%

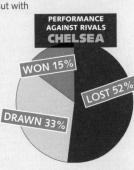

PERFORMANCE AGAINST RIVALS
CHELSEA

WON 15%
LOST 52%
DRAWN 33%

From the fans' point of view, Al Fayed has flirted somewhat too closely with the Chelsea board, having approached Ken Bates 'informally' about the possibility of a ground share of Stamford Bridge. The revamped Chelsea now sit within something of a derby vacuum. On the face of it, Abromovich's ambitions at Chelsea might be expected to draw the ire of many, but it has to be said that Fulham's chequebook-inspired rebirth doesn't really give them much right to sneer at their neighbours.

QUEENS PARK RANGERS

Ill-feeling between QPR and Fulham is only a notch above tepid, despite the mooted merger. Fulham chants of 'you all play in a blue tin pot' towards QPR came back to haunt them as they were forced to share Loftus Road for two years during the renovation of Craven Cottage.

'YOUR GROUND'S TOO BIG FOR YOU!'
RATING

LOVE/HATE

A 2-0 loss at home to Diadora League Hayes in 1991 prompted a 'Dicks out' campaign, not, as it sounded on the terraces, a novel protest involving mass trouser-dropping, but a stand against the person most fans consider their worst manager of all time, *Alan Dicks*. Kevin Keegan's departure to the England job didn't go down well either, particularly as Fulham had run up a string of nine straight victories at the beginning of the 2000 season.

CHANTS

Reasonably accurately, considering house prices in SW6, Fulham have been known to chant

'We're so rich it's unbelievable'.

DOH!!

Having suffered a 10-0 defeat in the League Cup at Anfield in 1986, the club's programme for the 2nd leg optimistically printed details of the replay date should the tie be 'level on aggregate'.

ATTENDANCE AS A PERCENTAGE OF CAPACITY
85%

100
80
60
40
20
0

GILLINGHAM

WHO ARE YA?

Here's a story that sounds like it should have had a distinctly unhappy ending. In 1995, Gillingham FC didn't have much of a history to look back on, and a bleak/non-existent future. Its mantle of the only League club in Kent had been broken in 1992, as Maidstone United, 'the squatters', had the cheek to rise from the Conference. Only three years later they disintegrated - proof that the county was not about to support two League clubs and provide Millwall and Charlton with some of their fan base as well.

In bounded a new chairman whose main ambition was to get financially involved with his first love...Millwall. Settling for what seemed like the booby prize, he coughed up £1 (or 1p, depending whose story you believe) for the privilege of owning a Gillingham outfit riddled with debt. His name, Paul Scally didn't inspire confidence either. With his own inimitable turn of phrase, he described the scene at the club as a 'derelict khazi', a situation that, in its literal sense, remained unresolved in 2003, when players found there was no loo paper at the training ground. But despite being dubbed the 'Ken Bates of the lower leagues', Scally's reign has seen The Gills rise to new heights. A team who had just two years previously narrowly avoided demotion to the Conference was, disputably, top of Level One at the beginning of 2001-02. Their achievement on August 11th isn't really officially recognised as their lofty status came by way of a 5-0 home defeat of Preston on the first day of the season, though dedicated followers still cherish cuttings from the few papers that bothered to print league tables after just one match.

Their rise to Level One was postponed after a nightmare last five minutes against Manchester City in the play-off final of 1999. With Gillingham 2-0 up, Light Blue's supporters trudged out of the ground in large numbers – a show of depression that meant them missing their comeback and victory by penalties. The Football League was less than impressed when Paul Scally was discovered to have had a flutter on City, fining him £10,000. The following year, Gills' fans stayed firmly put when 2-1 down to Wigan after the 90 minutes were up, and were rewarded by two ultra-late goals that ensured play-off success at the second time of asking.

The Priestfield Stadium has been virtually rebuilt since 1995, with the help of bits and pieces bought by Scally in a sell-off of equipment from the Millennium Dome. Scally's reputation locally is, at best, mixed. In a fit of pique, the head of the supporters' club, Alan Liptrott, was banned from attending games after Scally demanded he hand over the rights to the domain name of his internet site.

IN and AROUND

A good base for pesky windscreen washers, Gillingham is famed for its huge number of traffic lights.

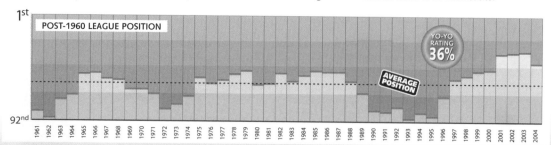

1st

POST-1960 LEAGUE POSITION

YO-YO RATING 36%

AVERAGE POSITION

92nd

1961 1962 1963 1964 1965 1966 1967 1968 1969 1970 1971 1972 1973 1974 1975 1976 1977 1978 1979 1980 1981 1982 1983 1984 1985 1986 1987 1988 1989 1990 1991 1992 1993 1994 1995 1996 1997 1998 1999 2000 2001 2002 2003 2004

PROGRESS REPORT

Such was Gillingham's dire early record, they were chucked out of the League in 1937 to be replaced by Ipswich. Their general pattern has been to survive reasonably happily in Level Two, but when sinking to Level Three they go all the way and end up fighting for survival. Life in Level One has been kinder than many commentators would have predicted, but they dangled perilously close when finishing fourth from bottom in 2004.

```
...In deference to most famous fan, fanzine was called 'Brian Moore's head
looks uncannily like London Planetarium'...Formerly called Excelsior FC...
```

RIVALS

Gillingham are amongst the least disliked Football League clubs, a slight surprise as they have a shopping list of hates, and can get antagonised by virtually everyone. The fact that their chairman has no qualms about publicly proclaiming his allegiance to Millwall has, not surprisingly, fuelled the fairly one-sided rivalry. The Gills are not amused to be portrayed as provincial bumpkins by the hardened 'inner-city' mob, especially as they have to put up with so many Lions' supporters in their turf of the Medway towns. Gillingham can point to a very respectable record against them, most notably subjecting Millwall to three straight defeats in 2000-2001, one of which Gillingham provocatively played in something very similar to Millwall's away strip. The argument goes that Gillingham's head-to-head-record is not grounds for claims that they are naturally the inferior of the two.

MILLWALL

SWINDON The bad feeling towards Swindon started largely on the pitch and fed through to the terraces. Gillingham felt a grudge after the perception in the 70s that Swindon always seemed to scupper their pushes for promotion. Tempers flared in the tunnel after a bad-tempered game which led Town to press charges. The two contrived to meet in the 1987 Level Two play-offs, a tense affair that was strung out to three games, as there was then a replay system in place. Under the more usual away goals rule, Swindon would never have got the chance of another crack at it.

Old lodgers Brighton are still named, with Stoke and Preston also getting a mention. Overall, Gillingham have no significant record of any fans' trouble, though the death of a Fulham supporter outside the ground in 1988 did little for their image.

BRIGHTON

Gillingham fans are faced with a series of onerous journeys when playing away. To add some spice to the trips, they have developed their own 'Cannonball Run' style competitions to see who can travel to the opposing turnstiles in the quickest time. There is the half-hearted advice that "We do not encourage the breaking of UK traffic laws or reckless driving".

PERFORMANCE AGAINST RIVALS
MILLWALL

WON 36%
LOST 36%
DRAWN 28%

SUPPORTERS' VFM **76%**

CHANTS

Gillingham became increasingly desperate to find a song to call their own to the extent that they have even been known to 'borrow' Millwall's *'No one likes us, we don't care'*. When an original tune finally emerged, a version of *'The Last Waltz'*, it wasn't exactly spirit-lifting stuff:

'I'll have the last waltz with you. Two lonely people together. I fell in love with you. The last waltz should last forever. It's all over now, nothing left to say'.

LOVE/HATE

Gillingham fans like to point out that their hatred of *Neil Warnock* predates most other people's, stemming from long before his outbursts over the Sheffield United/West Brom dismissals' saga. Fans commiserate with Blades' supporters, agreeing that they 'deserve better'.

DOH!!

In the days before motorways, Gillingham's travel pains were acute. Attempting to get to Barrow in 1961, the club made a series of logistical balls-ups leading to them having to charter a private plane to Blackpool and hiring a fleet of cars to ferry the players to the already delayed kick-off. In the pre-floodlight era, with the gloom descending, a jaded Gills' side might have been relieved when the referee abandoned the match. The League declared the result should stand...a 7-0 Barrow victory.

'YOUR GROUND'S TOO BIG FOR YOU!'
RATING

100
80
60
40
20
0

ATTENDANCE AS A PERCENTAGE OF CAPACITY
80%

GRIMSBY TOWN

A.K.A. THE CODHEADS

Recommended website: **www.electronicfishcake.com**

WHO ARE YA?

The phrase 'playing away at Grimsby on a Wednesday night' has become synonymous with the gloomy existence of an ex-Premiership side that have fallen on hard times. Characterised unfairly as a small town with a lingering odour of a cod's jockstrap, accompanied by strange green slime that finds its way onto the highways, Grimsby is a football outpost, clinging on where others with a similarly isolated coastal location have gone to the wall.

As every budding football anorak knows, Grimsby Town never play any games at home, though it could be argued that they are simply named after the wrong town. Since their inception in 1878 as Grimsby Pelham, they've played a couple of miles further down the estuary in Cleethorpes. To the uninitiated, their black and white stripes make them dead ringers for Newcastle United but close examination reveals that Grimsby have a black stripe down the middle, whereas the Geordies have white.

CELEBRITY FANS

HENRY KISSINGER
International Peace-Broker

DEAN REYNOLDS
Snooker player

IN and AROUND

Grimsby is home to frozen food giants Youngs, who are said to make more frozen pizzas a week than the whole of Italy does in a year.

Their best spell came under the temperamental Alan Buckley between 1988 and 1994. At a time when hoof-and-chase tactics had become the rage, Grimsby motored up two divisions with some pleasing on-the-eye tactics, helped on their way by virtually every fan in the Pontoon terrace waving an inflatable fish christened Harry Haddock. Buckley has since fallen out of favour though, willing to try anything to halt their recent slide, a new batch (shoal?) of Harrys are being manufactured.

Whilst in Level One, Grimsby were consistently undervalued by the bookies, who ritually put them amongst the favourites for relegation at the beginning of each season. But their biggest triumph lacked a sense of timing. On 1st September 2001, following a 1-0 home defeat of Barnsley, they topped the Level One table. However, this noteworthy achievement couldn't compete for column inches the following day, as four hours later, England walloped Germany 5-1 in Munich.

Grimsby Town may have played a part in securing the USA the finals of the World Cup in 1994. Diplomat Henry Kissinger was introduced to the game by the former MP and Mariners' fan Anthony Crosland. Kissinger would fly into RAF Waddington, Lincolnshire, to catch up with diplomatic events and accompany Crosland to Grimsby games. Whatever he witnessed obviously didn't put him off as he became a central campaigner to take the World Cup over the pond.

You would think a club the size of Grimsby couldn't afford the luxury of squad rotation. But in 2003, then manager Paul Groves seemed intent on signing goalkeepers. The 'Groves collection' consisted of at least seven goalies, though rumours suggested he could have had a dozen stashed away at the club. Continuing the dodgy pun theme, the club's supporters' group has the motto 'In Cod we trust'.

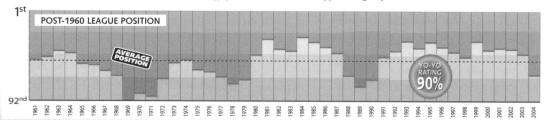

POST-1960 LEAGUE POSITION

1st ... 92nd

AVERAGE POSITION

YO-YO RATING 90%

1961 1962 1963 1964 1965 1966 1967 1968 1969 1970 1971 1972 1973 1974 1975 1976 1977 1978 1979 1980 1981 1982 1983 1984 1985 1986 1987 1988 1989 1990 1991 1992 1993 1994 1995 1996 1997 1998 1999 2000 2001 2002 2003 2004

PROGRESS REPORT

Grimsby's post-1960 record consists of a Himalayan series of peaks and troughs. When they start heading in one direction, up or down, they really go for it. For over 10 years, they batted (or perhaps battered) well above their station, maintaining their Level One status despite crowds that barely reached 6,000. But once the rot set in, it took hold. Consecutive relegation in 2003 and 2004 left the club with just six players under contract and a yearly deficit running at over £1 million.

```
...Didn't reach a Wembley final for 120 years - then played there twice in eight weeks (1998)...
...Fielded first pro footballer to wear contact lenses (George Hair)...Jointly responsible for the
highest ever attendance at Old Trafford (76,962) versus Wolves in the 1939 FA Cup semi-final...
```

RIVALS

As the crow flies, Hull City are the closest league club to Grimsby, though actually getting there requires a significant dog-leg over the Humber Bridge. The two have dodged each other in the league with The Mariners dropping down to Level Three just as Hull escaped. Nevertheless, unusually, they are fairly indifferent to each other. Grimsby tend to look to Yorkshire for their rivals, a product of their annoyance with being characterised as Yorkies. East Lincolnshire, as it is now called, is 'regionless'. It certainly isn't East Anglia (the jutty out bit), the East Midlands (the inland bit) or the Northeast (the Geordie bit). And it definitely has nothing to do with the hated Yorkshire to the west. The similarity with Hull's approach to choosing rivals is noticeable, i.e. if you're from Yorkshire and in the same division, we hate you.

PERFORMANCE AGAINST RIVALS
SHEFFIELD WEDNESDAY

WON 21%

LOST 39%

DRAWN 39%

SHEFFIELD WEDNESDAY
☠☠☠☠☠

A slight eccentricity is that Sheffield Wednesday are rated as slightly more loathsome than Sheffield United. Given the choice, other clubs will generally turn their attentions to The Blades, thanks almost entirely to the presence of Neil Warnock as manager. But Wednesday are seen as the antithesis of Grimsby – imagining that they deserve a place in the Champions League by virtue of possessing a 40,000 capacity stadium, even if it's only a quarter full. Since 2000, their meetings have been decidedly tense affairs. Being ultra-compact, Blundell Park can be an intimidating place to be when the mood turns ugly, and two visits by Wednesday in 2002 are etched on the locals' memories, as on both occasions shoppers scuttled out of the way of fans trying to confront each other in the town centre.

SHEFFIELD UNITED
☠☠☠☠

SUPPORTERS' VFM 29%

At the heart of the argument between the regions is the status of best fish and chip shop in the country. Residents will tell you self-styled champion Harry Ramsden's, near Leeds, serves up inedible slop compared to any of Grimsby's wonderful chippies.

Yet others are mystified as to how and why the Wednesday rivalry came into being – generally a sign that it is a bit of an inter-mob thing that doesn't reflect the views of true supporters. Now back in Level Three, Grimsby only have the less glamorous local company of Scunthorpe and Lincoln.

SCUNTHORPE
☠☠☠☠☠

'YOUR GROUND'S TOO BIG FOR YOU!' RATING

LOVE/HATE

The most unpopular manager in recent times arrived at the club following the sacking of the successful Buckley in 1994. *Brian Laws* is mostly known for a dressing room incident in which star foreign-signing Ivano Bonetti ended up with a black eye caused by a flying tray of chicken sandwiches.

CHANTS

Health and Safety alert:

'We p*ss, on your fish, yes we do, yes we do'

100
80
60
40
20
0

ATTENDANCE AS A PERCENTAGE OF CAPACITY 48%

DOH!!

Following the arrest of 30 Grimsby fans on the last day of the season in 1990, Chesterfield Police were forced to release them all on bail as their cells were full from the overspill caused by riots at Manchester's Strangeways prison.

HARTLEPOOL UNITED

A.K.A. MONKEY HANGERS

Recommended website: **www.inthenet-hufc.co.uk**

WHO ARE YA?

Hartlepool's history is best described as around 100 years of controlled underachievement. When automatic relegation to the Conference was introduced, they needed to smarten up their act in double-quick time. That is precisely what they did. They are amongst a handful of the 92 clubs that are enjoying the best spell in their history.

Hartlepool United has to endure the notoriety of being the club that has been re-elected to the Football League the most times. Put more starkly, the team has finished last more often than any of the other 91 English League clubs. Add to this the fact that they have never been higher than the bottom two divisions and the realisation dawns that supporting Hartlepool has been a thankless task. Revenues are not helped by the fact that the trip to the Northeast is one that comparatively few lower league away fans are prepared to make – though with crowds comfortably in the 6,000s, the change from the grim days is considerable. There is comfort in the fact that Hartlepool have never been relegated to the Conference, a claim which cannot be made by arch rivals Darlington.

IN and AROUND

Timmy Mallet rescued a woman from Hartlepool marina

The most well-known employee of Hartlepool United in recent years has been neither a player, coach, nor director. The story of club mascot H'Angus the Monkey standing for election to the post of Mayor of Hartlepool in 2002 has overshadowed the club's considerable on-field achievements; chiefly, that by 2004 the League's whipping boys had been transformed into serious contenders for Level One action.

But what started out as a bit of monkeying around (he included a manifesto pledge of free bananas for school children) turned into something of considerable constitutional significance. On a turnout of less than 30%, H'Angus, aka Stuart Drummond, was duly elected Mayor by a majority of 603 votes, pushing the Labour Party candidate into second place. Embarrassed at the mockery made of the mayoral elections, the government decided that they would concentrate instead on regional assemblies to promote local democracy. Under a hail of apathy, this too was abandoned in 2004, so H'Angus's indirect contribution to political history is perhaps far greater than he could ever have envisaged.

Before his political career, he was far from a model mascot. In 2001, he was ejected from the ground at Scunthorpe after simulating a sex act with a female steward, whilst a year earlier he had been asked to leave Bloomfield Road when, during the match against Blackpool, he offended the home supporters by engaging in an unsavoury practice with a blow up doll.

Though not having a huge 'Hall of Fame', Hartlepool can lay claim to the fact that they gave Brian Clough his first managerial post in 1965. During his reign at the Victoria Ground, Clough helped install corrugated iron roofing over the terraces, whilst assistant Peter Taylor repainted the stand. The duo left for Derby County in 1967, where presumably they were not called upon to help refurbish the Baseball Ground.

Victoria Park vies with Stoke's Britannia Stadium for the accolade of England's chilliest football ground.

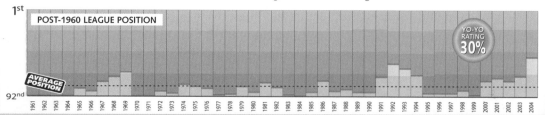

1st

POST-1960 LEAGUE POSITION

YO-YO RATING **30%**

AVERAGE POSITION

92nd

1961 1962 1963 1964 1965 1966 1967 1968 1969 1970 1971 1972 1973 1974 1975 1976 1977 1978 1979 1980 1981 1982 1983 1984 1985 1986 1987 1988 1989 1990 1991 1992 1993 1994 1995 1996 1997 1998 1999 2000 2001 2002 2003 2004

PROGRESS REPORT

Only promoted three times in their entire history, Hartlepool embarked on a regeneration that led to three consecutive play-off attempts from 1999 under Chris Turner, though their post-1960 average is still stuck in the lower reaches of Level Three.

```
    ...Went 13 consecutive games without scoring in 1992-93...
      ...Changed their name from Hartlepools United to Hartlepool in 1968...
...Still not entirely happy, they changed their name again to Hartlepool United in 1977...
```

RIVALS

The rivalry between Hartlepool and their near neighbours, Darlington, is a fully reciprocated one. A mirror of the Newcastle/Sunderland hatred, there are no other sides within reasonable travelling distance to care about. Carlisle had a minor thing going with both until their exit from the League in 2004. One fan told us when asked what or who Hartlepool supporters hate most, "Darlington FC and anything associated with them". With Darlo presently condemned to poverty and playing in a division lower, it is probably best that the two largely avoided each other during the ludicrous reign of Darlington chairman George Reynolds. His glorious plans for the club sat uneasily with a sort of mutual understanding that the two were destined to play out their time in or very near the basement.

DARLINGTON ☠☠☠☠☠

The Victoria Ground's relatively trouble-free reputation is only really challenged when Darlington come to town. Even then, the outbreaks of violence are sporadic and relatively minor. It seems that, though intense, the rivalry is reasonably good-natured and manifests itself more in the form of chanting than fisticuffs. For some reason best known to themselves, there have been occasional clashes between Hartlepool and Cheltenham fans.

There are, however, examples of outbreaks of peace between the two sets of supporters. In 2001, fans from each club's message boards played a match against each other to raise money for John Collingwood, a Hartlepool youth team player who lost the use of both of his legs in a road traffic accident. The event was such a success that it has now become a regular affair, with local charities reaping the benefit from the temporary suspension of hostilities.

PERFORMANCE AGAINST RIVALS
DARLINGTON

WON 41% LOST 37% DRAWN 22%

SUPPORTERS' VFM 86%

LOVE/HATE

There is nothing more guaranteed to pour oil on the troubled waters of local rivalry than a player leaving a club and jumping into bed with the fiercest adversaries. But this did not trouble midfielder *Ian Clark* when, in 2001, he left Hartlepool for the loathed Darlington. In doing so, he became the first player to leave Hartlepool for Darlington since Paul Olsson in 1994.

Clark had played over 100 games for Hartlepool, scoring some 18 goals in the process. The £10,000 transfer fee received by the club did nothing to temper the anger and hatred directed towards him by his former fans, with the situation being fuelled further by Clark managing to bag 13 goals in his first 30 appearances for his new club.

CHANTS

One of the longest chants in the Football League, Pool fans indulge in a rendition of all four verses of Rolf Harris's *'Two Little Boys'* – a parable of solidarity and kinship, in which (briefly): boy number one does a good turn for boy number two when his toy horse is accidentally decapitated. Years later, the favour is returned when boy number one is dying on the battlefield. Hartlepool have usually conceded a couple by the time the song finishes.

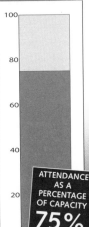

'YOUR GROUND'S TOO BIG FOR YOU!'
RATING

100
80
60
40
20
0

ATTENDANCE AS A PERCENTAGE OF CAPACITY 75%

DOH!!

The Victoria Ground was the victim of one the first German Zeppelin airship raids in 1916. A stand was hastily put up in its place that was supposed to be only a temporary structure.

They finally got round to building a permanent replacement in 1985.

HUDDERSFIELD TOWN

A.K.A. HUDDERSFIELD DOWN

Recommended website: **www.downatthemac.com**

WHO ARE YA?

Huddersfield swapped arguably the drabbest league ground, Leeds Road, for a stadium that ranks amongst the most space-age in the world – with a pitch that exactly mimicked the dimensions of the old Wembley stadium. The McAlpine is generally considered a design classic with its gigantic swooping arches of semi-circular tubing providing a focal point for an area not noted for its contemporary architecture.

When opened in 1995, the McAlpine Stadium was three-sided, allowing views of the game from the hillside to the north. But a bad-tempered horse did not take kindly to non-paying fans sharing its field. Many came away nursing bites and bruises.

However, the new look came at a cost that was unsustainable playing Level Three football, plunging the club into administration in 2003 after failing to pay its players for five months. Town are the masters of the swift catastrophe. Older fans will have seen them play in all four divisions and have witnessed two of the fastest collapses in league position to have befallen a British club.

IN and AROUND

Huddersfield's suburb of Fartown generally raises a smirk.

Before its demolition, Leeds Road suited the town's image quite well. Situated near the centre of an archetypal northern industrial town, the pitch suffered from a variety of noxious fumes in the air and constantly needed re-laying in the early days. By the 70s a new foe emerged, flocks of birds that swooped on the grass seed making maintenance nearly impossible.

The club got embroiled in a series of legal tangles in the 90s, notably the case brought by Bradford City for the injury to Gordon Watson. Less published was the fact that as soon as the Watson case was over, they were sued by Darren Pitcher for a 'late and reckless' tackle during a match with Crystal Palace. They managed to prevent court action when a 14-year-old girl had her arm broken by a wayward shot by Huddersfield's Kevin Blackwell during a match at Wycombe. In 1999, in a case that didn't detain the legal great and good, the Chairman announced his intention to sue a referee for not awarding Huddersfield Town a penalty.

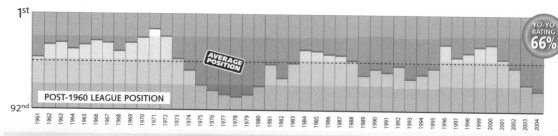

1st

YO-YO RATING 66%

AVERAGE POSITION

POST-1960 LEAGUE POSITION

92nd

1961 1962 1963 1964 1965 1966 1967 1968 1969 1970 1971 1972 1973 1974 1975 1976 1977 1978 1979 1980 1981 1982 1983 1984 1985 1986 1987 1988 1989 1990 1991 1992 1993 1994 1995 1996 1997 1998 1999 2000 2001 2002 2003 2004

PROGRESS REPORT

A glorious history as one of the great English clubs, including three consecutive championships in the twenties (ranking them alongside Arsenal, Liverpool and Manchester United), went horribly wrong with a dive from the old First Division to the basement in just five seasons from 1972. Under Mike Buxton, they staged a recovery and a jagged climb almost got them back to parity with West Yorkshire neighbours Leeds and Bradford in the 90s, before it all fell apart again amidst a manager's merry-go-round. In their new high-tech McAlpine stadium in late 1999, they enjoyed a spell at the top of the Level One. But a player clear-out proved to be the start of another incredible plunge, with a downward spiral into Level Three by 2003, accompanied by a spell in administration. Another fight back may have started with promotion to the Level Two in 2004.

```
...First team to win three league Championships in a row...
...Bill Shankly started his managerial career at Huddersfield...
```

RIVALS

In 2004 the region's football fortunes nearly took a previously unimaginable turn. With Halifax Town in the Conference, and Leeds United and Bradford's finances looking terminal, Huddersfield fans could be forgiven for dreaming that they would end up as the biggest and perhaps the only team in West Yorkshire. In some ways this left them in a quandary. Following the Gordon Watson incident, Bradford's ex-chairman, Geoffrey Richmond, was still subject to something of a footballing fatwa after refusing to let Huddersfield Board members into the posh bit of Valley Parade. Now, they were being asked to feel sorry for them – which to their credit, many did.

LEEDS UNITED

BRADFORD CITY

Until the mid 90s, the rivalry with 'Sadford' was reasonably low-key. Indeed, after the Valley Parade fire of 1985, Leeds Road was used for Bradford home games, as well as a fund-raiser against Manchester United. Town's odd relationship with their neighbours stems from the fact that until the late 90s, Bradford were serial underachievers, drawing mostly pity from Huddersfield's supporters. City could hardly be considered the larger, more successful local rival. Even when both teams were taking regular trips into the basement, there really wasn't a lot to hate as far as Town were concerned.

City's foray into the Premiership was sneered at as the club gained a new section of glory-seeking fans – and their woeful demise back into Level Two was seen as typical of a city who, at times, has barely seemed able to support a full-time professional team.

For older supporters, Leeds are still top rivals. It's easy to forget that in the eighties the clubs were level pegging, with both in Level One. The way their respective fortunes are developing, Town, City and Leeds could again be heading for a prolonged spell of each other's company.

PERFORMANCE AGAINST RIVALS
BRADFORD
WON 34%
LOST 26%
DRAWN 40%

BARNSLEY

With the constant chopping and changing of West Yorkshire's pecking order, Huddersfield have kept Barnsley, to the south, as a sort of reserve rival, waiting in the wings in case Leeds and Bradford bite the dust. Nearby Halifax have never bothered Town and are seen as having to mop up Huddersfield rejects just to stay afloat.

Huddersfield gained a slight reputation for violence during the 80s' 'casuals' fad that still occasionally raises its head nowadays. Lately, like Bradford, they have been involved in skirmishes at Hull City. In the tradition of English fans 'teaming up' with those over the Scottish border, there are rumours of a link with, of all sides, Aberdeen.

SUPPORTERS'
VFM
59%

LOVE/HATE

HATE

Bradford calling in the lawyers over the Gordon Watson injury by Kevin Gray, in 1997, has guaranteed *Geoffrey Richmond* pride of place on most fans' dartboards. Whatever the intensity of the challenge, it is argued, a sporting incident is hardly the sort of thing that should find its way to court.

CHANTS

At a particularly tiny contingent of Northampton supporters:

*'Are you waiting….are you waiting…..
are you waiting for a bus?'*

'YOUR GROUND'S TOO BIG FOR YOU!'
R A T I N G

100
80
60
40
20
0

ATTENDANCE AS A PERCENTAGE OF CAPACITY
43%

DOH!!

The club boasted a stuffed donkey as a mascot – until it was accidentally set on fire.

HULL CITY

Recommended website: **www.ambernectar.com**

WHO ARE YA?

With a population of nearly 250,000, Hull is considerably larger than the rather mediocre record of its football team would suggest. Dave Whelan's resuscitation of Wigan Athletic is perhaps the blueprint for amalgamating a town's football and rugby teams to the benefit of all parties, but attempts to create any unity between the two codes in Hull has a history of much kicking and screaming; that is until just a couple of years ago. The city's rather damning tag – that it is England's largest city not to host top-flight football – has become a millstone that finally has a faint hope of being laid to rest, thanks to the development of Hull City's super-stadium.

> **CELEBRITY FANS**
> **ROY NORTH**
> The one-time hand up Basil Brush
> **TOM COURTENAY**
> Actor - Billy Liar, Dr Zhivago

When former England Davis Cup tennis captain and leisure club boss David Lloyd acquired Hull in 1997, his plans for the town's sporting future weren't a million miles from the situation today; the football and rugby league clubs playing under one new roof. Buying both the football club and Hull FC, the confusingly named rugby league outfit, he suffered the usual chairman's syndrome of letting things slip on the pitch. Under Terry Dolan and Mark Hateley, Hull lurched from one disaster to another, flirting dangerously with a drop into the Conference. As things unravelled, the whole town turned against Lloyd. A protest by Hull fans at Bolton's Reebok involved the throwing of scores of tennis balls. It all culminated in a farcical lock-out, when Lloyd, no longer directly involved in the club but still owner of the ground, padlocked the gates of Boothferry Park in an effort to extract some rent. As the atmosphere deteriorated and the weeds started to take over the pitch, Hull's Council leader was moved to state "As far as I am concerned, he (Lloyd) can get on his bike and leave the city."

> **IN and AROUND**
> Hull isn't a boy racer's paradise. With 114 separate 20mph zones, it has more speed humps per head of population than any other British City.

The rejuvenation of Hull was remarkably swift. The council stepped in with plans for what was to become the first parkland ground in the country. The 25,000 capacity KC Stadium opened in late 2002, shared with Hull FC.

The fans poured in and, in 2003-04, Hull easily achieved the highest attendances in Level Three with an average gate of 16,800, easing themselves into an automatic promotion place to regain some pride in Level Two.

Hull City is hopeless for doodlers, as it is the only example of an English team's name without cavities – i.e. there are no letters to neatly colour in.

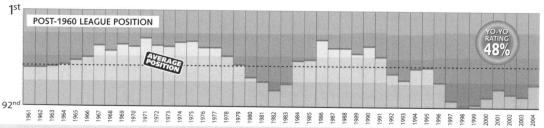

POST-1960 LEAGUE POSITION

1st

92nd

AVERAGE POSITION

YO-YO RATING 48%

1961 1962 1963 1964 1965 1966 1967 1968 1969 1970 1971 1972 1973 1974 1975 1976 1977 1978 1979 1980 1981 1982 1983 1984 1985 1986 1987 1988 1989 1990 1991 1992 1993 1994 1995 1996 1997 1998 1999 2000 2001 2002 2003 2004

PROGRESS REPORT

An early 80s' push ran out of steam halfway up Level One, giving way to a slide towards the nadir of the Hateley/Lloyd years in 1997 and 1998. Back in the safer waters of Level Two in 2004-05, Hull still need a top half finish to maintain a post-1960 average that is stranded somewhere below respectability. On the bright side, they are a reasonable tip to spring a Premiership challenge from next to nowhere.

...Lost Britain's first ever penalty shoot out (1970)...
...When opened, over 50% of supporters 'hated' the name KC (Kingston Communications) Stadium...

RIVALS

One side effect of slipping down the leagues is that you effectively say goodbye to your traditional rivals. A painful procession of clubs have managed to keep ahead of The Tigers – in the case of Leeds and the two Sheffield sides, this is hardly surprising stuff. But to be bottom of a pile that has included Bradford, Huddersfield, Grimsby, and, worst of all even Scunthorpe, was a grim reminder of how hard times had become.

LEEDS

Having struggled historically to maintain a regional identity separate from the Ridings and Lincolnshire, Hull have a natural antipathy to anything and everything in Yorkshire. Even in the worst times, they have rather optimistically continued to name Leeds as their first rivals, though seeing their respective league trajectories at the moment, this is beginning to look less fanciful.

The club realises it has a rump of highly undesirable fans – ones that have no qualms stoning visiting supporters' coaches or indulging in dubious nationalist chants. Despite the traditional animosity between the football and rugby clubs, there has been a strong suspicion that trouble-makers float between the codes. A pitch invasion at Huddersfield's McAlpine during the 2000 Silk Cut Challenge Cup semi-final, involving a mob of 500 mostly drunk Hull FC fans, was found to contain a number who'd previously been banned from Hull City. The ingredients for a stronger rivalry with Huddersfield Town are certainly there – as the two have an almost identical recent history on and off the pitch.

HUDDERSFIELD

PERFORMANCE AGAINST RIVALS
LEEDS
WON 30%
LOST 50%
DRAWN 20%

With the ever evolving pattern of rivalries, the local police have their work cut out knowing what, if any, numbers are required at each game. In 2000, it apparently required 160 officers with dogs, body armour and helicopter backup to police a crowd of just 6,000 at Scunthorpe. With concerns that their heavy-handed approach was unnecessary, the majority of games became police-free, with only the home clashes with Lincoln and Scunthorpe warranting any significant uniformed presence. But second guessing which matches are tense affairs often catches the authorities on the hop. The worst trouble in recent years occurred during a pre-season friendly with Middlesbrough, with 18 Hull arrests.

SCUNTHORPE

SUPPORTERS' VFM 94%

LOVE/HATE

Mark Hateley came to manage the club in 1997 with a strong reputation as a player. With the image of a man more concerned with personal grooming than football and with very few pennies at his disposal, his side carried somewhat more blubber than is generally considered appropriate for professional football, including not-so-star striker, Dean Windass. In 1999, Hull only just avoided the trap door, at the expense of their East Coast neighbours, Scarborough.

CHANTS

Manager for much of the barren spell of the 90s, Terry Dolan was the target for an immaculately constructed song adapted from Pulp's Common People;

'I wanna play in the Vauxhall Conference, I wanna do whatever Halifax do, I wanna to sign crap football players, I wanna watch this club just slide out of view'.

'YOUR GROUND'S TOO BIG FOR YOU!' RATING
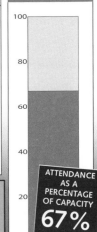
100
80
60
40
20
0

ATTENDANCE AS A PERCENTAGE OF CAPACITY 67%

DOH!!

As their nickname suggests, The Tigers play in amber and black, which should have given a reasonable clue when designing the colour scheme of their new KC stadium. When the gleaming edifice was revealed, jaws hit the floor on first sight of the 95% black seats with mere flecks of amber and white. To his credit, the chairman coughed up £50k to change them to something less funereal.

IPSWICH TOWN

Recommended website: **www.prideofanglia.com**

WHO ARE YA?

Considering their mutual hatred, an outsider might observe that the competitive fortunes of Ipswich and Norwich have more than a passing resemblance. For financial and managerial stability, Ipswich shade their Norfolk neighbours. With only ten managers since World War II (and two of those, Alf Ramsey and Bobby Robson, only leaving because of the offer of the England job) and some astute money management, the club has avoided the woes of others who have had fitful Premiership action. Both were late starters to professional football and the two clubs, whilst not exactly having a magnetic attraction, have similar patterns of promotion and relegation in recent times. On the field, it is possibly the closest matched significant British rivalry. Ipswich are ranked 17th overall thanks to a prolonged spell in the top division in the 80s, with Norwich only 4 places away at 21. The trophy count is 2-2.

CELEBRITY FANS
TREVOR NUNN
Theatre Director
KEITH DELLER
Former Darts champion
NICK KERSHAW
80s' pop idol was a regular at Ipswich during his heyday.

Ipswich are named as many fans' second favourite team. Their position of a smallish club with a limited budget managing to slug it out with the big boys (intermittently) is one that supporters of plenty of lower league teams aspire to. Ipswich players are amongst the more accessible breed of professionals. Encouraged to support community liaison programmes and living locally, fans comment on how easy it is to bump into members of the squad in and around the town. Taking interaction one step too far, midfielder Danny Sonner was caught urinating on the steps of the Town Hall.

IN and AROUND

For those tempted to insert an unnecessary 't' or 'h' into Ipswich, the phrase 'I put some water in Charlie's hat' supposedly aids spelling.

The club can boast an unlikely film star. The clunky but enjoyable 1981 war caper, *Escape to Victory*, required a handful of professional players to make the plot slightly more plausible. Remarkably, considering his complete lack of previous acting experience, John Wark was given a few lines, delivered with considerably more panache than any handled by the film's lead, Sylvester Stallone.

In latter days Bobby Robson has gained a reputation for forgetfulness, but it may not be anything to do with his advancing years, as he could be quite air-headed 35 years ago. Let loose in foreign cities during Ipswich's European away legs, the chairman ensured that Robson wouldn't totally lose track of where he was – by writing the hotel name on his cuffs.

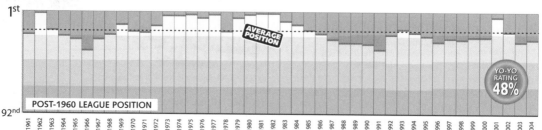

1st

AVERAGE POSITION

YO-YO RATING 48%

POST-1960 LEAGUE POSITION

92nd

1961 1962 1963 1964 1965 1966 1967 1968 1969 1970 1971 1972 1973 1974 1975 1976 1977 1978 1979 1980 1981 1982 1983 1984 1985 1986 1987 1988 1989 1990 1991 1992 1993 1994 1995 1996 1997 1998 1999 2000 2001 2002 2003 2004

PROGRESS REPORT

Ipswich have spent roughly equal periods of time in each of the top two divisions since 1960, with their golden age coming under Robson in the late 70s. Relegated twice from the Premiership, chairman David Sheepshanks has managed a fine balancing act between modest spending and keeping supporters on side. As a result, the club hasn't been drastically affected by their 'death zone' position.

```
          ...Have provided England's two most successful managers...
          ...Having scored the winner in the 1978 FA Cup final, Roger Osbourne
            promptly fainted through a combination of heat and over-excitement....
...When in the Premiership, tests revealed the Portman Road crowd as the loudest in the league...
```

RIVALS

At Portman Road, during a UEFA Cup tie, Helsingborg fans endeared themselves to the Ipswich supporters by starting the chant Stand Up if you hate Norwich. The degree of poisonous feeling between the two clubs is such that fans can reel off the names of those traitorous players who have appeared for both Ipswich and Norwich during their careers. The numbers of these turncoats are disputed because some go to extreme lengths to point the finger of guilt. The head of the club's training academy, Simon Milton, was 'discovered to have had a trial with Norwich as a schoolboy – forgiven only as a youthful indiscretion.

NORWICH

The fact that the towns are unusually far apart for derby status - it's over 40 miles up the A12 from Ipswich to Norwich - is said to make the rivalry worse. A Liverpool fan has to work with, meet, and possibly live with, an Evertonian. They know that rival fans tend not to have two heads. No such story in East Anglia. There is very little interaction between the two populations, so both sides are free to develop their own grim fantasies of what their rivals are like.

The two areas have developed along different lines. Ipswich is becoming something of a high-tech dormitory town of London; Norwich fans negatively characterise this as cockney overspill. In turn, Ipswich see themselves as wanting to break free of the country-bumpkin image that they see as being associated with Norwich.

David Llewellyn, the football coach at Glade Primary School, Brandon, discovered that being an Ipswich supporter had professional drawbacks. Pupil and Norwich fan Ester Roberts was so traumatised by the prospect of taking tips from the enemy, she pretended to lose her kit in order to avoid a session, and then pointedly refused to accept Ipswich players' autographs when handed round. Her punishment of a detention was reduced on appeal.

PERFORMANCE AGAINST RIVALS
NORWICH

WON 41% LOST 38% DRAWN 21%

SUPPORTERS' VFM 65%

LOVE/HATE

HATE

Ex-Norwich striker *Robert Fleck* was never a favourite for obvious reasons. Inevitably Norwich board member *Delia Smith* is a vocal target. One ditty, demonstrating fans are picky over their celebrity cooks, finished with the line 'Bring back *Two Fat Ladies*'.

CHANTS

Having landed a dream tie in the San Siro against Inter Milan, Ipswich fans were not going to let the 1-4 scoreline depress them too much. 10,000 joined in the chant of *'You're not singing anymore'* – which wasn't surprising as the game had finished and the Milan fans departed half an hour before.

DOH!!

It is always a sign of a 'real' rivalry when there is very little history of players moving between the two teams. Few have made the jump between Ipswich and Norwich, and the ones that did had trouble being accepted at their new club. In 2001, goalkeeper Andy Marshall left Norwich for Ipswich with the promise of a Premiership place and possible European action, the first player to move to their rivals since John Deeham in the mid 80s. His professional opportunism enraged City fans. More importantly, he also failed to win over the Ipswich faithful and is frequently named as the club's least favourite player. Marshall was eventually given a free transfer as part of a cost cutting exercise.

'YOUR GROUND'S TOO BIG FOR YOU!'
R A T I N G

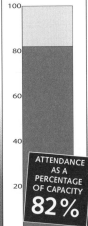

100

80

60

40

20

0

ATTENDANCE AS A PERCENTAGE OF CAPACITY
82%

KIDDERMINSTER HARRIERS

Recommended website: **www.harriers-online.co.uk**

WHO ARE YA?

Of all the clubs winning their League status in recent years, Kidderminster can at least point to better attendances than Macclesfield, but life at Aggborough boils down to a constant struggle just to break even. It was third time lucky, as they had previously won the Conference in 1994, but failed to satisfy the FA that the ground was up to scratch, despite much foot stamping from chairman David Reynolds that the work would be completed during the next season. Also in their favour was the fact that the ground of Northampton Town, who finished bottom, looked as if it had been the victim of an air-raid. Three years later, they threw away the Conference Championship to Macclesfield at the death. Their final accession in 2000 was tempered by the slight problem that promotion hero Mike Marsh accepted an insurance pay-out when it seemed as though his professional career had been ended by injury. Having made an unexpected recovery, he was eligible to play for Kidderminster in the Conference but would have had to pay back a lump sum if he'd wanted to turn pro again when they rose to Level Three. He took the financially prudent option of winding down his career with Southport and Boston United.

IN and AROUND

Don't mess with its hospital. Its downgrading caused one of the most furious political backlashes in modern political history when, in the 2001 general election, Dr. Richard Taylor, standing as the candidate for 'Independent Kidderminster Hospital and Health Concern', turfed out the government's David Lock, winning himself a 17,630 majority.

Jan Molby would be in line for a long service award if it weren't for the fact that he disappeared to Hull City for 17 games in 2002. Having masterminded their escape from the Conference, suspicious fans watched him battle to avoid another spell there as he steered them away from the relegation zone. Molby can probably claim to have the most constrained purse-strings of any League manager. With a board trying to keep the ship afloat on average crowds of 2,500, there are few illusions that the club is going to splash out on a bold promotion push. In July 2004, the entire playing staff consisted of nine outfielders and two goalkeepers.

Caterers at the club serve an allegedly very tasty thick broth dubbed Aggborough Soup. The subject of a certain amount of spin, the club likes to prefix its name with the word 'famous'.

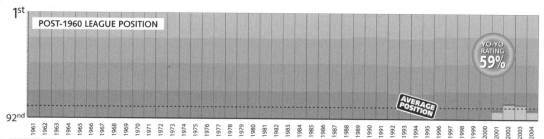

1st

POST-1960 LEAGUE POSITION

YO-YO RATING **59%**

AVERAGE POSITION

92nd

1961 1962 1963 1964 1965 1966 1967 1968 1969 1970 1971 1972 1973 1974 1975 1976 1977 1978 1979 1980 1981 1982 1983 1984 1985 1986 1987 1988 1989 1990 1991 1992 1993 1994 1995 1996 1997 1998 1999 2000 2001 2002 2003 2004

PROGRESS REPORT

Kidderminster's four seasons in Level Three have yielded a couple of 16ths, a 10th and an 11th, not the strongest foundation to make a push up the leagues, but they can point to the fact that their record in the Conference was fairly stuttering aside from their sudden surges. A clear-out of nine players at the end of 2003 doesn't inspire confidence though.

```
            ...Were formed as an athletics club...
         ...First non-league club to publish a fanzine...
   ...Season ticket holders were given free legal expenses insurance (1994)...
```

RIVALS

The most interesting aspect of Kidderminster's relationships is their strong bond with the two large clubs near their patch. Like their notable celeb supporter, Mr Plant, many are happy to swear allegiance to both Harriers and Wolves. A sizeable minority also support West Brom, meaning that, if anything, you'd have thought trouble was more likely to break out between Kidderminster supporters rather than with another side. Whilst not suffering much big clubitis, they don't have many legitimate rivals on the same par with them either. They are the only League side in Worcestershire, and have long left Worcester City and Bromsgrove Rovers (with whom they once shared a Conference place) far behind. Rushden and Diamonds became their Conference foes, having been perceived as a sort of non-league version of Chelsea, unashamedly spending their way into the Third Division, including a raid on playing and coaching staff from Aggborough in the 90s. As they faced up to each other, Rushden appeared to be slightly more favoured by the media for their (very slightly) more sexy tag.

RUSHDEN & DIAMONDS ☠☠☠☠☠

SUPPORTERS' VFM 43%

CHELTENHAM ☠☠

Their feelings towards Cheltenham are reasonably neutral, after all they are in roughly the same boat and, at 40 miles apart, barely deserving of the term 'local'. However, there is a slight sense that, with even fewer natural rivals than them, a few Cheltenham fans are trying to kick-start a bit of hatred. On the field, Kidderminster reckon they are somewhat more refined and like to characterise Cheltenham as long-ball merchants. But they are bound by a mutual dislike of Rushden and Diamonds. Shrewsbury v Kidderminster is often awarded derby status in the press, but evidently the supporters of the clubs aren't that bothered. With Shrewsbury regaining their League status, they are more likely to look north to Wrexham.

PERFORMANCE AGAINST RIVALS
RUSHDEN & DIAMONDS

WON 25%
LOST 50%
DRAWN 25%

Kidderminster's red and white strip has occasionally got them into a spot of bother, as trouble committed by similarly clad Stoke City supporters has been laid at the door of the very peaceable Kidderminster faithful. Like a number of smaller clubs, Kidderminster kept a close eye on Cardiff's progress up the Leagues, mainly because they did not fancy the prospect of hosting fans with the worst reputation in the League.

LOVE/HATE

Nothing particularly bitter to report. Financier of Rushden and Diamonds, *Max Griggs* was treated with utmost suspicion. 'Rats and Dogs' are seen as the first 'plastic' non-league team with a non-existent pedigree. Many wonder why he chose to sink his money into such a side and feel that there is something slightly fishy about their ability to pull in bigger crowds than themselves, though they stop short of any accusations of android infiltration.

CHANTS

'Stand up...if you love Kiddie'

Probably best it's not the plural

'YOUR GROUND'S TOO BIG FOR YOU!'
RATING

100
80
60
40
20
0

ATTENDANCE AS A PERCENTAGE OF CAPACITY 47%

DOH!!

Being a bit squeezed for cash, Kidderminster were keen to milk their home FA Cup draw to Wolves in 2004. But fans felt they had been well and truly fleeced. The hoops they had to jump through to get a ticket were: Go to a League match against Orient and buy a programme containing a stub. This entitled them to fork out for tickets to the next four home League games. Finally they were then granted the privilege of being allowed to buy a £20 (standing) or £30 (seated) ticket to see the Wolves clash. Total: £107.50p.

LEEDS UNITED

Recommended website: **www.lufcweb.com**

WHO ARE YA?

Back in 1975, most neutrals cheered Southern League Wimbledon after a 0-0 draw at Elland Road – an apparently impossible result against a Leeds team that was only four months away from appearing in the European Cup Final. Almost 30 years later, Leeds' fans were contemplating taking a leaf out of Wimbledon's book. Such was the despair over the club's disaster-strewn exit from the Premiership in 2004, many of the faithful seriously contemplated the idea of forming a new non-league version with a view to starting from scratch – a carbon copy of the idea behind the reconstituted AFC Wimbledon.

> **CELEBRITY FANS**
> **MEL B** – Ex-Spice Girl
> **CHRIS MOYLES**
> Radio 1 DJ
> **COLIN MONTGOMERY** – Golfer

Although it wasn't abundantly clear at the time, Leeds' woes were triggered by an apparently respectable fourth place finish in the Premiership in 2000-2001. In what transpired to be one of the less perceptive statements, then chairman, Peter Ridsdale, brushed aside the problems: "The absence of Champions League football this season will inevitably have a short-term impact on operating profit performance." It was one hell of a short term impact. By the autumn of 2003, Leeds had declared the largest loss of any English club in history, £49.5 million, with another £78 million debt hanging over them. Anything and everyone of any value was off-loaded in a gigantic sell-off, with some players fetching only half the value they had achieved on joining the club. Terry Venables should have probably gone before he did, but Leeds simply didn't have the cash to pay him off. Eventually he pocketed £7.2 million, though he had to put up with a lot: David Batty was threatening to sue the club after Ridsdale rubbished his fitness, Australians Mark Viduka and Harry Kewell weren't on speaking terms and there was a touch of unrest in the centre of defence. Michael Duberry had appeared for the prosecution in the trial of Jonathan Woodgate, charged with an attack with racial overtones that had brought nothing but scorn and terrible PR.

> **IN and AROUND**
>
> Leeds city centre is home to 'The Kremlin', the government building that is often considered to be the ugliest piece of modern architecture in the UK.

The Leeds' board and fans have a history of devotion to local lads that, in many ways admirable, has seen them fail to keep up with the development of the game. In the 1980s, with the club wallowing in the Level One, the rollcall of managers was like reading out a team sheet from the Revie era. A significant rump of fans would prefer as many Yorkshire accents throughout the team as possible, even in these days when you'd be surprised to witness any side without a clutch of foreigners – which made the defection of self-proclaimed 'supporter from birth', Alan Smith, across the Pennines, almost impossible to stomach.

With a reputation for toughness on the pitch and near lunacy off it, Leeds were helped by probably the most intimidating atmosphere to be experienced by any away side in the English League. Until Elland Road's conversion to all-seater when the ground was virtually silenced, the North Stand indulged in a particularly cruel trick that involved a spirited round of applause for the opposition goalkeeper as he took up his position for the beginning of the second half. Those not in the know would politely acknowledge the crowd – to be met with a hail of abuse and V signs.

Praise where it's due - Leeds United's official website is outside the premium tv network.

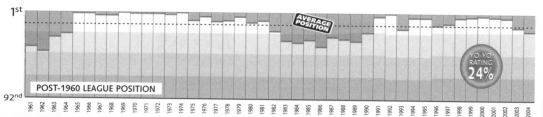

POST-1960 LEAGUE POSITION

AVERAGE POSITION

YO-YO RATING 24%

1st ... 92nd

1961 1962 1963 1964 1965 1966 1967 1968 1969 1970 1971 1972 1973 1974 1975 1976 1977 1978 1979 1980 1981 1982 1983 1984 1985 1986 1987 1988 1989 1990 1991 1992 1993 1994 1995 1996 1997 1998 1999 2000 2001 2002 2003 2004

PROGRESS REPORT

Leeds were the last winners of the old First Division, only two seasons after an eight-year spell in Level One. The Championship was immediately followed by an unnerving 17th, but stability was restored for a decade of reasonable finishes, though the spell included a wearisome 1996-97 season in which an 11th spot was achieved despite only scoring 28 goals. Warning bells started ringing with the 15th in 2002-03 before the unthinkable drop a year later.

```
...All white kit was based on Inter Milan...Two managers lasted 44 days (Brian Clough and
Jock Stein)...Fixture against Middlesbrough had to be rearranged 12 times due to bad weather...
```

RIVALS

It's fair to say that not many supporters of Manchester United or Leeds could give an authoritative account of exactly what the Wars of the Roses were all about, though the 15th century conflict between the Houses of York and Lancaster are still cited as the roots of the split between Yorkshire and Lancashire. The cultural gap between the two teams is only likely to be inflamed by Leeds dropping down a division.

SUPPORTERS' VFM 27%

MANCHESTER UNITED

Leeds have never been the beneficiaries of huge support outside the LS postcodes, even during their best years in the 70s – in stark contrast to The Reds' army of floating fans of dubious geographical credentials.

Leeds were involved in one of the original hooligan incidents of the modern age, when 32 were arrested after the 'and Leeds will go mad' offside goal of West Brom in 1971. Their trail of destruction since then has passed into the annals of hooligan history. Even recently, Manchester United are still the victims of 'Munich' chants, though Manchester United are not averse to displays of bad taste, such as the unfurling of a 'Galatasaray Reds' banner during their meeting in 2001 (following the death of two Leeds supporters in Turkey).

Leeds have simmered over their unwitting hand-outs to The Reds, particularly the transfer of Eric Cantona for what now seems like a pitifully small fee of £1.2 million, before he helped them to four Championships and was voted United's player of the century. In 1999, the title was gifted to them when Leeds beat Arsenal 1-0 in the penultimate game of the season.

PERFORMANCE AGAINST RIVALS MANCHESTER UNITED

WON 23% LOST 41% DRAWN 36%

The fixture itself, whilst extremely hostile between opposing supporters, has never been allowed to descend into full-scale violence, through massive police operations sometimes transporting the problems elsewhere. In early 2001, Leeds fans travelling to Maine Road, and Manchester United fans on their way to Bradford somehow contrived to meet in Rochdale town centre in the morning – with predictable results.

Mr Chinnaraja, who doesn't follow football, decided to sell his number plate M251 UFC, after his car was constantly vandalised when he was parked in Leeds City Centre. It didn't help that the BMW was bright red.

CHELSEA

Bad feeling towards Chelsea is a throwback to 70s' clashes where the two epitomised a north/south football and social divide. However, Chelsea were pleased to help out the old adversaries with their own chants of 'Judas...Judas..' at Alan Smith in 2004.

'YOUR GROUND'S TOO BIG FOR YOU!' RATING

LOVE/HATE

The car-boot sale of players by *Peter Ridsdale* was bad enough, but his airy insistence that the team would not be weakened appeared completely delusional. After his shoulder-top farewell in 2004, there were hopes that *Alan Smith* might have a season abroad, or at least at a neutral club, before returning to the fold when United were back in the Premiership. It's fair to say his choice of new team completely rules this option out..

CHANTS

The day after the off-loading of Jonathan Woodgate, Everton fans had a career announcement for Alan Smith:

'You're gonna be sold in the morning'.

ATTENDANCE AS A PERCENTAGE OF CAPACITY 91%

DOH!!

At £4.5 million from Parma, Leeds thought that they'd paid for a player who had graced Sweden's Euro '92 squad. Instead, they got an astoundingly overweight Thomas Brolin who waddled around for 19 appearances and got embroiled in a series of training ground bust-ups. A candidate for worst ever Premiership signing, he was still agile enough to demonstrate vacuum cleaners, his new job when returning to Sweden.

LEICESTER CITY

Recommended website: **www.forfoxsake.com**

WHO ARE YA?

Along with Middlesbrough this is the team whose name gives everyone the most spelling headaches. Their record, particularly in the years under Martin O'Neill, is better than their reputation. To the disinterested, the club's on-field character is not the most swashbuckling that can be imagined. They have been burdened with a slight reputation for being involved in dour goal-free encounters, provoking one Radio 5 commentator to remark during a game against Sunderland 'The score is Sunderland nil, Leicester nil, the temperature is nil and the entertainment value is not much above nil'. But they'd like to point out that their 4-4 draw at Spurs was voted the 2003-2004 game of the season.

Leicester cannot decide whether they belong at the top of the Level One or the bottom of the Premiership. Six changes between the two divisions have landed them with the 'yo-yo' tag, immortalised in a Manchester United song to the tune of Yellow Submarine 'You're going up...you're going down'. But at least they are constantly in the reckoning, unlike neighbours Derby and Nottingham Forest, who, once out of the Premiership, fell to pieces.

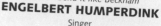

CELEBRITY FANS
PARMINDER NAGRA
Actress - *Bend it like Beckham*
ENGELBERT HUMPERDINK
Singer
DAVID NIELSON
Actor - Roy Cropper in *Coronation Street*

IN and AROUND

According to the BBC's Test the Nation, Leicester is Britain's most brainy city

Somewhat overlooked for Premiership TV coverage, even in their best moments they failed to attract much of an armchair audience. The club were dismayed that for their first foray into European competition, against Athletico Madrid in the UEFA Cup of 1997, no British broadcaster would offer a fee for taking the match.

Their tiny Filbert Street ground was the scene of one of the odder pitch protection systems in the 70s – a giant inflatable bubble with sci-fi overtones. Although effective in the short term, it was very labour intensive, requiring 50 people to man its stately deflation and packing away. Its sweating effect also encouraged the growth of fungus.

Anti-corporate fans from around the country - and some from Leicester itself - were less than impressed with the crispy name of the new stadium, a sop to sponsors Walkers. One supporter admitted to the Leicester fans being quite fickle with attendances moving up and down alarmingly depending on the club's standing. But there's no questioning the loyalty of their long-serving keeper, Mark Wallington, who played in every game possible in two spells with the club, between 1975 and 1981, and 1982 and 1983. So determined was he not to miss a match, he even turned out when injured for a game against Shrewsbury, to be replaced quickly by Alan Young.

No one seems sure how Leicester became the 'Foxes'. A lot of hunting goes on in the county, but the most interesting explanation is that, viewed in a certain way, the shape of Leicestershire looks like the head of the animal.

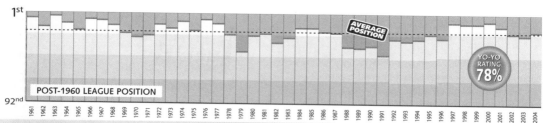

1st

AVERAGE POSITION

POST-1960 LEAGUE POSITION

YO-YO RATING 78%

92nd

1961 1962 1963 1964 1965 1966 1967 1968 1969 1970 1971 1972 1973 1974 1975 1976 1977 1978 1979 1980 1981 1982 1983 1984 1985 1986 1987 1988 1989 1990 1991 1992 1993 1994 1995 1996 1997 1998 1999 2000 2001 2002 2003 2004

PROGRESS REPORT

City avoided a first trip to Level Two by the skin of their teeth in 1991. In any other season, their 22nd place would have put them down but the re-jigging of divisional structure meant that only two were relegated. Since the formation of the Premiership, Leicester have twice performed the 'triple jump' – three consecutive seasons in which they changed between the top two divisions.

```
...Won 55 points, scored 55 goals and conceded 55 in 1999-00...
        ...Have lost all four FA cup finals they've appeared in...
...Earned nickname 'Leicester Nil' after failing to score in 23 out of 42 games in 1977-78...
```

NUTTER RATING
RANKED 33rd

RIVALS

Leicester are completely out of the loop of East Midlands' rivalries thanks to their neighbours' self-destructive inclinations. Unable to agree amongst themselves, fans seem to split down regional lines to decide who their real rivals are. In northern Leicestershire, Derby have generally been number one, though the struggling Rams are not currently seen as a serious threat. The urban area of Leicester itself has traditionally been more anti-Nottingham Forest, though, to a degree the same applies, "city fans merely smile at the mention of their name". Those living nearer the Warwickshire border tend to look more to Villa and Coventry, 'that concrete hellhole', aggravated slightly with the appointment of ex-light blues manager Gordon Milne back in 1982. Such is their 'spare part' status, Leicester are not considered to be anyone else's main rivals, with Nottingham Forest and Derby too busy at each other's throats.

COVENTRY

DERBY COUNTY

SUPPORTERS' VFM 29%

City's new-found family atmosphere has largely sidelined a small hooligan element, with a bulk of their number not the slightest bit interested in confrontation. One Leicester fan dismissed football violence as a dying phenomenon suggesting it was "a bit of a working class thing".

NOTTINGHAM FOREST

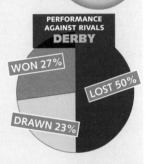

PERFORMANCE AGAINST RIVALS
DERBY
WON 27%
LOST 50%
DRAWN 23%

Struggling at the bottom of the Premiership in 2004, the club threatened to loose friends when members of the squad were held over, what turned out be, unfounded sexual assault charges in a luxury resort – their predicaments on and off the field leading neatly to the chant 'You couldn't score in La Manga'.

Having walked out on Leicester in 1997, the Wolves boss Mark McGhee was subjected to a postal bombardment by Foxes' fans who'd travelled to Spain to watch UEFA cup tie against Atletico Madrid. Thousands of postcards poured through McGhee's letterbox reminding him that whilst Leicester were hob-nobbing in Europe, his Wolves side had to visit Fulham, then considered the ultimate indignity.

LOVE/HATE

Former local market boy, England's greatest modern striker put cash into the club at a critical time, and manages to bear sitting so near Mark Lawrenson. It has to be *Gary Linneker*.

Players slagging off their previous clubs instantly get elevated to hate figures. Threatening legal action takes them to a different level. Following a card game row at a training camp in Finland, *Dennis Wise* punched team-mate Callum Davidson, breaking his jaw. Following a swift dismissal from the club, *Wise* demanded £2.3 million in lost earnings – not exactly lose change to the cash-strapped Leicester.

CHANTS

To woolly-minded Derby

'You only sing when you're shearing'.

'YOUR GROUND'S TOO BIG FOR YOU!'
RATING

100

80

60

40

ATTENDANCE AS A PERCENTAGE OF CAPACITY
95%

20

0

DOH!!

In 2002, the club mooted plans to reintroduce the old name of 'Leicester Fosse' (abandoned in 1920) after the Roman Way underneath the meeting house where the club was first formed. In latter days, more associated with the on-the-edge American choreographer, the name didn't appeal to fans and the idea disappeared without a trace.

LEYTON ORIENT

Recommended website: **www.leytonorient-mad.co.uk**

WHO ARE YA?

Leyton Orient could hardly be more hemmed in. With Arsenal four miles away to the south-west, Tottenham three to the north-west, and West Ham two to the south-east, it is remarkable that the club have survived [just] the financial chill, aided by snooker/boxing promoter, Barry Hearn, who paid a fiver for the club in 1995. Having lost the 'Leyton' tag in 1966, it was reinstated in 1987, taking over five years before the bulk of fans had become used to it again. But the faithful have been less flexible when it comes to the name of the ground. Hearn had it changed to his company name - but 'The Matchroom Stadium' is still generally referred to as Brisbane Road. Despite its seemingly small catchment area, only 2% of season ticket holders actually live within the local borough of Waltham. Support stretches along the Thames estuary through Basildon and into Southend.

IN and AROUND

Leytonstone is renowned as a popular hangout for the actors in *Eastenders*.

Hearn's arrival was typically flamboyant. Would he open his chequebook and bring glory, or try and make a quick buck from development? The truth, as is often the case with high profile directors, is neither. With a snooker-loopy board, including Steve Davis, Hearn has stuck with the club long enough to be loved by about 40% of the supporters, treated with neutrality by another 40% and still derided by the remainder. Hearn reckons it costs him £650,000 a year for the pleasure of running Leyton Orient. One of his imports was tannoy announcer Andrew Buonocore, whose notoriously partisan addresses to the crowd assisted by a PA system that the Beatles would have died for in 1964, are prone to wind-up away fans. Otherwise, Brisbane Road is known for being a bit of an away fans' paradise. Leyton Orient's home support is not noted for its volume, and the acoustics of the place seem to benefit the visitors. However, on their travels, their fans are known for their good-natured racket, accompanied in the 1995-96 season, by a sea of confetti, streamers and other paper (often courtesy of torn up American Express brochures liberated from service stations).

The craze was extinguished when Reading FC complained to the FA, after Orient supporters left a gigantic paper trail in gardens adjoining the ground.

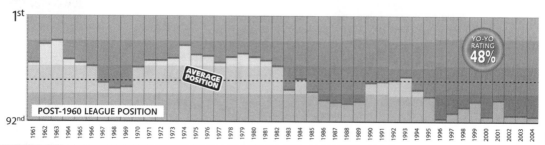

1st / 92nd — POST-1960 LEAGUE POSITION — AVERAGE POSITION — YO-YO RATING 48%

1961 1962 1963 1964 1965 1966 1967 1968 1969 1970 1971 1972 1973 1974 1975 1976 1977 1978 1979 1980 1981 1982 1983 1984 1985 1986 1987 1988 1989 1990 1991 1992 1993 1994 1995 1996 1997 1998 1999 2000 2001 2002 2003 2004

PROGRESS REPORT

The traumas of 1994-95, when for sometime it looked as though fixtures would have to be cancelled, marked a new low in a 30-year decline. Though riding high in the old First Division for a single season in 1962-63, that is the best that any supporter alive today could possibly have experienced. The post-1960 average places them mid-table in Level Two, but the arrival of Barry Hearn has, at best, managed to stabilise a sinking ship towards the foot of Level Three. Although not in serious danger of going through the trap door in 2003-04, their form in the latter part of the season was alarming enough to suggest that some more hair-raising moments lie around the corner.

```
...Have changed their name six times...Have played each of the other 91 league clubs...
                    ...Are the club nearest David Beckham's birthplace...
```

RIVALS

Leyton Orient are within the top ten of the least hated clubs in the league. In their early history, they were a semi-official feeder club for Arsenal, though, along with Spurs, they kicked up a fuss when the Gunners moved north of the river. These days, fans of London's major sides tend to look at them with a degree of fondness. Indeed there was a slight suspicion that the multitude of fans they mustered for their losing 1999 play-off final may have been bolstered by a large number from neighbouring clubs, particularly West Ham.

SOUTHEND

Traditionally, Southend are seen as their main rivals, though it is not really reciprocated – Southend are more bothered about Colchester and non-leaguers, Canvey Island, than they are about Leyton Orient. From Orient's point of view, things with Southend have cooled simply because they beat them so much. The games are famed for their tendency to produce own goals and Leyton Orient's habit of getting results with only ten men. Having grown bored with Southend, it is now more common to name West Ham as top rivals, though quite how they are planning to get to play them is another matter.

WEST HAM

Southend are seen as 'wannabe' Londoners. Although the fan bases are similar, West Ham are perceived as being slightly down-market socially as they draw a lot of support from the borough of Hackney.

BRIGHTON

There has also been tension with Brighton following a pitch invasion in 1997, where a Leyton Orient player was attacked by a Brighton fan. Barry Hearn was so incensed he voted for them to be kicked out of the league. Two years later, Brighton took 3,500 supporters to Brisbane Road. A huge smoke bomb landed on the pitch from the Brighton end and a pack of razor blades was later found, presumably not intended for personal grooming.

PERFORMANCE AGAINST RIVALS
SOUTHEND

WON 48%
LOST 28%
DRAWN 24%

SUPPORTERS' VFM 49%

LOVE/HATE

Unusually, one of Orient's highest scoring players, *Carl Griffiths*, ♡ 🤬 features prominently in both categories. Though a consistent goal-scorer, he was often accused of being a non-trier. Getting himself banned for a play-off final didn't help his cause with the anti-camp.

Barry Hearn ♡ 🤬 himself infuriated many fans with his comments on Nicky Campbell's radio phone-in, when his 'humour' on the subject of immigration, i.e. 'you would never be able to get your car windscreen cleaned', fell extremely flat on supporters' groups who had campaigned vigorously against racism on the terraces.

CHANTS

The O's have a rare example of an 'off-topic' song, a long ditty about Yogi Bear that has absolutely no connection with football.

'YOUR GROUND'S TOO BIG FOR YOU!'
RATING

100

80

ATTENDANCE AS A PERCENTAGE OF CAPACITY
37%

60

40

20

0

DOH!!

In 1996, Roger Stanislaus became the first senior player to be banned from English football for drug taking, whilst playing for Leyton Orient. What particularly irked O's fans was that he had just played his part in a dreadful 3-0 defeat at Barnet. The realisation that his performance that day might have been affected by performance-enhancing drugs made them wonder how bad he could get when he wasn't on them.

LINCOLN CITY

Recommended website: **www.lincolncity-mad.co.uk**

WHO ARE YA?

Although we know different now, at the time of the first automatic relegation from Level Three, it was widely assumed that the strength of the Conference sides was such that teams who went down would find it mighty difficult ever to return, and could even face extinction as a club. It was against this doom-laden background that Lincoln City found themselves rock bottom at the end of the last match in 1987, thanks partially to a confused police dog at fellow strugglers, Torquay, who gifted the home side some extra time by biting one of their players. But to the surprise of neutrals, they bounced straight back up from the Conference. Lincoln City were the forgotten victims of the Bradford Fire, where fans, officials and players were all affected, but whose involvement tended to be overlooked.

CELEBRITY FANS
JOHN INVERDALE
Sports Presenter

The recent history of Lincoln City mostly revolves around an ex-chairman with a sartorial taste in hats. John Reames came to the club spouting all the positive noises, though his impatience with managers didn't inspire confidence in the fans. The misjudgement he is most remembered for was the sacking of John Beck in 1997, when the team was in with a shout of a play-off place. Reames fulfilled the secret dream of many chairmen, appointing himself as manager – a spell which, with some inevitability, led to relegation. Breaking the mould, Lincoln became the first club to be owned by its supporters. With the new structure came manager Alan Buckley, whose odd tactics took the gloss off the excitement of the new financial setup.

IN and AROUND

There are two distinct designs of Lincoln biscuits, one where the nobbles are distributed randomly and another where they form concentric circles.

Sincil Bank, never in danger of bursting at the seams at the best of times, managed to record an official attendance of absolutely zero for a game between Bradford and Norwich during the Second World War. Worried that the draw of the game might keep workers away from the munitions' factories, the authorities ordered the gates to be locked. Around 200 people managed to find their way in anyway. A later conflict, in Iraq in 2004, caused the silencing of the infamous Sincil Bank siren that emitted a wail whenever the home side got a corner. Many were getting fed up with it anyway, as it seemed to glorify the long-ball technique despised under Buckley. The club reasoned that with so many of the local populace involved in some way in the Gulf War, the siren might be seen to be the wrong side of the good taste threshold.

Lincoln did mastermind one of the most lucrative lower league transfers of all time. Newcastle United paid £500,000 for Darren Huckerby in 1995, a figure that was larger than Lincoln's gate receipts for the entire season, transforming him overnight to a Premiership player from the depths of Level Three. Newcastle didn't get a particularly good deal – Huckerby made one appearance for them in his first season.

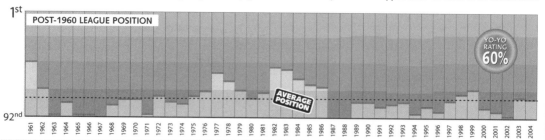

POST-1960 LEAGUE POSITION
1st
92nd
YO-YO RATING 60%
AVERAGE POSITION
1961 1962 1963 1964 1965 1966 1967 1968 1969 1970 1971 1972 1973 1974 1975 1976 1977 1978 1979 1980 1981 1982 1983 1984 1985 1986 1987 1988 1989 1990 1991 1992 1993 1994 1995 1996 1997 1998 1999 2000 2001 2002 2003 2004

PROGRESS REPORT

Lincoln's forays outside Level Three have been few and far between in modern times. Successive relegations took them to the Conference in 1987. Since then, a solitary season in Level Two in 1998 has provided the only respite.

...Seats have been sponsored by Gene Pitney, James Bolam and Lionel Blair...Became the 'Red Imps' as a reference to statues in Lincoln Cathedral and in an attempt to emulate Liverpool...After an early merger with cricket team, they became tongue-twisting Lincoln Lindum...

RIVALS

To those not familiar with the region, it's easy to imagine the collection of east coast teams are near neighbours. But Lincoln is comparatively stuck out on a limb, being as near to Nottingham as it is to Hull. Hull have always had fairly lofty pretensions with their choice of rivals, rather fancifully looking west to Leeds and picking fights with everyone in Yorkshire. Those that are left, namely Boston, Scunthorpe, Grimsby and Lincoln, form a complicated pattern that few fans, even within the same club, can agree on.

HULL CITY

SCUNTHORPE UNITED

Everyone in the region has a slight excuse to dislike Boston United, as they are seen as having 'cheated their way into the League'. The Imps have legitimate fears that their 'biggest club in Lincolnshire' tag is at risk, and get very jumpy at the idea of not being able to beat the newcomers.

BOSTON UNITED

SUPPORTERS' VFM 59%

PERFORMANCE AGAINST RIVALS
BOSTON

WON 40%
LOST 20%
DRAWN 40%

The biggest worry for Lincoln is that when there is the merest whiff of success, a load of headcases like to attach themselves to the club. There were a few gasps when Lincoln came top of the arrests' league for Level Three in 2002-03, considerably above Swansea who were generally seen as the basement's bad boys. There is an argument that the comparatively high number is the result of some strenuous 'zero-tolerance' policing, a factor that makes Sincil Bank safer to visit than it would suggest. But there's no denying that Lincoln have a disproportionately high number of troublemakers for their attendances, although almost all incidents have occurred outside the ground. The Barbican Hotel in Lincoln was ransacked when supporters of Hull and Lincoln City and the police fought a three-way pitched battle after the teams' meeting in 2004. Though not a name synonymous with a hooligan problem, the club were in hot water with the Football Association as early as 1897 when they received a suspension from the League.

Lincoln came face to face with 'downmarket' Scunthorpe in the play-off semi-final in 2003 amidst chaotic scenes. A Lincoln goal was greeted with a considerable number celebrating in what was supposed to be the home stand, resulting in brawls in the unsegregated section.

LOVE/HATE

HATE

Rarely a name mentioned in supporters' hate lists, Des Lynam has not been forgiven for his outburst on BBC's 'Grandstand' on the final day of the 1987 season. Displaying a rare preference, Lynam appeared to celebrate the fact that Burnley, a side with a great 'tradition', had survived at the expense of Lincoln.

CHANTS

Grimsby Town are welcomed with
'We smell fish',
cunningly adapted to
'We smell sheep'
for Swansea.

'YOUR GROUND'S TOO BIG FOR YOU!'
RATING

100
80
60
40
20
0

ATTENDANCE AS A PERCENTAGE OF CAPACITY
45%

DOH!!

Adam Buckley, son of former chairman, found it difficult to achieve a first team place at the club, so he embarked on some redistribution of wealth – by nicking small items off fellow players. In 2003, he was sentenced to 120 hours community service after admitting the theft of a pair of trainers, football boots, a watch and a mobile phone.

LIVERPOOL

Recommended website: **www.liverweb.org.uk**

WHO ARE YA?

The question of 'which is the greatest English team ever?' frequently does the rounds amongst the faithful of Arsenal, Manchester United and Liverpool. It all depends how you measure it. In terms of dominating a decade, United beat all-comers in the 90s in a very similar fashion to Liverpool's virtual monopoly on the 80s. Using the criteria of league positions since 1960, Liverpool have the edge as they have not suffered a wobble outside the top division. They were the first team to win a notable treble; the League Cup, FA Cup and European Cup (1984) and their overall record of honours is superior to both United and Arsenal. They were the game's first real super-team in Britain - a feat that arguably was more difficult then than now - as there wasn't the financial gulf between the top sides and the second-tier. Strictly speaking, Liverpool's league success of their golden decade just edges United's in theirs. With the astonishing average league position of 1.7 throughout 'their' decade, Manchester United hit back with the marginally less incredible 1.9 in the following 10 years.

CELEBRITY FANS
CILLA BLACK
Singer/Presenter
MIKE MYERS
Actor – Austin Powers
ELVIS COSTELLO
Rock Musician

But the manner in which the 80s' side was perceived in the world at large was quite different to the Manchester United of the 90s. The gently simmering hatred between the two has much to do with comparing how their spells of domination have been seen generally. United's domination coincided with a vast increase of TV coverage. With almost every kick of their season beamed around the world, their international standing broadened. Liverpool probably didn't benefit as much from their on-field brilliance.

Although famed for its political activism, the city is home to Britain's most apathetic parliamentary constituency. Riverside, that covers the city centre, recorded the worst turnout in the 2001 election, with just 34% of electors bothering to vote.

Unlike most clubs, Liverpool fans don't have a habit of turning on their heroes when they leave the club. Notably, Robbie Fowler and Steve McManaman's local status hasn't been dented by leaving the nest.

Liverpool's characterisation for being an international centre for petty crime and sponging off state benefits was largely popularised by Carla Lane's BBC comedy *Bread* in 1983 - an image that has stuck through a generation of anti-Liverpool chants. Clearly Lane wasn't bothered with immersing herself in the culture she was supposed to be reflecting; *Bread* was written at her home...in Kensington, West London.

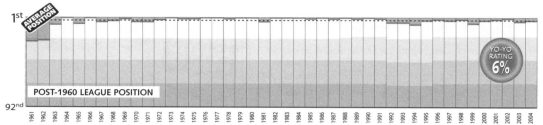

1st

AVERAGE POSITION

YO-YO RATING **6%**

POST-1960 LEAGUE POSITION

92nd

1961 1962 1963 1964 1965 1966 1967 1968 1969 1970 1971 1972 1973 1974 1975 1976 1977 1978 1979 1980 1981 1982 1983 1984 1985 1986 1987 1988 1989 1990 1991 1992 1993 1994 1995 1996 1997 1998 1999 2000 2001 2002 2003 2004

PROGRESS REPORT

Since 1972-73 Liverpool have experienced two distinct phases. Firstly, a spell of almost total dominance which included 11 championships, five second places, and a fifth place in the period up to 1991 and the resignation of Kenny Dalglish. Since then their best has been a solitary second place in 2002. In 2004 they finished a full 30 points behind Champions Arsenal.

```
...Largest club not to have been floated on the Stock Market...
...Liverpool's league championship trophy of 1964 was made of papier-mâché...
...Have remained unbeaten at Anfield in nine complete seasons...
```

RIVALS

NUTTER RATING
RANKED 67th

BBC North West News, produced in Oxford Road, Manchester, does its best to ensure that both Liverpool and its home city are given equal coverage and present a united front for northwest England. But they are fighting a losing battle. They might as well have border controls on the M62 between the cities such is the vast divide. The rivalry flourished in the 19th century when the two faced each other in an early version of the play-offs when United were still Newton Heath. More recently Liverpool are furious that their glory days were greeted with mild disinterest by the media compared to the incessant Manchester United mania from the early 90s. Tabloids are shunned generally, with both The Sun and The Mirror being labelled as United biased. Manchester's re-branding as the cool culture capital of the North doesn't impress either.

MANCHESTER UNITED

When playing for Manchester City, Robbie Fowler, the long-term darling of the Kop, was happy to remind United fans that Liverpool have won four European Cups to Manchester United's two, with a series of coded finger gestures at the crowd.

When Liverpool, in 2001, put a considerable dent in United's claim to be the country's top team - by scooping the FA Cup, League Cup and UEFA Cup - they became the victims of endless jibes from Manchester that it was merely a 'plastic treble', and a pale imitation of their epoch-making three trophies in 1999...blah...blah.

EVERTON

Despite the history between them, the two clubs managed to connive to keep Manchester United from relegation in 1915. With Liverpool safely in mid-division, they agreed to throw the game. United won 2-0. When the plot was uncovered, four players from each club were handed life bans, though these were later rescinded.

Revelations that Michael Owen had developed a prodigious gambling habit were quickly forgiven by Liverpool fans, but their patience was severely tested when it was discovered that one of his hefty wagers was on the arch enemy to beat Hungarians Zalaegerszeg in a Champions League qualifier (Manchester United lost 1-0; Owen lost £2,141).

The intensity of the rivalry with Everton depends on who you speak to. Many pointedly do not bother to name Everton at all in the top three, preferring to list the likes of Aston Villa and Newcastle before The Toffees. Others will claim that too much is read into the reputation of the Merseyside derby as being good-natured.

PERFORMANCE AGAINST RIVALS
MANCHESTER UNITED

WON 33%
LOST 35%
DRAWN 32%

SUPPORTERS' VFM
49%

LOVE/HATE

Fifteen years on from the Hillsborough disaster, it is still a rarity to see anyone in Liverpool holding a copy of The Sun. The Press Complaints Commission was deluged following the paper's coverage of Hillsborough in which it blamed drunk Liverpool fans for breaking into the stand, leading to the fatal crush. (It subsequently ruled against The Sun). After a public burning of copies in Kirby, the paper lost an estimated £10 million a year from lack of sales in Merseyside.

CHANTS

A plea to Manchester United fans;

'Support your local team'

DOH!!

Fans justifiably moan at clubs' premium rate ClubCall lines at the best of times, but in 1999 Liverpool's service managed to give pointers to a completely bogus, and impossible, transfer. ClubCall picked up press reports that Gerard Houllier was on the verge of signing French under-21 striker Didier Baptiste for £3.5 million.

The only problem was Baptiste was nothing more than a character in Sky's football soap-opera, The Dream Team, played by actor Tom Redhill. In an episode shortly before the surge of press interest, he mentions a possible move to a club managed by a Frenchman. The non-existent story was supplied to the News of the World via an agency, who held an 'urgent investigation'.

'YOUR GROUND'S TOO BIG FOR YOU!'
RATING

100
80
60
40
20
0

ATTENDANCE AS A PERCENTAGE OF CAPACITY
94%

LUTON TOWN

Recommended website: **www.hatternet.com**

WHO ARE YA?

Most people's awareness of Luton's history comes to a shuddering halt when they were relegated from the old First Division in 1992. But if anyone was under the impression Luton were trundling along minding their own business, a brief recap of their 'summer of hell' in 2003 will be enough to dissuade them. They enjoyed the PR benefits of having Eric Morecombe as a director, who memorably made Glenda Jackson wear a sash bearing the words 'Luton Town'. But the goodwill gave way to a period in the 80s, under pro-Thatcher MP David Evans, in which the club attracted little but negative comment.

At the root of Luton's woes is a Kenilworth Road ground where space is so tight that one side of it has nothing but corporate boxes, and the away supporters enter the ground through what once used to be someone's living room. The apparent 'redevelopment' opportunity has attracted the highest quality fruitcakes in the land. David Kohler got stuck in with his plan for…deep breath….The Kohlerdome, a gigantic sliding roof affair – that is until someone reminded him of supporters' power by depositing a fire bomb through his letter box. Their other difficulty was that, having experienced a decade in the top-flight and a 1988 League Cup win, most fans were unaccustomed to life in the lower Leagues.

IN and AROUND

London Luton Airport claims to be the 'fastest growing in the country'. Mind you, so do Stanstead, Manchester, Cardiff, Bristol, and…Bournemouth. However, it is the only one to feature in the title of a hit single - by Cats UK in 1979.

In May 2003, enter the 'mysterons', a consortium who, probably wisely, wished to remain anonymous. After sacking the highly popular backroom team of Joe Kinnear and Mick Harford, (who had achieved promotion from Level Three and a 9th spot in the Second), the men in grey suits organised a 'Pop Idol' style vote to decide who should become the new manager. Fans were urged to vote for, eh, Joe Kinnear, which they dutifully did. So obviously the next manager was… Mike Newell.

The mastermind behind the consortium was finally revealed as one John Gurney, whose CV included an acquittal for drug smuggling and a takeover of Bedford Rugby Club (that ended in tears). Gurney's blueprint for Luton's future was arguably the most unhinged document ever to have emanated from a football club. The highlights included a proposal for a revamped club housed in a Teflon roofed 50-75,000 capacity stadium up the M1, under the name Luton London FC (wilfully ignoring the town's wish to be seen as independent from the capital). This less than modest ten-fold increase in supporters would be achieved by a variety of wheezes, including the creaming off of north London fans – clearly believing Spurs' and Arsenal's faithful were becoming increasingly flaky. Failing this, they could always look north: "Let the 4,000 people who have bought Wimbledon season tickets at Milton Keynes come and watch the regional team called Luton play at Luton". (Why didn't the Bristol clubs think of this?) The stadium would also host the Grand Prix, and would be handily placed for the airport, so as to ensure the rapid passage of supporters from all over Europe.

After two months of this, a fans' boycott paid dividends and Gurney bid a hasty retreat, just as cans of four-star were being topped up in anticipation. Luton Town were placed in administration and in 2004, were close to new ownership by a supporters' trust.

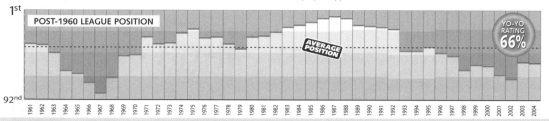

POST-1960 LEAGUE POSITION — 1st … 92nd — AVERAGE POSITION — YO-YO RATING 66% — 1961 1962 1963 1964 1965 1966 1967 1968 1969 1970 1971 1972 1973 1974 1975 1976 1977 1978 1979 1980 1981 1982 1983 1984 1985 1986 1987 1988 1989 1990 1991 1992 1993 1994 1995 1996 1997 1998 1999 2000 2001 2002 2003 2004

PROGRESS REPORT

In Level Two, Luton are slightly below their post-1960 average, but they've bounced around so much it's difficult to tell where their natural divisional home is. They are the only club to move through the divisional structure there and back in two separate spells.

...Hold record for most goals scored by one player in a single match (10 by Joe Payne v Bristol Rovers in 1936)...Players had a fight over who should take a penalty (versus York City in 2001)... ...First team in southern England to turn professional...

RIVALS

A couple of junctions of the M1 separate two towns that, on the surface, are similar, though the more northerly neighbours, Luton, tend to be looked down upon as verging on the nine-carat. History records that there was violence between the two stretching back to the early 20th century. However, many of the current day problems partly stem from a marked skew of results that has caused escalating tension. The pressure cooker started simmering after Watford's 2-1 victory back in November 1971 in Level One. By the time the two met in 1983, plenty of water had flowed under the bridge, with Watford at their historical high, lying second behind Liverpool in the old First Division. In between,

WATFORD ☠☠☠☠☠

Luton had won seven out of the nine games between them, with two draws. The Easter Bank Holiday fixture contrasted two very different styles, with 'long-ball' Watford triumphing in a 5-2 thriller.

The two met again, for the first time in four years, in the first round of the League Cup in 2002, when predictably the kick-off was held up for 15 minutes whilst brawls that had started in Watford town centre from lunchtime were continued with little concern about the game.

Luton's crusade against hooligan activity in the 80s, if anything, made the club somewhat more of a target. Conspiratorial theories abound concerning David Evans' 'clampdown' following the infamous Millwall pitch invasion of 1985. Luton are said to have requested Millwall not to bring too many travelling supporters. The call went unheeded and, anxious to show how much they cared for Evans' new breed of politicised, identity card culture, they wrecked the ground in a torrent of orange seats.

QPR ☠☠☠☠☠

Luton's subsequent ban on away fans got up the noses of other clubs and the FA, who banned them from the League Cup. In defiance of Evans' stand, Luton became a target for rival groups with Leeds, Cardiff and others going out of their way to cause trouble there. In turn, this probably led to a hardening of the Luton support that made the cycle of hooligan incidents get worse.

Luton are particularly stuffy about Wycombe and Rushden and Diamonds, utterly refuting any suggestions that they could be conceived as rivals, despite being reasonably close geographically. Luton have been forced to lower themselves into playing them a total of 19 times up to the beginning of 2004-05, though you can see their point as they've only lost once.

SUPPORTERS' VFM **45%**

PERFORMANCE AGAINST RIVALS **WATFORD**

WON 47% LOST 26% DRAWN 28%

'YOUR GROUND'S TOO BIG FOR YOU!' RATING

ATTENDANCE AS A PERCENTAGE OF CAPACITY **66%**

LOVE/HATE

Raddy Antic's last gasp goal against Manchester City in 1983 improbably ensured Luton's top-flight survival, leading to a fan's favourite video freeze-frame moment, the delightfully uncoordinated *David Pleat running onto the pitch to celebrate* with a spasmodic mix of forward motion punctuated with random jumps and excessive hand waving.

Ignoring the colourful cast of characters that have littered Luton's backroom history, which is difficult, the association of *Elton John* with Watford easily outweighs his musical attributes.

CHANTS

'10 years…It only took 10 years'

Luton's response to Watford bogey breaking win in 1997

DOH!!

Just the sort of words to endear the locals to the new regime. John Gurney's mission statement in 2003 included a reference to 'volatile fans in Bedfordshire' and the local paper, The Beds (Luton) on Sunday, making the 'worst tabloid look respectable'. In a nod to the classic episode of Dad's Army, he added, "They are on my list" [of people that he was taking court action against].

MACCLESFIELD TOWN

Recommended website: **www.macclesfieldtown-mad.co.uk**

WHO ARE YA?

Macclesfield's rise through the minor divisions to full league status in 1997 leads to some remarkable comparisons. By 1998, the town was hosting the mighty Manchester City. Thirty years before, City were winning the old First Division Championship ahead of Manchester United. In the same year, Macclesfield won the amateur Cheshire County League, finishing just above their old enemy Altrincham.

But the story is tinged with one of the more tragic tales of a chairman's bankrolling. 120 years of effort looked as if it might count for nothing as, in 1995, having finished top of the Conference, the club was barred from promotion for inadequate facilities at its tiny Moss Rose ground. It was a black moment for chairman Arthur Jones who had maintained a determined but somewhat secretive fantasy of seeing Macclesfield get league action. A year later, with the dream unfulfilled and his other business interests going to pot, he shot himself, having spent around £400,000 of his own cash on the club, but leaving a similar figure in debts. Manager Sammy McIlroy was forced to slash squad numbers to such an extent that, at the age of 42, he seriously contemplated having to come on as a substitute.

CELEBRITY FANS
GOD
Leading Deity
(Ex-chairman Alan Cash said
'we've got God on our side')

IN and AROUND

Latter day Macclesfield is best known for the yumminess of its cheese and onion pies.

The following year, the club was better prepared and having finished top again, they eagerly grasped their second chance, winning consecutive promotions to reach their zenith of Level Two. This led to the reasonable conclusion that the club had achieved more in one season than Rochdale had managed in 80 years. But the similarities are uncomfortable. Both suffer from their town being infested with fans of the relatively nearby Manchester clubs. With a Level Three average attendance hardly keeping its head above 2,000, Macclesfield have the poorest support of all 92 league clubs. Visiting fans can scarcely believe the non-league feel of Moss Rose (though this isn't necessarily an insult). It certainly didn't satisfy the picky German International squad for Euro '96, who were allocated the stadium as a training base. Complaining of its similarity to an allotment, they chose to retreat to the grounds of Mottram Hall Hotel instead.

You might do a double take if spotting a Town supporter with 'Rooney' on his back - but it is no glory-seeking gesture - Wayne's cousin, Tony, plays for them.

The very hardest of their minuscule hard core are three members of their Norwegian fan club who travel over every week to watch matches.

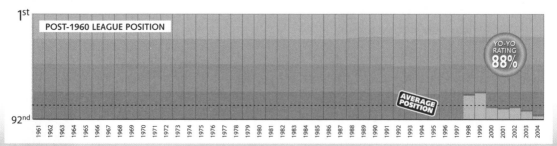

1st

POST-1960 LEAGUE POSITION

YO-YO RATING 88%

AVERAGE POSITION

92nd

1961 1962 1963 1964 1965 1966 1967 1968 1969 1970 1971 1972 1973 1974 1975 1976 1977 1978 1979 1980 1981 1982 1983 1984 1985 1986 1987 1988 1989 1990 1991 1992 1993 1994 1995 1996 1997 1998 1999 2000 2001 2002 2003 2004

PROGRESS REPORT

Macclesfield have serious concerns over their ability to remain a league club. Their trip to Level Two ended in ignominy, following which they have barely clung onto a mid-table place in Level Three. Their 18th position in 2004 has set the nerves jangling.

...Took out £30,000 insurance against a frozen pitch in order to guarantee TV revenue for FA Cup tie...
...Stewards have the word 'erection' on their jackets...
...Played most prolonged FA Cup shoot-out in history (a 24 spot-kick marathon against Forest Green)...

RIVALS

With Chester's promotion from the Conference in 2004, Macclesfield now have something approaching a local derby. Chester fans were not amused to be forced to share Moss Rose between 1990 and 1992 after the sale of their Sealand Road ground, at a time when Macclesfield were still in the Conference. In 1995, you might have assumed that the Football League would OK the use of Moss Rose for Level Three matches since there was no problem with Chester playing there, but with ground regulations tightening, it didn't make the grade. Macclesfield's logical response was to ask to share Chester's new Deva Stadium, but the League disappointed them again, leading to the reasonable charge that the whole saga had political overtones. Macclesfield's promotion to the Second was won with a 3-2 victory over their old lodgers.

CHESTER CITY
☠ ☠ ☠ ☠ ☠

ALTRINCHAM
☠ ☠ ☠ ☠ ☠

Viewers of Macclesfield's big TV moment, the televising of their FA Cup tie with West Ham in 2002, might have been flummoxed with the clearly audible chants of 'Are you watching Altrincham?' This is considered their traditional rivalry, though whether it could be strictly termed a Cheshire derby is a matter of dispute, since Alty has been surgically grafted onto South Manchester. For many years, the two were the leading lights of the non-league, with Macclesfield earning a reputation for having the biggest away support of any team outside the Football League. If anything, it was probably Altrincham who won most plaudits with a string of FA cup giant-killing feats. They suffered the misfortune of being the best of the non-league bunch before automatic promotion from the Conference. But having shadowed each other for years, there was a dramatic divergence in the late 90s. The same day Macclesfield played Manchester City, Altrincham were losing to Worksop in the Unibond Premier. There has always been plenty of transfer traffic between the sides to heat things up, and regrettably, a fair amount of hooligan incidents.

SUPPORTERS' VFM
55%

PERFORMANCE AGAINST RIVALS
CHESTER CITY

WON 33%

LOST 17%

DRAWN 50%

Today, Moss Rose has a family atmosphere i.e. only a couple of grades above total silence. The only significant trouble in recent times was an unlikely meeting of Macclesfield Town and Leeds United supporters in a pub in Alsager where 80 men exchanged bits of broken glasses.

Macclesfield deserve a significant footnote in the tally of British rivalries. Aside from now non-league Exeter, they are the only club who have ever had any significant dislike of Torquay United. There is a historical link between Stevenage Borough and Town, as both were refused League entry on account of substandard grounds. Torquay, who had most to fear from Borough as they had finished bottom of the league, lobbied aggressively to keep out the Conference upstarts. So the minor rivalry uses the principle of 'my friends' enemy is my enemy'.

'YOUR GROUND'S TOO BIG FOR YOU!'
R A T I N G

LOVE/HATE

CHANTS

Although far from unanimous, ex-manager Dave Moss, who later turned up at Chester, is accused of some bad mouthing of home fans during his spell at Macclesfield.

'Hello... hello... it's good to be a Macc, it's good to be a Macc'

suddenly fell out of favour upon the conviction of its original writer, Gary Glitter.

ATTENDANCE AS A PERCENTAGE OF CAPACITY
38%

DOH!!

The club's nickname, The Silkmen, is based on the town's best known industry. So not to miss out on the inflatables' craze, giant blow-up silkworms were manufactured, but their phallic qualities were judged too ridiculous to catch on (unlike the eminently sensible collection of bananas, hammers and assorted wild animals wielded by other clubs).

MANCHESTER CITY

A.K.A. THE MASSIVES

Recommended website: **www.bluemoon-mcfc.co.uk**

WHO ARE YA?

If sharing a Manchester bus with football supporters, an experienced spotter could distinguish between a bunch of United and City fans without needing to know the colour of the shirts. United supporters possess a confident and laid back air - interpreted as arrogance in other quarters. Those in light blue, even when they are doing well, can sometimes be mistaken for people travelling to their own execution.

It is slightly typical that arguably the second best goal in Wembley's history, a rocket of a volley from City's Steve MacKenzie in the FA Cup final replay against Spurs in 1981, was swiftly followed by a winner from Rickie Villa that is generally considered a couple of notches better still.

Even by 2004, the club's reputation for amazing back-room bust-ups had yet to be extinguished, with ex-manager Joe Royle winning a £500,000 payout in compensation for his sacking in 2001. Wisely, he had nothing but praise for the fans themselves commenting "the only class at City is on the terraces". Falling out with the faithful here is not recommended - previous victims, chairman Peter Swales, his replacement Francis Lee, and to a lesser extent Lee's mate, Alan Ball, suffered concerted hate campaigns involving the posting of so much dog excrement that the pavements of Moss Side must have been the cleanest in northern England.

In and Around

Fracture victims at North Manchester General Hospital can choose between light blue or red plaster casts.

CELEBRITY FANS

RICK WAKEMAN
AOR Musician
JOHN STAPELTON
BBC Current Affairs Presenter
LIAM & NOEL GALLAGHER
Oasis

For a major club, City's fall into Level Two in 1998 was virtually unprecedented. Many fans have their personal low points - but the 2-1 home defeat to Mansfield in the Auto Windscreens trophy in 1998 takes the biscuit, particularly as Manchester United were preparing to face Bayern Munich in the Champions League. Turn the clock forward to March 2004; just as Maine Road was being demolished, along with accompanying graffiti celebrating the 5-1 victory over United in 1989, they repeat the trick, smashing Manchester United 4-1 in their new City of Manchester Stadium - a result that symbolically seemed to consign their foe to a new age mediocrity. However, you have to go back to 1990-91 to find the last time City finished higher in the league than United, but more painful still are the 34 years (and counting) since they last won a major honour.

City fans started the craze for inflatable toys, dating back to an appearance of a solitary blow-up banana against Plymouth in 1987. The culmination was around October 1988, by which time sharks, penguins, toucans and a paddling pool became regular terrace features. The police reaction was generally favourable, as they took the sting out of potential confrontations (the then hated Stoke turned up with blow-up Pink Panthers). In a majestic sense of humour bypass, Arsenal banned them.

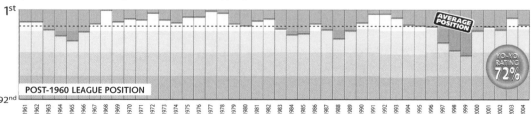

1st

AVERAGE POSITION

YO-YO RATING 72%

POST-1960 LEAGUE POSITION

92nd

1961 1962 1963 1964 1965 1966 1967 1968 1969 1970 1971 1972 1973 1974 1975 1976 1977 1978 1979 1980 1981 1982 1983 1984 1985 1986 1987 1988 1989 1990 1991 1992 1993 1994 1995 1996 1997 1998 1999 2000 2001 2002 2003 2004

PROGRESS REPORT

Manchester City's dips outside the top division have been infrequent and short-lived. In 40 years up to 1995, they had changed leagues only seven times, but the following seven seasons saw them clock up six separate moves. Even when looking well established in the Premiership in 2003-04, they got dragged into a dog-fight with ex-Liverpool stalwarts McManaman and Folwer performing considerably below par.

```
...Only club to score and concede 100 goals in the same season (1957-58)...
...City player Andy Morrison was sent off for 'licking' Stan Collymore...
...Level Two attendances in 1998-99 were higher than they'd been in the Premiership...
```

RIVALS

City's second string rivalries are a hotchpotch of Liverpool, Bolton, Middlesbrough, Birmingham and Millwall, depending on who you talk to. But with the biggest football club in the world three miles to the southwest of your stadium, there's not much energy left for anyone else other than the old enemy, Manchester United. In terms of the shirt count, City are swamped by their neighbours. A nine-year old at school sporting a light blue strip might be outnumbered by ten to one in some areas. Being a City supporter in Manchester means accepting minority status - something that breeds arguably the most dedicated and obsessive football supporters in the land.

MANCHESTER UNITED

LIVERPOOL

United are perceived as 'hateful, arrogant and ungracious'. Pithily, one City supporter noted that when Liverpool were world beaters, they didn't attract the same degree of dislike from neutrals. The charge that a bulk of United fans aren't from Manchester has to be conceded - the sea of red scarves on Piccadilly station waiting for the Euston train after matches provides conclusive evidence. There is a rather lame retort that City fans flood in from Stockport, but it's not quite the same thing. The two are at daggers drawn over their political roots. Both like to claim a solid working class, socialist tradition. This partly explains why they always bicker about where their supporters live, a debate that is fuelled by the fact that until recently, both clubs were situated just to the south of the city centre, with no strong demarcation lines. If anything there was a slight east/west split, with United dominating the sprawl of Salford, leaving the east to display light blue leanings. Their move back to nearer their old stomping ground of Ardwick might promote a more north/south divide, as was the case during the clubs' early years.

BOLTON

PERFORMANCE AGAINST RIVALS
MANCHESTER UNITED

WON 24% LOST 44%

DRAWN 31%

SUPPORTERS' VFM 84%

United are specifically charged with refusing to accept that they can be outplayed. On the occasions that they are beaten, fans point to the fact that they never seem to credit the opposition - a defeat comes with a series of excuses - something that appears to break the footballing code. The 'grey shirts' incident at Southampton in 1996 is frequently named as a typical 'Unitedism'.

City like to point to the fact that they gave United a helping hand in letting them play at Maine Road when Old Trafford was bombed during World War II, and even 'gave' them their club captain, Matt Busby.

'YOUR GROUND'S TOO BIG FOR YOU!'
RATING

LOVE/HATE

CHANTS

Roy Keane displays loyalty, determination and single-mindedness – the qualities fans drool over in a footballer. He is a notable absentee from most clubs' hate lists - except City's, where they are in no mood to forgive his grotesque revenge tackle on Alfie Inger Harrland.

Bordering on the suicidal during the dark period:

*'Oh, we never win at home, and we never win away
We lost last week, and we lost today'*

100

80

60

40

ATTENDANCE AS A PERCENTAGE OF CAPACITY
98%

DOH!!

City are specialists in last-day cock-ups. In 1996, they had clawed their way back to 2-2 against Liverpool. Knowing that they needed a better result than Southampton and Coventry to survive, manager Alan Ball was under the impression that both were losing. He ordered City to play keep-ball by the corner flag - until Niall Quinn ran out from the dressing room to let them know they were mistaken. City were relegated.

20

0

MANCHESTER UNITED

Recommended website: **www.red11.org**

WHO ARE YA?

Travellers from Britain who have visited isolated tribes in the Serengeti or peasant farmers of South America are frequently astonished that, on first meeting the locals, they are greeted with the names of mis-pronounced Manchester United players – a show of recognition that the backpacker is from the golden isle that gifted the world Manchester United. The majority of the population of the planet probably knows Britain for little more than the fact that it is home to the club that is, in their opinion, the best football team in the world. In some ways, it matters little that they are currently probably not the best team in Britain, as United's global presence transcends even their fairly earth-shattering recent record. There are anecdotes a plenty supporting their incredible popularity. A Coca-Cola promotional competition, held in the Philippines, had as its prize an all-expenses paid trip to Old Trafford. It attracted 12 million entries.

The first impressions of the Theatre of Dreams itself depend on how you approach it. From United's traditional supporters' breeding ground of Salford, Old Trafford is the gleaming temple at the far end of the classy Quays development.

CELEBRITY FANS
STEVE COOGAN
Comedian
MICHAEL CRICK
Journalist and serial Jeffrey Archer pursuer
BERTIE AHERNE
Irish Prime Minister

IN and AROUND

Eagle-eyed soap fans will have noticed an addition to the title sequence of Coronation Street. A Metrolink tram purrs its way across the bridge in the background. The sequence is, however, a TV cut-and-paste job, as the railway is half a mile from the Granada set where the programme is filmed.

From the south, you get snarled up in traffic somewhere near Stretford's brutalist 1960s' shopping centre, with the stadium appearing to be tagged on to a dull retail development. Oh, and don't even think about parking in PC World. Sitting inside Old Trafford, its totally enclosed design impresses fans from smaller clubs, i.e. everyone. But a result of the distorting effect of TV cameras is that, on first inspection, the ground seems much smaller than the first-time visitor would imagine.

The club's unapologetic attempts to 'broaden the appeal of the brand' stick in the throats of the majority of League teams' fans, who struggle to broaden the appeal of their home clubs within their own town's boundaries, thanks mainly to being swamped with youngsters wearing red shirts.

United's Level One Championship in 1975 has largely been obliterated from the club's official records, though interestingly, older supporters remember their spell out of the big time with some affection, as away days became a memorable ritual of fans completely taking over the 'little' towns. Though others routinely talk of the arrogance of United's fans, they will often concede that their away support is the best in the land, although their habit of standing up in all-seater stadia doesn't always endear them to the locals.

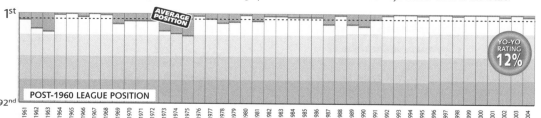

YO-YO RATING **12%**

POST-1960 LEAGUE POSITION

1961 1962 1963 1964 1965 1966 1967 1968 1969 1970 1971 1972 1973 1974 1975 1976 1977 1978 1979 1980 1981 1982 1983 1984 1985 1986 1987 1988 1989 1990 1991 1992 1993 1994 1995 1996 1997 1998 1999 2000 2001 2002 2003 2004

PROGRESS REPORT

United's only dip outside the top division occurred in 1974-75. Their worst finish since then was 13th in 1990. Their spell of domination of the English game started at the beginning of 1992-93, from which time they recorded eight Championships in 11 years up to 2004. They played 468 League games during the period, losing just 69 of them.

```
        ...In 1979, it cost £1 to stand on the terraces at Old Trafford...
...When in Level One, they still maintained the highest average attendance of all clubs...
      ...Many dead season ticket holders still seem to attend matches...
```

RIVALS

United were generally well liked in the period after the Munich Air disaster and into the 1970s. Refusing to put others' dislike of them down to anything more than mean-minded jealousy, there continues to be widespread confusion in the outside world as to who their real rivals are. In the eyes of the majority of fans, Liverpool have been the number one hates going back to the 70s and beyond, yet the media continuously prefer to build up the bad blood with City.

LIVERPOOL

MANCHESTER CITY

The rows with Liverpool continue over which club's golden era was greater. United assert that Liverpool have a huge chip on their shoulders over the issue, and that contrary to Liverpool's claim, it is a myth that they were more popular during their best years than Manchester Unitedhave been through theirs. Liverpool are the target of the usual regional stereotypes of being work-shy 'wide-boy' types.

There is a slight perception that United form the Protestant part of a religious split with City. Whilst the local issue isn't of much importance, wider relationships, particularly with the Scottish giants, are very mixed. United's historical connection with the Irish Republic is very strong, and at one stage in the 60s, there were rumblings of discontent from Protestant players who claimed that they weren't getting a fair chance to establish themselves. Since George Best was Protestant, this seemed unfounded, but it didn't put off Rangers' fans from trashing Old Trafford at a friendly in 1974, as well as giving United an extremely hostile welcome in the Champions League in 2003.

ARSENAL

Their relationship with Arsenal is quite perplexing. Some United fans will admit to a faint glow of recognition for the Londoners' achievements, though on the pitch the temperature when the clubs meet is perhaps the highest there has ever been between two sides in the Premiership.Wenger and Ferguson's war of words is not stage managed, as there is clearly real animosity, but it is not reflected in the stands quite as much as you might expect. Indeed many United fans will ignore Arsenal when asked for their top rivals and insert Leeds' name in their top three instead.

Despite protests that City are of exceedingly minor interest, United occasionally give an airing to perhaps the most comprehensive vocal demolition of another club – countering the image of The Reds only able to muster up spasmodic cheers of 'U-nit-ed'. The 'City are a massive club' epic runs to approximately 53 verses and contains every damning indictment imaginable, a mixture of the 'factual', through the ironic, to the accusatory. To the tune of 'He's got the whole world in his hands', highlights include 'They take 25,000 to every away', 'They've got Bernard Manning as their fattest fan', and the particularly sarcastic 'They had Ryan Giggs on schoolboy forms'.

PERFORMANCE
AGAINST RIVALS
LIVERPOOL

WON 35%

LOST 33%

DRAWN 32%

SUPPORTERS'
VFM
49%

LOVE/HATE

Who could resist a dream move to Old Trafford? Not many, but the ones that do are guaranteed a poor reception. *Alan Shearer* is particularly disliked for his curt rebuttal of the club's overtures. On the same theme, oldies remember that Peter Shilton got the same treatment. Purchased for a pittance from Leeds, *Eric Cantona* leads the list of recent gods, probably more so than Becks himself.

CHANTS

To those visiting fans who can actually get in:

'You've only come to watch United'

DOH!!

At a press conference following his masterly kung-fu display against an abusive Crystal Palace supporter in 1995, Eric Cantona contrived to produce one of the most perplexing analogies in literary (and certainly footballing) history. When pressed for a quote, his reply amounted to: "When the seagulls follow the trawler, it is because they think sardines will be thrown into the sea. Thank you." The deep meaning appears to be, the press (the seagulls) hound Cantona/United (the trawler) because they are a source of good stories (the sardines). Absorbing stuff.

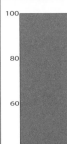

'YOUR GROUND'S
TOO BIG FOR YOU!'
R A T I N G

100

80

60

40

20

0

ATTENDANCE
AS A
PERCENTAGE
OF CAPACITY
100%

MANSFIELD TOWN

Recommended website: **www.ftybr.co.uk**

WHO ARE YA?

Traditionalists got a bit concerned, when, in the 1990s, Mansfield Town started wondering whether they should renovate their existing Field Mill Ground or look to move somewhere completely different. Had they chosen the latter option, they would be abandoning a site that had hosted football since 1840, making it, disputably, the second oldest football ground in the entire world. But after what seemed like eternal discussions, they stayed put. Mansfield have an unorthodox history of nefarious goings on, which started when they muscled into Field Mill behind the back of the town's other side, Mansfield Mechanics, who they'd been in merger talks with.

CELEBRITY FANS

DALEY THOMPSON
Olympic Decathlete and
ex-Mansfield Player

The Football League didn't seem keen to want them at all, having refused their application to join their happy band on five separate occasions. It was only after they had beaten a couple of League teams in the FA Cup in 1928-29 that they sat up and took notice. Having spent most of their existence in Level Three, the club won promotion in 1963, but the media was closing in on a match-rigging scandal that had involved most of the playing staff. The People newspaper did some digging and named five of the club's players as being implicated, including the captain Brian Phillips. Investigations dragged on until 1965, when the ringleader was revealed as Jimmy Gauld, who owned up to have pocketed around £1,000 per week from fixing matches, receiving a four-year jail sentence for his trouble. Mansfield players accounted for three of the ten professionals who were sent down for what remains the biggest match-rigging case in British football.

IN and AROUND

Mansfield lies at the southern edge of Sherwood Forest, which may or may not have been the home of Robin Hood. He brings in around £120 million of tourist revenue to the area, though a House of Commons' motion was tabled suggesting that his true home was Wakefield, West Yorkshire.

Ironically, Mansfield were to benefit from others' misdemeanours shortly afterwards. In 1968, they finished rockbottom of Level Two but were handed a lifeline when Peterborough were deducted points after being found to have been making illegal payments to players.

Mansfield's relegation from Level Two in 2003 ended in high farce at Tranmere. Both teams were looking to results elsewhere, in Tranmere's case because they still had hopes of promotion. With Mansfield 2-0 down, the game was abandoned when a local loon scaled the floodlights. Both teams watched from the dressing room as results elsewhere went against them. They were then forced to come back for a replay, to which fans were admitted for free, though by now the game was entirely meaningless as their destinies had already been sealed.

A lifelong Mansfield fan, Geoff Smith beat the world record for being buried alive for 150 days in a glorified coffin dug into the ground at a pub near Field Mill. He said he felt most isolated when hearing the cheers for a Mansfield goal on a Saturday afternoon – so he probably stayed quite cheerful throughout.

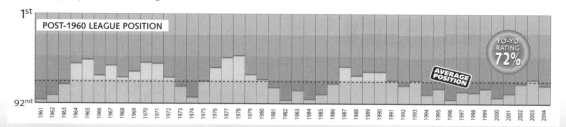

1st

POST-1960 LEAGUE POSITION

YO-YO RATING 72%

AVERAGE POSITION

92nd

1961 1962 1963 1964 1965 1966 1967 1968 1969 1970 1971 1972 1973 1974 1975 1976 1977 1978 1979 1980 1981 1982 1983 1984 1985 1986 1987 1988 1989 1990 1991 1992 1993 1994 1995 1996 1997 1998 1999 2000 2001 2002 2003 2004

PROGRESS REPORT

If anything, things have got slightly worse for the club in latter days. Before the 90s, they had spent more time out of the basement than in it, but after relegation from Level Two in 1993, Mansfield have spent all but one in the lowest division.

```
...Were involved in the first penalty shoot out at Wembley (Freight Rover trophy, 1987)...
     ...Having won the 1987 final, they were the last team to receive a trophy by climbing
                          the 39 steps before redevelopment...
...Constantly swapped between the northern and southern sections of the old Third Division...
```

RIVALS

It's not exactly the Berlin Wall, but the M1 provides a distinct physical boundary between Chesterfield and Mansfield. The intensity of the rivalry is clear by looking at the attitudes of the opposition. The Spireites have largely led life in a division higher than Mansfield, but still have no doubt that it is they who are their number one hates. Often in this situation, the club who were doing better would lose interest quickly, but there seems little risk of this happening with these two.

CHESTERFIELD ☠️☠️☠️☠️☠️

Mansfield's place in miners' strike folklore confuses those who are not scholars of the industrial unrest of the early 80s. Chesterfield see Mansfield as responsible for much of the strike-breaking, hence the constant litany of 'Scabs', whereas Mansfield are simultaneously characterised as violent revolutionaries in Scargill's army – a perception sometimes held in the south of Nottinghamshire and in the rest of the country. There was considerable merriment at Chesterfield's predicament when, in 2001, the Football League announced the results of an investigation into 90 allegations of mismanagement under the reign of ex-chairman Darren Brown. Some assumed that, like Swindon years before, they were at risk of being chucked out of the League entirely, a result which would have brought the streets of Mansfield to a standstill. The penalty of a nine-point deduction wasn't even enough to prevent Chesterfield getting promoted that year, leading to the constant accusation of 'cheats'.

NOTTS COUNTY ☠️☠️☠️☠️☠️

SUPPORTERS' VFM 65%

PERFORMANCE AGAINST RIVALS CHESTERFIELD

WON 42% · LOST 33% · DRAWN 26%

Mansfield are now embroiled in a minor row with Notts County as to who can claim to be Nottinghamshire's second best club. There is a distinct pecking order involved whenever the local media round up the region's action – and it's always Mansfield that comes last. Mind you, having any sort of row with Mansfield is not to be recommended. The way in which hooligan bad-boy tables are presented, Mansfield don't look too awful because of their comparatively tiny size. But if you balance out troublemakers per head of average attendance, then Mansfield's record of arrests was, until 2001, worse than the likes of Cardiff, Millwall and Stoke. Of the 4,000 or so that regularly watch Mansfield, there is a sizeable minority willing to stir things up. An operation to curb Nottinghamshire's hooliganism in 2003 netted 18 men, six of whom were banned from all football matches for life. A disproportionate number were Stags' fans. Eight were from Mansfield; nine were from Forest, though Forest have gates of five times that of Mansfield.

DONCASTER ROVERS ☠️☠️☠️☠️☠️

'YOUR GROUND'S TOO BIG FOR YOU!' RATING

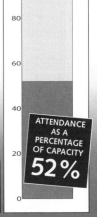

ATTENDANCE AS A PERCENTAGE OF CAPACITY **52%**

LOVE/HATE

Mansfield Town don't get too many on-field heroes to get excited about, so when one comes along, they're not happy when he suddenly disappears to Sunderland. *Liam Lawrence* gets the booby prize here after scoring 22 goals for them in 2003-2004.

CHANTS

*♪**♪*!*

'You all look like deckchairs'

An interpretation of Notts County's black and white strip.

DOH!!

Mansfield hold the record for the most bookings at one time. Following a dodgy penalty awarded to Crystal Palace in 1962, all the outfield players gave the referee a heavily ironic round of applause as he was leaving the field. He paused briefly to book all ten of them.

MIDDLESBROUGH

Recommended website: **www.boro.rules.it**

WHO ARE YA?

The uninitiated might have imagined that when Boro picked up the League (Carling) Cup in 2004, it was another addition to a reasonably well-endowed trophy cabinet. In fact, it was the first time they'd won any major honour – a sign that their current status of Premiership middlemen is a vast improvement on what has gone before.

Boro got off to a faltering start in their early history when a bunch of renegade players staged a breakaway to become the oddly named Middlesbrough Ironopolis. It was this team that was the first to turn professional, joining the Football League in 1893 whilst the 'real' Boro held on to their amateur status. What could have turned out to be one of Britain's most bitter rivalries fizzled out when Ironopolis became an early casualty of the overspending syndrome – going bust after just one year with the elite.

CELEBRITY FANS
CHUBBY BROWN
Comedian
DAVID SHAYLER
Ex-MI5

When they graced the top-flight in the 70s under Jack Charlton, they were not everyone's idea of a thrilling, free-flowing team and, pre-dating Arsenal's tag, picked up the 'boring' label. By 1986, having slipped to the Second Division, the wheels had fallen off completely. Ayresome Park was closed down, a particularly humiliating development as Boro had just offered the use of their ground to Hartlepool, who were going though their own traumas. Instead, Hartlepool ended up letting Boro squat at their Victoria Ground.

The City is plagued with double spelling trouble. It's 'Middlesbrough' not Middlesborough (the latter of which accounts for 58,400 hits on google.co.uk) and it's Teesside not Teeside (110,000 hits). The NHS Careers website manages to get them both wrong.

Onto the board came Steve Gibson and the turnaround began, symbolised by the daring signings of Juninho (who spent three separate spells with the club) and Fabrizio Ravanelli, together with the construction of the Riverside Stadium. In 1994, it seemed like a gleaming modernist temple, though as so many came out of the same mould it became synonymous with the new brand of identikit stadium. It has received one piece of particularly unfortunate branding. British Telecom's support came at the cost of having the ground officially called the 02 Riverside Stadium. Some felt the ordering of the numbers might be a dark omen of future scorelines in games it hosted.

For the 1966 World Cup, Ayresome Park was chosen to stage matches ahead of Newcastle's St James' Park, as the club were involved in a lease wrangle with the local council. After hosting North Korea's dramatic 1-0 victory over Italy, around 3,000 fans from Teesside made the journey to Goodison Park to support the Asian minnows in their quarter final against Portugal. After what in those days was a gruelling trek, they were rewarded by seeing one of the great World Cup final matches, with Eusebio and co pulling back from 3-0 down to win 5-3.

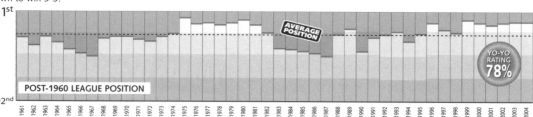

1st

AVERAGE POSITION

YO-YO RATING 78%

POST-1960 LEAGUE POSITION

92nd

1961 1962 1963 1964 1965 1966 1967 1968 1969 1970 1971 1972 1973 1974 1975 1976 1977 1978 1979 1980 1981 1982 1983 1984 1985 1986 1987 1988 1989 1990 1991 1992 1993 1994 1995 1996 1997 1998 1999 2000 2001 2002 2003 2004

PROGRESS REPORT

Middlesbrough reacquainted themselves with the Premiership for the third time in 1998 and, considering their past record, they've made a good fist of it. In 14 years from 1960, they were little more than Level One fodder before an eight-year spell in the top-flight, from 1974, suggested they were capable of better things. A prolonged wobble set in with nine changes in 13 seasons after 1986. But coming up again in 1998, they have maintained a steady-as-she-goes Premiership record, finishing between 9th and 14th in the last six seasons.

```
...First English team to buy a player for over £1,000...Original nickname was The Scabs...
   ...In triumphing in the 2004 Carling Cup, Steve McClaren was the first English boss to
              manage to win an English League trophy in eight years...
```

RIVALS

There is certainly a derby atmosphere at matches between Boro and Newcastle as well as Boro and Sunderland. But according to the other two, they are definitely not derby games. Geographically, the Northeast's two great adversaries are virtually joined at the hip, with Middlesbrough a clear 30 miles to the south, countering the southerners' perception that they are all part of one 'Geordie' conurbation (Geordie is used as an insult in Middlesbrough). Newcastle and Sunderland fans protest that they still hate each other more, even on the occasions when Boro have been in a higher division than them. Many at Sunderland even do Boro the disservice of naming Leeds their second rivals. All of which leaves Middlesbrough exasperated and with no 'proper' derby at all. Chelsea are sometimes named as a bit of an afterthought, as Boro have had three major battles with them, the League Cup final of 1998 (lost), the FA Cup final of 1997 (where they were wiped-out within 43 seconds by a di Matteo goal) but most notably a dogfight of a two-legged play-off in 1988, in which they reversed a 1-0 deficit from the first leg.

SUNDERLAND

NEWCASTLE

CHELSEA

The only real nod in their direction from their neighbours is the nickname 'Smoggies', derived from the fact that Teesside is a centre for petrochemical production, perceived as a polluting influence. Putting up with chants of 'Have you ever seen the sun?', the club was unhappy when rival fans started to don chemical suits and surgical masks. In 2003, they found a reason to chuck out anyone in such attire on the grounds that it was 'inappropriate' given the current world situation. However, the police weren't bothered and confirmed that it wasn't an arrestable offence.

SUPPORTERS' VFM 84%

PERFORMANCE AGAINST RIVALS
NEWCASTLE

WON 33%
LOST 43%
DRAWN 24%

Middlesbrough had the dubious honour of being supported by the first person to be barred from every football match in the world. 38-year old Lee 'Oathead' Owens received the three-year ban in 2004 after police spotters pinpointed him as being involved in clashes with fans in Bristol following Boro's appearance in the Carling Cup final in Cardiff. He wasn't that difficult to spot – he had the words 'Made in Stockton' tattooed prominently on his usually exposed stomach. The police's case was strengthened by alleged references to him, under a false name, in a book about Boro's Frontline hooligan firm.

LOVE/HATE

Bryan Robson was part of an ex-Manchester United contingent that found its way to the Riverside. For most fans, his spell in charge dragged on far too long and descended into farce with the appointment of Terry Venables as an expensive shadow. The boozy culture that is whispered to have existed didn't play well with the faithful when the on-field performances suggested there was absolutely nothing to celebrate.

CHANTS

'There's only one Job on Teesside'

Not a summary of the state of the local economy, but a reference to striker Joseph-Desire Job.

DOH!!

With a virus sweeping the club, Boro were forced to cancel a fixture at Blackburn in December 1996. Claiming they still had 17 fit, the FA docked them three points for their no-show. They finished 19th in the Premiership. Had they kept the three points, they would have escaped relegation.

'YOUR GROUND'S TOO BIG FOR YOU!' RATING

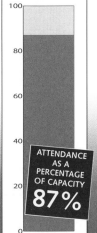

100
80
60
40
20
0

ATTENDANCE AS A PERCENTAGE OF CAPACITY
87%

MILLWALL

Recommended website: **www.hof.org.uk**

WHO ARE YA?

A single *Panorama* documentary about goings-on at Millwall FC, broadcast in late 1975, defined how football hooliganism was reported for a generation. A sensational account of a quasi-military structure on the terraces countered beliefs that football violence was random and unorganised, culminating in a scene with a group of supporters dubbed 'The Treatment' decked out in surgical coats and masks. The medical garb is now considered to have been crudely staged for the camera's benefit. Ever since, Millwall have felt up against the wall and the ability to tell the difference between truth and fiction has been increasingly difficult.

In a region sometimes seen as being home to swaying supporters happy to latch onto whichever club is on a good run, Millwall stand out as being markedly different from other London outfits. If you put aside the catalogue of violence for one moment (which admittedly takes a leap of imagination), many Millwall fans have qualities that most would applaud. They rabidly hate the injection of commercial values into the modern game. Their siege mentality leaves them open to particularly vicious mood swings depending on results, with reports of outbreaks of despair and self-harm when things don't go their way – and that's just pre-season friendlies.

CELEBRITY FANS
DANNY BAKER
Radio/TV Presenter
MIKE REID
Actor - *Eastenders*

IN and AROUND

Millwall Inner Dock was a prominent location for the James Bond flick, *The World is not Enough*.

Appearing in the Cup Final in 2004 against Manchester United, they had the perfect opportunity to garner neutrals' support, though Denis Wise's extremely robust performance did nothing to promote a new cuddly image. Despite the impression that there are thousands of them ready to demolish any town they see fit, Millwall's away following is actually quite sparse for a Level One club, with ticket sales regulated zealously. Many local police forces and newspapers have been caught out, not by being unprepared, but by talking themselves into a frenzy of concern which has proved unfounded when a handful of bedraggled supporters turn up.

Their fans' reputation for racism and far-right links depends on whose account you believe. The anti-Nazi League reported that there was an 'overwhelmingly good response' from supporters when they were organising opposition to a National Front march in 2001. A particular moan is that they are pilloried by the press for booing black players. Millwall would like to stress that they routinely boo all players.

Millwall's infamous 'No one likes us. We don't care' chant often has caveats attached to it by fans eager to explain the club's view on the world. Sometimes it is softened to 'We do care, but we've given up trying to get a fair deal', or alternatively affirming its meaning; as one fan reminded us, "We REALLY don't care".

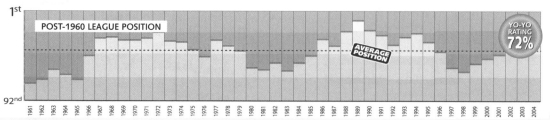

1st

POST-1960 LEAGUE POSITION

AVERAGE POSITION

YO-YO RATING 72%

92nd

1961 1962 1963 1964 1965 1966 1967 1968 1969 1970 1971 1972 1973 1974 1975 1976 1977 1978 1979 1980 1981 1982 1983 1984 1985 1986 1987 1988 1989 1990 1991 1992 1993 1994 1995 1996 1997 1998 1999 2000 2001 2002 2003 2004

PROGRESS REPORT

Millwall have spent the majority of their time zipping around in the middle two divisions. From a base of the Level Two in 1985, they launched an impressive run that saw them go up to the top-flight for the first time in their history in 1988. After finishing 10th in their first season, they didn't survive the next, and a downward trend set in that nearly saw them retreat all the way to the basement. On getting back to Level One in 2001, they achieved a play-off place at the first time of asking and have been hanging around the top half of the table since.

```
...Topped the old First Division table in 1989-90 and were relegated in the same season...
    ...Attendances at the New Den were initially worse than those at Cold Blow Lane...
              ...The 'New' Den reverted back to The Den in 2004...
```

RIVALS

Considering Milwall's record of trouble is often put down to a fanatical devotion to the club's local region, it's odd that their geography is not clear-cut. The name Millwall is generally reserved for the Isle of Dogs area – the jutty out bit to the north of the river that is now home to an uncomfortable mix of executive developments and a decreasing number of its indigenous population. For a time after their formation, the club was based on the Isle before progressively moving south, ending up at Cold Blow Lane, which, loosely, is in Deptford, south of the Thames. The area called Millwall is usually considered to be East London, but plenty of supporters strongly identify themselves as being a South London outfit, which sort of explains the hatred of West Ham. But in the past, the name Millwall FC has become entwined with the excesses of East End inspired violence. The cockney 'purity' of the 'cor blimey guv' culture at West Ham is sneered at, but to an extent, the two sides share a common history, particularly as the population of the area was virtually bombed out of existence in World War II. This confuses a rivalry that, though short of actual fixtures, is one of the 'all police leave cancelled' moments in the calendar.

WEST HAM

CHARLTON ATHLETIC

The cultural gulf between Charlton and Millwall is exceptional considering their proximity. Charlton are seen as 'short-termers' in anoraks; a collection of ridiculous "happy smiley dweebs". Millwall's nickname, 'Spanners', was given to them by Charlton after the said item was chucked onto the pitch in the middle of a game. At the heart of Millwall's collective psyche is a dislike of 'middle-class' values, apparently typified by Crystal Palace (routinely called Parlarse), who are said to have a "holier than thou" air of superiority about them.

CRYSTAL PALACE

PERFORMANCE AGAINST RIVALS
WEST HAM

WON 20%
LOST 50%
DRAWN 30%

SUPPORTERS' VFM 82%

Millwall's catalogue of violent incidents only rarely corresponds to arguments with their local rivals. In fact, many of the most publicised incidents involving Millwall supporters have relatively little to do with attacking other 'ordinary' fans. The club's early history of trouble generally involved intimidating and attacking officials and opposing players. The unbelievable footage of Millwall supporters invading the pitch at Kenilworth Road in 1985 showed a deliberate attempt to have the match stopped rather than an anti-Luton gesture. Similarly, massive trouble after the club's play-off defeat against Birmingham in 2002 was directed mostly at the police, borne out of the sheer frustration of losing on the pitch. Trouble has tended to concentrate itself at fixtures where rival mobs are trying to assert some type of supremacy, hence the repeated problems with the likes of Bristol City, Stoke and Birmingham.

Without much hint of irony, Millwall point to the fact that their fanbase doesn't consist predominantly of hardened white racists – footage of the Luton riot shows plenty of black fans chucking seats at the police.

'YOUR GROUND'S TOO BIG FOR YOU!'
RATING

LOVE/HATE

HATE

Millwall have an unnervingly hard-core opinion on the subject of their hates. Many profess to have little interest in footballing life outside their own club and don't hold particularly strong views on opposing players, managers or any of the usual hate figures. Spooky.

CHANTS

The 2002 ban on away supporters robbed Millwall of the chance to chant at the opposition, though it didn't stop them gesticulating to a totally empty area and baiting the non-existent Manchester City fans with

'Is that all you bring away?'

100

80

60

40

20

0

ATTENDANCE AS A PERCENTAGE OF CAPACITY 52%

DOH!!

The move to The New Den, at New Cross in 1993, was supposed to symbolise a new modern image, with the stadium marketed as the New London Stadium, a venue for all sorts of events including pop concerts. Initially, there were no signs indicating that the stadium had anything to do with Millwall whatsoever, a fairly serious omission for a club so hyper-aware of its identity. A short, sharp fans' protest put things right.

MILTON KEYNES DONS

Recommended website: **www.mkdonsclub.co.uk**

WHO ARE YA?

The area around Wimbledon has, for some time, attracted expat Norwegians, a consortium of whom thought it was a neat idea to buy the football club of the same name, even though the price was astronomical as they had no stadium, a fan base that compared to a Conference side, zero prospects on the pitch, and were arguably the most unpopular team ever to feature in the League. And then it got really bad.

Even at Plough Lane, Wimbledon FC were strangely rootless, drawing well-heeled support from a ragbag of south London boroughs and Surrey towns. Arguments still rage over whether there was ever any intention to move back to Merton by either Sam Hammam or Charles Koppel, the South African front man for the Norgie owners. Koppel appeared to be caught red-handed when telling a residents' meeting that football supporters weren't the sort of types they wanted in their neighbourhood. His comments were from bitter experience, having claimed to have suffered a Blue Peter style attack of vandalism on his garden that he laid at the door of disgruntled Mertonites. By 2002, Wimbledon fans organised an effective boycott of games that helped bring things to a head. Radio 5 dolefully reported that they had counted 26 Wimbledon supporters at a Level One match at Coventry. During their protracted spell at Selhurst Park, the club held a vote to decide on the name of the club's Womble mascot. Pointedly, the fans voted for 'Merton'.

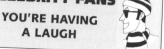

IN and AROUND

Stoney Stratford is a serious boozers' paradise, with 13 pubs on its High Street, including The Cock and The Bull – the tales from which gave rise to the popular expression.

After previously rejecting the plan, the FA conceded to the club relocating to the National Hockey Stadium in Milton Keynes, taking some players and staff, though not Koppell. The date of their turnaround, 28th May 2002, is seen by many as the death of the Wimbledon FC that came through the Southern League to win the FA Cup in 1988. With local groups forming the alternative AFC Wimbledon, another twisted chapter was opened creating a diabolically complicated row over which club held the rights to Wimbledon's glorious playing history. According to the FA, MK Dons are supposed to retain the record of the 'old' club, though they have effectively cut all ties with south London – a fact that will give almighty headaches to compilers of soccer annuals for years to come.

Under new chairman, pop promoter Pete Winkleman, the new Frankenstein-like club changed its name from Wimbledon FC for the 2004-05 season, and got itself a new white strip. In administration, with a threadbare squad and attracting the hatred of just about every football supporter in the land, even their plans to construct a new stadium were threatening to run out of steam as contractors McAlpine wrangled over insurance in the event that the club should go to the wall completely.

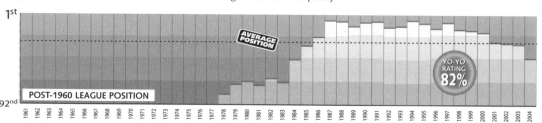

1st

AVERAGE POSITION

YO-YO RATING 82%

POST-1960 LEAGUE POSITION

92nd

1961 1962 1963 1964 1965 1966 1967 1968 1969 1970 1971 1972 1973 1974 1975 1976 1977 1978 1979 1980 1981 1982 1983 1984 1985 1986 1987 1988 1989 1990 1991 1992 1993 1994 1995 1996 1997 1998 1999 2000 2001 2002 2003 2004

PROGRESS REPORT

A grotesque on-field slump has set in, which has delighted all and sundry not connected with the club. Wimbledon propped up Level One for most of 2003-2004 and promptly struggled to keep their heads above water at the beginning of 2004-2005 in Level Two.

...Milton Keynes' original concrete cows now live at the Dons' ground...
...Lowest ticket prices in League...
...Wimbledon ladies team refused to go to Milton Keynes and affiliated with AFC instead...

RIVALS

Trying to determine who MK Dons' rivals are, and might be, is made more difficult by the fact that the identity and origin of their supporters (who number around 4,000) is shrouded in mystery. The old Wimbledon had no known adversaries and a deserved reputation for good humour and impeccable terrace behaviour. Clearly the vast majority of the club's original fans have stuck their colours on the AFC Wimbledon mast. It is this club, now playing in the Isthmian League South Division One at Kingston (not Wimbledon, as is pointed out by MK fans) that claim the heritage of the team – organising a re-run of the 1988 FA Cup final with many of the combatants of the time. The MK version can probably count on around 25% more fans. The prospect of them meeting in the future is too delicious to contemplate. For the time being,

AFC WIMBLEDON

the distinction between the two is a complete mess. The websites on the 'Rivals' and 'Footy Mad' networks have been set up with the operating company's template of MK Dons, though they are actually now connected with AFC. This leads to the ultimate absurdity of a section entitled 'Directions to the National Hockey Stadium' providing the route to AFC's home at Kingsmeadow, the name of which 'The Fans' Stadium' causes MK supporters to jab their fingers down their throats. Those wishing to post insulting messages directed at MK Dons tend to end up doing so when the sites are actually AFC supporting.

SUPPORTERS' VFM 27%

PERFORMANCE AGAINST RIVALS
AFC WIMBLEDON

There are distinct sub-groups to the current MK Dons' support. A small number were undoubtedly fans of the old club, mostly those who have moved away from south London or never lived there in the first place. Some who moved to Milton Keynes retain loyalties to their clubs in other areas, but find it convenient to now cheer on the 'local' boys. A substantial number of children from the area have taken to the club and have persuaded their mildly interested Dads to take them. There are also a smattering of defectors from Northampton and Oxford. The rest are made up of locals who would otherwise be kicking their heels on a Saturday afternoon.

LOVE/HATE

A reasonably good-natured civil war has broken out over *the name Milton Keynes Dons* ♡ 👊, roughly splitting the fans 50/50. Winkleman's shotgun decision caused spluttering from those with any loyalties to the old club, as they had hoped that the word 'Wimbledon' would find a way into the mix.

CHANTS

Constructing new chants is a bit of a pain when you are not quite sure of the name of the club. By 2004, there were rival factions singing the praises of both Milton Keynes and Wimbledon. Highlight of the old club's repertoire was probably the shopping list orientated *'Wimbledon is lovely'* in which various items available for purchase locally were listed along with how much they cost, i.e.

'Chicken Tikka…Two pounds ninety-five'.

'YOUR GROUND'S TOO BIG FOR YOU!'
RATING

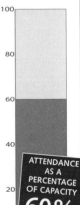

100

80

60

40

ATTENDANCE AS A PERCENTAGE OF CAPACITY
60%

20

0

DOH!!

Demonstrating a tenuous grasp on reality, Charles Koppel was quoted as saying "Palace and Wimbledon are the only two teams to ground-share, apart from the two Sheffield clubs of course".

A.K.A. THE BARCODES

Recommended website: **www.nufc.com**

WHO ARE YA?

Newcastle have a legitimate claim to the title of England's best supported club, if not the most supported club. The cauldron-like St James' Park can fill its 52,000 seats whoever the opposition. When languishing in Level One in 1974, they still managed to pull in average crowds of 48,389, well above that of the best supported top-flight club of the time, Liverpool. The ferocity of the fans' protests was instrumental in turning the club around. Sit down pitch protests booted out the fossilised old guard of 80s' directors, infamous for losing a host of influential players down south. Newcastle already had something of a tradition in this respect – it's easy to forget that the native Charlton brothers made their name elsewhere. Considering their recent status as Champion's League hopefuls, it is a surprise that as recently as 1991, their departing manager, Jim Smith, branded the club 'unmanageable'.

CELEBRITY FANS
SID WADDELL
Darts Commentator
JOHN MCCRIRICK
Racing Presenter
TONY BLAIR
has expressed a loose allegiance

IN and AROUND

The Lonely Planet guide to Britain uncharitably lists Newcastle as possessing 'no major attractions'.

Far from taking an insular attitude to foreign signings, Newcastle have a colourful history of international dabbling. Sir Bobby Robson, in his pre-dotage, developed a bit of a thing about South American players, though the arrival of the first major Latin signing, the totally barking Fausitno Asprilla, coincided with a slump in early 1996 that took Newcastle from the heights of a 12-point lead in the Premiership to mere bit players. The sagas of Frenchies' Didier Domi and Alain Goma are still a sore point. Domi was loathed locally for going AWOL, having criticised Robson's training techniques. He stropped off back home claiming he was pilloried for his religion and the fact he was teetotal.

The term geordie is always used exclusively to describe those from Newcastle only – and is used as a minor insult by Sunderland fans.

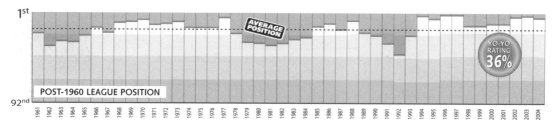

1st

AVERAGE POSITION

YO-YO RATING 36%

POST-1960 LEAGUE POSITION

92nd

1961 1962 1963 1964 1965 1966 1967 1968 1969 1970 1971 1972 1973 1974 1975 1976 1977 1978 1979 1980 1981 1982 1983 1984 1985 1986 1987 1988 1989 1990 1991 1992 1993 1994 1995 1996 1997 1998 1999 2000 2001 2002 2003 2004

PROGRESS REPORT

Compared to the calamities of Wolves and Manchester City, Newcastle's torrid experience of the late 70s and 80s was far from the worst 'big club' disaster in recent history, but it left much of the population of the Northeast scarred and fuming for just under two decades. With four league Championships under their belt by 1927, they confidently held on to a run of top five finishes in the post-war period with only short terms blips into Level One. But in the 50 years since 1955, only one trophy has come their way; the 1969 Fairs Cup success – the first time they had entered a European competition.

Between 1978 and 1993, the club only spent four seasons in the top-flight – despite producing a wealth of home-grown talent, including Beardsley, Gascoigne and Waddle. But once Premiership promotion had been secured under Kevin Keegan in 1994, Newcastle were in no mood to join the in-betweenies, and have maintained consistent top half finishes.

...Won the first ever floodlit match (1956 at Portsmouth)...Never won a match on an artificial surface...St James' Park has the largest cantilever structure in Europe...

RIVALS

It is no accident that the stark alternative names of 'North Side' for Newcastle and 'South Side' for Sunderland have slightly military undertones. The most passionate football culture in England leads to among the most crazed derbies. This is intensified by the fact that apart from the big northeast trio (adding in Middlesbrough), there is no other decent sized club within bearable travelling distance. As the teams' fortunes go through cycles, there is never anyone else to temporarily form a rivalry with, so the mutual dislike in the northeast is set and relatively unchanging.

SUNDERLAND

MIDDLESBROUGH

The worst recent violence between sets of Newcastle and Sunderland supporters occurred in March 2000 – associated (loosely) with a match between Boro and Sunderland. The disorder, involving 70 men, at the landing area for the Tyne ferry, was one of the few occasions when the elements that most excite the tabloids actually came together in a recorded incident. Described in court as 'like a scene from Braveheart', there was evidence that trouble was pre-arranged. Some combatants had travelled specially from Manchester(!) and were older than the general profile of headcases – one of the ringleaders was a 39 year-old with children.

Other than these exceptional cases, there is a distinctive pattern with northeast football related trouble. Newcastle and Sunderland have a high proportion of drink-related offences – around fifteen times the rates recorded at Arsenal – and vastly higher than all the southern clubs.

Public displays of hatred included pub landlady, Yvonne Mann, receiving a £580 fine when officers on a routine licensing visit discovered a scarf hanging in the bar emblazoned with the words 'Sunderland are Shite'. The joy of Sunderland's exit from the Premiership in 2003 was heightened for a Newcastle fan from Gateshead who scooped a £1,400 win from Ladbrokes having placed a fiver on Sunderland losing their last 10 league games of the season.

MANCHESTER UNITED

The geographical boundaries between the northeast clubs are indistinct – with many areas such as Gateshead split between Newcastle and Sunderland fans, meaning that workplace atmospheres after derby games can get particularly rancid.

Alan Shearer's lack of interest in overtures from Manchester United has, not surprisingly, irked Reds' followers. His reluctance is symbolic of the cultural gulf between the clubs. Newcastle can genuinely claim to have a massive and fanatical fan base within 10 miles of the ground, whereas Manchester United's is more transient. Kevin Keegan's refreshingly unhinged "I would love it...I would just love it" [if they were beaten to the Championship] rants at Sir Alex Ferguson in a TV interview in 1996 gave the official touch to the bad feeling.

PERFORMANCE AGAINST RIVALS
SUNDERLAND

WON 32%

LOST 23%

DRAWN 45%

SUPPORTERS' VFM 78%

LOVE/HATE

If *Andy Cole* wanted to be remembered fondly on Tyneside, he wouldn't have picked Manchester United as his new club. But he performed the ultimate snub to his former club when spotted joining in a stirring version of *'Daydream Believer'* to the words 'Cheer Up Kevin Keegan'.

CHANTS

A nice example of an action chant;

'Shoes off if you hate Man U'.

DOH!!

Though perhaps unfair to characterise as a mistake, the signing of the player with one of the more smirk-inducing names in football history ended in tears. Dutch winger Brian Pinas bore the brunt of an onslaught of media and fans' wisecracks. Under the weight of the hilarity, his career at Newcastle amounted to no more than a pre-season friendly. Having endured a season in the reserves, he skulked off to the Dutch Second Division.

'YOUR GROUND'S TOO BIG FOR YOU!'
RATING

100
80
60
40
20
0

ATTENDANCE AS A PERCENTAGE OF CAPACITY 100%

NORTHAMPTON TOWN

Recommended website: **web.ukonline.co.uk/ntfc**

WHO ARE YA?

Although 1966 is generally recalled for something else, the year also marks the pinnacle of the greatest 'there and back' escapade of any League team. In 1961, Northampton Town were promoted from Level Three before having a couple in Level Two, and two more in Level One. By the time England had won the World Cup, Northampton had finished their only season in the highest division. They took just four years to go back to Level Three. Only Swansea and Wimbledon have had a faster ascent, and no club has yet to beat the rapidity of their decline.

The town tends to be cited as one that most of the British population have seen signs for, but few have actually visited. Prior to 1994, when the club moved to their current Sixfields Stadium, those that made the trip to watch their team play Northampton could hardly believe the scene that greeted them. The County Ground was, by some distance, the worst football venue in the league. Shared with Northamptonshire County Cricket Club, who was the dominant partner, the football club was forced into having to juggle the fixture list around the willow and leather merchants. The playing areas overlapped and when The Cobblers weren't in town, their portion of the pitch was used as a car park.

> Opened in 1959, Watford Gap was the first motorway service station in the UK. It is named after 'another' Watford, a village in Northamptonshire just off the motorway, and has nothing to do with its larger namesake 60 miles south in Hertfordshire.

Ground safety regulations led to the construction of the notorious 'Meccano Stand', seemingly made out of bits of old scaffolding material – not that there were many wanting to avail themselves of the facilities in the first place. In March 1985, only 942 fans turned out for a League match versus Chester, a then record.

Northampton are now controlled by a Supporters' Trust, and have the proud boast that in 1992, they had the first two elected supporters' directors on the board of a League club. During the (rare) promotion season in 2003-2004 they managed a series of results that, if it were not for a local eagle-eyed statto type, might have gone unnoticed. During the course of the season, they beat Norwich, Plymouth and Doncaster Rovers in one competition or another. These sides won each of the three (as they were) Nationwide Leagues. They didn't manage to complete the collection by taking the scalp of Premiership champions Arsenal, though they happen to have a respectable record against the Gunners of won one, lost one, and drawn two.

CELEBRITY FANS
JO WHILEY
DJ
BOB HARRIS
DJ

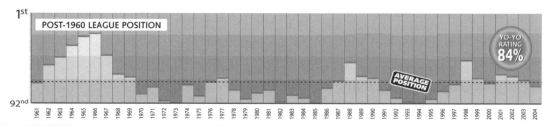

1st

POST-1960 LEAGUE POSITION

YO-YO RATING **84%**

AVERAGE POSITION

92nd

1961 1962 1963 1964 1965 1966 1967 1968 1969 1970 1971 1972 1973 1974 1975 1976 1977 1978 1979 1980 1981 1982 1983 1984 1985 1986 1987 1988 1989 1990 1991 1992 1993 1994 1995 1996 1997 1998 1999 2000 2001 2002 2003 2004

PROGRESS REPORT

Northampton's trip to the old First Division stands out in a sea of very little. Since 1960, half of their time has been spent in the basement. In 1994, they should, by rights, have gone down to the Conference, except Kidderminster's ground was considered substandard, so it was just as well they had Sixfields to move to early in the next season. The supporters' trust can point to better placings since they took over, with The Cobblers spending much of the last 10 years in the relative comfort of the Second.

```
   ...Went to Wembley for the first time in their anniversary year of 1997, and won...
...Des O'Conner played once for the reserve team...Played match in baseball boots (1962)...
```

RIVALS

Talk about being shot from both sides. At the turn of the Millennium, Northampton could at least draw comfort from the fact that they had a potentially huge fan base, with the nearest League clubs being Coventry, 30 miles to the northwest and Luton, a similar distance to the south. But they were about to have company.

PETERBOROUGH

It's sometimes difficult to distinguish between the club's dislike of Peterborough United and that directed personally at Barry Fry. Northampton's gripe at the man himself goes back to his days at Barnet, when dressed in only red shorts, he performed a celebratory dance along the touchline after his side got a late equaliser. Some Cobblers' fans are still in therapy.

SUPPORTERS' VFM 47%

RUSHDEN & DIAMONDS

The appearance from nowhere of Rushden and Diamonds on the League scene in 2001 was a severe shock. Only 13 miles up the A45, Northampton, whose financial hardships had left them in administration, were not best pleased that R&D had exploited the millions of Max Griggs to create their 'manufactured' club. Worse was the fact that Griggs had been a board member at Northampton and had scarpered when fans' unrest forced him out. The two met in their first competitive fixture in 2004-2005, with Northampton winning 1-0, though Rushden and Diamonds had won a pre-season friendly in 1994 and had triumphed in something called the Maunsell Cup in 2001, a fixture that was only taken semi-seriously by the teams, but was made all-ticket just in case. Northampton can console themselves that R&D's name lends itself to endless variations, with the upstarts referred to variously as 'Rats and Dogs', 'Rancid and Dismal', and with reference to their weirdly sub-rural base of Irthlingborough, 'The Village People'.

PERFORMANCE AGAINST RIVALS PETERBOROUGH

WON 32%
LOST 43%
DRAWN 25%

MK DONS

…And then it happened again. In 2002, the FA granted permission for Wimbledon to up sticks to Milton Keynes, one junction down the M1. The anger was barely disguised in their official statement, "We, at Northampton Town Football Club, are surprised and disappointed at this decision". By 2004, it was clear that a handful of ex-Cobblers' fans had sneaked off into the MK camp, though with Northampton instantly maintaining a higher league position in the Second Division, the turncoat supporters may have inadvertently downgraded themselves.

LOVE/HATE

Needless to say, the formation of the supporters' trust came after the standard behind the scenes farce. In this case, the villain was chairman *Michael McRitchie*, who was well known locally for selling china out of a barrow at the market. Having taken over in 1991, his popularity was such that the entire playing staff went on strike. With the club considered a serious credit risk, there was nothing in the kitty for printing programmes so the reading material for a match against Burnley amounted to a photocopied sheet of A4, neatly folded.

CHANTS

Said to be one of the most stirring songs in the League, Northampton's version of the Red Flag:

'No finer town they'll ever be,
No finer town you'll ever see,
Big city lights don't bother me,
Northampton Town I'm proud to be.'

Fans admit that they need to be doing supremely well on the pitch to be motivated enough to sing it…which isn't very often.

'YOUR GROUND'S TOO BIG FOR YOU!' RATING

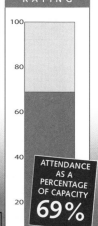

100

80

60

40

ATTENDANCE AS A PERCENTAGE OF CAPACITY 69%

20

0

DOH!!

For his first game as director, Michael McRitchie came on the tannoy and announced that the match against Darlington was a 'home banker'. Northampton were three down in 17 minutes.

NORWICH CITY

Recommended website: **www.pinkun.com**

WHO ARE YA?

Norwich City, along with their bitter rivals Ipswich, became successful relatively late in their history. The club escaped permanent obscurity by achieving promotion to the old First Division in 1972. They occupy a nightmarish position in the football pecking order. With a post-1960 rank of 20, they are in the grey area between the rewards of the Premiership and the relative destitution of the lower leagues. Other clubs in a similar position have coped less well, and although threatened with insolvency in 1984 (following a stadium fire), Norwich have shown a degree of skill in keeping the receivers away.

One of the ugliest fan/director spats occurred when Robert Chase was finally removed from the club after a prolonged and bloody supporters' campaign. Though credited with rescuing the club from likely bankruptcy in 1984, Chase concentrated their meagre resources on developing the ground and surrounding land, selling players liberally in the meantime. Chase put up a good fight, outstaying his welcome by a full two years. Onto the board came TV cook and lifelong supporter Delia

CELEBRITY FANS
STEVEN FRY
Comedian/Actor
DELIA SMITH
Joined the Norwich City board in 1997
SOPHIE ELLIS-BEXTOR
Feline-like Singer

IN and AROUND

From the moment comedian Steve Coogan chose Norwich as the base for Alan Partridge, Norfolk hardly gets a mention in the media without having the fictitious DJ/chat show host name-checked in the same sentence. The one recognisable East Anglian location is Bickling Hall, which Partridge attempts to pass off as the home of Bono. Despite the characterisation of petty small-mindedness, real residents and visitors hardly have a bad word to say about Norwich.

Smith. Initially treated with extreme caution by fans, her involvement is now acknowledged to have turned around more than just the club catering.

Their unusual green and yellow strip is derived from their nickname, The Canaries, (after the area's flourishing 1900s bird trade), rather than the other way round. The nickname is shared with Hitchen Town and Turkish side, Fenerbache. Generally considered to hold a place in the top five most ghastly kits of all time, Norwich's home strip of 1993 was basically yellow but with the additions of green and white smears - which pithily, considering their nickname, looked uncannily like bird excrement.

Candidate for the oldest currently heard football song in Britain, 'On the Ball', City dates from 1905, just three years after the club's foundation.

Norwich pulled off perhaps the most incredible European club competition victory in living memory when, in 1993, they beat Bayern Munich in their Olympic Stadium - the only British club to achieve the feat.

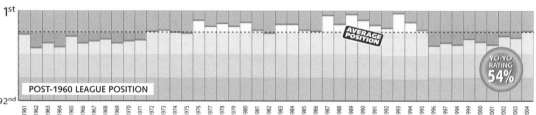

POST-1960 LEAGUE POSITION

AVERAGE POSITION

YO-YO RATING 54%

PROGRESS REPORT

Norwich may feel aggrieved that they have haven't enjoyed a longer Premiership existence. Having been reasonably established in the top flight for 20 years, they survived only three more seasons after the big-money Premiership was formed, suffering relegation in 1995, with the small consolation that Ipswich went down with them. The phrase 'on loan to the Endsleigh League' became a common adornment to fans' shirts, but it took nearly 10 years before they stormed Level One to achieve promotion in 2004.

```
...Highest finisher in the Premiership with a negative goal difference (3rd in 1992-93 with 61
scored but 66 conceded)...Won promotion immediately after relegation three times in 12 years...
...Previous ground 'The Nest' featured cliff behind field of play, from which wide shots
would bounce back into play...
```

RIVALS

Despite the tabloid titillation with middle-class hooligans, clubs involved in particularly bad-tempered rivalries are generally from poorer areas - which makes it all the more remarkable that Norwich and Ipswich (neither exactly known for their grinding poverty) have such a thing about each other. Despite the intensity of bad feeling, it has rarely boiled over into anything serious, thanks mainly to very heavy policing. There was, however, prolonged seat-throwing at Portman Road in 1996 when a fan decided to drag the Norwich keeper Bryan Gunn into the crowd. (Gunn had just let in a laughably soft goal). In fact the worst recent violence in Norwich city centre occurred when Sheffield United were the visitors in 2004.

Having endured years of abuse from Ipswich along the lines that they were all land loving 'farmers', it was ironic that on promotion to the Premiership, Ipswich re-invented themselves as the decidedly rural 'Tractor Boys'.

There were joyous scenes in Norfolk when an episode of the BBC antique drama *Lovejoy* featured a refuse collector wearing an Ipswich scarf that he'd found amongst the rubbish. The unofficial nickname 'The Binmen' has stuck ever since. Such was the jumpiness of police over the risk of trouble, they sent letters to known suspects in Norwich warning them to stay away from an England international against Croatia played at Portman Road.

A scoreboard operator at Carrow Road was disciplined for displaying the scoreline 'Man Utd 1 Scum 0' when Ipswich had gone behind at Old Trafford.

There were raised eyebrows when, in January 2004, Norwich supporters were fingered in a FA observer's report for racist chanting. No one else present at the FA Cup game against Everton seemed to witness it, including the police. The consensus emerged that the offending chant (directed at Wayne Rooney) was a reference to him being 'fat', not to anyone else being 'black'.

Australian rugby fans have reason to be irritated with the club having endured chants of Are you Norwich in disguise? by England supporters during the last World Cup, who saw similarities between the Aussie gold colours and Norwich's garish yellow.

IPSWICH

PERFORMANCE AGAINST RIVALS
IPSWICH

WON 38%
LOST 41%
DRAWN 21%

SUPPORTERS' VFM 71%

CHANTS

'You only sing when you're cooking' from Birmingham City very nearly hit the mark, though strangely, Delia Smith virtually never prepares meals for herself.

Another Birmingham ditty aimed at Norwich,

'Ooh, ahh, it's Ambrosia',

must rate amongst those with the poorest geographical sense. The famed rice pudding is, of course, marketed as a Devon product.

LOVE/HATE

It has taken a while for the faithful to really take her to their heart, but finally in 2004, the bulk of the Norwich fans feel compelled to actually chant *Delia Smith's* ♡ name.

Kevin Muscat, former Wolves defender, was for a long time the biggest hate figure. Twice sent off whilst playing against Norwich - once in 1996 when playing for Crystal Palace notoriously sparking what has been described as the worst player brawl of all time.

'YOUR GROUND'S TOO BIG FOR YOU!'
RATING

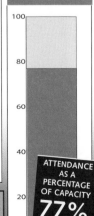

ATTENDANCE AS A PERCENTAGE OF CAPACITY
77%

DOH!!

Such was the hangover of being crowned Level One Champions in 2004, nobody at the club thought to apply for planning permission to extend the car-park at Carrow Road. A children's play area with swings and a roundabout was concreted over, provoking furious protests from local mums.

NOTTS COUNTY

Recommended website: **www.nottscounty.net**

WHO ARE YA?

Even the most hopelessly unrealistic County supporter would have to admit that, for the world's oldest club, their record is decidedly underwhelming. Officially formed in 1864, the club staged its centenary two years early in 1962, pointing to the fact that some games had been played a couple of years before. Nottingham is the smallest city in the English league to host two clubs. Since 1960, County have only enjoyed four seasons in the top flight (with Forest to keep them company each time, though Forest managed to gain a higher league place in all four). Former chairman Derek Pavis once pithily commented that "most of the people who can remember when we were a great club are dead". Perhaps the most telling stat was that prior to their appearance in the play-offs in 1990, the club had never played at Wembley. But they developed a taste for it and achieved a unique double by winning another Wembley play-off the following year.

CELEBRITY FANS

NOTTS COUNTY HAVE AN ENVIABLE RECORD OF ATTRACTING NO KNOWN CELEBRITY FANS.

Considering Nottinghamshire's role in the miners' strike of 1984, it will come as no surprise to learn that Notts County's hideous re-branding of Meadow Lane in 2002 as the 'Scargill Stadium' was not a tribute to the former NUM leader, but a £100,000 sponsorship deal with a local estate agent (who subsequently went bust, leaving the club in the lurch). Reverting to its former name, the gound now tops many visiting fans' list of best in the lower leagues. Twenty years on County still occasionally have to put up with chants of 'Scab' from the opposing fans, many of whom were probably not born at the time of the miners' strike.

IN and AROUND

There are 1,928 more women than men in Nottingham (2001 Census), a very rare imbalance as males form the majority of the general population. But bachelors champing at the bit should note that the over-supply of ladies is mostly in the over 85s' age group.

The highlight of their lower league exploits was to win the Level Three title by the unfeasible margin of 17 points, in 1998, meaning they had the luxury of taking it easy from March onwards.

Along with Oldham and Oxford they start an alphabetical trio of clubs with average positions anchored very close to half way in the divisional pecking order.

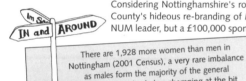

POST-1960 LEAGUE POSITION

1st

AVERAGE POSITION

YO-YO RATING 78%

92nd

1961 1962 1963 1964 1965 1966 1967 1968 1969 1970 1971 1972 1973 1974 1975 1976 1977 1978 1979 1980 1981 1982 1983 1984 1985 1986 1987 1988 1989 1990 1991 1992 1993 1994 1995 1996 1997 1998 1999 2000 2001 2002 2003 2004

PROGRESS REPORT

Notts County's pinnacle was two seasons in the old First Division in the early 80s. A steady downward slide has afflicted County for the past 10 years, sinking to the lowest division for the first time since 1971.

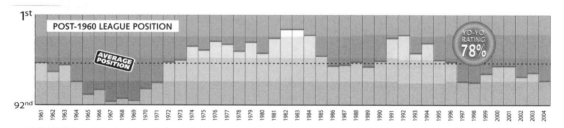

```
...Presented Juventus with their distinctive black and white striped kit...
        ...County are the oldest senior football club in the world...
        ...Have suffered relegation more times than any other club...
```

RIVALS

The feelings of County and Forest supporters towards each other form perhaps the most bizarre unrequited rivalry in Britain. The trend of smaller clubs naming larger outfits as rivals (when the larger club couldn't care less) is mirrored here, but seeing as they have spent so little time in the same leagues, there are relatively few matches on which to reminisce.

Although not an issue in recent times, on formation, there was a definite rich-man/poor-man split, with County attempting to take the mantle of the more upmarket outfit. In fact, much time and effort was spent in the club's formative years squabbling with Forest over real estate.

Bad feeling was not long in coming. Even before they played each other in 1886, tensions were rising with the choice of nicknames. County's seemingly pastoral choice of 'The Lambs' was in fact the name of a violent Nottingham gang of the time. Forest opted for the equally provocative 'The Garibaldis', after the Italian Nationalist Revolutionaries.

The impression of the club's early history is one of County attempting a bit of social climbing. County chose not to include Forest on their fixture list for 1877, seeing their neighbours as a poorer and paler imitation. Having been beaten by Forest in a FA Cup tie, County got stroppy, leaving Nottingham altogether for the more gentile county cricket club at Beeston.

In latter days, County supporters hate the fact that Forest look down on them condescendingly as their smaller brother. There is the implied assumption that Forest are permanently going to be in a higher league - though with Forest plunging from their historical highs, County fans can occasionally dream of parity.

NOTTINGHAM FOREST

PERFORMANCE AGAINST RIVALS

NOTTINGHAM FOREST

SUPPORTERS' VFM **41%**

WON 32%

LOST 36%

DRAWN 32%

MANSFIELD TOWN

BRISTOL ROVERS

Following a tetchy Leyland Daf semi-final of 1990, things blew up again in 2000 when County scored following a throw-in that should, under the unwritten laws of sportsmanship, have been collected by a Rovers player. The ball was put out of play so Rovers defender Steve Foster could receive treatment. But the throw was collected and crossed for County's Mark Stallard to make the score 1-1 with one minute left on the clock. Rovers hit the roof and protested to the FA, demanding a replay (which was turned down). In recognition of the fact that some might say that the matter should drop, County sing 'If you still hate Bristol Rovers clap your hands'.

CHANTS

County possess one of the shortest but most talked about songs in the football league. The saga of the *Wheelbarrow Song* and its origins is disputed, but the best guess dates it from 17th April 1990, away at Shrewsbury. Losing 2-0, a small group of Notts County fans began parodying the opposition chant, which they heard, wrongly, as being something to do with gardening. The full lyrics amount to no more than '*I had a wheelbarrow...the wheel fell off*' sung ad infinitum. The chant coincided with County fighting back to 2-2, helping them to gain promotion. The legend soon grew that the team never lost when the song was sung - a claim that might not stand up to independent analysis.

LOVE/HATE

Jimmy Sirrel was first appointed manager in 1969 and helped County to the Level Three title the following year. In fact he liked the place so much he had three separate spells at the club. He was renowned for a Scottish accent so thick that it rendered much of what he said unintelligible to locals.

Though manager *Sam Allardyce* improved the club's fortunes, the love quickly soured when he flew the nest to Bolton Wanderers, a move that infuriated the Notts County board (who asked for compensation) and the fans, who now name him as one of their top hate figures.

'YOUR GROUND'S TOO BIG FOR YOU!'
R A T I N G

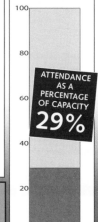

ATTENDANCE AS A PERCENTAGE OF CAPACITY **29%**

100

80

60

40

20

0

DOH!!

When Juventus celebrated their anniversary, they planned a visit to the club that gave them their distinctive image. They got the strip roughly correct, but a major communication failure, possibly caused by both teams' nicknames being The Magpies, saw them end up playing Newcastle United.

NOTTINGHAM FOREST

Recommended website: **www.lostthatlovingfeeling.co.uk**

WHO ARE YA?

Whereas the standing of some British cities suffers from the lack of a League team, Nottingham owes its enhanced status largely to its two football clubs. With a population of under 300,000, the city is smaller than Wakefield in West Yorkshire, a town never to have a league team of its own. Essentially, Forest and County make Nottingham seem bigger than it really is.

CELEBRITY FANS
SU POLLARD
Actress - Hi-di-Hi
KENNETH CLARKE
Tory Politician
LEE WESTWOOD
Golfer

From the bare stats of their league finishing positions, it has to be said that Forest have the look of a one-man club. Having been sacked from Leeds after just 44 days, Brian Clough stepped down a division to join a Forest side threatened with relegation. But with the addition of his right-hand man from Derby, Peter Taylor, with whom he'd won the First Division Championship the previous season, Clough embarked on an 18-year reign that is unsurpassed in terms of a manager exerting such influence. Clough inherited a solidly Level One outfit. Four years later, they won the European Cup (and retained it the following year), becoming the smallest city ever to hold the crown – a record that is unlikely to be broken.

In and AROUND

Visitors to Nottingham Castle are disappointed to learn that they've arrived 360 years late. The castle itself was burned down in 1649, leaving a stately home/museum that somehow retains the 'castle' tag.

Although he was in charge when they finally left the top-flight in 1993, their wallowing since points to how influential Clough was. His magic was not instantly obvious. Ultimately to admit that he enjoyed a few bevvies, he was tetchy with the media at the best of times, and quite capable of descending to the antics of a tap-room bore. Having aimed punches at two Forest supporters during a pitch invasion, he deemed the most appropriate apology was to smother the already abused pair in kisses (on TV).

Forest's Achilles heel in recent years has been a clutch of mediocre strikers. Jason Lee suffered public assassination at the hands of Baddiel and Skinner, but worse was the man he replaced, Andrea Silenza, who cost the club £8,000 per week, an absolute fortune in 1995. Candidate for awful Premiership player ever, his utterly lethargic approach to the game saw him loaned to Venezia, from where he refused to come back.

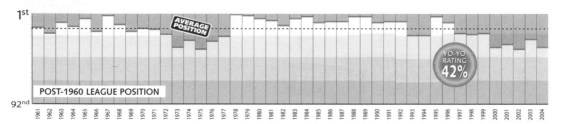

POST-1960 LEAGUE POSITION — AVERAGE POSITION — YO-YO RATING 42%

1st ... 92nd — 1961 1962 1963 1964 1965 1966 1967 1968 1969 1970 1971 1972 1973 1974 1975 1976 1977 1978 1980 1981 1982 1983 1984 1985 1986 1987 1988 1989 1990 1991 1992 1993 1994 1995 1996 1997 1998 1999 2000 2001 2002 2003 2004

PROGRESS REPORT

Currently in their worst phase in living memory, Forest have a post-1960 rank safely in the lower reaches of the Premiership but are stuck in the mire at the foot of Level One. Catastrophe was narrowly averted for the second time in two seasons with Joe Kinnear steering them away from Level One relegation zone in 2004. Amazingly their League Championship came immediately after promotion from the Level One. During their yo-yo days, they weren't too far from emulating the feat in 1995 – finishing third in the Premiership having come up the year before – an achievement that is unlikely to be bettered in the foreseeable future.

```
        ...Pioneered use of shin-pads...
   ...Forest's old Town Ground was first to use a crossbar...
...Forest player first suggested use of whistle to replace ref's white flag...
```

RIVALS

The ultimate example of the little brother syndrome, the rivalry between County and Forest is remarkably one-sided, both in terms of strength of feeling and past results/league positions. One of a handful of high points in Notts County's 140-year history was their appearance in the 1990-91 play-off final against Brighton. For a club with distinctive black and white colours, there were very suspicious patches of red in the County section. Far from hostile intentions, Forest fans had turned up in numbers as a genuine sign of affection for the city's smaller club. There is absolutely no chance that County supporters would return the compliment.

DERBY COUNTY

The rivalry with Derby predates the Clough saga, but his sudden departure to Forest added to its intensity. If anything the bad feeling is a bit stronger with Derby fans, who still have a lingering suspicion that had Clough not defected, it would be them, not Forest, who would have been crowned European Champions – a theory treated with contempt at Forest. Despite not being most people's idea of a rural town, Derby are characterised with the "mutton worriers' label". Never a purist's favourite, Pride Park is dubbed variously the Temple of Meccano and Prideless Park.

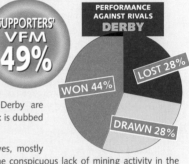

SUPPORTERS' VFM 49%

PERFORMANCE AGAINST RIVALS
DERBY

WON 44%
LOST 28%
DRAWN 28%

Wolves and Liverpool have been recent minor players on Forest's hate list; Wolves, mostly because of the previous antics of the notorious Kevin Muscat. Liverpool, despite the conspicuous lack of mining activity in the history of Merseyside, were prone to use the 'scabs' taunt as a hangover from the 1984 miners' strike. More significantly, in the late 70s, Forest stole Liverpool's thunder in Europe. With Derby increasingly seen as not worth their energies, a search for new rivals has thrown up Sheffield United, on the basis of their managerial equivalent of Muscat, the rarely loved Neil Warnock.

SHEFFIELD UNITED

NB If you want to avoid local scowls, don't refer to the club as *Notts Forest*.

LOVE/HATE

Stuart Peace, stalwart from the glory days, exhibited guts and passion for his club, a combination that pushes the right buttons with supporters everywhere

HATE

CHANTS

The Forest faithful can go one better (or worse) than the phonetically notorious chant of 'Eng-er-land'. Sung to the tune of Paul McCartney's Christmas hit, fans manage to stretch the phrase 'City ground' to fit the first line of the chorus of *Mull of Kintyre* - an excruciating attempt at using three syllables where four are needed.

DOH!!

Transferred from Celtic, Dutchman Pierre van Hooijdonk was a huge hit when scoring 24 goals for Forest in 97-98, aiding a return to the Premiership. But having commented that the club lacked the ambition and financial clout to survive the big time, a war of words with manager Dave Bassett ensued, conducted mostly in the press. Van Hooijdonk absconded for three months demanding a transfer.

With a buyer not found, he returned to a decidedly chilly reception from the fans and team-mates. Training alone, his reappearance on the pitch culminated in a predictable farce. Playing against Derby at home, he got on the end of a corner and scored with a looping header. Looking around for a full 30 seconds for a colleague to celebrate with, he received a couple of half-hearted pats, whereas the rest of the team, in a pre-planned move, congratulated the corner-taker instead. Forest went down, never to return.

'YOUR GROUND'S TOO BIG FOR YOU!'
RATING

100

80

60

40

ATTENDANCE AS A PERCENTAGE OF CAPACITY
81%

20

0

OLDHAM ATHLETIC

Recommended website: **www. latics.cjb.net**

WHO ARE YA?

According to local folklore, Manchester only became 'Greater' when they put Oldham in it. Whatever the town's political geography, it has the distinct disadvantage of only being uncomfortably close to a couple of significantly larger clubs...and we're not talking Stockport County.

Oldham have been cursed by the fact that they have previously not owned their ground, making the setup a fairly unattractive proposition for the well-heeled. Finally, in 2003, they managed to purchase Boundary Park in an unconventional deal that saw the supporters' trust gain a windfall of £1 million to plough back into the club, though there is still the small question of needing an estimated £2 million to scrape through a single season. Then manager, Iain Dowie was clearly confused when he publicly announced that some officials were attempting to 'feather their own nests'. Before plumping for Exeter City, renowned bender, Uri Geller was spotted at Boundary Park sizing up the club for a possible bid. But not even he had enough positive energy to contemplate turning around the club's perilous finances.

IN and AROUND

Nobody is sure of the derivation of Britain's most unappealing sounding railway station, Oldham Mumps, but local historians have ruled out any link with the acute viral illness.

Despite semi-permanent poverty, Oldham enjoyed a prolonged spell of managerial stability. Joe Royle led the club through an adventure that saw the pinnacle of three years in the top-flight. In the haze of history, it's easy to forget that they were one of the founding members of the Premier League. Royle's 12-year spell neatly corresponds to the best period in the club's recent history. Oldham were probably the victims of Steve MacMahon's sudden change of mind in 2004, when, 20 minutes after Blackpool announced his resignation, he decided he wasn't going anywhere, including Oldham to which it was strongly rumoured he had applied.

In 2000, against Peterborough, Chaddy the Owl was given his marching orders after being flagged offside. The linesman claimed to have had difficulty distinguishing the mascot from legitimate Oldham players. The dejected owl commented "Fair enough, I did have a replica shirt on – but I also have a big furry head". In a more standard mascot incident in the same year, Chaddy was reprimanded for mooning at Cardiff fans.

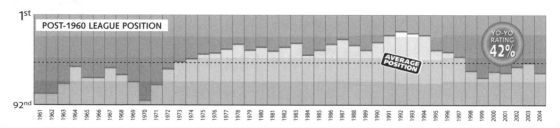

POST-1960 LEAGUE POSITION — 1st ... 92nd — 1961–2004 — AVERAGE POSITION — YO-YO RATING 42%

PROGRESS REPORT

Oldham have three mid 90s' seasons of Premiership action to fondly reminisce on, in stark contrast to a 19th place finish in Level Three in 1970. To find their best ever League performance, you have to go all the way back to their runners-up place in the old First Division in 1915, an achievement they never looked like matching when in the top-flight in the early 90s, where they stumbled to three bottom half finishes. They have been anchored in Level Two for eight years having one stab at the play-offs in 2003.

```
...Formed under the name Pine Villa...
...Had match abandoned when player refused to leave the field (1915)...
```

RIVALS

If your club was more or less equidistant from the two Manchester clubs, you might feel a strong dislike of United to be the logical reaction. In fact, Oldham manage to reserve bile for both of them, with a suggestion that City might just edge it in the hate stakes, despite their second-string status in the song 'We hate Man United...and City too'. Oldham fans tend to have bitter memories of being baited at school, either by hordes of 'plastic' Manchester United fans or City moaners who comforted themselves with the thought that at least what they were experiencing wasn't quite as bad as the antics at Boundary Park.

MANCHESTER CITY
☠ ☠ ☠ ☠ ☠

MANCHESTER UNITED
☠ ☠ ☠ ☠ ☠

Oldham's place in the Manchester pecking order is becoming set in stone – well behind the big two, roughly on par with Wigan (hence the general dislike) and miles ahead of Bury and Rochdale (hence the indifference).

But no one can accuse them that their dislike of United isn't simply the petulance of a tiny near neighbour. The two were involved in some significant matches in the early 90s with Oldham's fall from grace signified by an equalizer from Mark Hughes in their FA Cup semi-final clash in 1994. United went on to easily win the replay. With Oldham relegated from the Premiership that year, many still view the game as the moment Oldham went on the skids.

WIGAN ATHLETIC
☠ ☠ ☠ ☠ ☠

SUPPORTERS' VFM 47%

PERFORMANCE AGAINST RIVALS MANCHESTER CITY

WON 28%
LOST 39%
DRAWN 33%

Wigan Athletic have muscled in on the Manchester scene, much to the chagrin of Oldham fans who are highly fed up with the musings of Dave Whelan and his cohorts as they assume they can breeze into the Premiership with the help of his millions. Wigan are consequently characterised as glory seekers of the highest order whose ridiculously under-capacity attendances are a sure sign that the whole illusion of near-greatness is shortly to be exposed as a cruel dream.

LOVE/HATE

Ex-chairman *Ian Stott* became the target of a concerted and successful campaign to eject him from the hot seat when, in 1999, he dared to answer an innocent question in a Manchester Evening News interview. He made the mistake of mentioning a casual conversation on a train with his counterparts at Bury and Rochdale in which, briefly, the idea of a three-way merger was mooted. The subject was apparently never revisited to, but by the time the press got hold of it, it was reported as virtually a done deal, much to the horror of the Oldham faithful, for whom it would mean an instant relegation.

CHANTS

Oldham and Wigan now share the same nickname, though Oldham consider it nicked, justifying the chant,

'2-1 to the real Latics'.

'YOUR GROUND'S TOO BIG FOR YOU!'
R A T I N G

100
80
60
40
20
0

ATTENDANCE AS A PERCENTAGE OF CAPACITY 48%

DOH!!

An unforeseen colour clash occurred when Oldham sported a glowing orange strip for a match at Millwall in 1996. Though there was no problem telling the difference between the two teams, Oldham players were virtually indistinguishable from the stewards and photographers in their florescent jackets. The snappers had to make do with turning their garments inside out and a bunch of natty green waistcoats were found for the stewards.

OXFORD UNITED

Recommended website: **www.rageonline.co.uk**

WHO ARE YA?

Clubs that lurch from financial crisis to crisis tend to have something in common; semi-floating populations. And they don't come much more floating than those in Oxford (and Cambridge, where the club has been similarly afflicted). 50,000 students and largely non-football minded academics – all of temporary residency - account for 60% of the town's population. But it is not a declining base of support; Oxford have enjoyed better attendances in their recent spell in Level Three than they did in Level One. After a five year struggle to move out of their tiny Manor Ground, considered by many visitors to be the worst ground in the football league, Oxford finally have a new home in the albeit three-sided Kassam Stadium. The Chairman's decision to name the ground after himself caused understandable alarm, but local hotelier Firoz Kassam has qualified support from most fans, since without his millions there would probably be no Oxford United.

CELEBRITY FANS
JIM ROSENTHAL
Ex-ITV Presenter
THOM YORKE
Radiohead
TIMMY MALLETT
80s Children's TV Presenter

IN and AROUND

The senior partner of Henman's Solicitors in the city centre is Tim's dad.

On the basis of past experience they have a right to be suspicious. Robert Maxwell's Headington Hall estate, near Oxford, was the perfect base to launch one of his now notorious rescue bids, mooting the idea of a merger with Reading until it was howled down. But his limited concentration span made it inevitable that he would be eyeing up something bigger and took over the reins at Derby instead, leaving son Kevin in charge at the Manor Ground – though not before a bit of barely hidden asset stripping. Star striker Dean Saunders was informed straight after an Oxford match that he was 'required' at Derby – and was gone in an instant.

Fans have had a constant struggle with the club over the Oxford strip. Traditionally they wore gold and black, à la Wolves. This turned to yellow and blue in the seventies. The blue tuned to navy, and more recently the yellow became transformed into a fluorescent green.

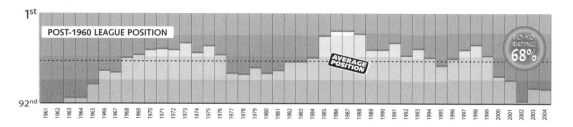

1st

POST-1960 LEAGUE POSITION

AVERAGE POSITION

YO-YO RATING 68%

92nd

1961 1962 1963 1964 1965 1966 1967 1968 1969 1970 1971 1972 1973 1974 1975 1976 1977 1978 1979 1980 1981 1982 1983 1984 1985 1986 1987 1988 1989 1990 1991 1992 1993 1994 1995 1996 1997 1998 1999 2000 2001 2002 2003 2004

PROGRESS REPORT

Oxford's story is basically one of a steady climb from obscurity to the top-flight followed by a slightly faster descent. Muddling around at the foot of Level Three in the early 60s, the next 20 years saw two dramatic spurts take them to the heights of the 18th spot in the top division, two seasons in a row in 1986 and 1987. The next period was a painful mirror of their rise – a slow decline followed by a dramatic slump which saw them come full circle to finish 21st in Level Three by 2002.

```
...Were put out of FA Cup by non-league opposition in five consecutive seasons...
            ...Share nickname 'The U's' with Cambridge United...
    ...Only club to win divisions in consecutive years (1984 and 1985)...
```

RIVALS

SWINDON TOWN ☠☠☠☠☠

Oxford and Swindon are both centres of car manufacturing, but they share little else. A fully requited and intense rivalry has engulfed more than the football teams. The Oxford Mail pitched in with a piece '20 reasons why you wouldn't want to live in Swindon'. Swindon's local paper retaliated and the temperature rose further. On the field, the two were involved in an incident that possibly robbed Oxford of promotion in 1982. With minutes to go, a smoke bomb appeared from the Swindon end landing in the Oxford penalty area. With the defenders losing their bearings, Swindon forced the ball in the net. To vehement protests, the goal was allowed handing Swindon a 3-2 victory. Seething Oxford fans, of the type that would normally steer clear of trouble, started perhaps the worst violence seen at the Manor Ground. Otherwise, the club have a record of minor trouble, aided by a few local nutters who occasionally latch onto the club particularly when Swindon are in town. Oxford have an admirable record of combating racism – with any fans tempted to start dubious chants likely to be slapped down by their own fans. If anything, Oxford's exceptionally poor record against Swindon (only eight wins in 40 meetings since 1960) has contributed to the rivalry from the 'U's point of view. The proposed merger with Reading should perhaps have caused long term bad feeling, but they also name Swindon as their biggest rivals.

Swindon's utilitarian feel doesn't cut much ice with those fans used to the highbrow university town; "Swindon's not the sort of place you'd go for shopping...or entertainment" commented one fan.

PERFORMANCE AGAINST RIVALS SWINDON

WON 20%
LOST 42%
DRAWN 38%

SUPPORTERS' VFM 49%

LOVE/HATE

A contender for the most inspired signing ever, *John Aldridge* ♡ came for next to nothing from Newport County during the Jim Smith/Maxwell years. His arrival in 1984 to joining Liverpool in 1998 coincided with the club storming up from Level Three to the top flight, with a record-breaking 34 goals in his first complete season and a league Cup win in 1986. Even when the team was struggling in the old First Division, he still managed 31 goals.

Having regularly given the Vs' up to the home end when he was at Newcastle, manager *Willie McFaul* was happy to offload Billy Whitehurst to Oxford, even paying half his signing-on fee from his own pocket. Oxford got what many consider to be the worst striker ever to grace the football league with a reputation for using his fists to iron out any contractual problems with managers.

Unpopular with fans for his lumbering ineptitude, he spent much of his time at the club watching greyhound racing. He managed eight months there until moving on to Reading, but still has strong memories of his time at Oxford; "the fans were a bag of shit".

CHANTS

Songs about questionable parentage are common, though not when they're about your own side:

'We are the bastards in yellow and blue'.

'YOUR GROUND'S TOO BIG FOR YOU!'
RATING

100

80

60

40

20

0

ATTENDANCE AS A PERCENTAGE OF CAPACITY
50%

DOH!!

Such was the scale of the financial chaos in 1999, players went for 10 weeks without pay, and supporters' groups coughed up to cover some backroom expenses. Every match could have been the club's last. A relatively innocent colour-clash cock up at Watford saw Oxford trotting out in the home side's change strip. But in the gloomy atmosphere, rumours and conspiracy theories grew – leading to the consensus that the club could no longer afford the laundry bill, signalling that the fat lady was testing the microphone.

PETERBOROUGH UNITED

Recommended website: **www.talkingposh.net**

WHO ARE YA?

Back in 1937, fans put pressure on the club to change from an all-green strip, believing it to be unlucky. If their record in blue is in some way enhanced, one shudders to think of how bad it could have been in their old kit. Peterborough's league record is hardly earth-shattering considering a town of its size and central location. The one instance of the club making a real effort to escape from life in the lower two leagues ended in ignominy. Rumbled by the FA for illegal bonus payments to players in 1967-68, they were demoted to Level Three. The supporters launched one of the original 'sack the board' campaigns. It met with a similar reaction to most of the subsequent ones. Director Jack Vernon stated that resignation would be a 'coward's way out' – and generously stood for re-election.

CELEBRITY FANS
ADRIAN DURHAM
Sports Presenter
Assorted members of
THE PRODIGY

With its long history of boardroom strain and pain, Peterborough are an unlikely candidate for stability of management. Despite frosty relations with the local press and a significant chunk of the fan-base, Barry Fry is closing in on a long-stayer award having survived since 1996. He's had plenty of sticky moments, chiefly the Peterborough Evening Telegraph revealing details of his contract and pay. Seeing as the Premiership wasn't exactly a realistic prospect, most fans felt his remuneration of around £230,000 per year wasn't deserved. In his defence, Fry's almost bewildering rate of transfers has netted the club a substantial profit – though somehow there never seems to be much left in the kitty to actually spend on the field.

Peterborough's nickname, The Posh, derives from the founders' meeting when a call was made for 'posh players for a posh club', though financially the club has a decidedly down-market record. Their bid for the big time in the early 90s was scuppered by a board suddenly obsessed with increasing revenue from all manner of corporate wheezes, rather than keeping their eye on what was happening on the field. By 2002, the club was considered such a dubious commercial proposition, they couldn't find a shirts' sponsor. With debts of around £5 million, Fry was playing the chirpy chappy as ever in 2002, expecting to surprise a few people. However, he admitted he was hampered by "no assistant manager, no reserve team manager, no personal assistant and no club secretary", and he "couldn't sign players or extend the contracts of existing ones". Considering all this, their 11th place finish was more than respectable.

Landlocked Peterborough was the unlikely location for the discovery of what may be the largest fish in the world (a 35-metre fossil).

Fry's endless transfer tinkerings have, inevitably, led to a few howlers. Scottish Asda checkout worker David Craig was surprised to get a call up to Peterborough in 2002. The 21-year old was playing for a five-a-side team when offered a contract by Fry. An elated Craig said "One minute I was swiping toilet rolls and sausages, the next, a professional footballer". But barcode hell soon beckoned again. Training at this level was beyond him – and Fry despatched him back to Scotland with a month's wages as a pay-off.

Former Nottingham Forest player Jason Lee, infamously savaged by Badddiel and Skinner for, amongst other things, his pineapple barnet, turned up playing for Posh, this time sporting the even more startling combination of a bald head and a beard.

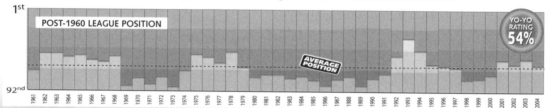

1st — POST-1960 LEAGUE POSITION — AVERAGE POSITION — YO-YO RATING 54%

92nd — 1961 1962 1963 1964 1965 1966 1967 1968 1969 1970 1971 1972 1973 1974 1975 1976 1977 1978 1979 1980 1981 1982 1983 1984 1985 1986 1987 1988 1989 1990 1991 1992 1993 1994 1995 1996 1997 1998 1999 2000 2001 2002 2003 2004

PROGRESS REPORT

The drabness was punctuated by one Herculean effort in 1991 and 1992, with successive promotions up to the heady heights of Level One – but the decline was nearly as rapid, consigning The Posh back to an uneasy life again pivoting around the bottom of Level Two and top of the Level Three.

```
...Won promotion from Fourth Division in their first league season (1961)...
    ...Barry Fry is the most active manager in the transfer market...
        ...Like to play large number of pre-season friendlies...
```

RIVALS

Older Posh fans will tend to point to Northampton as traditional rivals, as Cambridge United, elected to the league in 1970, are just new upstarts. Behind the unusually fierce lower-league rivalry are the similar records of both clubs. Cambridge experienced a very similar 'there and back' trip to Level One in the early 90s.

CAMBRIDGE UNITED

NORTHAMPTON

Derby games have a unique edge as their London Road Ground is well liked for its old-style feel with open terraces. This might lead to the behaviour of Posh fans to veer towards the old school as well; considering its comfortable social background, Peterborough has a grim history of football arrests. In the last published figures for Level Two, The Posh clocked up enough arrests to place them in the top five for hoolie problems for the division, putting them in the same dubious bracket as Stoke and Cardiff. A hardcore of Peterborough fans are associated with England violence, or would be if they still had their passports.

The full force of the law did little to dissuade 20-year old Barry Johnson, who, along with 17 others, received bans from all football grounds following incidents at Peterborough's pre-season friendly with Nottingham Forest in 2001. He greeted the news of four months in a young offenders institution and a seven-year bar from attending any matches in the UK with the cheerful reaction, "I think I'm going back to it…once a hoolie, always a hoolie". Could be a menace with a Zimmer frame.

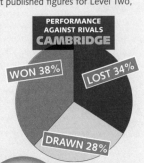

PERFORMANCE AGAINST RIVALS
CAMBRIDGE

WON 38%
LOST 34%
DRAWN 28%

RUSHDEN AND DIAMONDS

There is a distinct pattern of teams promoted from the Conference getting the cold shoulder from League fans, who feel it is beneath them to get worked up about newbies. But Peterborough now name Rushden and Diamonds amongst their hates, helped by the fact that long-term Peterborough player and then captain Andy Edwards chose to defect to R&D, slagging off the Posh board on his way out.

SUPPORTERS' VFM 65%

LOVE/HATE

Victoria Beckham (aka Posh) and Peterborough United (aka Posh) handed the tabloids such a perfect tale that it looked as though it had the hands of an over-enthusiastic PR agency all over it. But a spokesman from the UK patents office really did receive an objection from Mrs Beckham to Peterborough's proposal to trademark their nickname. It was later withdrawn on the basis of representations that their use of 'Posh' had predated the Spice Girls by 70 years.

CHANTS

QPR greeted Peterborough goalie Carl Tiler with
'You should be mending our roof'

'YOUR GROUND'S TOO BIG FOR YOU!'
RATING

ATTENDANCE AS A PERCENTAGE OF CAPACITY
34%

100
80
60
40
20
0

DOH!!

A confidence boosting lift from manager Chris Turner before Peterborough's League Cup semi-final in 1992; "I've told the players that we need to win so that I can have the cash to buy some new ones".

PLYMOUTH ARGYLE

Recommended website: **www.greensonscreen.co.uk**

WHO ARE YA?

Of cities that have not tasted top-flight action, only Hull is larger. Hull's excuse is their rugby tradition. Plymouth are simply dogged by their location. Plymouth's travelling/hotel budget is disproportionately huge. Their total mileage to all other 23 clubs of Level One is approximately six times greater than that of the average British side. Apart from finding it difficult to coax fans hundreds of miles to away games, there is the added difficulty of attracting significant signings and loan players.

The far southwest exists in something of a travel black hole, the scale of which is not fully appreciated by outsiders. Everywhere is a significant trek. With the relegation of Exeter City to the Conference, Plymouth have just four league clubs within two-hours travelling distance. In theory, their catchment area is one of their best assets – to the west of the River Tamar lies Cornwall where no League football has ever been played. In reality Plymouth can garner massive support when tasting success, but are prey to finding the locals turn their affections to the major Premiership teams like Manchester United when fortunes aren't so good – demonstrated by average gates of barely 5,000 when they endured a spell in Level Three.

CELEBRITY FANS

MICHAEL FOOT
Ex-Labour Party Leader

IN and AROUND

Plymouth is further south than the French port of Boulogne

Considering it's such an unusual name, it's odd that nobody is really sure how they came to be known as 'Argyle'. A plausible guess goes back to the fact that the meeting that founded the club took place in Argyle Terrace. Whatever its origin, no current day supporters would refer simply to Plymouth. Green is generally seen as unlucky for a football team. Argyle have the distinction of being the only club to have originally opted for the colour, and kept it through thick and thin, though in 2001 they came perilously close to a white strip with the green element reduced to a few pinstripes. Fan power soon forced them to see the error of their ways. Plymouth's identity took a bit of a knock with the promotion of Boston United from the Conference, who share their 'Pilgrims' nickname.

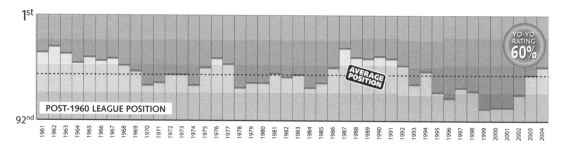

1st

YO-YO RATING 60%

AVERAGE POSITION

POST-1960 LEAGUE POSITION

92nd

1961 1962 1963 1964 1965 1966 1967 1968 1969 1970 1971 1972 1973 1974 1975 1976 1977 1978 1979 1980 1981 1982 1983 1984 1985 1986 1987 1988 1989 1990 1991 1992 1993 1994 1995 1996 1997 1998 1999 2000 2001 2002 2003 2004

PROGRESS REPORT

Plymouth have a reasonably static historical average – poised in the top half of Level Two. Any variations have quickly been evened out. Twice since 1960 they have escaped to Level One only to be dragged back down soon after. The worst spell has come comparatively lately with four seasons in Level Three from 1998. But an ingrained habit of not being able to win outside Devon was finally laid to rest with the appointment of Paul Sturrock in late 2000. At the end of 2001-2002, Argyle were promoted as Champions with an unprecedented 10 away wins under their belt. By 2004, they were riding high in Level Two, when Sturrock was poached by Southampton. If they can hang on in Level One for just a single season, it will be their best spell for a generation.

```
...Beat a Santos team that included Pele...
   ...Nearly became 'Plymouth Pickwick'...
...Used to give free tickets to residents of psychiatric hospital...
```

RIVALS

In 2003, Plymouth were in the apparently happy position of seeing their neighbours and historical rivals, Exeter City, disappear from the Football League altogether. Cautious gloating was the order of the day, though in the back of their minds was the fact that it demonstrated Devon and football didn't necessarily go together. Exeter's shenanigans with Uri Gellar caused mirth with Argyle fans, though for most of their history Argyle have had good reason for seeing themselves as a cut above both their Devon neighbours. In 1999, however, for the first time in their history, they finished in a lower league position than both Exeter and Torquay. Otherwise, Plymouth's good record against both has generally taken the sting out of any ill-feeling from their point of view. West Country derbies have never been known for their off or on-the-field passion, and have remained both low key and irregular. It may be the case that the strength of regional identity is such that inter-town squabbles are kept to a minimum. Nearest neighbours Torquay have always been off the radar for Plymouth, despite the towns being markedly different. Torquay has gained a reputation as a haven for northerners wearing gaudy jewellery with nefarious reasons for leaving their home towns. Barring an Auto-Windscreens victory, Torquay haven't beaten Plymouth since 1972.

PERFORMANCE AGAINST RIVALS
BURNLEY

WON 19%
LOST 43%
DRAWN 38%

BURNLEY

Burnley have picked up a ragbag of rivals, locally to them and others further afield – most of them not directly connected with actual results. But Plymouth's recent loathing of them stems from two humiliations at the hand of the Lancastrians. The first, in 1994, in the play-off semi-final was galling because Burnley had finished the season a full 12 points behind. Following a 0-0 draw away, the second leg at Home Park turned to disaster. An early lead was squandered, with Burnley running out 3-1 winners.

Four years later, it was Burnley who sent them back to Level Three. Rubbing salt into the wounds, Burnley's pitch invasion at the end of the game was seen as unnecessarily hostile.

SUPPORTERS' VFM 98%

Being of a similar size and within bearable travelling distance, both Bristol clubs are named as rivals. Older fans remember the 'battle of the ports' with Portsmouth.

BRISTOL CITY

BRISTOL ROVERS

'YOUR GROUND'S TOO BIG FOR YOU!' RATING

LOVE/HATE

Tommy Tynam's 120 goals in six 1980s' seasons guarantee him long-term hero status.

A Plymouth fans' message board ran a 'Who would you like to punch in the mouth?' thread – mostly consisting of a variety of annoying minor celebs – though *Rupert Lowe*,  the Southampton chairman, received plenty of name checks. Accused of doing to Plymouth what Tottenham did to them (in poaching Glen Hoddle), the alarm that Sturrock's departure might lead to an end of the good times is understandable.

CHANTS

As the most southern league town in the country, Plymouth are entitled to sing

'You dirty northern bastards'

at everyone – including, as they have been known to, Torquay United, the second most southern team.

DOH!!

In 2000, ex-chairman Dan McCauley, prickly with the fans at the best of times, had a notorious run-in with fans ringing a Talksport chatshow. Berating many of them for their stupidity, he suggested to one that he must be a member of the National Front.

ATTENDANCE AS A PERCENTAGE OF CAPACITY 63%

PORTSMOUTH

Recommended website: **www.pompeyweb.co.uk**

WHO ARE YA?

Portsmouth fans are frequently named as the most vocal in the land - even in defeat. In Level One their away support invariably gets into four figures, with the home fans guaranteed to get stiff competition. Supporters lucky enough to see their team thrash Portsmouth are frequently amazed that they are out-sung even when the game is decided. Portsmouth's genuine belief that the level of singing can affect the result probably stemmed from one of their many escape acts, whilst in Level One in 1998. Able to keep up the monotone of 'Alan Ball's blue and white army' for the entire second half and beyond, it started a series of ultra-high volume matches that saw the side pull clear of relegation on the final day. It may be a regional thing: Southampton have a similar vocal reputation. The level of fanaticism for Pompey may derive from something of a social siege mentality. The town, essentially a down-to-earth navy port, is slightly at odds with the surrounding prosperity of the southern seaside stretch.

IN and AROUND

The term Pompey is used as a name of the town and football club. It doesn't derive from the word Portsmouth itself, but other theories differ. It might have originated from a group of Portsmouth sailors scaling 'Pompey's Pillar' in Egypt in 1781, or come from the name of a captured French ship ' La Pompee' that was later to stand guard over Portsmouth harbour.

Chairman Milan Mandaric's large bank balance isn't the only reason he gains the respect of the fans. In keeping with a run of genuinely popular South Coast chairman, his reputation has been helped by a willingness to meet with and chat casually to fans. His one eccentricity was to register the company as 'Portsmouth City FC'. Amongst the club's most devoted fans is John Westwood, accompanied by a bell (!) that he brings to most games. Courtesy of deedpoll, he is now John Portsmouth Football Club Westwood.

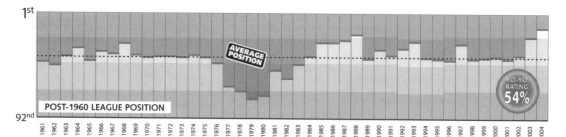

1st

AVERAGE POSITION

POST-1960 LEAGUE POSITION

92nd

YO-YO RATING 54%

1961 1962 1963 1964 1965 1966 1967 1968 1969 1970 1971 1972 1973 1974 1975 1976 1977 1978 1979 1980 1981 1982 1983 1984 1985 1986 1987 1988 1989 1990 1991 1992 1993 1994 1995 1996 1997 1998 1999 2000 2001 2002 2003 2004

PROGRESS REPORT

Portsmouth have basically been a middling Level One team, with very brief forays into the top flight. Much of the last forty years has been taken up by a series of relegation battles to prevent slipping any further. The plodding along was punctuated by a decline in the mid-seventies that saw them reach the nadir of mid-table in Level Three followed by a rapid rise to the Premiership in 1987. But over-spending in the top-flight plunged them into administration when relegated. But saviour Chairman Milan Mandaric poured cash into the club, culminating in promotion to the Premiership for 2003-04, soured slightly at the end by a majestic bust-up with manager Harry Redknapp.

```
...Were involved in England's only recorded match without a corner (1931)...
   ...Won first match in which players were numbered 1 to 11(1939)...
            ...Originally played in salmon pink...
```

RIVALS

About the only thing that Southampton and Portsmouth fans have in common is the wish for the rivalry to be seen as serious as the more public spats, such as between Arsenal and Spurs. In local folklore, the rivalry dates back to the breaking of a dockers strike by workers in Southampton during the depression of the 20s, much to the annoyance of Portsmouth workers who stood firm. There is an apocryphal tale that the scabs were named 'Southampton Community Union Members' resulting in the unfortunate/apt acronym, SCUM.

SOUTHAMPTON

Although aped by many club's fans, Portsmouth have a strong aversion to the word Southampton - 'an obscenity to all Pompey'. Dubbed Scumhampton, the proper name of the 'northern neighbours' is considered too strong to print. The first outbreak of actual violence at matches probably dates back to 1969.

An unfortunate set of circumstances has led to the rivalry becoming so intense. Justifiably, Portsmouth consider themselves equally as large and important a club, but Southampton's unusually elevated league status is clearly a running sore. Portsmouth's worst moments have tended to coincide with their best. 1976 particularly sticks in the throat. Whilst in Level One, Southampton's 1-0 victory at Fratton Park consigned Pompey to relegation. Within weeks Southampton were the darlings of virtually everyone outside Manchester, having remarkably picked up the FA Cup. Oddly, the goalscorer of that day, Bobby Stokes, was born in Portsmouth and moved to his 'home' club shortly afterwards, but was given a very mixed reception.

SUPPORTERS' VFM 84%

PERFORMANCE AGAINST RIVALS
SOUTHAMPTON

WON 19%
LOST 57%
DRAWN 24%

Pompey's case against Southampton, though not easy, is heartfelt. They point to the fact that Southampton have failed to capitalise on their 'good fortune'. Portsmouth, they argue, were historically the major club in the region, with Southampton stuck hopelessly for 50 years mucking around in lower divisions. Their one honour, the 1976 FA Cup is not much to show for 120 years of their existence, comparing unfavourably with Pompey's three major honours, hence their 'superiority' is a temporary blip and not based on performance.

If anything, the rivalry has intensified through lack of actual fixtures - there have only been seven league and cup meetings of the sides in the 28 years since Southampton won the FA Cup - most of them marred by trouble of some sort. In March 2004, the fixture at Fratton Park led to what the police described as 'large scale public disorder', with bottles of ammonia discovered before the match. On the field, the 1-0 victory was the first home win Portsmouth had inflicted on the old enemy for 41 years.

CHANTS

Now much copied, Portsmouth originated the 'bell peal' chant of 'Play up Pompey, Pompey play up', based on the chimes of the city's Guildhall clock. The song was first noted in 1900, and is often cited as the most irritating for the opposition to have to endure.

LOVE/HATE

'Anyone who has ever played for Southampton, or anything that is the same colour as their strip'. Presumably sales of Mcewans Export are sluggish locally.

HATE

DOH!!

Portsmouth's Noel Blake scored possibly the most farcical own goal ever, when, in 1984 v Wimbledon he rolled a ball from near the halfway line back to keeper, Alan Knight. Knight was more interested in nursing an injury and never even saw the ball trickle past him, and only realised it had gone in when he wondered what the Dons fans were laughing at.

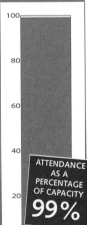

'YOUR GROUND'S TOO BIG FOR YOU!'
RATING

100
80
60
40
20
0

ATTENDANCE AS A PERCENTAGE OF CAPACITY
99%

PORT VALE

Recommended website: **www.onevalefan.co.uk**

WHO ARE YA?

Port Vale's obscure claim as the only side in the League not to be named after a 'proper' town or area is muddled further by a convoluted early history. No part of the phrase 'Port Vale' can be discovered on a map of the Stoke area, though their early life as Burslem Port Vale provides a clue. Typically they weren't actually based in the market town of Burslem at the time, and there are distinct doubts as to whether the club that was formed in 1876 can strictly be considered the same outfit that plies its trade today. The mists don't clear until 1919 when they took the place of the disgraced Leeds City. Vale nearly suffered the same fate, having been expelled from the League in 1965 for paying players illegal bonuses, but the FA had a change of heart and lessened their sentence to a slapped wrist.

CELEBRITY FANS

PHIL TAYLOR
Darts Player

Vale have never topped fifth place in Level One, but had their best chance to better that in latter years under the reign of manager John Rudge whose 15-year stint from 1984 saw Vale progress from Level Three to Level One and go to Wembley three times. He developed a talent-spotting habit that was the toast of the lower leagues, netting Vale very tidy profits along the way. This made his sacking in 1999 all the more gutting for fans, especially as the board's statement of appreciation amounted to a stuffy two-paragraph memo. After his departure, Vale slid into the buffers, going back down to their natural home in Level Two in 2001.

IN and AROUND

Pointedly, Rudge, the archetypal footballing gentleman, was immediately offered the top job at Stoke City, but turned it down in favour of becoming their director of football, as he considered the move would be seen as a kick in the teeth for Vale fans who had given him a spirited send-off.

Burslem is home to a prestigious arts school, attended by famous ceramicist, Clarice Cliff. Its website has the mildly rib-tickling URL, www.schoolofart.co.uk

Ex-chairman Bill Bell survived a period of being public enemy number one, not helping his cause in 2001 by ditching the club's traditional black shorts in favour of an all-white kit, in an effort to emulate Real Madrid – a trick successfully pulled off by Leeds United in the 60s. Since it coincided with relegation, Vale fans were doubly unimpressed and the black was reintroduced.

Vale fans have become slightly exasperated at the association of ex-Take That front man, Robbie Williams, with the club. In his rise to galactic superstardom, Williams proudly sported a Vale shirt on stage – a fact that helped sell the said item to teeny-boppers around the globe. But with the club up for sale and back in Level Two, they weren't such a sexy proposition, and Mr Williams was suddenly noticeably absent from Vale Park and stayed silent on the matter of his loyalties.

Vale have had a craze for fans turning up for matches in kilts – although as Vale Park is the second highest ground in the League, it can get decidedly chilly around the Potteries.

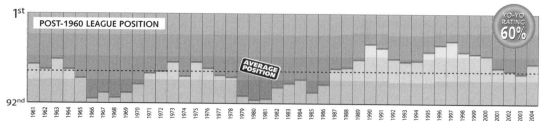

POST-1960 LEAGUE POSITION

1st ... 92nd

AVERAGE POSITION

YO-YO RATING 60%

1961 1962 1963 1964 1965 1966 1967 1968 1969 1970 1971 1972 1973 1974 1975 1976 1977 1978 1979 1980 1981 1982 1983 1984 1985 1986 1987 1988 1989 1990 1991 1992 1993 1994 1995 1996 1997 1998 1999 2000 2001 2002 2003 2004

PROGRESS REPORT

A somewhat suspicious pattern of being a 'one man club'. Before the arrival of John Rudge, Vale were embarked on a rocky ride in the lower two divisions. Their trip to Level One neatly coincides with his time with the club. The net effect is a post-1960 average planted in the middle of Level Two.

```
      ...Achieved highest number of points for a non-promoted team (89 in 1993)...
...The roof on the Cauldwell Stand was purchased from Chester City when they moved from
    Sealand Road...Fixture backlog in 2001 saw them playing six games in 11 days...
```

RIVALS

STOKE CITY

Everyone assumes that the Stoke/Port Vale derby is one of the most hotly contested in the League, a view supported by the degree of trouble there has been in previous meetings. But, very oddly, fans of both sides appear to be reluctant to admit its existence. The reason for this peculiarity lies in the fluctuating balance of power between the two. It's fair to say that as the second oldest club in Britain and a reasonably successful record in the 70s, Stoke City had little to fear from their neighbours. Port Vale feel their development was badly hampered by them, particularly as their early attempt at a youth development scheme, under Stanley Matthews in 1965, flopped, as the majority of the town's promising young players only had eyes for a contract with Stoke.

Partially accepting their lot, Port Vale had little to get excited about until they achieved promotion to Level Two in 1989. There they met a disintegrating Stoke for the first time since 1956. By the end of the 1990 season, Stoke were in complete turmoil having gone down to the Third, much to the mirth of the local 'minnows' who had no qualms about mocking them relentlessly. But they spoke a bit too soon and found themselves meeting up again in 1992, with the unfortunate (for the police) quirk of being drawn to play each other in the FA Cup. The meetings were marked with widespread disorder, including a mass breaking of almost all Burslem's pub windows.

SUPPORTERS' VFM 49%

PERFORMANCE AGAINST RIVALS STOKE CITY

WON 32% LOST 21% DRAWN 47%

CREWE ALEXANDRA

Although 1990 was only the second time that Vale had played in a higher division, their fans appeared to grow comfortable with the idea that they were now the top club in Stoke, a feeling that is still widespread today, despite them being leapfrogged finally in 2002. This leaves the almost unique state of affairs that both feel markedly superior to one another. As is the pattern with other rivalries, this leads to a sort of detached indifference.

But Port Vale continue to be racked with worry over the possibility of a merger. In 2003, the supporters' group took over the club, but the threat of a second dose of administration constantly looms, with the prospect of a buy out by Stoke's Icelandic owners making the fans queasier still. It is agreed that such an outcome can result in only one thing, a move to the Britannia Stadium, with the eventual swallowing up of Port Vale entirely. In this respect, Stoke fans could turn out to be their saviours, as inevitably, they are just as opposed to any reorganisation.

LOVE/HATE

HATE

Not entirely happy with their own big celeb name, Port Vale understandably start throwing soft objects at the TV whenever *Nick Hancock* appears. In the words of one fan, the high profile Stoke supporter must be considered "a terrible advert for the town".

CHANTS

Confused away supporters have been known to put words to the Big Ben chimes:

'Where is Port Vale?...you don't exist'

'YOUR GROUND'S TOO BIG FOR YOU!'
RATING

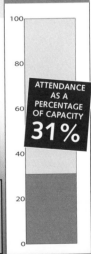

ATTENDANCE AS A PERCENTAGE OF CAPACITY

31%

DOH!!

Building of the Lorne Street Stand started in 1998 and was immediately hampered by the discovery of an old mine shaft. As the club's debt worsened, work had to be abandoned completely leaving one half open to spectators, the other, nothing more than a sad steel framework. By late 2004, hopes were once again raised that work could recommence, especially as fans had given generously to a previous 'buy a brick' campaign.

137

PRESTON NORTH END

A.K.A.
PRESTON NOB END

Recommended website: **www.lilywhites.net**

WHO ARE YA?

Preston's 19th century history is of great importance to the club, particularly as the 20th century was nowhere near as kind to them. But they appeared to 'forget' their anniversary, celebrating it in 1981-82, whereas the game's historians might have expected it a year before. Preston might have assumed that their record of winning the 1889 Championship without losing a game would remain unbroken – until Arsenal came along in 2003-2004, playing nearly twice as many games. Preston's official tourist information website proudly lists the football club's greatest claim to fame, that they hold the English game's scoring record with their 26-0 victory over Hyde in the first round of the FA Cup in 1887.

CELEBRITY FANS
ANDREW FLINTOFF
England Cricketer

However, the factoid receives a lower billing than the essential information that Preston was home to the first Spar '8 til late' shop. Preston's one moment of glory in the last 100 years was when beating the then mighty Huddersfield in the 1938 Cup Final. Before the game, a BBC radio commentator had fatefully promised to eat his hat if Preston won. The BBC broadcast some munching noises afterwards.

IN and AROUND

A people v planners battle is raging over Preston's enormous bus station, due for demolition to make way for 'yuppie' flats. A rare example of popular 60s' architecture, some hardy residents have plans to squat in front of the bulldozers.

Under David Moyes, Preston enjoyed their best period for a generation, pulling up from Level Two to achieve a play-off place in Level One in 2001. But with Moyes spirited away to save Everton from the Premiership drop, a downturn has set in, much to the chagrin of fans, who are beginning to gang up on chairman Derek Shaw. Every statement and financial report is being pored over in forensic detail in an attempt to uncover anything amiss; usually the first symptom of a full-scale rebellion.

David Beckham played five games on loan for the club in 1995 – an attempt by Alex Ferguson to toughen up the teenager. Becks scored twice for them, one, a trademark free kick, and could have been snapped up for £1 million if Preston had the cash. It is said that, during his black moment following the Simione sending-off saga, Preston would have been the only team in Britain (apart from Manchester United) where he would have got a good reception, as he had gone out of his way to say nice things about his previous club.

Preston installed an artificial pitch in 1986, famed for its carpet-like appearance. Never popular with visiting teams and only slightly less hated by fans, by 1994 the club had become sick of it and had a celebratory final game on plastic (or whatever it was), at the end of which supporters poured onto the pitch and did a decent job of ripping the thing up themselves. Like others who had artificial surfaces, Preston strenuously deny that they derived any advantage from it. However, an impartial look at their results from the period would suggest otherwise. The key is in the ratio of games they won at home to those won away. Generally, home wins account for slightly less than twice the number of wins away from home, but in Preston's case during the period, they clocked up a suspiciously disproportionate number of home wins, i.e. 12 home victories in 1991-92 and just three wins on their travels.

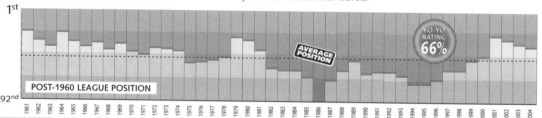

1st

YO-YO RATING 66%

AVERAGE POSITION

POST-1960 LEAGUE POSITION

92nd

1961 1962 1963 1964 1965 1966 1967 1968 1969 1970 1971 1972 1973 1974 1975 1976 1977 1978 1979 1980 1981 1982 1983 1984 1985 1986 1987 1988 1989 1990 1991 1992 1993 1994 1995 1996 1997 1998 1999 2000 2001 2002 2003 2004

PROGRESS REPORT

Relegation from the old First Division in 1961 gave way to a gentle decline, getting dramatically worse towards the end, with a 23rd position in Level Three in 1986. Moyes steered them to Premiership contenders by 2001, but that appeared to be their peak, as they had three progressively worse finishes after that.

```
...Fielded Britain's first black footballer, Arthur Wharton, in 1886...
    ...Have had the longest time at one ground of any League team...
        ...First club to do the League and Cup double...
```

RIVALS

It's fitting that one of the earliest incidents of trouble at a football ground dates back to a match against Blackpool at Deepdale in 1905, in which a drunk and disorderly 70-year-old lady was arrested. As former leading lights, Preston and Blackpool have been reduced to bickering like a pair of old women over which of the two is going to take over the world. In some ways, Preston's concentration on Blackpool is quite praiseworthy as they have been out of contact since 2000. A particular source of scorn towards everyone at 'Gloomfilled Road' was Blackpool's LDV Vans Trophy win in 2002. As far as Preston are concerned, it brings shame and humiliation on the Seasiders as even the competing teams "don't take it seriously" – suggesting you have to be real mugs for even turning up. And as for the placard spotted at the welcome home party bearing the words "Preston – Look and Weep"; clearly a pitiful statement of the club's meagre ambition. And so it goes on…Matthews was hopelessly in Tom Finney's shadow…Matthews never scored…the Blackpool stand named after him couldn't hold a busload of midgets.

BLACKPOOL

SUPPORTERS' VFM 88%

PERFORMANCE AGAINST RIVALS BLACKPOOL

WON 39%

LOST 36%

DRAWN 25%

Despite the current day bitterness, there is plenty of evidence that the Matthews/Finney days saw a large contingent of floating supporters who would travel from all over the Northwest to see the two greats play, without a particular sense of loyalty towards their respective clubs. In the 1950s, coaches were laid on from Preston to both Blackburn and Blackpool when North End were not at home. In those days, Lancashire solidarity was everything, and there is still a sizeable minority who refuse to dislike Blackpool.

BURNLEY

Feelings towards their nearest League neighbours, Blackburn, are surprisingly neutral, but Burnley are motoring up the hate list. Here, the explanation is that they are not a Lancashire club at all, but should 'go back' to Yorkshire. Despite Burnley's protests that they only have hostile intent towards Blackburn, that didn't stop 200 of them running amok in the centre of Preston in 2002

LOVE/HATE

Sir Tom Finney ♡, currently Preston's life president, has a rather fine 'splash' statue in his honour outside Deepdale. Essentially a sculpture within a fountain, it depicts a Finney tackle during an actual game at Chelsea in 1956 where the pitch was waterlogged.

CHANTS

The chant that never was became immortalised in the title of a fanzine:

'Hyde, Hyde, what's the score?'

'YOUR GROUND'S TOO BIG FOR YOU!' RATING

100

80

60

40

ATTENDANCE AS A PERCENTAGE OF CAPACITY 69%

20

0

DOH!!

Preston's mascot, Deepdale Duck, used to be a sorry looking character in a costume that seemed as though it might have had a variety of other small creatures residing within its feathers. But having appeared to boost attendances in reserve games, he had something of a makeover for his first team appearances, though his outrageously large feet aren't suited to the mascots' Grand National where he has a supremely poor record.

In 1995, a Preston fan at Deepdale nearly landed himself a highly collectable and valuable item during the warm-up. Clasping the match programme and a pen, the fan managed to get David Beckham's attention.

He asked Becks to get him the autograph of fellow Preston player, Alan Smart.

QUEENS PARK RANGERS

AKA
QPHa

Recommended website: **www.queensparkrangersfc.com**

WHO ARE YA?

The usual wisdom that geographically isolated clubs get into the worst financial scrapes hardly applies to QPR. Close to BBC headquarters in Shepherd's Bush, the club is sitting on a juicy piece of real estate, though the Loftus Road site is a bit too small to really set the pulses of Tesco and friends racing. Its tightness has proved a virtue in an age of cavernous super-stadia and, when full, leads to a super-charged atmosphere. The trouble is, Rs' fans have spent so much time complaining about their own players, managers and directors, they don't have much energy to shout at anyone else. In turning Loftus Road to all-seater, the designers weren't very generous with the legroom - and though there are no reported cases of deep-vein thrombosis, there is the added hassle of trying to get in, as there tends to be a snail's pace procession into the away end.

In 1981, the BBC's *Tomorrow's World* carried a feature previewing the installation of a revolutionary Omniturf surface at Loftus Road, one that supposedly accurately mimicked the natural qualities of grass and would save clubs from the drain of winter weather postponements. FIFA suspected it might give the home side a distinct advantage and ordered QPR to play UEFA Cup ties at Highbury. QPRs' home form during the life on the pitch was suspiciously good compared to that on their travels. Its absurdly high bounce and habit of giving players multiple burns did not endear the club to neutrals and, fraying at the edges and looking like a bit of tatty carpet, the thing was ripped up in 1988.

> **In and Around**
> Queens Park itself is actually in South Kensal.

Considering the last 20 years, you have to pinch yourself when you remember how good QPR actually were. In 1975-76, they were within a whisker of picking up the Championship with one of the most thrilling sides put together by any British club. QPR were sitting pretty at the top of the table with Liverpool needing to beat Wolves in the last game of the season. 1-0 down with 13 minutes to go, Liverpool poured forward to end up 3-1 winners, overtaking a side that, with the likes of Stan Bowles and Gerry Francis, was a great favourite of neutrals - and did a passable impression of the Dutch national side of the 1970s.

Following relegation from the Premiership in 1996, a series of almost comic book disasters on and off the pitch left them in Level Two - with a catalogue of ludicrous rescue plans. In making an offer to buy Loftus Road, Ron Noades drew accusations that his intentions were to take his club, Brentford, and QPR off to Heathrow to form a newly merged team. By the time Wimbledon came knocking at the door with the dreaded 'm' word, QPR fans were ready to keep the interlopers from the door with sit-down protests and some pre-planned pitch invasions. On the field, the team was beset with a string of plodders past their best with questionable commitment, unlike the fans, who through the formation of supporters' groups had clung together through adversity, making them some of the most committed, though angst-ridden, in London.

It was with a slight twist of irony that QPR got (partially) out of the mire. The club came out of administration in 2002, thanks to a few million quid from Panama (!) and valuable revenues from Mr Al Fayed's disliked Fulham, who were forced into a groundshare to get Craven Cottage up to scratch.

CELEBRITY FANS
GLEN MATLOCK - Sex Pistols
MICK JONES - The Clash
BILL BAILEY - Comedian

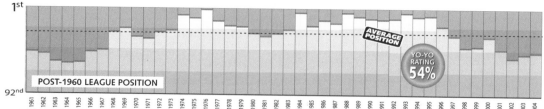

POST-1960 LEAGUE POSITION

1st

92nd

1961 1962 1963 1964 1965 1966 1967 1968 1969 1970 1971 1972 1973 1974 1975 1976 1977 1978 1979 1980 1981 1982 1983 1984 1985 1986 1987 1988 1989 1990 1991 1992 1993 1994 1995 1996 1997 1998 1999 2000 2001 2002 2003 2004

AVERAGE POSITION

YO-YO RATING 54%

PROGRESS REPORT

Until the mid-80s QPR were the sexiest thing in West London - in marked contrast to the hoolie infested Chelsea and Fulham, who were sinking without a trace. The rot set in with relegation from the Premiership in 1996, a take-over that saw Loftus Road being shared with Wasps Rugby Union Club and an awful transfer policy.

Against the background of almost incessant talk of mergers, sit-ins and fan unrest, QPR slipped to Level Two where they stayed for an agonising three seasons, enduring a period of administration, before finally escaping to the relatively calm waters of Level One in 2004.

```
...The most nomadic league team, with 18 changes of ground...Forgot to enter FA Cup (1927)...
...Current pitch is 5% artificial...
```

RIVALS

With the possible exception of Fulham, QPR may be the largest club not to have any deep-seated rivalries with anyone. This can annoy their fans as it gives the impression that they simply aren't enough of a threat to dislike. In the 70s the walk to and from Loftus Road, past the down at heel White City Estate, was one of the more nerve-wracking for visitors as QPR had a significant hooligan element. But as their fortunes slumped the club fell back to its hard-core fan base - not like others a neanderthal element, but a relatively gentile bunch.

FULHAM

Before 1967, when QPR were a very minor force, fellow minnows Brentford were natural rivals. Success in the 70s allowed Chelsea and Fulham to come into the picture but when QPR plummeted they were again left with only Brentford spitting blood at them by which time they couldn't lower themselves to 'small fry'. In turn, these days QPR are totally ignored by Chelsea and not really of much interest to tenants Fulham either.

BRENTFORD

Fulham survived an awful patch similar to QPRs' that does draw a degree of admiration (through gritted teeth). But now, with Al Fayed bankrolling them, black and white scarves are everywhere. Of irritation to QPR is that they have picked up a lot of the floating Surrey support - a significant catchment area that tends to go wherever the silverware is likely to turn up. The combined fortunes of Al Fayed and Abramovich have seen their neighbours reach the stratosphere - a sore point when QPR were recently having to let 20 players go on free transfers.

Watford are not particularly keen on QPR, though most of their energies are concentrated on Luton. In the words of one fan, QPR 'had a go' at hating Charlton, but it 'didn't work out'.

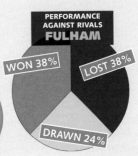

PERFORMANCE AGAINST RIVALS
FULHAM

WON 38%

LOST 38%

DRAWN 24%

SUPPORTERS'
VFM
71%

LOVE/HATE

When Brentford started a chant of 'Stand up if you hate *Ron Noades*'. QPR fans were more than happy to oblige. Aside from the takeover/merger wrangling, Noades didn't endear himself to QPR by objecting to them trying to bring in players whilst in administration.

CHANTS

A comment on Louis Saha's distinctive headgear
'He's got an innertube . . . on his head'
was swiftly followed by
'Saha's got a puncture',
when the then Fulham striker fell over.

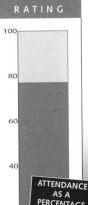

'YOUR GROUND'S TOO BIG FOR YOU!'
R A T I N G

100

80

60

40

20

0

ATTENDANCE AS A PERCENTAGE OF CAPACITY
77%

DOH!!

A feast of dodgy signings to choose from, but the one that still gives Rs' fans nightmares, is Mark Hately's attempt at taking the centre forward's role. Desperate to turn things around, the sight of Hately clumping around looking as if he'd rather be elsewhere made fans despair.

READING

Recommended website: **www.royals.org**

WHO ARE YA?

Reading are about the only club in the land who can claim to have had a re-birth because of the late 80s' economic depression. Local squillionaire, Jon Madejski, became that way thanks to the sudden surge in used car sales as the recession started to bite. The mag he published, Autotrader, became the bible of the second-hand trade, allowing him to indulge in some free-form, though never reckless, spending on Reading FC. His credentials as a bona-fide fan are less than perfect, in fact it is generally accepted that his bankrolling of the football club has more to do with his allegiance to the town rather than any great love of football, or sport in general.

CELEBRITY FANS
KATE WINSLETT
Actress
ANDREW LLOYD WEBBER
Composer of Musicals

In history, Reading have never been much more than a very moderate Level Two and Level Three outfit, with, in Elm Park, a ground to match. Although named after the chairman, Madstad, as the Madejski Stadium has come to be known, is a high-tech wonderland, which is possibly the best outside the Premiership. Opened when the side was in Level Two in 1998, attendances have blossomed until levelling out in 2003. They certainly needed to – the Madejski's 25,000 capacity was wildly above the average gates and with a usual turnout of 13,000, remains eerily empty for home matches.

IN and AROUND

Reading holds an annual 'beard day'.

The club's first attempt at modernisation was the attempted ditching of the nickname 'The Biscuitmen', bequeathed to them by H&C biccie manufacturers. The fans chose 'The Royals' as a reference to the county's close relationship with the monarch, i.e. Windsor Castle, but older fans stuck their heels in and stubbornly refused to adopt the name.

Reading's ability to claw its way into the headlines was, for much of the 90s, limited to reporting the antics of Uri Gellar, who indulged in a number of tiresome public demonstrations of his supernatural abilities to affect the club's fortunes. In the face of a welter of evidence to the contrary, Geller seems to be under the illusion that the club 'did well' under his spiritual guidance and lost its way since he turned his attention to Exeter City. (Exeter were relegated to the Conference in 2003).

At that point, utterly starved of any cup success, fans organised an attempt to rig The Observer's poll of the 100 greatest sporting moments. Unfortunately, Reading's victory over Luton in the Simod Cup final of 1988 wasn't deemed quite worthy of inclusion. By 1995, they rightly should have been celebrating a far bigger prize. But finishing second in Level One wasn't enough to claim a Premiership place as the League structure was undergoing yet another minor adjustment.

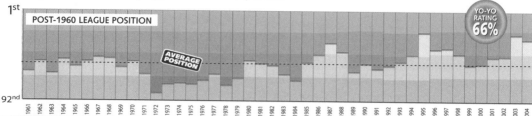

1st

POST-1960 LEAGUE POSITION

YO-YO RATING 66%

AVERAGE POSITION

92nd

1961 1962 1963 1964 1965 1966 1967 1968 1969 1970 1971 1972 1973 1974 1975 1976 1977 1978 1979 1980 1981 1982 1983 1984 1985 1986 1987 1988 1989 1990 1991 1992 1993 1994 1995 1996 1997 1998 1999 2000 2001 2002 2003 2004

PROGRESS REPORT

Reading's progress to within shouting distance of Level One play-offs in 2004 can be traced all the way back to their low point of 16th in Level Three, back in 1972. A series of very jagged peaks and troughs since have almost imperceivably sent them towards the promised land. Madejski's aim to steer them straight to the Premiership came unstuck with relegation from Level One in 1998, but they were transformed into genuine Premiership hopefuls by 2003.

```
...There is a dead hamster buried under the southern goal...
...George Best, Sir Matt Busby and Martin Peters are ex-players...
...No other league team ends in a 'g'...
```

RIVALS

Despite not exactly being in the sticks, Reading, as Berkshire's only League team, are 30 miles away from any serious competition, giving them a densely populated catchment area from which to draw in the masses. Unfortunately, aided by a speedy rail route into Paddington, it is suspected that a lot of potential Reading faithful have drifted off to the big London teams instead. It is a measure of how far they've come that long-term fans bemoan the demise of Aldershot, their natural geographical rivals.

OXFORD ☠☠☠☠☠

Otherwise, Reading have largely been frozen out of hostilities between Swindon and Oxford. Younger Reading fans fantasise that the Reading/Swindon rivalry is of huge national importance, but Swindon and most of the Reading fans know otherwise. There

SWINDON ☠☠☠☠☠

have been isolated violent incidents between Reading and Oxford, and the visit of Bristol City is not a quiet affair with Reading being easy to get to.

There is a nod of recognition towards Bournemouth's dislike of them, but as far as Reading are concerned, they are wasting their time. The most bitter atmosphere at any Royals' game in recent memory was probably the visit of Wolves to the old Elm Park in 1996. Due entirely to the presence of ex-manager Mark McGhee, Wolves became a temporary rival. The previous hero was given a send off from 11,000 fans in full voice chanting something along the lines of 'Go away, Mark McGhee'.

WYCOMBE ☠☠☠☠☠

Wycombe enjoy pouring scorn on Reading, but as befits a relatively new League club, Reading don't give back much in return, even admitting to 'secretly liking them'.

SUPPORTERS' VFM 100%

PERFORMANCE AGAINST RIVALS OXFORD

- WON 36%
- LOST 58%
- DRAWN 6%

LOVE/HATE

Fans acknowledge that without *John Madejski* ♡, Reading would still be plying their trade in the lower Leagues, or not at all. They can occasionally be heard to moan that his other expensive loves, fine art and classic cars, could possibly take second billing in his life when just a few more quid might guarantee Premiership action.

Mark McGhee was the architect of Reading's revival in the early 90s that saw them winning the Level Two title in 1994. Midway through the following season, after expressing his apparently heartfelt wish to stay at the club, he suddenly decided that Leicester were more to his liking.

CHANTS

'Bill Oddie, Bill Oddie, Rub your beard all over my body'

In deference to the king of the beardies.

'YOUR GROUND'S TOO BIG FOR YOU!' RATING

ATTENDANCE AS A PERCENTAGE OF CAPACITY **63%**

DOH!!

The designers of Reading's change strip of 1992 seemed to ignore the principle that it should necessarily be a significantly different design to the first team kit. Reading's choice at the beginning of the season was between blue and white hoops and the blue and yellow hoops. The result was total confusion when they met another team playing in blue. When up against Wigan and Huddersfield, the referee ordered that Reading should don the opposition's change strip.

ROCHDALE

Recommended website: **www.rochdaleafc.com**

WHO ARE YA?

If the planning process finally grinds its way to a conclusion, it will take around half an hour on a swish Metrolink tram to travel from the largest club in the world to England's most obscure football outpost. Already bursting at the seams with professional clubs, Greater Manchester is not the sort of place where it's easy to gain a new generation of supporters if you're one of the minor players on the scene – and they don't come any more minor than Rochdale FC.

Though possessing the worst long-term record of any of the 92 League clubs, Rochdale's survival deserves plenty of credit. Good relations with the local council have seen them avoid the usual ground difficulties and despite attendances best described as derisory, they have experienced reasonable financial stability. The authorities did embark on one bit of monumental bad taste, renaming Spotland 'The Denehurst Park Stadium'. The change was simply ignored.

CELEBRITY FANS
TOMMY CANNON
Of 'Cannon and Ball' comic fame is not held in high regard after he resigned from the Rochdale board.

IN and AROUND

The National Grid's pylon ZP 226, just off the A680, is a classic for electricity transmission enthusiasts. It is the only one in Britain, and possibly the world, that is painted pink.

Rochdale are permanent fixtures in Level Three. At the start of each season, the aim is generally that of mid-table respectability, something that has become more of an imperative with the recent automatic demotion of two sides, rather than one. In 2002, they had one of their rare sorties up the table to finish fifth, qualifying for a nail-biting but unsuccessful 4-3 aggregate defeat in the play-off semi-finals against Rushden and Diamonds.

Their giant-killing acts have, strangely, come mostly against the same team. Coventry City just can't stop losing to them – in the FA Cup in 1920, 1971 and 2003, the League Cup in 1991, and in their only league meeting in 1926. Rochdale have boasted internationals Leo Bertos of New Zealand and Paddy McCourt of Northern Ireland, as well as Marcus Hahnemann, whose status of being the USA's third choice keeper was overshadowed by his startling resemblance to Fabian Barthez.

Unable to cover expenses from gate receipts, the club has occasionally dreamed up some interesting commercial wheezes, including, controversially, nude female models for its merchandise catalogue. The commercial manager admitted the club had received complaints, lamely explaining "but we took the decision to use the girls because sex sells".

Visiting fans appreciate the authentic football flavour of Spotland and it has been voted the best away-day in the League. Apparently the pies are top-notch as well.

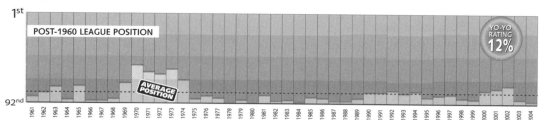

1st

POST-1960 LEAGUE POSITION

YO-YO RATING 12%

AVERAGE POSITION

92nd

1961 1962 1963 1964 1965 1966 1967 1968 1969 1970 1971 1972 1973 1974 1975 1976 1977 1978 1979 1980 1981 1982 1983 1984 1985 1986 1987 1988 1989 1990 1991 1992 1993 1994 1995 1996 1997 1998 1999 2000 2001 2002 2003 2004

PROGRESS REPORT

Normal service was resumed after the top 10 finishes of 2001 and 2002. The next two seasons saw them cling onto their League status in 19th and 21st. Rochdale's only break from the drudgery was a five-year spell in Level Two from 1969. However, they have the unlikely honour of being the only basement side to appear in a major final, the 1962 League Cup, where they lost to Norwich, though in reality the competition didn't have much clout in those days as it had yet to gain the support of the big clubs.

```
        ...Had lowest post-war English League attendance (450 v Cambridge in 1974)...
...Were managed by a committee (1920-22)...Michael Owen's dad was their top scorer in 1978...
```

RIVALS

Realistically, Rochdale can't really claim superiority over any current League side regarding their record or status. Bury, which lies roughly on the same longitude to the north of Manchester, are the only conceivable rivals at present. Their beef with Bury goes along the lines that whereas Rochdale fans have continuously supported their club with a variety of ongoing fund-raising efforts, Bury made a financial drama out of a crisis, suddenly running around shaking their buckets when they should have had a better long-term survival plan. Their bad feeling isn't really thrown back at them though. Nobody, it seems, can be that bothered about The Dale, though Halifax like to bait them that they look forward to meeting them in the Conference (which possibly shows the limits of 'Scallyfax's' ambitions.) The most memorable dust-up between the two was a cocking-of-the-leg on the goalpost incident leading to an altercation between Rochdale mascot Desmond the Dragon and Halifax's Freddy the Fox, in which, according to an official police statement, Freddy was "punched on the snout".

BURY ☠☠☠☠☠

HALIFAX ☠☠☠☠☠

Anti-Burnley feelings still run high, but it seems unlikely that the two will find themselves in the same division for the foreseeable future.

BURNLEY ☠☠☠☠☠

In 1999, the Oldham chairman Ian Stott mooted the merger of Oldham, Rochdale and Bury under the umbrella of Manchester North End, threatening gloomily that it would be the only means by which there could be survival for any of them. Inevitably, this sparked a degree of rivalry that hadn't really existed previously. In fact, it would have been Oldham and Bury who would have suffered the most as, under League rules, the new outfit would have started at the level of the lowest ranking club, Rochdale, who at the time were two divisions beneath the other two.

The only recent trouble involving Rochdale fans came during the two-legged play-off against Rushden and Diamonds in 2002. Tensions rose at the first game at Nene Park, after which a Rushden fan attacked Dale striker Lee McEvilly. The return leg saw a pitch invasion at the final whistle with the usually peaceable Dale fans having a go at Rushden players.

SUPPORTERS' VFM 67%

PERFORMANCE AGAINST RIVALS BURY

WON 24%
LOST 41%
DRAWN 35%

'YOUR GROUND'S TOO BIG FOR YOU!' RATING

ATTENDANCE AS A PERCENTAGE OF CAPACITY **32%**

100
80
60
40
20
0

LOVE/HATE

The Godfather of lower league football, *Tony Ford* ♡, started his career with Grimsby in 1975 and was still going strong for The Dale as a player in 2001 at the age of 42. Managing an England 'B' team place and an OBE, his longevity is celebrated with the chant 'He's big...he's blue...he fought in World War II'

CHANTS

In front of the Sky cameras, some of the Hull contingent made a beeline for Rochdale fans, though their choice of targets wasn't considered very impressive:

'Well done, you took the family stand'.

DOH!!

Sponsored in the mid 80s by a local firm, 'All-in-one Garden Centres', Rochdale had to suffer the embarrassment of sporting a shirt with a huge watering can on the front.

145

ROTHERHAM UNITED

Recommended website: **www.rotherhamunited-mad.co.uk**

WHO ARE YA?

In recent years, Rotherham have experienced one of the most rapid climbs of any League club. But they are definitely not happy little bunnies. Badly hemmed in by nearby Sheffield, only Crewe endure lower attendances in Level One, and fans are getting increasingly jumpy that the club is homing in on another spell of lower league drudgery that will be witnessed by fewer than half their already meagre base of supporters. As usual, it's a mix of TV money woes and wrangling over the ground that lies at the heart of their problems. And if anyone needs their ground tarting up, it's Rotherham. For some, it's a refreshing change from identikit stadiums; to others, it's a 'call in the demolition ball' job. A few can't moan though, as there is a handily placed railway bridge where skint folk can get a good view for free.

CELEBRITY FANS

THE CHUCKLE BROTHERS

frequently sneak in a mention of Rotherham FC into their kids' TV show

IN and AROUND

Rotherham gave the world Jive Bunny, a rabbit who shares the record of having three number one singles from his first three UK releases.

With Rotherham slumbering at the foot of Level One in 2004, they are not so keen to give the club's saviour, Ken Booth, much credit. In 1997, Booth cleared the club's £800,000 debt and has had to service a colossal overdraft ever since. It all looked very suspect when he arrived, as his scrap metal business virtually surrounded Millmoor. But with things on the pitch looking rosy and no sign of any underhand property dealings, nobody was complaining. After whispers of lack of ambition, Booth started looking to bail out, but two take-over attempts have seemingly come to grief over a mysterious 'bit of land' – the car park behind the main stand. Local chap Neil Freeman thought the deal was in the bag, until he blamed the aforementioned piece of tarmac for a last minute hitch, as it apparently had done in a previous negotiation with another consortium.

Some of the biggest press coverage for the club occurred in 2000, when two men went to court for 'stealing the penalty spots', having clambered into the ground after dark. The court was given the rather fanciful estimate that the penalty spots were worth £1,000...each.

Rotherham are one of a long list of clubs whose fans suspect that they are victims of a 'bogus famous fan' – in their case, Paul Shane, famous for *Hi-Di-Hi* and infamous for a ridiculously over-wrought vocal on *'You've Lost that Loving Feeling'*. In fans' eyes, he commits the ultimate sin of associating with the club for official functions but is conspicuous in his absence on actual match days.

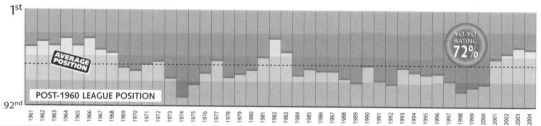

PROGRESS REPORT

Rotherham's natural home has generally been in Level Two. They fell into Level Three in 1997, but emerged in fighting form with consecutive promotions in 2000 and 2001. Life in Level One has not been plain sailing with three low positions before propping up the table for the early part of 2004-2005.

```
...Reached first ever League Cup Final...
...Recently supported Oxfam campaign to stop the spread of weapons...
...Beat Chelsea 6-0 in first game of 1981...
```

RIVALS

Frequently, rivalries seem to exist for the flimsiest of reasons, chiefly because teams need someone else to dislike, but Rotherham really do have quite a lot to complain about, having to endure one of the most unfortunate footballing locations. The town of Rotherham is very close to being welded onto the northeastern tip of Sheffield. Compared to most people's perception, it is huge, with a population of 250,000 that will probably see it acquiring city status before very long. In latter days, it is probably Rotherham, rather than Sheffield, that can claim to be the centre of steel production. Considering how difficult the relationship is, some credit is deserved on both sides for keeping things going with nothing more serious than a war of words.

SHEFFIELD WEDNESDAY
☠️☠️☠️☠️☠️☠️

SHEFFIELD UNITED
☠️☠️☠️☠️☠️

When there has been trouble at Millmoor, it has tended to happen randomly, outside the web of local rivalries. In one bizarre incident, an estimated 80 Aberdeen fans did a quick, destructive tour of South Yorkshire, stirring up problems in a pre-season friendly with Rotherham before moving on to cause problems with supporters of the two Sheffield clubs, where they had made an overnight stop. In 2000, a visiting fan died after being accidentally trampled by a police horse trying to quell incidents at the end of season home game with Swansea.

It would make sense if Rotherham's main current rivals were Sheffield United as the two have kept each other company in Level One for the last four years. In fact, all the nastiness is directed at Wednesday – a hangover from their Premiership days, when they were seen to have dominated the local media coverage to the exclusion of everyone else.

SUPPORTERS' VFM 57%

PERFORMANCE AGAINST RIVALS
SHEFFIELD WEDNESDAY

WON 30%
LOST 55%
DRAWN 15%

There is little agreement over their second rivals. Although again there are no particularly hostile intentions, Chesterfield are named, largely on the basis of having an astonishingly good record against them. In August 2004, Rotherham's 2-1 League Cup victory managed to prevent The Spireites completing a 20 match unbeaten run dating back to September 1979. A sign of how transient rivalries can be, Barnsley's flirt with the big-time made them number one hates, but as soon as they went down to Level Two it was as though they never existed.

CHESTERFIELD
☠️☠️☠️☠️☠️

LOVE/HATE

HATE

It's never a great idea for goalkeepers to get caught up in inter-club squabbles as the job requires standing for long periods close to baying supporters. In 2000, *Mike Pollitt* ♡ 👊 seemed secure having said he was planning to stay at Rotherham, and apparently agreeing a new deal. It was, therefore, a shock when he suddenly appeared on the books of Chesterfield. When Chesterfield visited Millmoor in December, Pollitt was subjected to various objects thrown from the terraces, including wastefully, hot pies. Amazingly, everyone kissed and made up and he returned to Rotherham a year later.

CHANTS

Injured players from either of the Sheffield clubs tend to be met with cries of '*Dee-dah, Dee-dah*', a reasonable impression of an ambulance and also a parody of the Sheffield accent in which, it is claimed, vowels become ludicrously flattened and many words that don't warrant it begin with a 'Dee' sound.

'YOUR GROUND'S TOO BIG FOR YOU!'
RATING

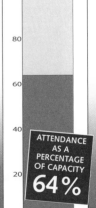

100
80
60
40
20
0

ATTENDANCE AS A PERCENTAGE OF CAPACITY
64%

DOH!!

One of those tales that could only end one way. In the excitement of promotion from Level Two in 2001, manager Ronnie Moore pledged not to shave until the club won their first game. A forlorn and increasingly Neanderthal Moore had to wait until a 2-0 victory at Grimsby on 6th October, 12 games into the season, by which time Rotherham were a doleful 24th in the table.

RUSHDEN & DIAMONDS

A.K.A.
RUBBISH & DUSTBINS

Recommended website: **www.rdfcnet.co.uk**

WHO ARE YA?

It's fair to say that R&D are a fine example of a club that were cobbled together – in more ways than one. Their existence is mainly the product of ex-chairman, Max Griggs, making a mint in footwear manufacturing. The rebirth of the Dr Martens brand helped fund a club that didn't even exist in early 1992. Eleven years after their formation and at an estimated bill of £30 million, they gained promotion to Level Two. To the envy of their opponents, Rushden and Diamonds have generally been the best funded side in whichever league they've graced. With Griggs gone in 2004, leaving his son in charge, it won't be long before we know whether their glorious rise will be a blueprint for others to spend their way out of the lower leagues, or a quick path to financial ruin.

CELEBRITY FANS
NO LUCK YET...THOUGH THE PLAY ON WORDS **RUSHDEN ANNE DIAMOND** DOES THE ROUNDS WITH RIVAL SUPPORTERS.

In front of 315 spectators, the club made its debut against Bilston Town in the Southern League Midland Division. The club was the unlikely merger of Southern League Rushden Town, (average gate 250) who'd been around since 1889, and Irthlingborough Diamonds of the United Counties League (average gate 90). Griggs set out from day one to create a League outfit. The involvement of the town of Irthlingborough was mainly a tactic to grab their ground, the only one in the area suitable for the modernisation that would be needed if the new baby was to start shooting up the leagues.

IN and AROUND

Caught on a cusp of ITV's network, Rushden has the unlikely pleasure of being in the Anglia TV region, though it's closer to London and Birmingham than it is to Norwich.

By January 1999, they were hosting Leeds United in the FA Cup in the, by now, palatial Nene Park (pronounced 'Nen' not 'Neen'). Their entrance to Level Three in 2001 provided away fans with one of the odder days out. The capacity of Nene Park stands at 6,441, but the population of Irthlingborough is only 6,310. This means that on some match days, there are probably more people inside the ground than in the town. For some, the term 'town' is stretching the meaning of the word. More often it is characterised as a village in the middle of nowhere whose main features are a roundabout and a shop selling wicker furniture. It also leads to the essential trivia that Irthlingborough is the smallest place whose name is embodied in an English Football League team. This fact is made pithier as Milton Keynes, 20 miles to the south, and with a population 32 times greater, didn't have a side to call their own...and it's a matter of conjecture whether that is still the case. Oh, and Irthlingborough hasn't got a railway station either.

Having scaled the heights of Level Two, the 'what goes up must come down' adage hit with a vengeance in 2004. With manager Brian Talbot deserting to Oldham and the board off-loading players to make the club a sweeter proposition for a potential buyer, R&D at least looked safe from relegation. In mid-March, they came into a match with Brentford in 13th place. They promptly lost eight and drew one of their remaining games to finish in 22nd.

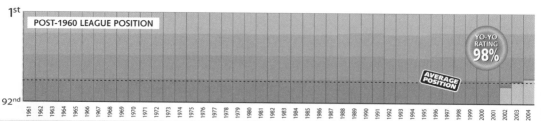

POST-1960 LEAGUE POSITION

1st

92nd

YO-YO RATING **98%**

AVERAGE POSITION

1961 1962 1963 1964 1965 1966 1967 1968 1969 1970 1971 1972 1973 1974 1975 1976 1977 1978 1979 1980 1981 1982 1983 1984 1985 1986 1987 1988 1989 1990 1991 1992 1993 1994 1995 1996 1997 1998 1999 2000 2001 2002 2003 2004

PROGRESS REPORT

Five changes in division in nine years have made it an explosive early history for the club. Their entry to Level Three could have been even sooner, with two Conference fourth places and a second before becoming Champions in 2001. They gained a play-off place in their first League season, before winning the division outright a year later. 2003-2004 doesn't bear thinking about.

```
...The club's function room has hosted European Snooker League events...
   ...The roofs of Nene Park feature statues of owls to scare birds...
      ...Paid Millwall £20,000 for their old electronic scoreboard...
```

RIVALS

The Rushden and Diamonds/Northampton rivalry has a unique quality, in that it appeared to exist well before a senior fixture between the two sides. Northampton were the only League side in the county and they would have preferred to keep it that way. As an (intermittently) Level Two side, they seemed to have little to fear. But they looked over their shoulder in trepidation as The Diamonds' express train rattled its way up to their status. But Northampton never even got the chance to halt their progress, as, in 2003, they contrived to get themselves relegated from the Second just as R&D won the Championship of the Third. Finally, with both in the basement, they got to meet each other in August 2004 with Northampton edging a 1-0 win.

NORTHAMPTON TOWN

KETTERING TOWN

Kettering Town, who joined them in the Conference in the run up to The Diamonds' promotion to the League, have reason to believe that 'it could/should have been us' to have benefited from Griggs' seemingly bottomless wallet. Barely six miles away, Kettering (formed 120 years before their neighbours and with their long history of FA Cup giant-killing) watched in disbelief as Rushden and Diamonds swanned their way into the League. Their noses were thoroughly rubbed in it as The Diamonds only lost one of their ten Conference meetings and, even more joyously, were promoted in the very same season that Kettering lost their footing in the top-flight of non-league action for the first time in 30 years.

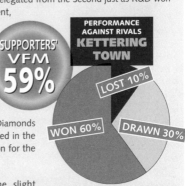

SUPPORTERS' **VFM** **59%**

PERFORMANCE AGAINST RIVALS
KETTERING TOWN

LOST 10%
WON 60%
DRAWN 30%

KIDDERMINSTER

Kidderminster and, to a degree, Cheltenham have become slight adversaries as both continuously go on about how they didn't 'buy themselves' into the League. As far as Rushden and Diamonds are concerned, they are all a bunch of arrogant whingers who would jump at the chance of some proper funding.

Rushden and Diamonds' arrest rate is negligible. If anything, lack of vocal support is more of a problem than anyone getting remotely carried away. The county collected 15 banning orders for Euro 2004; three of them being Diamonds' supporters, tellingly one less than was handed out to Northamptonshire's lunatic fringe of Manchester United and Chelsea fans.

LOVE/HATE

Harking back to their Conference local derbies, *Brett McNamara* of Kettering Town got into The Diamonds' bad books after alleging an assault in the tunnel by Duane Darby in a match in late 2000.

CHANTS

The lack of singing causes some angst amongst the die-hards. In fact, the most enthusiastic vocal action ever heard at Nene Park was probably when *Songs of Praise* was filmed at the stadium in 2000.

'YOUR GROUND'S TOO BIG FOR YOU!'
RATING

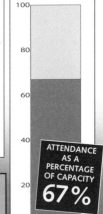

ATTENDANCE AS A PERCENTAGE OF CAPACITY
67%

DOH!!

Billed as the Conference 'game of the season' in 1999-2000, Rushden and Diamonds visited Kidderminster in April for a match that would go a long way to deciding which of the two would win the Championship.

Having taken advantage of an early booking discount, Max Griggs was on holiday in Egypt.

SCUNTHORPE UNITED

POLITELY WRITTEN AS S**HORPE UNITED**

Recommended website: **www.iron-bru.net**

WHO ARE YA?

Comedian Ali G's painful interview with the Beckhams included a gag where he asked Victoria whether the best looking women got the top footballers. After she answered yes, his follow up was "so does Sporty Spice go out with someone from Scunthorpe United?". As secondary targets of the slur, Scunthorpe can claim not to have the worst League record of the current League clubs – that honour going to Rochdale. However mediocre on the field, Scunthorpe have occasionally been well ahead of the time off it. After a stadium fire in 1958, the club's Old Showground was rebuilt with the first cantilever stand in Britain. In 1985, they were the first British club to build a new stadium since the 1950s. Their daring plan has been the blueprint for just about every ill-conceived takeover since, but for pioneers Scunthorpe, the plan actually worked. It was 1988 when they moved into their new Glanford Park ground, having sold off the previous site to Safeways. Though there were a few gripes, attendances took a leap.

IN and AROUND

Scunthorpe residents occasionally tire at people laughing at the town's name. But in world terms, they are quite lucky. Spare a thought for the good folk of Knob Lick, Missouri.

Scunthorpe have gone down in history as something of a two-fact club. The first, that Kevin Keegan played for them before going to Liverpool, became the leading trivia nugget for most of the 70s and beyond. But the club only received what even Bill Shankly considered the derisory sum of £35,000. Their other pub-quiz contribution, that they provided three different England captains, Keegan, Ray Clemence and ahem...Ian Botham (who made 11 non-contract appearances for them in the early 80s), had bigger consequences for cricket than it ever did for football. At the time, the authorities were worried that cricketers were risking their delicate frames by indulging in such a rough out-of-season sport. By 2003, the England and Wales Cricket Board effectively banned professional cricketers from playing football by issuing absurdly limiting guidelines for cricketers wanting to take up the game (at any level) during the winter.

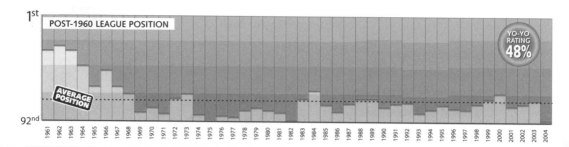

POST-1960 LEAGUE POSITION

1st

YO-YO RATING 48%

AVERAGE POSITION

92nd

1961 1962 1963 1964 1965 1966 1967 1968 1969 1970 1971 1972 1973 1974 1975 1976 1977 1978 1979 1980 1981 1982 1983 1984 1985 1986 1987 1988 1989 1990 1991 1992 1993 1994 1995 1996 1997 1998 1999 2000 2001 2002 2003 2004

PROGRESS REPORT

At the turn of the 60s, Scunthorpe were quite a force, narrowly missing out on promotion to old Division One in 1962. But that was about the extent of the glory days. They slipped into the basement in 1968 and have been there ever since, bar a couple of seasons – their last one-year escape coming in 1999-2000. Oddly though, since the introduction of automatic relegation to the Conference, they have managed to avoid any dogfights for survival.

```
        ...Were called Scunthorpe and Lindsey United until 1958...
    ...Sacked manager Brain Laws, only to re-appoint him three weeks later...
  ...Raffled pig to raise funds, but it escaped and ran around the pitch (1924)...
```

RIVALS

Scunthorpe's seemingly permanent residence in Level Three has left them in the unenviable position of having to pick fights with anyone who joins them in the basement. Hull's descent in the mid-90s caused them to meet their natural geographical rivals in 1996 for the first time in 12 years. As is often the case where a 'bigger' club drops down to the same level as 'inferior' locals, Scunthorpe gave them a fairly bloody nose during their time together, allowing Hull to win only three out of 12 senior meetings, until Hull clawed their way to Level Two in 2004. In fairness, Grimsby are probably entitled to think they are a few notches above Scunthorpe, having enjoyed plenty of Level One action, but unusually, given their previously elevated status, they have traditionally named Scunthorpe as their first hates. The two have managed to maintain the rivalry through meetings in the Lincolnshire Cup. Even though the clubs treat it as little more than a reserve fixture, crowds of around 700 are common for the final.

GRIMSBY TOWN ☠☠☠☠

HULL ☠☠

LINCOLN CITY ☠☠☠

Back in 1920, Scunthorpe were well and truly shafted by Grimsby and Lincoln who remained in the League at their expense nearly causing the club to fold altogether. In terms of League position, Lincoln City make logical adversaries, though it brings them into conflict with one of the most volatile sets of supporters. The Level Three play-offs of 2003 were marred with scenes involving around 450 supporters, made worse by the ropey ticketing arrangements, which saw a mass of Lincoln fans taking up their positions in the home end for the first leg at Glanford Park. In 2001, a local hotelier was left to regret his decision to decorate the bar in Scunthorpe's claret and blue colours. The Larchwood Hotel sustained £2,500 of damage when the front of the building was covered in tar in what looked suspiciously like a football-related incident of vandalism.

SUPPORTERS' VFM 59%

PERFORMANCE AGAINST RIVALS
HULL
WON 40%
LOST 40%
DRAWN 20%

Scunthorpe's buried obscenity, which causes many computers to automatically insert asterisks into their name, has its payoffs. Its teenage giggle factor is probably one of the main reasons, along with the club's underachievement, for the side to be named as many supporters' second team – or at least the one whose results they look out for on whatever the tele-printer is called these days. As such, at a push, Scunthorpe United might be the most liked team in the entire League.

A less pleasant member of their fan base hit the news in 2004. A refuse collector won £4.3 million on the lottery after purchasing his ticket from a Spar shop in Scunthorpe. After pronouncing that he intended to devote his life to football, he chose to pursue his interest at the sharp end, managing to get himself arrested after Grimsby fans 'diverted' to Scunthorpe on their way back from Stockport. As bricks, bottles and the obligatory pool cues went flying, lucky lotto winner Andrew Simpson was alleged to have got stuck in.

LOVE/HATE

After Safeway built their store on the Old Showground, a wall plaque was installed commemorating Scunthorpe's history at the site. When *Sainsbury's* took over the store in 2004, they had it removed as it was emblazoned with the former company's name – and continue to drag their heels over a replacement.

CHANTS

'They come from near meggies,
They can't afford a telly,
They're dirty and they're smelly,
The Coddie family'

An amended version of the theme from The Adams Family, especially for Grimsby.

'YOUR GROUND'S TOO BIG FOR YOU!'
RATING

100 —
80 —
ATTENDANCE AS A PERCENTAGE OF CAPACITY **42%**
60 —
40 —
20 —
0 —

DOH!!

Manager Brian Laws made the foolhardy promise to bear his buttocks in Scunthorpe town centre if Alex Calvo-Carcia scored from outside the penalty box in the team's meeting with Southend in 1998. You can guess the rest.

SHEFFIELD UNITED

A.K.A. THE BLUNTS

Recommended website: **www.redandwhite-wizards.co.uk**

WHO ARE YA?

Sheffield's pecking order was established when the two clubs entered the Football League in 1892, with Wednesday going into the old First Division and United, to their displeasure, the next one down. Though their long-term records are similar, United bear a slight inferiority complex, which, if anything, has probably spurred them on. Their nicknames have a convoluted history. In their formative years, the local press would refer to both as Blades or Cutlers. The right to use the term Blades was fought over, with United finally getting their way in 1907 when Wednesday settled for The Owls after their home turf of Owlerton.

Sheffield United have good reason to be irked at Manchester fans singing 'there's only one United'. The South Yorkshire version was the first 'United' that remains today– in fact they'd adopted the name when the lot across the Pennines were still at Newton Heath. More generally the 13 other League Uniteds up and down the land moan that commentators use the term exclusively to mean Manchester United.

CELEBRITY FANS
SEAN BEAN
Actor
RICK ALLEN
Def Leppard
JOHN RAWLINS
Radio 5 Commentator

IN and AROUND

Sheffield was the setting for the 1984 BBC drama *Threads* - a programme that traumatised a generation – in which the city is destroyed in a nuclear attack.

United have seen a couple of particularly agonising final games of the season. They were relegated in 1981 having missed a penalty in the last minute that would have ensured survival. They also spectacularly crumbled on their way out of the Premiership in 1994. 2-1 up at Chelsea with five minutes to go, they contrived to lose 3-2. The subsequent arrests of Bruce Grobbelaar and Hans Segers did nothing to ease the hurt, as one of the suspect results, Everton's 3-2 defeat of Wimbledon, worked against the Blades.

Most of the talking points of the club's recent history have revolved around manager Neil Warnock, one of very few League managers who can claim to be in charge of the team that he has supported fervently since boyhood. Not afraid to launch into a tirade, his highlights include a (perfectly accurate) reference to David Elleray as a 'bald-headed bloke'. He has a spectacular record of FA misconduct charges, mainly from his bating of officials (he is a qualified referee himself), but really rose to prominence after the 'Battle of Bramall Lane' in 2002, when, following the dismissal of three Blades players, West Brom manager Gary Megson strongly hinted that Warnock had encouraged some feigning of injuries in order to get the game abandoned, which it was after Rob Ullathorne limped off with eight minutes left. Warnock dubbed Megson 'one of the biggest moaners in the game' – again, not a statement that would trouble the libel courts.

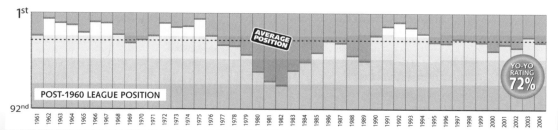

POST-1960 LEAGUE POSITION

1st ... 92nd

1961 1962 1963 1964 1965 1966 1967 1968 1969 1970 1971 1972 1973 1974 1975 1976 1977 1978 1979 1980 1981 1982 1983 1984 1985 1986 1987 1988 1989 1990 1991 1992 1993 1994 1995 1996 1997 1998 1999 2000 2001 2002 2003 2004

AVERAGE POSITION

YO-YO RATING **72%**

PROGRESS REPORT

United's rise to the top-flight sprung from nowhere, with consecutive promotions in 1989 and 1990. After their two-season stay, their fall back into Level One has seen them regularly challenging for promotion, with eight top ten finishes in ten years and three unsuccessful play-off appearances.

```
...Attempted to buy Diego Maradonna after the 1978 World Cup...
...Robert Carlyle wears a Blades shirt in 'The Full Monty'...
...Won 28 corners in one game (v West Ham 1989) - and still lost 2-0...
```

RIVALS

Depending who you speak to, the Sheffield rivalry is either a seething hatred with no middle ground, or an out of fashion and artificial situation that is whipped up by a minority. It is generally acknowledged that when the two met in the FA Cup semi-final at Wembley in 1993 (won by Wednesday), the occasion had a remarkably good-natured atmosphere. With its space-age metro system, the city centre must rank as one of the most improved in Western Europe. Yet unlike Manchester, and to a lesser extent Liverpool and Leeds, it has never really gained a chic northern tag, something that might be expected to create a degree of unity between the factions.

The fact that rugby has never gained much of a hold on the city has eased the usual northern club difficulties, but Sheffield remains around 100,000 people short of being a city that can support two clubs with Premiership ambitions. With both outside the top-flight, the merger/groundshare proponents are more in number than at any time in recent history. The staunch United view on this is that it's odd that Wednesday are only showing any enthusiasm for the idea now that they are suffering in the depths of Level Two. The most scurrilous advice is that they should go and seek a merger with Chesterfield, as they are now roughly equal. Wednesday's retort is that, by the same token, United's true footballing equivalent is currently Rotherham. The considered opinion was mooted to the astonishment of many by the Blades' chairman, John Thurman. 1997 figures revealed that the two headed the list of loss-making clubs with a combined debt of £17 million, so the whole city would be better served by redeveloping the Don Valley Stadium and flogging Hillsborough and Bramall Lane, but the chances of ever reaching a fans' consensus seems remote in the extreme.

LEEDS UNITED

BARNSLEY

SHEFFIELD WEDNESDAY

SUPPORTERS'
VFM
53%

PERFORMANCE
AGAINST RIVALS
SHEFFIELD WEDNESDAY

WON 29%
LOST 29%
DRAWN 42%

But there are plenty of anecdotes that point to no let-up in the rivalry. An advertising hoarding outside Bramall Lane depicting a pig (Wednesday's caricature of United) soon got the treatment from paint-pot wielding locals. United fans were not amused to be sent a flyer promoting ITV's new sports' channel, prominently featuring a picture of a Wednesday player celebrating a goal. Mailed out with a letter from the United chairman, the club knew it was asking for trouble. A Blades fan commented "If ITV wanted to stop us watching the channel, they couldn't have come up with a better idea".

CHANTS

A favourite at Bramall Lane is a rather heavy-handed celebration of Yorkshire culture:

'You fill up my senses like a gallon of magnet [molten steel]
Like a packet of Woodbines;
Like a good pinch of snuff
Like a greasy chip butty'

LOVE/HATE

With not a vast number of admirers from other teams' supporters, it's fortunate that the single-minded devotion of *Neil Warnock* to the club is repaid by the fans.

DOH!!

One piece of corporate sponsorship incensed supporters. In 1979, the Blades' traditional red and white stripes were ditched in favour of a radically different design featuring larger blocks of colour. The reason? So the new sponsors' name would show up better. The kit lasted one season, and coincided with relegation.

'YOUR GROUND'S TOO BIG FOR YOU!'
RATING

100
80
60
40
20
0

ATTENDANCE
AS A
PERCENTAGE
OF CAPACITY
70%

SHEFFIELD WEDNESDAY

Recommended website: **www.anzowls.com**

WHO ARE YA?

The most exciting sounding league name has a fairly routine explanation. Looking for an excuse to stay together during the winter months, a cricket club had the idea of playing footie as well. Formed in 1867, the club was unimaginatively named after the day of the week they met on. The Sheffield prefix was only added later.

As one of the oldest clubs in the world, Wednesday's golden era was around 100 years ago. Though the establishment of the modern day Premiership heralded the true age of the yo-yo phenomenon, Wednesday managed an early version of this effect, being promoted to the old First Division four times and relegated to Level One three times during the 1950s. Finding themselves in the Level Two with United in 1979, 49,309 packed into Hillsborough for a derby game, a record for that league.

CELEBRITY FANS
MICHAEL VAUGHAN
England Cricketer
PRINCE NASEEM HAMED
Boxer

Their first, brief, exit from the Premiership was something of a howler. In 1989-90, they reached the semi-comfort zone of 13th place, before a slump left them needing to look elsewhere for a last day salvation. Wednesday players had already completed a lap of honour following a 3-0 defeat by Nottingham Forest, as they thought that strugglers Luton had only drawn 3-3 at Derby, allowing Wednesday to stay up. But Derby's equaliser had been completely bogus – in fact Luton had won 3-2, putting them down.

IN and AROUND

Sheffield's Town Hall extension, variously known as the 'Frog's-eye building' and 'The egg-box', was so universally hated that the local authority bowed to pressure to have it demolished.

Attitudes towards the club's resident band are decidedly mixed. Designed to inspire the home fans into more noise, some argue that the effect of their tooting is to embarrass everyone else into near silence. When Wednesday are losing, their racket does little to soothe the spirits.

If there's one thing you don't need as a manager, it's a statement of support from your chairman. But Danny Wilson received calls for his head that actually improved his position – albeit temporarily. In 2000, four Labour MPs, including David Blunkett, went on the record to say he should go. Enraged by the unwarranted political interference, Owls fans reacted by giving the hapless Wilson plenty of encouragement before the axe finally fell two months later.

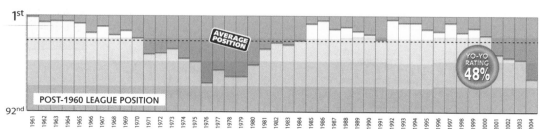

AVERAGE POSITION

YO-YO RATING 48%

POST-1960 LEAGUE POSITION

1st ... 92nd

1961 1962 1963 1964 1965 1966 1967 1968 1969 1970 1971 1972 1973 1974 1975 1976 1977 1978 1979 1980 1981 1982 1983 1984 1985 1986 1987 1988 1989 1990 1991 1992 1993 1994 1995 1996 1997 1998 1999 2000 2001 2002 2003 2004

PROGRESS REPORT

It says something about the plight of the club, that those unfortunate enough to be relegated from the Premiership talk of the threat of 'doing a Wednesday' i.e. dropping even further. If you overlay both Sheffield clubs' graphs on top of one another, they have distinct similarities, with both dropping like stones through the 70s, only to recover spectacularly in the 80s. Wednesday enjoyed a prolonged period of superiority in the Premiership, only to wave briefly to The Blades on the way down, as they spent just two seasons in the First before sinking to the depths of Level Two – to join the likes of Swindon Town as those catastrophically unable to cope with losing their top-flight status.

```
...Lost largest ever half-time lead, drawing 5-5 with Everton in 1904 after being five up...
...Goalkeeper Kevin Pressman was subject of the fastest league sending-off in 13 seconds (2001)...
                    ...Were originally called The Blades...
```

RIVALS

In latter days, Wednesday's rows with other clubs have barely risen above arguing with Huddersfield over who has the best stadium in the lower divisions. Parity with Sheffield United is eagerly awaited so ancient hostilities can resume. However, the city is not quite as starkly split as some. Celeb fans Michael Palin and ex-boxer Prince Naseem Hamed express loyalty to both clubs, a situation mirrored by a sizeable number who consider solidarity for the city as a whole is more important than internecine squabbles. There is an interesting theory as to why the rivalry has strengthened. It is argued that the bad feeling wasn't particularly evident before the advent of rampant ticket price inflation. Able to afford to see a game every week, Sheffield fans would happily watch both teams at home, alternating their support each Saturday. But increasingly, as this became too much on the pocket, they were forced to choose between the two, leading to a hardening of attitudes.

SHEFFIELD UNITED

LEEDS UNITED

But hostility towards the Piggies, as United are known, is now deeply entrenched. A 4-0 victory over them at Christmas of 1979 became known as the Boxing Day Massacre. Tee-shirts were printed to celebrate its 25-year anniversary.

SUPPORTERS' VFM 43%

PERFORMANCE AGAINST RIVALS SHEFFIELD UNITED

WON 29%
LOST 29%
DRAWN 42%

The presence of Neil Warnock in the top job at United is not the sort of thing to help the atmosphere between the two. Warnock's ability to wind up fans of virtually all clubs is unique. Legions of supporters from all clubs interviewed for this book named him as their number one irritant, mostly for his perceived endless capacity to whine to TV cameras when things haven't gone United's way. He misjudged the mood of the city when making supposedly light-hearted comments in a magazine interview. He later admitted to expressing the jocular view that if he was the Wednesday manager he would 'buy some bad players, get the sack and then move to Cornwall'. FourFourTwo's version of the quote was "I'd love to manage Wednesday. I'd buy so many tosspots - their current squad would do - and f*** 'em up so badly. Then I'd retire to Cornwall and spend the rest of my life laughing my f***ing head off."

BARNSLEY

A local design company irked the Equal Opportunity people by placing a recruitment ad with the words 'e-mailed CVs accepted. No personal callers. No Blades'.

LOVE/HATE

Ron Atkinson clearly wasn't all that impressed by what he called 'the best job in the world'. By the end of 1991, his words seemed to reaffirm a commitment to get Wednesday back into the Premiership at the first opportunity. He left for Aston Villa a week after making the comments. Amazingly, he returned to a muted reception in 1989 until sacked at the end of the season, having got Wednesday clear of Premiership trouble.

CHANTS

To Barnsley:

'You're just a town full of scrubbers'

slightly echoing the thoughts of their ex-player Georgi Hristov who undiplomatically said he preferred Yugoslav women to those from the ex-mining capital.

'YOUR GROUND'S TOO BIG FOR YOU!'
RATING

ATTENDANCE AS A PERCENTAGE OF CAPACITY
56%

DOH!!

The club were ready with a consignment of tee-shirts proclaiming 'Division Two Champions 03-04'. They finished 17th.

SHREWSBURY TOWN

Recommended website: **www.blue-and-amber.co.uk**

WHO ARE YA?

Shrewsbury made a significant contribution to the early development of the game as in 1848, representatives from the public school got together with their counterparts at Eton, Harrow, Winchester and Rugby to throw together a few rules that roughly approximate the modern game. Shrewsbury's quaint image has been helped by their minuscule Gay Meadow ground, beloved for the tendency of footballs to end up in the River Severn, requiring a bloke in a boat with a long stick to go and retrieve them. But the tree-lined ground is falling out of favour as it is looking increasingly ropey, having had no significant spruce-ups in over 20 years.

CELEBRITY FANS
PETE
POSTLETHWAITE
Actor

In 2000, perilously stuck within the drop zone, the local newspaper, The Shropshire Star, dreamed up a last-minute incentive scheme where it pledged to pay £500 to the scorers of all Shrewsbury's goals in their last four fixtures. The offer resulted in some unseemly jostling for the ball when the team was awarded a penalty against Southend. Whilst the bonus payments might have played a part, it needed a huge slice of good fortune to keep them up, with defeats for Carlisle and Chester – on the last day – proving their salvation.

IN and AROUND

Shrewsbury residents are unlikely to get pestered by people trying to sell them house insurance. Such is the frequency and ferocity of floods when the River Severn bursts its banks, many houses near the river are becoming uninsurable.

The side's greatest moment in recent years came in the same season as their worst. In the third round of the FA Cup in 2002-03, they stunned a full-strength Everton side, Rooney and all, with a 2-1 defeat at Gay Meadow. But things in the Third Division went rapidly downhill. Their goodbye to League football was confirmed when Rotherham became the eighth consecutive side to notch up a win against them. Ironically, Shrewsbury's first League game, 53 years before, was against the same side. The relegation was taken with as much good grace as fans could muster, which wasn't much, as the police had to be called in to quell minor trouble at demonstrations outside the ground.

A single season of rubbing shoulders with the other Shropshire club, Telford, was as much as they had to put up with as, in 2004, they emerged triumphant from a nerve-shredding penalty shoot out with Aldershot in the Conference play-offs. The huge number of welcome back messages from fans of other clubs was a symbol of their general popularity. But it was not always such backslapping stuff. At one stage in 1996, the team mustered the less than shining record of played 21, scored 21, conceded 21 and won 21 points. The drab uniformity of the results was matched by the team itself, as their official height measurements were all 5ft 10". Some reckoned that they all looked exactly the same as well.

Their place in pseudo rock history was assured when the team's blue and amber strip made a cameo appearance in the spoof Rockumentary, *This is Spinal Tap*. The best known scene, in which bassist Brian Smalls passes through an airport metal detector, sees him having to admit to secreting something resembling an iron cucumber in his trousers in an attempt to improve the appearance of his natural assets. Collectors of footie trivia were thrilled by the fact that he is wearing a Shrewsbury Town shirt.

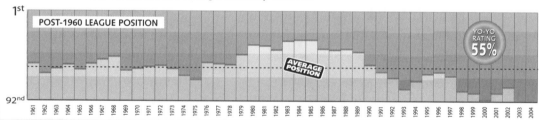

1st

POST-1960 LEAGUE POSITION

YO-YO RATING **55%**

AVERAGE POSITION

92nd

1961 1962 1963 1964 1965 1966 1967 1968 1969 1970 1971 1972 1973 1974 1975 1976 1977 1978 1979 1980 1981 1982 1983 1984 1985 1986 1987 1988 1989 1990 1991 1992 1993 1994 1995 1996 1997 1998 1999 2000 2001 2002 2003 2004

PROGRESS REPORT

In 1979, 29 years after their entry to the Football League, Shrewsbury got into the top half for the first time and remained comfortably ensconced within Level One. But from the mid 80s onwards, they slipped towards lower half finishes culminating in relegation in 1989, and then down again under John Bond in 1992. The drop to the Conference was the final humiliation in what had effectively been a 20-year decline.

```
       ...Locals often refer to the club as Salop...Before Manchester United cavorted off to
South America in 1999, Shrewsbury were the last League team not to enter the FA Cup (1950-51)...
    ...Ex-player Arthur Rowley achieved the highest tally of goals in English football, 434...
```

RIVALS

Many lower division clubs have a natural aversion to the new age of Premiership-obsessed, Sky-dominated, seven-figure-salaried football. But at Shrewsbury, the feeling seems unusually strong. In this respect, they share the characteristic with the likes of Millwall. Amazingly, there are indications that they share another of Millwall's less wonderful traits – a fairly strong inclination to misbehave. Per head of supporter, Shrewsbury scrape into the top ten in the arrest stakes, though, as usual, these figures have to be taken with a substantial pinch of salt, as they can simply reflect different degrees of police tolerance.

WREXHAM
☠☠☠☠

Though, to their irritation, some from the East seem to think that Shrewsbury is in Wales, it is undisputedly an English club, despite the fact they've won the Welsh Cup six times. If it weren't for the border, there is no particular reason why there should be so much bad blood between Shrewsbury and Wrexham. It is not a 'media-friendly' rivalry, based as it is on dubious regional stereotypes and an undercurrent of semi-digestible nationalism. The mobile boozing population doesn't help the atmosphere, with lads from Wrexham gravitating towards Chester for a night out, and in turn, many from Shrewsbury choosing Wrexham as a drinking hole – a situation that inevitably blows up into drunken insults on the dance floor. You might imagine that Shrewsbury bond with Chester against the common enemy of Wrexham, but they hate them as well, tending to think of Chester as long-ball bores who cheated their way out of the Conference.

CHESTER
☠☠☠☠

TELFORD UNITED
☠☠☠☠

SUPPORTERS' VFM 31%

PERFORMANCE AGAINST RIVALS WREXHAM

WON 34%
LOST 43%
DRAWN 23%

Whilst outside the League, Shrewsbury became embarrassingly acquainted with Telford, Shropshire's other club. For the year they were flung together, a war of words broke out as Shrewsbury were accused of being smug and condescending to their neighbours. A few have tried to talk up problems with Kidderminster, but The Shrews are united in their disinterest.

LOVE/HATE

Although the hero of their FA Cup beating of Everton, most fans didn't think a lot of *Nigel Jemson*, who chose to commute from Nottingham (where he was at Forest) rather than risk the rising waters of delightful Shrewsbury. Some felt his performances could have been improved by cutting down on the consumption of 'high calorie pies'.

CHANTS

'Are you watching BBC?'

rang out as Everton were being humbled in the 2003 FA Cup tie. They weren't, as to the disgust of Shrews fans, they hadn't deemed the tie interesting enough to send a camera or two.

'YOUR GROUND'S TOO BIG FOR YOU!' RATING

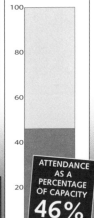

100
80
60
40
20
0

ATTENDANCE AS A PERCENTAGE OF CAPACITY 46%

DOH!!

Nigel Jemson astonished fellow players when unexpectedly turning out for what was supposed to be a good-natured bridge-building match between fans and staff in 2000. His ungentlemanly performance consisted of a number of searing tackles, arguing with the ref, and indulging in grossly OTT celebrations for a jammy deflected goal.

SOUTHAMPTON

Recommended website: **www.upthesaints.com**

WHO ARE YA?

Even the most hardened Saints supporter would admit that Southampton is possibly the least glamorous Premiership club, but they have worked wonders with a comparatively small catchment area and years of decidedly un-Premiership attendances at The Dell. But the new St Mary's Stadium needed the kick-start of an exorcism ceremony in 2001 to dispel a poor home record. Today, visiting fans remark on it's similarity to Middlesbrough's Riverside, though it's not entirely clear whether this is a complement.

In a scientific study of the tunefulness of Premiership supporters' songs, Southampton came top of the league with Professor David Howard praising their ability to hold their pitch well, producing a 'consistently outstanding performance'.

IN and AROUND

According to Angus Calder's *The People's War*, Southampton was probably the worst affected English city in the Second World War with constant air raids causing a near collapse in morale.

CELEBRITY FANS
DICKIE DAVIS
Ex-World of Sport Presenter
DAVID FROST
Versatile TV Presenter
Craig David
Singer

Their transfer policy has sometimes looked like that of a high-flying nursery club. In 1992 Alan Shearer went to Blackburn for a then record of £3.3 million. Tim Flowers went the same way shortly afterwards for a goalkeeper transfer record of £2 million. But the club's profile was raised by the remarkable loyalty of Matt LeTissier, whose exclusion from the England national side in general, and the 1998 World Cup in particular, is still is sore point.

On the basis of 'my enemies' enemy is my friend', The Saints drew plenty of neutral admirers with their ability to beat Manchester United, including the notorious 3-1 win in 1996, blamed by Alex Ferguson on United's grey strip, followed in 2002 by a 6-3 drubbing, blamed on Roy Keane's 22nd minute sending off.

For around 20 seasons Coventry and Southampton were generally mentioned in the same breath as the teams most likely to get dumped from the Premiership at any time. With Coventry finally taking the plunge in 2001, the Saints tenure of 27 seasons in the top-flight looks even more incredible, particularly as they came through a sticky spell in the 90s, a period when their best finish was 10th, and they suffered three last days reprieves in four seasons.

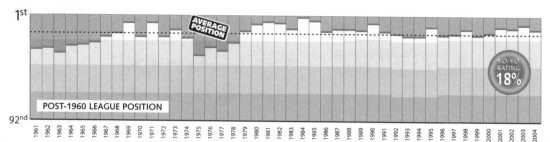

1st ... AVERAGE POSITION ... POST-1960 LEAGUE POSITION ... 92nd

YO-YO RATING 18%

1961 1962 1963 1964 1965 1966 1967 1968 1969 1970 1971 1972 1973 1974 1975 1976 1977 1978 1979 1980 1981 1982 1983 1984 1985 1986 1987 1988 1989 1990 1991 1992 1993 1994 1995 1996 1997 1998 1999 2000 2001 2002 2003 2004

PROGRESS REPORT

Since the turn of the millennium they've managed four seasons of mid-table respectability, boosted by bigger revenues from their relocation to St. Mary's, a much delayed move that seemed quite risky as their improbably tight ground at the Dell might have been their best asset. The departure of Gordan Strachan and Paul Sturrock in rapid succession seems to some an indication that The Saints are unravelling, but they are well versed in the art of escape acts.

...First club to field three brothers in same team - Danny, Rod and Ray Wallace...
...Fielded a team with five players who served as England captains - Peter Shilton, Mick Mills, Mike Channon, Kevin Keegan and Dave Watson...Have never finished higher than Liverpool in League...

RIVALS

Southampton only have eyes for 'The Skates', 20 miles to the east. Quite how Portsmouth got lumbered with the nickname is open to question. The most lurid explanation is that Royal Navy sailors from Pompey would use skate fish as a romantic 'aid' during long voyages - though the image is not really worth conjuring up. This has led to the frankly ludicrous claim of Saints fans that, more recently, specimens had to be removed from the Southsea's Sealife Centre because they had been 'interfered with'.

PORTSMOUTH

According to Southampton, Portsmouth are simply jealous. Whilst The Saints were winning the FA Cup, promoted to the top-flight and playing in Europe, Pompey were struggling in the lower leagues. Portsmouth's claim to be the naturally 'big' club of the South Coast is, it's said, a sad illusion based on a mediocre early history followed by 50 years of nothing. Their aspirations to greatest don't really tally with the facts - notably the club once being sued for payment by their own pie supplier. Their hailing of Terry Venables shows blind faith, and similarly their Chairman was more interested in acquiring the club for a retail development than a successful team.

SUPPORTERS' VFM 59%

PERFORMANCE AGAINST RIVALS PORTSMOUTH

- LOST 19%
- WON 57%
- DRAWN 24%

The intensity of the rivalry is often understated. There has been trouble at every meeting of the teams for 35 years - including the Premiership in 2004, one of very few recent incidents in the top division. In the absence of actual fixtures against each other, Saints and Pompey hooligan element have found 'opportunities' elsewhere. During the worst days of the 70s, Southampton coaches travelling east to matches in Brighton were at constant risk of being greeted by a reception committee chucking things from road bridges. Trouble has flared in a variety of unlikely places, including amongst England supporters during both the 1982 and 1988 World Cup final stages.

There is a history of both sides masquerading as supporters of other clubs in order to cause trouble. In 1978, a Southampton contingent turned up as Chelsea fans for a pre-season friendly with Portsmouth. In 1985/86 Portsmouth fans suddenly became supporters of Millwall. Going one step further, a 1986 Sunday League game between The Tabbycat and The Air Balloon (pubs) descended into chaos when members of Portsmouth's hooligan 657 crew made an unexpected appearance.

'YOUR GROUND'S TOO BIG FOR YOU!' RATING

LOVE/HATE

Understandably, *Glenn Hoddle's* 'here today, gone tomorrow' departure to Spurs was difficult to stomach. Often derided for being a bible-basher, Hoddle's dim musings were actually a form of half-baked spiritualism and nothing to do with religion at all.

Former manager, *Ian Brantfoot* (1991-94) is seen as presiding over the club's darkest spell in recent history. His 'hoof and chase' tactics relegated Le Tissier to a spectator's role - a cause of further irritation.

CHANTS

The first female line official, Wendy Tomms, was given some career advice following a dubious offside decision,

'You should be washing up'.

DOH!!

Probably the most classic cock-up in British football befell Southampton in the winter of 1996. Having taken an enthusiastic phone call from someone claiming to be George Weah, manager Graham Souness was talked into signing a promising 'Senegalese international', Ali Dia. On a week's trial, he debuted as a first-half substitute in November in a league game against Liverpool. It became horribly apparent that he wasn't actually a pro footballer at all, running around gamely but not really getting a sniff at the ball. A rare occasion when a substitute was substituted, he was quickly shown the door - though he managed to spend a few weeks at non-league Gateshead over Christmas.

ATTENDANCE AS A PERCENTAGE OF CAPACITY 99%

100
80
60
40
20
0

SOUTHEND UNITED

Recommended website: **www.shrimpers.net**

WHO ARE YA?

There's hardly a club in the country that doesn't complain that the end of terracing ruined a once decent atmosphere, but the redevelopment of Southend's sprawling North Bank and the removing of home fans into a small all-seater stand quelled what little excitement there was in the first place. Roots Hall's capacity in the 1970s was 35,000, around ten times their current average crowd as they depressingly drift around the lower echelons of Level Three. It is difficult to think of Southend as anything other than bobblers between the bottom two divisions, but the best spell in their history happened between 1992 and 1997, when they clung onto Level One status. In fact, an early kick-off allowed themselves to top the table for a few hours on New Year's Day 1992, thanks to a 4-0 beating of Newcastle. Looking back, students of the club's history tend to grumble that they simply weren't ready for it. Their best spell on the pitch coincided with perhaps their worst spell off it. Roots Hall was being touted around supermarket chains and many of the floating East London fans had deserted to the increasingly respectable West Ham.

CELEBRITY FANS
TEDDY TAYLOR
Eurosceptic Politician
ALISON MOYET
wrote 'Blue', a song about her beloved team

Southend fans are particularly hard on players who have flown the nest. They also enjoy laughing at the misfortunes of managers who come a cropper after they have left Southend. Barry Fry's fruitless spell at Birmingham came immediately after a few months at Roots Hall in 1993, but though regarded as something of a traitor, he did give Southend a much needed injection of cash through his transfer exploits bringing, for better or for worse, Stan Collymore into the limelight. In one of the great lower division pieces of profiteering, Collymore arrived for £750,000, netted a goal per game, and was bought by Nottingham Forest for £3.5 million just six months later.

IN and AROUND

The Essex-girl tag has some statistical basis, as Southend battles against one of the highest rates of teenage pregnancy in the country.

Southend were one of a number of clubs to have suffered from the illusion that an ex-England World Cup winner would be just the man to catapult them to the big-time. In 1984, Bobby Moore might have looked a catch but at the time of his appointment, the managerial records of his 1966 teammates didn't inspire confidence. He joined a club consisting of Bobby Charlton (relegated Preston), Martin Peters (relegated Sheffield United), Ray Wilson (quit Bradford within two months for a career as an undertaker) and Geoff Hurst (terrible at Chelsea). Moore presided over one of Southend's dire periods as they went down from the old Third Division the season he joined and continued in free-fall towards the foot of Level Three, before he, the board, and the fans could take no more.

The club's nickname, 'The Shrimpers', doesn't really lend itself to many merchandising/promotional avenues, though they persevered with 'Sammy the Shrimp', voted the League's ugliest mascot.

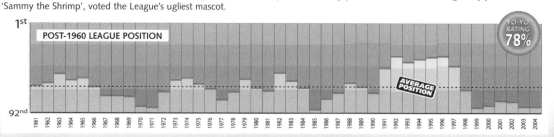

POST-1960 LEAGUE POSITION — 1st ... 92nd — YO-YO RATING 78% — AVERAGE POSITION — 1961 1962 1963 1964 1965 1966 1967 1968 1969 1970 1971 1972 1973 1974 1975 1976 1977 1978 1979 1980 1981 1982 1983 1984 1985 1986 1987 1988 1989 1990 1991 1992 1993 1994 1995 1996 1997 1998 1999 2000 2001 2002 2003 2004

PROGRESS REPORT

On the couple of occasions that Southend have broken their pattern of lower division mediocrity, they have done it in big leaps. Two consecutive promotions in a row in 1990 and 1991 were mirrored by the ultimate decline, ending last in Level One in 1997 and last in the Level Two a year later.

```
...The only League team to still be playing at their original ground...
    ...Roots Hall was turned into allotments in the First World War...
        ...Suffered longest run of missed penalties (seven in 1991-92)...
```

RIVALS

At least one Southend fan harbours extreme hard feelings towards 'carrot-crunching' Colchester United, their combatants for the slightly hollow claim to be 'pride of Essex': "Rather than us win promotion, most supporters would like to see the anguish and pain of Colchester United being relegated". From Southend's point of view, the suffering has been fairly intense as The U's, with a division in hand, have consistently managed to dodge them. The two haven't met in the League since 1990, but they did cross each other's paths twice in 2004 in the Associate Members Cup. Neutrals may like to stay away from their pre-season friendlies as they give the nutters on both sides the only opportunity to get at each other.

COLCHESTER

WEST HAM

Southend frequently has a feel of the East End-on-Sea, and the smallish band of Shrimpers are outnumbered by West Ham fans in their own town, causing particular resentment with the younger Southend fans. West Ham had the cheek to put a merchandise shop in the centre of the town, an undiplomatic move as Upton Park lies 35 miles away. The Southend media are increasingly seen as West Ham obsessed.

LEYTON ORIENT

Southend's periods in Level Three have led to new-found friction with Leyton Orient, though it is treated with only semi-seriousness on both sides, as historically, they have enjoyed a friendly relationship with players regularly moving between the two. Some, on both sides, point to their similarity, in both being in The Hammers' shadow. When West Ham are playing away, both Brisbane Road and Roots Hall 'benefit' from the attentions of Hammers' fans. Less charitably, Southend gave Orient some stick on a teletext message board in 1999 when the club was facing relegation to the Conference, which didn't go down too well.

SUPPORTERS' VFM 47%

PERFORMANCE AGAINST RIVALS COLCHESTER

WON 29%
LOST 39%
DRAWN 32%

LOVE/HATE

HATE

Former Chelsea defender *David Webb* ♡ was hopelessly attracted to the club, spending three separate managerial stints there. On his third return in 2000, his assessment was tinged with perhaps too much realism. "Southend has been a sick patient over the last few years". Whatever the diagnosis, it was probably contagious, as Webb resigned a year later pleading poor health.

CHANTS

'Oh Southend Pier
Is longer than yours
Oh Southend Pier is longer than yours
It's got some shops and a railway
Oh Southend Pier is longer than yours'

Can justifiably be sung at any seaside team in Britain...or even, at a push, Wigan Athletic.

'YOUR GROUND'S TOO BIG FOR YOU!' RATING

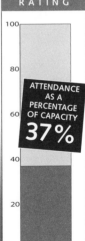

ATTENDANCE AS A PERCENTAGE OF CAPACITY
37%

DOH!!

Terry Alderton's career in comedy was slightly more glittering than his spell in between the sticks for Southend United. His talent for impersonations led to a slot with Lulu on the National Lottery show. But an ill-conceived performance against Colchester led to the death of his football career. Clinging onto the ball from a penalty save, he did an impromptu imitation of Michael Jackson's moonwalk. Penalising him for taking too many steps, the referee awarded Colchester an indirect free kick in the area, from which they scored.

STOCKPORT COUNTY

Recommended website: **www.stockportcounty-mad.co.uk**

WHO ARE YA?

Even the most devout County fans would admit that their recent five-season stay in Level One was a high watermark, the like of which they might have to wait a while to witness again. Despite their mock-rural name, County are the nearest club to the Manchester big two, leading to a necessarily stoical character, though their 'small club' features are a mixture of the laudable and the slightly shady. When it comes to the legal side of things, Stockport have a record of sailing extremely close to the wind under their property developer chairman, Brendan Elwood. In 2003, following a torturously long FA inquiry, the club finally admitted to dishonestly claiming £18,000 of public Football Trust money for the purchase of a PA system in 1995. The dodgy deal involved the contractors submitting over-inflated invoices, 75% of which could be claimed from the Trust. The net effect was to somehow end up with a £3,000 'profit'. The FA delivered what many neutrals considered to be a staggeringly meek punishment of a £10,000 fine and a reprimand. A string of lost tribunals to ex-managers has dogged the club, most notoriously when fans' favourite Danny Bergara was sacked following an altercation with Elwood at a hotel. The club implied that Bergara had thrown the first punch, though subsequently this was demonstrated to be the precise opposite of what really occurred.

CELEBRITY FANS
MIKE YARWOOD
Impressionist

IN and AROUND

Stockport County were the original Hatters (before Luton), the name being a reference to the region's history of making headwear. The term 'mad as a hatter' probably derives from the descent into psychosis suffered by some industry workers when they were exposed to mercury – at one time a key ingredient in the moulds.

The positives are generally the responsibility of the fans. Stockport have a deserved reputation for having the wittiest chants of any League club, including one of the longest – a twelve verse epic singing the praise of faithful County supporter of 30 years' standing, Arthur Brownlow, who rose to prominence because of his habit of charging up and down the touchline abusing officials. A special effort is made at away games – the quality of their songs inversely proportional to their League fortunes, hence a particularly fine vocal spell when they were propping up Level One with 'The relegation conga...Division One no longer'. When prevented from forming the customary snake at Selhurst Park, this turned into 'The stationary conga'.

In 1999, Gary Megson was one of the managers to leave under a cloud. When his new club, West Brom, were scheduled to play at Edgeley Park, the writers of the programme notes felt unable to churn out the usual pleasantries for the opposition's biographies. Under the heading 'West Brom's Coach' was an entirely accurate description; "West Brom make the journey to Edgeley Park today on the tried and trusted 1996 Volvo Bio M Jonckheere Deauville, which comprises 35 reclining seats each with adjustable footrests".

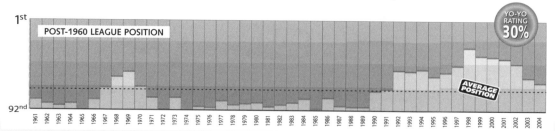

YO-YO RATING 30%

POST-1960 LEAGUE POSITION

1st ... 92nd

AVERAGE POSITION

1961 1962 1963 1964 1965 1966 1967 1968 1969 1970 1971 1972 1973 1974 1975 1976 1977 1978 1979 1980 1981 1982 1983 1984 1985 1986 1987 1988 1989 1990 1991 1992 1993 1994 1995 1996 1997 1998 1999 2000 2001 2002 2003 2004

PROGRESS REPORT

Since their formation in 1883, nothing has surpassed their 8th place in Level One in 1998. From 1971, they endured 19 consecutive basement seasons in which they failed to finish higher than 11th. Uruguayan manager Danny Bergara took them through a whirlwind of four play-off places and one promotion in five seasons from 1989 with the job finished by Dave Jones who eased them into Level One. Relegation in 2002 didn't mark the end of the downturn and they have plied their trade in the wrong half of Level Two since.

...The club features as the answer to perhaps the greatest football trivia question of all-time 'Whose ground is closest to the River Mersey?'...Fielded the only father/son combination in same League team (1951)...Recorded lowest League attendance of 13 (1921)...

RIVALS

Stockport might be expected to be even-handed in their hatred of the two Manchester teams, but their bile is reserved only for the blue half. When City were on a downer, travelling to Macclesfield was the ultimate low, but the trip to Edgeley Park was only slightly less humiliating. The fact that the Blues went round with a hang-dog 'we really shouldn't be here' attitude didn't help their cause – particularly at Stockport where the locals battle against being culturally and geographically swallowed up by Manchester. Stockport lost its official status as a Cheshire town in the 1974 Local Government reorganisation, though you won't find many residents referring to the town as being in 'Greater Manchester'. The town of Stockport is positively bulging with City fans, themselves something of a repressed minority within the region

MANCHESTER CITY
☠☠☠☠☠

as a whole. To be a County supporter is like being marginalised within someone else's ghetto. When the two met up in Level One, the fixture started to cause City real agony with County winning their first meeting for nearly 90 years, 3-1. By the time they parted company in 2002, City had only managed victory in one out of their six fixtures, making their constant promise that 'we'll never play you again' look extremely irritating and hollow.

County have twice had to put up with plans for the two clubs to cosy up to one another. A proposed full-scale merger under the banner of Manchester South FC was particularly loathsome. When City were due to move to their new stadium, rumours started flying of a plan to take over the Maine Road site under the genetically modified name of Manstock County. It is alleged that, despite denials of any official backing, the domain name www.manstockcounty.co.uk was registered to someone at the club.

BURNLEY
☠☠☠☠☠

With their jocular outlook, Stockport fans are not well disposed towards what they see as the thuggish seriousness of Burnley. Far from a traditional rivalry, it mainly stems from some ill-tempered matches in the 1990s and had some petrol poured on it when Stockport's marketing manager wrote that he'd been the subject of some shabby treatment in the Burnley directors' box. A Burnley fanzine re-printed the comments leading to a predictable rise in tension.

CREWE
☠☠☠☠☠

Crewe are seen as the annoying 'goody goodies'. One trip to Gresty Road was flung into chaos when hundreds of County fans were ordered off a train at Sandbach and told to walk home – an appetite-sharpening 25-mile ramble.

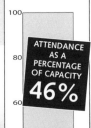

**SUPPORTERS'
VFM
53%**

**PERFORMANCE
AGAINST RIVALS
MANCHESTER
CITY**

WON 43%
LOST 29%
DRAWN 29%

LOVE/HATE

The managerial reign of *Carlton Palmer*, taking them from the bottom of the First to the bottom of the Second, is considered to have made the club 'a laughing stock'. Palmer is seen to have tried to use Stockport as a stepping stone to something more glamorous.

DOH!!

Caught up in the ticker-tape frenzy of the 1978 World Cup, Stockport emerged wearing a clone of the Argentina kit. It had a hasty re-design in 1982 when General Galtieri's lot invaded the Falklands.

CHANTS

Spoilt for choice:

At Gillingham, the mocking chant of

'Going Down…Going Down…
Going Down…'

was met with

'So are we…so are we…
so are we…'

**'YOUR GROUND'S
TOO BIG FOR YOU!'**
R A T I N G

**ATTENDANCE
AS A
PERCENTAGE
OF CAPACITY
46%**

100

80

60

40

20

0

STOKE CITY

AKA
SJOKE CITY

Recommended website: **www.potters-und.co.uk**

WHO ARE YA?

For Northerners making the torturous train journey back from London, the sight of Stoke's Britannia Stadium looming three miles south of the city centre signifies that they are back in civilisation. Sandwiched between the major cities of the Midlands and the North, Stoke is a geographical and cultural grey area. The accent is a unique mix of Brummie, Scouse, Mancunian and South Yorkshire.

For its loyal followers, watching Stoke has largely been a labour of love. They hold the record of the worst old First Division performance ever when picking up just 17 points during the whole of the 1984-85 season - although with typical Stoke irony, their three victories included the notable scalps of Arsenal and Manchester United. By the time they moved into The Britannia in 1997 (contender for the coldest ground in England) they were cash-starved and floundering in Level Two playing in a shiny, but only half-full, new stadium.

Considering the status of its legendary ex-players, including 1966 World Cup goalkeeper Gordon Banks, Stoke's collection of silverware is actually smaller than many casual observers realise. Although founding members of the Football League, they have yet to pick up the FA Cup - their solitary major success coming in the League Cup of 1972.

CELEBRITY FANS
Dominic Cork -
England Cricketer
Sybil Ruscoe -
Radio Presenter
Nick Hancock -
Presenter - *They Think It's All Over*

IN and AROUND

Stoke is not known for the standard of its architecture though locals can point to the fact that those who refer to Stoke as a shithole would, if it was not for the ceramics pioneered in the Potteries area, be literally shitting in a hole now.

Taken over by an Icelandic consortium in 1999, the omens looked bleak as the new owners stuffed the side with a collection of Scandinavian players. At one point, the first team featured five Icelandic players, one Dane and a Norwegian. Animosity grew between board and fans but with promotion to Level One, they weathered the storm and the prospect of Premiership action is no longer a complete pipe dream. The benefit of an Icelandic board is that the club is massively popular...in Iceland. A third of football fans on the island support Stoke. Anyone from the Potteries who visits is said to receive a regal welcome.

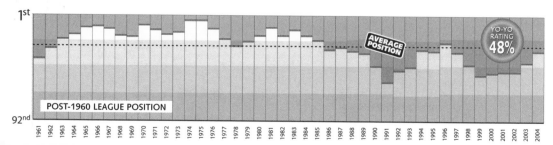

1st

AVERAGE POSITION

YO-YO RATING 48%

POST-1960 LEAGUE POSITION

92nd

1961 1962 1963 1964 1965 1966 1967 1968 1969 1970 1971 1972 1973 1974 1975 1976 1977 1978 1979 1980 1981 1982 1983 1984 1985 1986 1987 1988 1989 1990 1991 1992 1993 1994 1995 1996 1997 1998 1999 2000 2001 2002 2003 2004

PROGRESS REPORT

Respectable top-flight placings for nearly 20 years unexpectedly ended in relegation in 1977. Though it only took two seasons to return, the wobbles set in again. Stoke left the old First Division in 1985, never to return.

```
...Stoke were presented with a wooden spoon having finished last in the first ever football
                league - leading to the expression's popular usage...
     ...Stanley Matthews was 50 years and 5 days old when he played his last Stoke game...
          ...Have had two knighted players, Sir Geoff Hurst and Sir Stanley Matthews...
```

RIVALS

Stoke's geography is confused enough as it is without the factor of one of the most notorious local derbies in the country. Although many cities claim to be a series of distinctive towns, Stoke really is five, or possibly six, separate places - in fact the old number plate prefix for the area, VT, was, if you count the V as a Roman numeral, short for five towns.

SUPPORTERS' VFM 61%

PORT VALE

In their heyday of the 70s Stoke had a right to feel superior towards Port Vale. As the teams were generally separated by two divisions, there was a lot of 'dual supporting', with Stoke fans happy to watch Vale when their team was out of town. But as the two clubs converged, Stoke got a double dose of trouble. As they slipped down the divisions, the 'normal' fans drifted away leaving a hard-core of hooligan support. The relatively dispossessed Vale fans started to see Stoke as legitimate rivals, and now with a significant proportion of hyper-aggressive supporters, things have frequently boiled over.

The rivalry is crudely split down an east/west line with Stoke dominant in the Fenton and Longton areas to the west. Vale's strongholds are Burslem and Tunstall, with Hanley, home of the Britannia Stadium, split roughly down the middle. Vale use the term 'lardies' as an insult towards Stoke fans, an accusation with some grounding in reality, as Stoke was named in a study of obesity as the second fattest city in the UK (after Manchester).

The older school of supporters still sees Manchester United very negatively, but newer fans have been subjected to many smaller sides in their fall from grace. Crewe Alexandra, for so long synonymous with Level Three obscurity, have met Stoke in the league enough times for them to be considered genuine rivals, whereas in the past they were no more than a mild irritant.

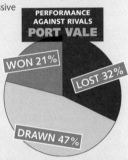

PERFORMANCE AGAINST RIVALS
PORT VALE

WON 21%
LOST 32%
DRAWN 47%

CARDIFF CITY

The hooligan element has turned its attentions largely to Cardiff City, partly due to the fact that a disproportionate number of good players have left the club for South Wales, but also because they vie for the top-dog status of British football mobs. Fixtures between the two are littered with serious incidents leading to the Stoke authorities insisting on increasingly draconian measures of control. In 2000, entry for the Cardiff match was limited to those who could produce a utility bill as proof of ID. Lately, a more sophisticated means of tackling trouble at away games has been introduced - a club ID card that must be produced to buy tickets and gain entry to away matches. Its ridiculously condescending name, 'The True Supporters card', has infuriated many fans, who feel they are now being discouraged to see them at all, having endured years of borderline misery supporting the club.

'YOUR GROUND'S TOO BIG FOR YOU!' RATING

LOVE/HATE

Graham Kavanagh moved from Stoke to the already loathed Cardiff, with the hint that he considered Cardiff a far better long-term proposition, guaranteeing him a cult-hate status at his former club.

CHANTS

Home of the rendition of Tom Jones' *'Delilah'* - first popular in the dark days of the 80s when something was needed to distract from what was happening on the field. Although heard less at the new Britannia Stadium, the ritual of the song is peculiarly detailed. One particular supporter, known as PJ, (who fell out of favour with the club) would get to his feet and shh the crowd. His solo lines were punctuated with the crowd's whoooas at the end of each, with the chorus a joint effort. Although originally adapted to include the line *'Forgive me Stoke City, I just couldn't take anymore'*, the lyric reverted back to *Delilah*. Stirring when a rendition goes to plan, a cacophony when it doesn't, supporters give themselves a round of applause at the end.

100

80

60

40

ATTENDANCE AS A PERCENTAGE OF CAPACITY

52%

20

0

DOH!!

Stoke's 70s' downhill path was largely due to the selling of most of their best players (including Jimmy Greenhoff in 1976). This was suddenly necessary after a gale left the roof of a stand scattered around the neighbourhood. When the insurance documents were dusted down, it was discovered the damaged stand was not covered; hence the need for a fast injection of funds.

SUNDERLAND

Recommended website: **www.readytogo.net**

WHO ARE YA?

'Passionate' and 'dedicated' are adjectives liberally applied to football fans everywhere, but no one can dispute their use in association with Sunderland AFC. From the legendary 'Roker Roar' of their former stadium, to the manic atmosphere in a frequently sold out Stadium of Light, there is no escaping the fact that hopeless devotion to their beloved club is almost a classifiable disease. Sunderland's fan base is exceptional, as, to be fair, is Newcastle's. They accounted for the third and fourth highest Premiership attendances, and if at home the same day (something that the schedulers largely manage to avoid), around one sixth of the two cities' official populations would be attending a football match. Sunderland's ground easily brushes off its 'Stadium of Shite' billing from Newcastle fans, as it is generally considered the swankiest in the country. Legend has it that 50,000 crammed in for the Level One trophy presentation game of 1999, a tight squeeze as its official capacity at the time was 42,000.

CELEBRITY FANS
STEVE CRAM
Athlete
PETER O'TOOLE
Actor - Lawrence of Arabia

IN and AROUND

The city of Sunderland has a larger population than Newcastle by around 20,000.

In their early history, Sunderland were a semi-Scottish outfit, enticing players from across the border where professionalism was still frowned upon. Their succession into the League in 1890 wasn't well received by clubs from the south, who didn't fancy the trek to away games, seeing as, until that point, there were no clubs from outside the Midlands or the Northwest. A clutch of pre-war championships gave way to not a lot, until Ian Porterfield attempted to break the Leeds net with the winner in the 1973 FA Cup final, making them the first side for 40 years to win the trophy from outside the top division.

Sunderland's 'Makems' nickname may have originally been an insult invented by Newcastle shipworkers during World War II. With experienced men from Sunderland drafted in to the Tyneside yards, Geordies felt aggrieved that locals were being deprived of jobs, hence the Wearsiders would 'mak[e]'em and tak[e]'em', (takeaway jobs). However, there is a variation which suggests that it was the Geordies who were the 'Tak'ems' (consumers of goods made by those in Wearside). Alternatively, the whole thing may be completely contrived, as some local historians say that the terms have only sprung to prominence relatively recently. But like a handful of other sides' nicknames, it has been taken up by those it was supposed to ridicule.

The club shop sells 'Sunderland' chocolates and wine, possibly earmarked for fans needing to placate the many wives who are virtually widowed by their men folk's obsession with the team. Their prominent football branding might only serve to dilute the peace offering; it's surprising that more have not needed to visit the casualty unit at Sunderland Royal Hospital to have them surgically removed.

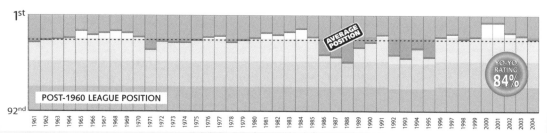

1st

AVERAGE POSITION

YO-YO RATING 84%

POST-1960 LEAGUE POSITION

92nd

1961 1962 1963 1964 1965 1966 1967 1968 1969 1970 1971 1972 1973 1974 1975 1976 1977 1978 1979 1980 1981 1982 1983 1984 1985 1986 1987 1988 1989 1990 1991 1992 1993 1994 1995 1996 1997 1998 1999 2000 2001 2002 2003 2004

PROGRESS REPORT

Sunderland's bobbing between the top two divisions is symptomatic of the gulf in class. They were able to runaway with Level One in 1999, beating every other team at least once, but four years later, they were relegated from the Premiership with the worst ever record for the division.

```
        ...The fans chose their nickname 'The Black Cats'...
            ...Stadium of Light is built on an old coal mine...
   ...Tally of 105 points was the highest ever in English League football (1998/99)...
```

RIVALS

One might expect that the three biggest clubs in the Northeast, Newcastle, Sunderland and Middlesbrough, would share some sort of intertwined triangular rivalry, but this is not strictly the case. Sunderland fans are keen to stress their ambivalence towards Boro, the 'small town in Yorkshire'; in fact, they can get quite shirty if it is suggested that they might even acknowledge their existence. This is to emphasise the undiluted and savage hatred of Newcastle. The overused 'life and death' expression became rather literal for one fan, who, following the Mackems' defeat of Newcastle at St James' Park in 2001, had worked himself up into such a frenzy that he suffered a heart attack and dropped down dead. The unfortunate widow was quoted as saying "I'm just glad he died happy".

NEWCASTLE

MIDDLESBROUGH

To get a historical grasp on the animosity between the two towns, it is possible to delve back into the era of roundheads and cavaliers, or more recently, the founding of the Tyne and Wear Development Council. The two fought each other in the English Civil War (Newcastle were the Royalists), exchanging canon fire over the Wear in the mid 17th century. Originally, Sunderland was little more than a fishing village, whilst Newcastle was a trading centre of international importance. Geordies were horrified when their 'little' neighbour began to rival them as a major port.

SUPPORTERS VFM 73%

PERFORMANCE AGAINST RIVALS
NEWCASTLE

WON 23%

LOST 32%

DRAWN 45%

Opposing gangs, the Gremlins (Newcastle) and the Seaburn Casuals (Sunderland), clash on numerous occasions, whether the sides are meeting or not. With both groups displaying far-right leanings, the ringleaders tend to be the subject of close police scrutiny.

LEEDS

Barry Welsh's Vauxhall Cavalier was easy to spot on Wearside with its distinctive red and white stripes, the Sunderland strip, and pictures of Peter Reid (when he was still in favour). Almost inevitably, when parked up one day, the car had a quick makeover, which saw it re-sprayed black and white.

Sugar Puffs' mascot, The Honey Monster, appeared in a TV commercial wearing what appeared to be a Newcastle United shirt. The effect on sales in the local area was devastating.

CHANTS

Sunderland have a fairly vicious selection of chants to call upon, many of which are unsuitable to print – particularly those aimed at ex-Newcastle boss Bobby Robson, whose mortality and continence were frequently called into question.

LOVE/HATE

The strength of feeling towards their rivals alone would be reason enough to loathe Newcastle's star striker, but the hatred of *Alan Shearer* has more tangible roots. At the end of a derby game, Shearer allegedly antagonised the Fulwell End by gesticulating and smiling smugly at the fans as he left the pitch. Supposedly, he also claimed to not enjoy playing alongside Kevin Phillips whilst on England duty.

'YOUR GROUND'S TOO BIG FOR YOU!'
RATING

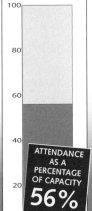

100

80

60

40

ATTENDANCE AS A PERCENTAGE OF CAPACITY
56%

20

0

DOH!!

Remembered for one of Wembley's greatest moments in 1973, Sunderland also contributed a Cup stinker, the song for their final against Liverpool in 1992. Forgetting that recent football records had gained semi-respectability, their ghastly rendition of Ain't No Stoppin' Us Now sent the genre back to the Stone Age.

Liverpool didn't take heed of the title, beating them 2-0.

SWANSEA CITY

Recommended website: **www.scfc.co.uk**

WHO ARE YA?

Swansea have done all the usual 'small club' things, once having suffered the indignity of being sold for a pound...twice in one year. But regardless of their uncertain future, at least they can reminisce on one of the more incredible fairytale seasons. The fact that they reached the top-flight in 1981-82 was good enough, but once there, they started their campaign with a 5-1 win against Leeds, topped the table on three occasions and never left the top six. If it hadn't been for them losing five of their last six games, Swansea were on target to be the most unlikely Champions in the League's history. At the time, the club was supplying the majority of the Welsh national side and Toshack earned a session with Eamonn Andrew's big red book for his trouble.

CELEBRITY FANS
ROBERT CROFT
Cricketer
RUTH MADOC
Actress - Hi-di-Hi

IN and AROUND

Swansea is the wettest city in Britain.

Unfortunately, the whirlwind of swapping leagues hadn't been completed. Within ten years, the club had gone all the way up, and had fallen all the way back. In the final game of 1985, Swansea managed the point they needed to prevent a slippage from old Division One to Level Three in successive seasons. Redevelopment of the Vetch Field was scuppered by residents who objected to the view from their houses being blocked. By December of that year, Toshack had done a runner to Sporting Lisbon and the club was officially wound up, requiring some grovelling to the League authorities to be permitted to play a derby fixture against Cardiff on Boxing Day. Over a year of wrangling in the High Court followed just to ensure the club's existence. In 2002-03, they had a spell propping up the entire League (the first time this had happened in their history), and with on-field stability totally gone to pot, 21 different players made their debuts for the club in just the one season.

Swansea's nickname, The Jacks, is not, as one Cardiff City supporter claimed, simply 'the name of one of their pubs'. It is a strange brew of fact and legend surrounding a black retriever named Jack who, during the depression of the 20s, would make a habit of rescuing people who'd fallen in the North Dock. His final tally has been put at 27.

Swansea's most famous old boy was given a free transfer in 1966. Not considered good enough for the first team of a, then, Level Two side, striker Georgio Chinaglia returned to his native Italy to be picked up by Lazio where, by 1974, he had become top scorer in Serie A. After a stint with New York Cosmos, he became president of Lazio in 1983.

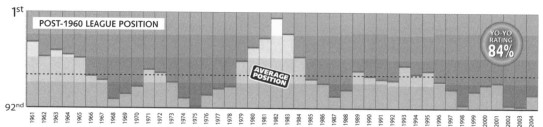

1st

POST-1960 LEAGUE POSITION

AVERAGE POSITION

YO-YO RATING 84%

92nd

1961 1962 1963 1964 1965 1966 1967 1968 1969 1970 1971 1972 1973 1974 1975 1976 1977 1978 1979 1980 1981 1982 1983 1984 1985 1986 1987 1988 1989 1990 1991 1992 1993 1994 1995 1996 1997 1998 1999 2000 2001 2002 2003 2004

PROGRESS REPORT

A Himalayan post-1960 chart reveals that the period after the peak of the early 80s is split into two distinct phases. Swansea managed to hang around in Level Two for a prolonged spell for much of the 90s, but despite a solitary season back there in 2000-2001, they now have the look of a basement outfit – and had trouble even hanging onto that status when finishing 20th and 21st in 2002 and 2003 respectively. A 10th spot in 2004 did something to relieve the gloom.

```
...Changed their name from Swansea Town (1970)...Beat Real Madrid 3-0 (1927)...
          ...'Vetch' (as in Vetch Field) is a type of cabbage...
```

RIVALS

CARDIFF CITY
☠️ ☠️ ☠️ ☠️ ☠️

BRISTOL ROVERS
☠️ ☠️ ☠️ ☠️

SHREWSBURY
☠️ ☠️ ☠️

Seasoned derby watchers are fairly unanimous that Swansea v Cardiff is the most venomous rivalry in the League, with only Celtic v Rangers in the same bracket in the British Isles. The first difficulty with these two is trying to sort out the thorny issue of which is the more successful club historically. When things really began to get nasty between the two in the 80s, it could have been reasonably argued that Swansea were top of the pile. Even with Hammam's mad dash up the divisions, there isn't a lot of difference between their league placings over time, but the impression lingers that Cardiff have always been seen as more important. Swansea were, and are, incensed that, even when they were in the top-flight, their exploits were virtually ignored by the Welsh media. The constant bias is said to have been partially responsible for the demise of Newport County, Wales' fourth club. Many Swansea fans are reasonably well disposed towards Wrexham, feeling that they are similar victims of the pro-Cardiff lobby. The situation is mirrored outside football. Cardiff was the first to be granted city status, became the capital in the 1950s, was chosen as the base for the Welsh Assembly and has been the recipient of European Aid that has transformed it into a sleek cultural centre – whilst Swansea residents fume ever more deeply.

Violence at the derby fixture has, over the years, been guaranteed. The number willing to turn up for each side ready to break the law accounts for a high proportion of the fan-base, with Swansea frequently heading the bad boys table for the lower leagues. In 1992, such was the ferocity of the rivalry, 13,000 turned out to see an otherwise meaningless Autoglass Trophy fixture. The following year saw some of the ugliest scenes ever seen in Britain as Cardiff won a Level Two match at Ninian Park in December. It was a surprisingly rare on-field victory for them. Since 1990, Swansea have enjoyed more success in League and Cup games, losing just three of 13 meetings. After 1993, away supporters were banned from entry to derby games, which in 1999 dried up completely as the two drifted apart in the League. The two got together in 2002 for the FAW Cup final at Ninian Park where fans pelted each other with anything that came to hand. This despite the 'hand of friendship' gesture by Sam Hammam in laying on free coaches for Swansea fans at a cost of £7,500.

Interestingly, there is a slight feeling that Swansea has a less anti-English culture than the capital, leading, strangely, to the 'baiting' of Cardiff supporters with Union Jacks fluttering in the Swansea end.

SUPPORTERS' VFM 63%

PERFORMANCE AGAINST RIVALS CARDIFF

WON 46%
LOST 30%
DRAWN 24%

LOVE/HATE

Ex-chairman *Tony Petty* (HATE) made plenty of enemies, not least amongst the players, who he told would not get paid...on Christmas Eve. Ex-manager *John Hollins* (HATE) for demanding compensation. *Regional TV football programmes* (HATE) that display blatant Cardiff bias. More positively, *Liverpool* ♡ are seen in favourable light for writing off some of Swansea's crippling debt in the 80s.

CHANTS

Not known for its match-day cuisine, Swansea were asked

'Why are your pies so shit?'

by Burnley.

DOH!!

The lowlight of the 1995-96 relegation season was the appointment of PE teacher and former manager of Cradley Town (it's in the West Midlands), Kevin Cullis. He lasted seven days before Jan Molby was drafted in, making him the second shortest managerial appointment in League history. (He is pipped for the ultimate honour by Dave Bassett, who struggled through four days at Crystal Palace in 1984).

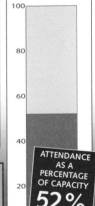

'YOUR GROUND'S TOO BIG FOR YOU!'

RATING

100
80
60
40
20
0

ATTENDANCE AS A PERCENTAGE OF CAPACITY

52%

SWINDON TOWN

Recommended website: **www.swindon-town-fc.co.uk**

WHO ARE YA?

Swindon's main offbeat claim to fame is that rival supporters appear to have very little idea where the town actually is. Many labour under the illusion that Swindon is very near, or even, in Wales – demonstrated by the usual chanted accusations that the town's residents are over-familiar with livestock of the woolly variety. But its mention in the BBC comedy, *The Office*, where members of the Swindon branch parachute in on the grim corporate world of David Brent's Slough paper merchants, goes someway to identifying the town's true location – 30 miles east of Bristol and an extremely long walk from the Welsh border.

CELEBRITY FANS
MELINDA MESSENGER
Doubly-blessed Model
WILLIE CARSON
Ex-Jockey, is currently the chairman

Swindon Town comprehensively wins the title of 'team that nobody remembers being in the Premiership'. More unfairly, one of the great Wembley shocks, when beating Arsenal in the League Cup final in 1969, tends not to loom very large in the footballing consciousness either. The club's history is littered with extremes of both the heroic variety (as FA Cup giant-killers) and the downright terrible – of which the worst must be the fact that the club holds the record for the least points won in a Premiership season. Their promotion to the top-flight for the 1993-94 season was the long-term reward for some audacious managerial appointments, Lou Macari, Ossie Ardiles and, notably, Glenn Hoddle, who, as player-manager, encouraged the team to develop a slick passing game.

IN and AROUND

Approaching the County Ground from the south, visiting supporters are faced with the ultimate urban driving thrill – Swindon's infamous 'Magic Roundabouts' – five 'sub' roundabouts encircling a sort of 'daddy' roundabout. Experts advise treating each as an entirely separate entity and give way to traffic to the right.

But with Hoddle lured to Chelsea during the close season, his comparatively inexperienced assistant, John Gorman, took over the reins. With just five wins in their first and only Premiership season and a record 100 goals conceded, Swindon secretly hope that the future will serve up another, even more hapless, side to exorcise the ghosts of 93-94. Their top-flight existence had been postponed, as in 1990 they had already won a Level One play-off final against Sunderland when an enquiry reported that there had been illegal payments made to players during Lou Macari's spell as manager. In one of the harshest judgements ever passed, the club was effectively relegated two divisions, though the sentence was later 'halved', leaving it where it was.

Swindon have at least shaken off the dubious honour of being the only club to have been placed in administration twice. Seeing its record of improbable internal wrangles, the 2002 High Court ruling that dissolved the board (after it was discovered that the proper election procedure hadn't been followed) could probably only happen to Swindon Town.

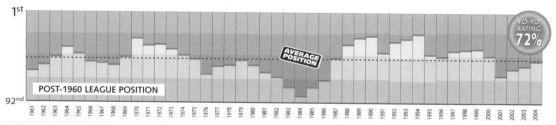

1st

YO-YO RATING 72%

AVERAGE POSITION

POST-1960 LEAGUE POSITION

92nd

1961 1962 1963 1964 1965 1966 1967 1968 1969 1970 1971 1972 1973 1974 1975 1976 1977 1978 1979 1980 1981 1982 1983 1984 1985 1986 1987 1988 1989 1990 1991 1992 1993 1994 1995 1996 1997 1998 1999 2000 2001 2002 2003 2004

PROGRESS REPORT

Swindon have been everywhere and done just about everything. It's a fitting reflection of their perpetual bouncing around that their post-1960 average is very nearly in the centre of the four divisions. It took nine years from a low point of 17th in Level Three to a Premiership place in 1993, but their one season with the big boys was followed by a consecutive relegation to Level Two. After an undistinguished spell back in Level One, they have really only found their legs again very recently, achieving a play-off place from the Level Two in 2004.

...Were the first to trademark their badge...Managed to be promoted and relegated in the same season (due to financial irregularities)...'Swindon Town' is the only English club name not to contain any letters from the word 'mackerel'...

RIVALS

The Thames Valley/Wiltshire rivalries form a complex web with fans of opposing clubs unable to agree on the intensity of feelings. The Swindon/Reading rivalry tends to be maintained by the younger fans of both clubs, though the majority of Swindon supporters point the finger at Oxford United.

OXFORD UNITED

Part of the confusion was that Reading lost their biggest rivals, Aldershot, when the Berkshire club disappeared out of the League. Prior to them going bust, fans of the three enjoyed compiling their own 'Didcot Triangle' league, based only on results between the three. Reading gradually turned their attentions to Swindon, only for the latter to be already preoccupied with Oxford. However, a Swindon v Reading match in 1997 saw a serious outbreak of violence, with an estimated 5,000 fans barricaded in their respective car parks by police in riot gear. The extent of the injuries overwhelmed Swindon's casualty unit and Reading's walking wounded were sent back to their own hospital for treatment.

READING

The entry of Wycombe into the equation complicates things further. Both they and Reading like to see Oxford United as realistic rivals, though at The Manor there is little interest in anyone other than Swindon.

More positively, during a League game in 2000, it was noted that Swindon fans cheered a group of Reading supporters when they did a lap of honour following a charity walk to raise funds for a meningitis sufferer.

SUPPORTERS' VFM 47%

PERFORMANCE AGAINST RIVALS OXFORD

WON 42%
LOST 20%
DRAWN 38%

♥ LOVE/HATE

The insult hailed most often at Oxford's centre-half, *Joey Beauchamp*, was that he is a 'Mummy's boy'. The origin of this feeling and why it is so important to his detractors lies in his transfer from Oxford to West Ham for £1 million in June 1994. Beauchamp, having got his break into the big-time, was loathed to move out of his parents' house in Oxford, giving him a long commute to work. He didn't make a single appearance for The Hammers and just 58 days later was sold to Swindon for £800,000. After a fairly dismal season, he went back to his beloved Oxford for a fraction of the price West Ham had paid just over a year earlier, where his performances picked up.

CHANTS

*♪**♫*!*

'I can't read or write, but that don't really matter
'Cos I come from Swindon Town....
and I can drive a tractor'

One of the more oddly self-deprecating chants. The claim of being able to handle farmyard equipment might be an exaggeration as agriculture only employs 3% of the town's population.

Do 'matter' and 'tractor' rhyme?

'YOUR GROUND'S TOO BIG FOR YOU!'
RATING

100
80
60
40
ATTENDANCE AS A PERCENTAGE OF CAPACITY
54%
20
0

DOH!!

Betting on your side to win is often a sign of misplaced confidence. Putting money on your side to lose, particularly if you are the chairman, has a distinct whiff of impropriety. In 1988, the Sunday People printed revelations that chairman Brian Hillier had bet on Swindon to lose in an FA Cup match against Newcastle. Swindon lost 5-0. On 5th January 1989, both manager Lou Macari and Hillier were charged with unauthorised betting. Hillier was suspended from football for six months. He appealed. So irritated were the FA by the matter being strung out by the appeal process, they increased the ban to three years. The club was fined £7,500, and Macari £1,000, for what the FA described as a minor role in a "foolhardy misdemeanour".

TORQUAY UNITED

UNREADY TO QUIT
(ANAGRAM)

Recommended website: **www.mervo.com/torquay-united**

WHO ARE YA?

It doesn't seem natural to talk of only two Devon clubs. More surprising is the fact that the missing member of the trio is Exeter City, not Torquay – a side whose league record allows them only to look down on Rochdale. But their neighbour's fall into The Conference seems to have scared the remaining two into their best seasons in living memory.

Torquay United have turned the last day of the season drama into a specialised subject. In the last 20 years, they have finished last of the 92 on three occasions– surviving via re-elections and a huge let-off in 1996, thanks to the Conference champions, Stevenage, having their ground condemned as inadequate for League football. They have survived a couple of last day 'great escapes'. Having hung on the previous two years, it looked like third time unlucky as they found themselves bottom on the last day of the 1986-87 season (the first with automatic relegation). They were famously saved by an over-zealous police dog who mistakenly thought a Torquay player was about to attack his handler, rather than the goal. Pooch dutifully took a chunk out of him. The resulting injury time was used very effectively, scoring an equaliser against Crewe to send Lincoln City out of the League. Torquay also managed an improbable last day win in May 2001 to stay up.

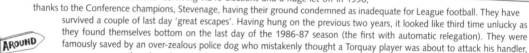

Torquay's microclimate allows palm trees & other sub-tropical plants to flourish, though botanical types point out that they can also grow in parts of Scotland.

The chairman, Mike Bateson, can politely be described as a colourful character who has brought inspiration, optimism and cash to his club. It is rumoured that his belief in colour psychology saw the home and away dressing rooms given, respectively, a blue and pink makeover in a cunning ploy to help results...it didn't. Popular with fans, the businessman is permitted to indulge in some mild eccentricities, allowing Algernon (a ventriloquist's dummy sporting a club blazer and tie) to attend and make sage-like contributions to interviews.

Following an unseasonably chilly day in November 2001, the chairman was forced to abandon the use of ball boys following a complaint from an off-duty education officer that it was too cold for a school boy volunteer to be wearing shorts rather than a tracksuit. After screams of 'political correctness', the council apologised with only one FA Cup match going ahead without them.

The club has a deserved reputation for being welcoming, a prime example coming in 2000 when the locals joined in the celebrations of Northampton fans who had just gained promotion...by beating Torquay into a play-off place. However, there are occasionally gripes at Plainmoor's rather jobsworth stewarding. There was a literary protest when a fan was refused admission – for carrying a paperback book. The following home game saw supporters defiantly brandishing a selection of popular fiction. Similarly, inflatable starfishes were outlawed for their potential to cause injury.

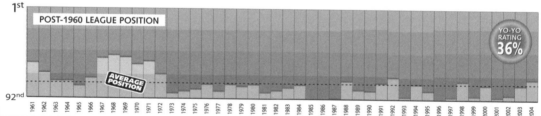

POST-1960 LEAGUE POSITION

1st

92nd

AVERAGE POSITION

YO-YO RATING 36%

1961 1962 1963 1964 1965 1966 1967 1968 1969 1970 1971 1972 1973 1974 1975 1976 1977 1978 1979 1980 1981 1982 1983 1984 1985 1986 1987 1988 1989 1990 1991 1992 1993 1994 1995 1996 1997 1998 1999 2000 2001 2002 2003 2004

PROGRESS REPORT

Steady and frequently lucky since 1960, Torquay United have spent all but nine years in the basement. Promotion to Level Two in 2004 puts them well above their long-term average. If they can finish third or better, it will be their highest ever League placing. They have timed their infrequent movements nicely to coincide with tinkering of the league structure, having been relegated from Division Three ...to Division Three in 1992 and jumping from Division Three to League One in 2004.

```
...The only league club to be knocked out of the FA Cup by non-league opposition in four
consecutive seasons from 1991 - Farnborough Town, Yeovil Town, Sutton United and Enfield...
       ...Became 'The Gulls' as Brighton had already nabbed first choice 'Seagulls'...
              ...Helen Chamberlain has a tattoo of a gull on her arse...
```

RIVALS

The least hated club in the football league, your chance of being assaulted by a Torquay United supporter is close to absolute zero. Torquay weren't amused at being barracked after a lock-in following the meeting with Argyle in 1995, but even when the Devon clubs have been at parity in Level Three, the derby games have been played in a fairly calm atmosphere. The only occasion when police at Plainmoor thought it wise to bring a few shields and extra padding was for the visit of Wolves. Otherwise all the anecdotal evidence points to Torquay folk being entirely peaceable.

PLYMOUTH ARGYLE

Plymouth clearly weren't exactly expecting an invasion in 2001, as they allocated a mere 138 seats for Torquay fans. Relations between the Devon clubs have always been reasonably cordial, particularly between Exeter and Torquay, with Gulls fans happy to contribute to the fundraising efforts of their neighbours in times of trouble. The two chairmen are known to be good mates.

Torquay fans don't seem keen on confrontation. In the absence of recognisable local derbies, the trip to Cardiff is a stroll round the block. But a noticeable lack of numbers on the away terraces at Ninian Park in 2001 suggested that Gulls fans were happy to swerve the notoriously hostile atmosphere – and those that made the trip were happy to leave asap. However, the message apparently hasn't got through at Villa. In 2002, a group of fans started their 600 mile round trip to Carlisle, only to discover that the game had been postponed as they were approaching the Midlands. Taking a quick detour to Villa Park, who were hosting Spurs, they arrived at the ground satisfied that at least they'd get to see some sort of football. But the sight of a handful of amber-clad Torquay supporters was too strong for the stewards to stomach and they were turned away as a 'security risk'.

PERFORMANCE AGAINST RIVALS
PLYMOUTH

WON 21%
LOST 50%
DRAWN 29%

SUPPORTERS' VFM
73%

LOVE/HATE

Travelling to away games requires stamina and more petrol money than any other league club, bar Plymouth. Their play-off final at Wembley in 1991, on a Friday evening, dragged on to nearly 11pm following extra-time and penalties, meaning travelling supporters could witness the sun coming up on Saturday morning as they made the trek home.

CHANTS

To pasty-faced land-locked clubs:

'Have you ever…
have you ever…
have you ever seen a beach?'

'YOUR GROUND'S TOO BIG FOR YOU!'
RATING

100
80
60
40
20
0

ATTENDANCE AS A PERCENTAGE OF CAPACITY
55%

DOH!!

In 1996, Gulls' fan Mike Beresford bought a house on Warbro Road, overlooking Plainmoor. Reasoning that he was effectively buying an armchair view of matches every Saturday for life, he was gutted when the club erected a mobile screen during the critical 90 minutes of every home game. This was done for 'health and safety reasons' after he and some mates had dimly shouted abuse at Dawlish fans during a pre-season friendly.

TOTTENHAM HOTSPUR

Recommended website: **www.mehstg.co.uk**

WHO ARE YA?

Although seen as fairly neutral in national terms, Tottenham are, perhaps unfairly, generally portrayed as the least popular team in London. This is no reflection on their supporters or their on-field style which, even in the worst times under the charge of Ossie Ardiles, was anything but dull. But the never ending saga of the club's backroom squabbles through the Scholar/Maxwell/Sugar/Venables/bung era of the 90s, with its associated hand-wringing, is seen as tiresome by outsiders. Tottenham's cause was not particularly helped by gifting England Darren Anderton, a player with the reputation of getting injured if the wind changed direction, and who was partly responsible for Spurs being dubbed 'Tottenham Hospice'.

Despite their moans that Alan Sugar has been more interested in milking the club for cash than building Championship contenders, Spurs' fans are keen on their reputation for bringing young players through the ranks and supporting those going through a lean patch. They point to their continued encouragement of players such as Helder Postiga as evidence of patience and a lack of the fickle nature that bedevils so many supporters. Ramon Vega was beyond help though.

CELEBRITY FANS
EMMA BUNTON
Spice Girl
SALMAN RUSHDIE
Novelist

Their high expectations are understandable, as many of the Spurs' faithful can recall the League, Cup and European successes of the 50s and 60s, including being the first British team to win a European trophy (Cup Winners Cup 1963). A solitary League Cup in 1999 is their sole piece of silverware of the last decade.

The send off for the area's radical Labour MP, Bernie Grant, was the largest black funeral ever seen in Britain.

The legend that Spurs won major honours in years that ended with a '1' is not a particularly recent thing. As early as 1979, in 'Shoot', it was noticed that Spurs tended to bag trophies in the year after the turn of each decade. Even since the first observation, they triumphed in the FA Cups of 1981 and 1991. Spurs have won 15 major honours since 1900. If evenly distributed between the 10 years of the decades, we'd expect one or two to coincide with each digit. In fact, Tottenham have won eight trophies in '01s, the only exceptions being 1911, 1931 and 2001. (There were no competitions played in 1941.)

Although a charge primarily aimed at Manchester United, Tottenham are no slouches at making the most of any commercial opportunity they can find – leading to criticism of the club's official website as little more than a tool for selling various knickknacks to fans. Alan Sugar got off to a difficult start with the redevelopment of the 'Shelf' terrace as executive boxes. However, White Hart Lane's conversion to all-seater is generally acknowledged to be one of the more successful stadium re-builds, with some even claiming the atmosphere has improved with the abolition of standing areas.

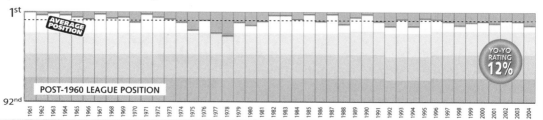

1st

AVERAGE POSITION

YO-YO RATING 12%

POST-1960 LEAGUE POSITION

92nd

1961 1962 1963 1964 1965 1966 1967 1968 1969 1970 1971 1972 1973 1974 1975 1976 1977 1978 1979 1980 1981 1982 1983 1984 1985 1986 1987 1988 1989 1990 1991 1992 1993 1994 1995 1996 1997 1998 1999 2000 2001 2002 2003 2004

PROGRESS REPORT

Considering the boardroom traumas, Spurs' Premiership record is a model of consistency – though perhaps a little below what their fans consider they deserve. Aside from their Cup exploits, Spurs have remained solidly stuck in the middle of the top-flight – not deviating between 7th and 15th since 1990, but without ever looking serious title contenders and constantly falling short of a European place. If anything, their trajectory is pointing very slightly downwards, and their 14th place finish in 2003-04 was the lowest of any of London's four Premiership teams

```
...White Hart Lane was used as a rifle range during World War II...
      ...Were the last non-league team to win the FA Cup (1901)...
...When playing for Spurs, Les Ferdinand scored Premier League's 10,000th goal...
```

RIVALS

Spurs' loathing of Arsenal is at least based on a tale more lively than simply proximity. With admirably long memories, Spurs point to the fact that Arsenal were originally from South London, as a team for workers at a munitions plant, and should have stayed there, instead of trying to muscle in on Tottenham's supporters' base by locating themselves within three miles of White Hart Lane. Arsenal's then chairman, Henry Norris, pushed through the move to howls of protest from both Spurs and Orient. Things turned really nasty on the resumption of football after the First World War in 1919 when the old First Division was enlarged from 20 to 22 teams.

Having finished bottom of the First, Spurs expected to be allowed to remain with two being promoted from the Second to make up the numbers. This was thought even more likely as Manchester United, who had finished two points ahead of Spurs, had 'arranged' to beat Liverpool 2-0 in an effort to avoid the bottom spot. In a suspiciously matey arrangement, other top clubs from the Second Division were invited to apply for promotion. Despite finishing only fifth, Arsenal got the nod on what are seen as spurious grounds that they had been established longer than other applicants, whilst Spurs were relegated. (The Gunners have a different take on the saga).

Norris went on to be discredited, having been found making illegal payments to Arsenal players. Spurs' fans were convinced that there was bribery involved in getting Arsenal their place in the top-flight, a position they've maintained ever since.

SUPPORTERS' VFM 67%

PERFORMANCE AGAINST RIVALS ARSENAL

WON 32%

LOST 40%

DRAWN 28%

The rivalry was responsible for some of the darker moments of hooliganism during the 70s and 80s. Today, Wenger is seen as a little too cock-sure, particularly his very early hint that Arsenal could go through a season unbeaten (even though it later proved possible). The most jaw-dropping managerial move, with Arsenal stalwart George Graham being appointed as Spurs' boss in 1998, led to the rare situation of virtually the entire fan-base hating both the manager and the chairman simultaneously.

Increasingly galling for Spurs is the fact that the rivalry is threatening to become unreciprocated, with many at Arsenal tending to name Manchester United as their top hate. Spurs have a poor record against their fiercest London rivals – but then again, most have. Even harder to swallow are their 23 matches against Chelsea since the Premiership was formed – without a single win.

'YOUR GROUND'S TOO BIG FOR YOU!' RATING

LOVE/HATE

Tottenham's excitement at appointing two of their on-field heroes to management was, with hindsight, unjustified. But tactfully ignoring what happened during their spells in charge, *Ossie Ardiles* and *Glen Hoddle* are still seen as gods.

It is said that Jimmy Greaves, Steve Perryman and Glen Hoddle would have never considered pulling on the hated Arsenal shirt. The appointment of *George Graham* as manager in 1998, straight from an illegal payments scandal at Arsenal, pushed loyalties to the limit. But the defection of *Sol Campbell* to Highbury in 2001 was met with astonishment and vehement hatred.

CHANTS

At odds with the image of the French as sensitive lovers:

'Don't bend down when Wenger's around'.

100

80

60

40

ATTENDANCE AS A PERCENTAGE OF CAPACITY 96%

20

0

DOH!!

Spurs received £15,000 after their opening fixture of the 1988-89 season had to be postponed because work on the ground had not been completed on time.

TRANMERE ROVERS

Recommended website: **www.whitereview.co.uk**

WHO ARE YA?

At the first sign of the club gaining a bit of momentum in the 90s, Prenton Park was suddenly the place to be. A rare stay in Level One saw attendances swelled by floating Merseysiders, not that you'd have thought that there was any such thing. But the flip side was that many deserted Tranmere when the good times came to an end/were temporarily halted. Tranmere's renaissance coincided with a mammoth financial struggle in 1989. The buckets were shaken at local businesses just to pay the players' wages, and a chunk of the squad was transfer listed.

Tranmere's FA Cup heroics, most memorably a comeback from 3-0 down at half-time to beat Southampton 4-3 in 2001, were aided by the man with the longest throw-in in the world. Record-breaking Dave Challinor could effectively turn any throw-in won in the opposition half into a corner. At home, the FA allowed him to use a towel to wipe the ball (with the stipulation that players from both sides could use it). Playing away, it was suspected that clubs would try and scupper him by shifting advertising hoardings a bit closer to the pitch than normal. Barnsley were so concerned that they had substitutes limber up in such a way as to try and put him off.

CELEBRITY FANS
RAY STUBBS
BBC Football Presenter
ELTON WELSBY
ITV Football Presenter
HALF MAN HALF BISCUIT
Rock group

IN and AROUND

There wasn't much of a buzz around Birkenhead before the Industrial Age. In 1801 its population was recorded as 110.

Supporters put pressure on the club to turf out away fans from the huge Kop end (it had been shared), a move they took in 2002.

In 2003, Prenton Park saw one of the oddest abandonments ever when a serial climber scaled a floodlight pylon and went for a breezy jog along the roof of the Cowshed end. With minutes to go, and Tranmere beating Mansfield 2-0, the game was called off. Prenton's Spiderman had previously got form for clambering up assorted churches in Birkenhead.

Half Man Half Biscuit, (whose best known song 'All I want for Christmas is a Dukla-Prague Away Kit' betrays more than a passing interest in football) are in a different league of true celebrity fans. On the verge of the big time, they refused to go on Channel 4's *The Tube*, opting instead for the delights of Tranmere v Scunthorpe in a Level Three league match. Even the thoughtful offer of a helicopter which would have ensured that they could see the second half was turned down.

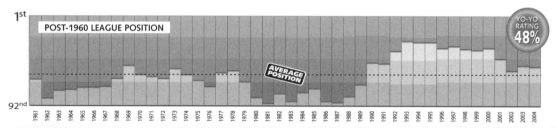

1st — 92nd

POST-1960 LEAGUE POSITION

AVERAGE POSITION

YO-YO RATING 48%

1961 1962 1963 1964 1965 1966 1967 1968 1969 1970 1971 1972 1973 1974 1975 1976 1977 1978 1979 1980 1981 1982 1983 1984 1985 1986 1987 1988 1989 1990 1991 1992 1993 1994 1995 1996 1997 1998 1999 2000 2001 2002 2003 2004

PROGRESS REPORT

On paper, Tranmere have a passing similarity to another club squeezed for support by two major names within easy distance, Leyton Orient. If you ignore the 1990s the two share an undistinguised league record – but Tranmere's league and cup exploits of that decade are a top drawer fairytale. It could have been even better. John Aldridge, homesick for Merseyside whilst managing Real Sociedad, came home as player/manager to take the club to three Premiership play-offs in a row – only to lose all of them in the semi-finals. Another 'nearly' occurred when losing the League Cup Final to Leicester in 2000. To get one step below the top-flight was incredible enough – a position they hadn't managed since 1938. In the 50+ years between, Tranmere were just above the hardcore basement boys, flitting anonymously between the Level Two and Level Three. The noughties haven't been quite so kind – with a slip back into Level Two.

```
...Conceded the fastest ever league goal in four seconds against defunct Bradford Park Avenue...
        ...Won record aggregate score match 13-4 against Oldham (1935)...
```

RIVALS

It's taken a bit of ingenuity for Tranmere to gain a rival at all. With Everton and Liverpool to the east (who, to be fair have bigger fish – like each other – to fry), Wrexham to the south, nothing to the north, and just the Atlantic to the west, Tranmere lies on the geographical sidelines.

Then, handily, along come Bolton. One of the odder non-traditional rivalries to appear on the scene, it's also notable because it seems to engulf the two clubs behind the scenes as well as the fans. Like a growing number, it is based largely on the rancour inducing play-off system. In 1991, having finished fifth in Level Two, Tranmere beat Bolton, who'd finished fourth, with a goal in extra-time.

BOLTON ☠️☠️☠️

This was followed by Tranmere ruining Bolton's chances of amassing 100 league points with a late equaliser in 1997. A bitter and niggly League Cup semi-final between the two in 2000 saw an argument over the use of Dave Chalinor's helpful towel. But the low was reached with a smash and grab raid on Prenton Park in August 2000. In what was seen as a deliberate refusal to use Tranmere's facilities, the Bolton coach turned up with just 35 minutes to go until kick-off. The players were already changed and ready to go, proceeding to secure a 1-0 victory. At the final whistle, they jumped straight back on the bus without troubling the changing rooms.

Aware of the media interest in the bust up between the clubs, at the start of a press conference before their meeting in 2001, Aldridge announced that he wouldn't take any questions about Bolton or Sam Allaydyce.

EVERTON ☠️☠️☠️

Of the Merseyside big-boys, Tranmere tend to dislike Everton more than Liverpool and fondly remember a 3-0 drubbing of The Toffees in 2001.

PERFORMANCE AGAINST RIVALS
BOLTON

WON 27%
LOST 43%
DRAWN 30%

SUPPORTERS'
VFM
78%

LOVE/HATE

HATE

John Aldridge ♡ has the unusual distinction of being a hero at all the British clubs he's been associated with. He is Britain's leading scorer with 474 goals in 882 appearances and spent 13 years at Tranmere as player/manager throughout their most successful period in their history. Oxford and Liverpool worship him as well.

Even Tranmere's Chief Executive, Lorraine Rogers, managed to have a dig at Bolton manager *Sam Allydyce*, suggesting, in 2000, that he may be "a little peculiar". Tranmere fans tend to use slightly stronger expressions.

♪**♫**♪*!

CHANTS

Wishing to distance themselves from anti-Merseyside chants, Tranmere would like to point out:

'Don't be mistaken, don't be misled, we are not Scousers, we're from Birkenhead'.

'YOUR GROUND'S
TOO BIG FOR YOU!'
R A T I N G

100

80

60

40

20

0

ATTENDANCE
AS A
PERCENTAGE
OF CAPACITY
46%

DOH!!

Tranmere were lucky not to have been ordered to replay an FA Cup tie against Sunderland in 2000 when throwing on a substitute for a player who had been sent off. Having had Clint Hill dismissed for a second bookable offence, Tranmere's Stephen Frail came on, without anyone else coming off, leaving them with 11 players to defend a corner.

WALSALL

CONFUSED WITH: CAPITAL OF POLAND

Recommended website: **www.walsallindependent.co.uk**

WHO ARE YA?

In the roll call of West Midlands clubs, the 'oh and' afterthought is likely to be reserved for Walsall. Though sometimes lumbered with the 'lack of ambition' tag, there is a positive side; the club has avoided the money problems that beset virtually every other lower league outfit, and routinely show a modest profit for each season's endeavours. Walsall do all the 'small club' things very well. Their 2-0 defeat of Arsenal in the third round of the FA Cup 1933 is still regarded as the greatest giant-killing act of all time, with Walsall in the Division Three North and Arsenal about to win three consecutive old First Division Championships. Their recent transfer policy has also paid dividends. Losing £2.5 million of ITV Digital revenue, the shortfall was partially eased by an astute clause inserted in the sale contract for Michael Ricketts. Ricketts started his career at Walsall, playing 31 games before being snapped up by Bolton for £400,000. Having fallen out with Sam Alladyce, he went to Middlesborough for £2.5 million, netting Walsall a £420,000 windfall from the sell-on.

CELEBRITY FANS
PETE WATERMAN
Pop Producer – ITV's *Pop Idol*
KENNETH CLARKE
Tory Politician

IN and AROUND

Walsall is home to one of the few genuinely liked pieces of public art in the country – a stone hippo that stands in the pedestrian precinct.

Their stability is remarkable considering the degree that they are squeezed for support. The town itself suffers a sort of four-way split. Walsall fans are suffocated by the predominance of other West Midlands teams within their own boundaries. Wednesbury and Darlaston, immediately to the west, are mostly West Brom. Brownhills and Aldridge to the north and east are overrun with Villa, and Bloxwich to the northeast carved up by Wolves. Within this mix, Walsall tends to be every other West Midlands teams' supporters' second favourite club.

On hearing it for the first time, outsiders collapse with the hilarity of the similarity of the name Walsall with the Polish capital Warsaw. But for locals it tires after the 50th hearing and chants of 'You're just a small town in Poland' are met with yawns.

The Bescot is a stone's throw from the most notorious stretch of motorway in the UK, the M5–M6 interchange, making visiting fans particularly at risk of missing the kick-off. But it proved a blessing for apprentice Ian Gaunt, who was forced into an unintentional debut against Wigan in the Autoglass Trophy in 2001. With two players snarled up in traffic, Gaunt took his chance, scoring the winner.

Walsall claim to be the first stockists of the cult footballing snack, the balti pie.

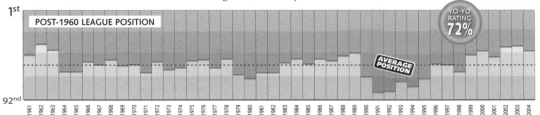

POST-1960 LEAGUE POSITION — 1st / 92nd — YO-YO RATING 72% — AVERAGE POSITION — 1961 1962 1963 1964 1965 1966 1967 1968 1969 1970 1971 1972 1973 1974 1975 1976 1977 1978 1979 1980 1981 1982 1983 1984 1985 1986 1987 1988 1989 1990 1991 1992 1993 1994 1995 1996 1997 1998 1999 2000 2001 2002 2003 2004

PROGRESS REPORT

Walsall had an incredibly static spell of almost 30 years in Level Two until one of their rare backroom bust-ups led to a takeover by hard living, high spending Terry Ramsden in 1998. But wiped out by the Black Monday stockmarket crash, he became bankrupt, heralding a spell that saw the club finish bottom of Level One in 1989 and bottom of Level Two a year later. A steady rise has seen them reach the heights of Level One again – and gaining their best league placing for a generation in 2003. Their 21st century record would look superb if it weren't for a trip back into Level Two in 2004-2005.

```
...Hold the record for the most number of applications from the old regional Third Division...
   ...Won Level One championship in 1923 by scoring just 1.1 goals per game...Radically changed
the bird logo on their club badge in 1995 so its beak optimistically pointed up instead of down...
```

RIVALS

Before going overboard with Walsall's friendly, small club persona, it's worth remembering that for decent periods, they were ahead of both Stoke and Wolves in the league. Wolves, who are supposed to have a soft spot for their neighbours, are wounded by all the abuse they get on radio phone-ins from Walsall fans. "They have always been a bigger club than us and god don't they know it. All 23,000 who go to Wolves now swear blind they continued through the bad times, although the average crowd in the mid-80s was just over 5,000. Strange that, eh?" The unofficial nickname, The Dingles, was first used by a Walsall fanzine within three weeks of the archetypal dense rural family appearing in *Emmerdale* in 1993. Up to 2000, Walsall could be proud of their record against them: no defeats in 100 years, but they've lost all four since.

WOLVES

STOKE

As far as Walsall are concerned, Wolves have the ultimate fickle supporters. After a win, they're convinced that Arsenal will be quaking. When they lose, it unleashes a torrent of bile, regret and anger that soon becomes monotonous. The stadium is said to give a false impression of the club's true standing.

Strictly speaking, Villa's turf is closer to Walsall than Wolves, yet many Walsall fans have a grudging admiration for the Premiership perennials. West Brom and Birmingham are only mentioned in passing – possibly surprising in The Blues' case as many of the late 90s' ructions at Walsall were caused by ex-chairman Ken Wheldon's plan to merge the two. Stoke are more likely to be named as number two rivals as they are seen to share similar bleating characteristics with Wolves.

ASTON VILLA

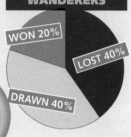
PERFORMANCE AGAINST RIVALS
WOLVERHAMPTON WANDERERS
WON 20%
LOST 40%
DRAWN 40%

SUPPORTERS' VFM
53%

LOVE/HATE

H♥TE

Alan Buckley ♡ holds the record of scoring 20 goals in five consecutive seasons between 1973 and 1978. A long-term club hero used to be immortalised in the name of the *Gilbert Alsop* ♡ stand until the corporate bods got their fingers on it and re-christened it the Purple Stand.

Ex-boss *Colin Lee* de-camped to Plymouth Argyle after slagging off director Jeff Bonser, and is perceived as someone ready to blame everything and everyone except himself. Despite giving Walsall a financial boost, *Michael Ricketts* is not exactly highly thought of.

CHANTS

♪**♫♪*!

Walsall fans have the pleasure of/suffer from a lone chanter – a gentleman who belts out the

'Stop the Pigeon'

theme from *Wacky Races*.

'YOUR GROUND'S TOO BIG FOR YOU!'
R A T I N G

100

80

60

40

ATTENDANCE AS A PERCENTAGE OF CAPACITY
70%

20

0

DOH!!

Walsall's director, Roy Whalley, was inadvertently caught out admitting what most British fans think about their club's administration. "That's what we're paid to do – make bad decisions". Whalley is renowned as a bit of a multi-tasker, officially listed as the Chief Executive/Secretary, Marketing/Commercial Manager and Media Relations Manager.

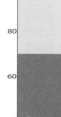

WATFORD

Recommended website: **www.bsad.org**

WHO ARE YA?

When Pink Floyd sang, somewhat cynically, "think I'll buy myself a football team" in their 1973 track, 'Money', there hadn't actually been much precedent for high-profile buy-outs. Shortly afterwards, Elton John's purchase of Watford FC became the first example of a monied celebrity dipping his toes in the water. The partnership of the pop star and Graham Taylor is, on paper, one of the more successful in the game. This is a reality that contradicts the image of the club, Taylor, and to an extent, the town itself, as workmanlike and unremarkable. The story of Watford's latter day triumphs breaks down into two completely separate spells under the same chairman/manager combination.

CELEBRITY FANS
DOUG & EDDY BRIMSON
Authors
BRIAN CONLEY
Comedian

The dream team was flung together in the mid-70s, with the side barely twitching in Level Three. Two consecutive promotions saw them knocking on the door and, by 1982, they'd entered the top division for the first time, where they proceeded to finish second, behind Liverpool. Hero of the time, Luther Blissett, became a slightly unlikely recruit of AC Milan, an anomaly that was solved as it became increasingly clear that they really meant to buy John Barnes. With Taylor trotting off to Villa, and Elton bailing out, Watford drifted back to from where they came, only for the pair to chum up again in 1997 – with virtually the same results, another frantic push that earned them a solitary Premiership season in 1999-2000.

IN and AROUND

Both tube trains and normal Network Rail choo-choos run on the same tracks from Watford to London.

Watford are a particularly independent spirited bunch. Perhaps the effect of seeing so many 'plastic' fans of the north London teams has stiffened their resolve, but ever since Taylor originally took charge, there has been an almost religious pursuance of community involvement. This should have won them many friends in the purist supporters' category, though Taylor's other mantra, to get the ball up the field as swiftly as possible, burdened them with a tag of footballing outcasts – a fact that became even more accentuated when Taylor took over the England job, with a notably unsuccessful outcome.

Watford's Harry Hornet came first in the second mascots' Grand National, though his opponents were cheesed off that he wore training shoes rather than the traditional over-sized, and often furry, feet.

Elton John's lovers' site, *eltonfan.net* reports his continuing obsession with the club in a slightly pointed way, informing readers that he regularly calls his mother, Sheila, when he his abroad to find out "if his favourite football team has won *any* of its matches".

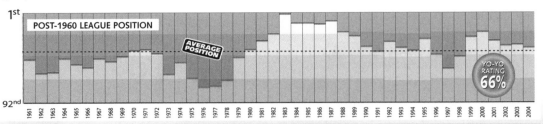

1st

POST-1960 LEAGUE POSITION

AVERAGE POSITION

YO-YO RATING 66%

92nd

1961 1962 1963 1964 1965 1966 1967 1968 1969 1970 1971 1972 1973 1974 1975 1976 1977 1978 1979 1980 1981 1982 1983 1984 1985 1986 1987 1988 1989 1990 1991 1992 1993 1994 1995 1996 1997 1998 1999 2000 2001 2002 2003 2004

PROGRESS REPORT

Watford were stuck into a Level Two grove until falling into Level Three in 1975. Their ascent to the old First set a blueprint for rapid rises at a time when divisional changes were much less frequent than they are today. Their spell in the top-flight lasted six years. When Taylor returned to lead another charge, with promotion in 1999, life was much crueller on Premiership newcomers and they lasted just one season. Since then, they have failed to make any sustained challenge in Level One.

```
...In 1997-98, Steve Palmer successfully completed his dream of playing in all positions...
    ...Gained fewest ever number of Premiership points (24 in 1999-2000)...
        ...A business on Vicarage Road is called 'Taylor Made Tattoos'...
```

RIVALS

Watford have a major advantage over their rivals in providing the world with the noticeably anti-Luton writers, Dougie and Eddy Brimson, whose texts are punctuated with the incomplete form of the unpalatable name, L*t*n. Both Watford and Luton suffer the indignity of a national reputation for being utilitarian London dormitory towns, but there isn't much doubt which of the two feel they are, socially, a cut above. A joke circulates in Watford that Luton was chosen as a sight for an international airport because of the easy availability of tarmac layers – ouch. Luton's standing wasn't helped over the coverage of the town's recruits volunteering for duties in Afghanistan to fight the US military, leading to the terrace chant 'Where's your Taliban?'

LUTON ☠️ ☠️ ☠️ ☠️

At the heart of the Bedfordshire/Hertfordshire derby is the fact that each set of supporters have had to put up with the other side utterly dominating fixtures between them for long periods, breeding ever-deeper resentment. The pattern started with their first League fixtures in which Watford had the upper hand. Their first 11 meetings resulted in just one Luton win until The Hatters clocked up their biggest margin of victory, crushing Watford 5-0 in 1926. Ever since, there has been a similar pattern; one side going unbeaten for a prolonged spell until the opposition stages a big win.

In recent history, Watford have suffered two separate non-winning runs. The first spanned the whole of the 70s and only came to an end with a 5-2 win in 1983 that much of the town's people reflect on as the greatest moment in the club's history. But the trials started again with a 12-game barren spell that was only ended with a 4-0 away victory in 1997, a result that heralded Luton's drop into Level Two obscurity.

Watford particularly scoff at Luton's 'apology of a ground', 'The Kennel'.

Web-based fans from the Luton Town Mailing List and www.bsad.org dreamed up a variety of mean anti-Luton tactics, including an attempt to translate the 'wings of a sparrow' song into as many different languages as possible. Aside from the standard French, German etc, highlights include 'Harlem', "I'd fly ova' Luton tomo'row an' shit on de bastards below" and, if you should ever require it, the computer programming language, Cobol; "for wIndex:= 0 to (NUM_SHIT_ONS - 1) do ShitOn(sWho, sWhereY); end."

Watford were also responsible for perhaps the longest message-board thread in history. At the time of writing, responses to the message "Post here if you hate Luton" ran to a full eight pages.

SUPPORTERS' VFM 67%

PERFORMANCE AGAINST RIVALS
LUTON

WON 26%
LOST 46%
DRAWN 28%

LOVE/HATE

Elton John 💙 is forgiven for his semi-absent role in the club, as he has the pleasing habit of putting his hand in his pocket when circumstances require. Graham Taylor 💙 instigated the type of rule that many fans of other clubs would drool over; that players under contract with Watford FC should reside in Watford.

HATE

CHANTS

Not much gratitude to their Versace clad ex-manager:

'Vialli...He came from Italy
He spent all our money'

'YOUR GROUND'S TOO BIG FOR YOU!'
RATING

100
80
60
40

ATTENDANCE AS A PERCENTAGE OF CAPACITY
72%

20
0

DOH!!

Preparations for the 1987 FA Cup semi-final were thrown into disarray when the club's two senior goalkeepers fell injured at the last minute. Graham Taylor was forced to call upon Gary Plumley, a restaurant owner whose professional appearances amounted to a handful of games for Halifax Town. He conceded three goals in the first half hour, with Spurs running away 4-1 winners.

WEST BROMWICH ALBION

Recommended website: **www.baggies.com**

WHO ARE YA?

Their Baggies nickname probably (though not certainly) comes from their taste for knee-length shorts in their early history – though they were all the rage again by the late 1990s.

West Brom had an unfortunate sense of timing. Just as money flooded into the game the club endured the worst spell of its history. Having been one of the founder members of the Football League, they have scooped all three major honours at one time or another and were consistent top-flight performers until the beginning of the wilderness years in 1986, when they tumbled out of the old First Division. By 1991, they had slumped into Level Three and experienced their darkest hour in front of *MOTD* cameras, going down 4-1 at home to non-league Woking in the FA Cup. The Hawthorns became a manager's graveyard, with the club maintaining a steady average of one per season for over a decade.

IN and AROUND

According to Tesco, West Bromwich has the highest sales of baked beans per head of population in the UK, hence the label 'Windy City'.

They are the only league team to play in blue and white stripes, (explaining the 'Tesco' tag), a kit that has seen only minor variations through the years. Continuing the retail analogy, the 1992 version narrowed the stripes drastically, leading to the temporary nickname 'The Barcodes'.

They look upon Birmingham's resurgence with something approaching disbelief, imagining that the club had been consigned to the footballing dustbin. They comfort themselves with the fact that The Blues still haven't picked up a single Championship or FA Cup.

The history books record that Ron Atkinson, as manager in 1979, unleashed a trio of the best black players ever to have played in the league, Cyrille Regis, Laurie Cunningham and Brendan Batson. It's therefore, even more of a mystery that he was caught making off-mike racist comments about Chelsea players during an ITV live commentary in 2004 – a gaff that finished his media career in an instant.

Apart from constant references from Frank Skinner, the club can count on plenty of name checks from the BBC's Adrian Chiles, now a *MOTD* presenter. An episode of his series *What do you do all day?* had him cavorting around with the British ambassador to Romania. Cooing over his collection of West Brom memorabilia, Chiles admitted that it was only the fact that they supported the same club that got him such unfettered access to the normally closed world of the diplomatic service. An even more bootlicking performance was reserved for West Brom's then manager Gary Megson...profiled in the same series.

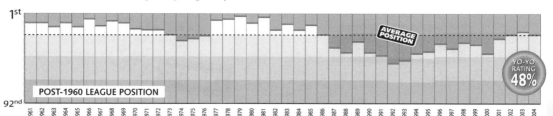

1st

AVERAGE POSITION

POST-1960 LEAGUE POSITION

YO-YO RATING 48%

92nd

1961 1962 1963 1964 1965 1966 1967 1968 1969 1970 1971 1972 1973 1974 1975 1976 1977 1978 1979 1980 1981 1982 1983 1984 1985 1986 1987 1988 1989 1990 1991 1992 1993 1994 1995 1996 1997 1998 1999 2000 2001 2002 2003 2004

PROGRESS REPORT

The recent similarity with the hated Wolves is striking. West Brom memorably pipped them to Premiership status in 2002, where, like Wolves a year later, they hardly caused a murmur, going straight back down in their first season. The yo-yo between the two clubs continued in 2004 with West Brom getting another crack at it, having stormed Level One. Survival for just a couple of Premiership seasons will put their post-1969 average back in the top-flight.

```
...At 542ft above sea level, The Hawthorns is the highest English football ground...
   ...Only club to gain promotion and win the FA Cup in the same season (1931)...
             ...First British club to play in China (1978)...
```

RIVALS

WOLVES

Virtually joined at the waist in terms of their recent league records, it is about the only thing that unites West Brom and Wolves. The two have maintained a seething hatred of each other for over 30 years. In recent times, the games have had an added 70s feel – as the atmosphere is a throwback to the worst days of hooliganism. The concentration of the clubs in the West Midlands poses a uniquely difficult web of rivalries that has probably contributed to the degree of violence. Until the 70s, West Brom would always name Villa as their first hate. Wolves and West Brom represent the region popularly called The Black Country, stretching to the south and western borders of the conurbation and distinct from the city of Birmingham itself.

ASTON VILLA

BIRMINGHAM

With Villa and Birmingham City fighting it out for Brummie supremacy, the other two are involved in something of a sub-battle for the region – and the right to claim that they are the main opponents of Villa, who have topped the West Midlands' achievement league for over a generation. The problem is that, Villa aside, the other three have never established any clear blue water between themselves and the other two. The dream of both Wolves and West Brom is to be perceived as the real opposition to Villa. However, as soon as one club gets ahead, the old foe bite them when they least expect it – i.e. West Brom overhauling Wolves in 2002 to gain their Premiership place.

The loathing of Wolves spills out to other games. When Graham Taylor was manager at Watford, following a doomed spell with the neighbours, West Brom fans showed their appreciation: 'Thank you very much...for f***ing Wolves up'. West Brom now claim that it was only their benevolence that saved Wolves from extinction, with the sale of key players, including Steve Bull in 1986.

Reacquainted in the Premiership, West Brom will certainly turn their attentions more on Aston Villa, characterising the clash as the best of the Black Country against the best of Brum. In fact some fans are quite wary of the perception that it is Wolves and not Villa that are number one rivals, suggesting that the obsession with Wolves is relatively recent and for those more interested in fighting than football, whereas West Brom/Villa can claim to be the oldest rivalry in the English league.

The pattern of rivalries splits the West Midlands into a bewildering patchwork of loyalties with West Brom (and Walsall) stuck in the geographical centre. Wolves account for Dudley, Stourbridge and (though with a league team of their own) Kidderminster, to the west and south of them. To the north, Cannock and Brownhills are fairly solidly Villa.

PERFORMANCE AGAINST RIVALS
WOLVERHAMPTON WANDERERS
WON 35% / LOST 28% / DRAWN 37%

SUPPORTERS' VFM 69%

LOVE/HATE

HATE

The people of Sandwell were asked to nominate a local luminary whose name could grace a new Metro train, which is why you can now chug around on *Geoff Astle*. He is considered as the prime mover behind the club's purple patch in the 1960s. He is better known to younger fans as the bloke who couldn't sing at the end of Baddiel and Skinner's *Fantasy Football League*.

CHANTS

Unlikely to suffer chants of *'You're not singing anymore'* as West Brom are well known for being enthusiastic singers even when losing. But they are the targets of what is frequently named as the favourite football song doing the rounds: *'Oh I do like to be beside the seaside'* contains the unexpected twist "Oh I do like to stroll beside the prom prom prom...where the brass band plays 'f*** off West Brom'".

'YOUR GROUND'S TOO BIG FOR YOU!'
RATING

100 / 80 / 60 / 40 / 20 / 0

ATTENDANCE AS A PERCENTAGE OF CAPACITY 88%

In 1999, West Brom's Fabian De Freitas turned up for the league match against Crewe an hour after it had finished. He was under the impression that it was an evening kick off.

WEST HAM

A.K.A. THE HAMSTERS

Recommended website: **www.kumb.com**

WHO ARE YA?

Until 1961 when Ron Greenwood took over, West Ham were looked down upon as a 'family club', but those virtues came in handy when money and outside interests seeped into the game later. The Hammers' stability has allowed players and staff to grace the heights of the game, where others have lurched between boom and bust. But since losing their Premiership status in 2003, there is irritation that there has been no easy route back.

The club came to prominence by reaching the first FA Cup final to be played at Wembley in 1923. Famed for its chaotic conditions with the stadium full well beyond capacity, the game became synonymous with the legendary 'white horse clearing the pitch' episode. More recently, this over-egged story is considered hugely exaggerated.

CELEBRITY FANS
MARTIN BRUNDLE
F1 Driver, Commentator
PHIL JUPITOUS
Comedian - *Never Mind The Buzzcocks*

For those who remember football from the period, the sight of Clyde Best donning the West Ham shirt was history in the making. Recently, there has been publicity about the earliest black players in the English game, but Best, who signed for the club in 1968, featured on TV regularly at a time when black football players were almost unheard of, but, more significantly, a black face on British TV was a rarity. Alf Garnett was regularly featured dishing out racial abuse to Best by name, probably the least glorious moment in the BBC's history.

IN and AROUND

The residents of Barking may inherit the earth (along with cockroaches) as it is a rare example of an urban area that lies below sea level – reputedly making it 'safe' from nuclear attack.

The club's hooligan following of the late 70s dovetailed with the emergence of hard core punk rock. There was a significant crossover between fans of The Cockney Rejects and the much feared Inter-City firm, who had named themselves after their preferred way of travelling to games. In those days the trains were quite fast.

West Ham have a place in the history books of having the most obscure FA Cup final winning goalscorer. Netting twice to secure a 2-0 win over Fulham in 1975, Alan Taylor barely achieved a long-term place in the first team and had no career to speak of away from West Ham.

If David Beckham had spent his professional career in the area of his birth, West Ham would have a virtual monopoly of English football heroes. In Bobby Moore, Geoff Hurst and Martin Peters, the club produced the backbone of the most successful England side in history.

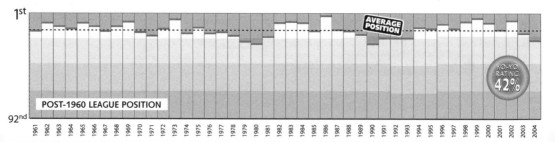

1st

AVERAGE POSITION

POST-1960 LEAGUE POSITION

YO-YO RATING 42%

92nd

1961 1962 1963 1964 1965 1966 1967 1968 1969 1970 1971 1972 1973 1974 1975 1976 1977 1978 1979 1980 1981 1982 1983 1984 1985 1986 1987 1988 1989 1990 1991 1992 1993 1994 1995 1996 1997 1998 1999 2000 2001 2002 2003 2004

PROGRESS REPORT

Their 4th position in Level One in 2004 was only three places above their post-1960 low, with their average finish comfortably mid-table in the top division.

```
...West Ham's managers have the longest average time in their job of any League club...
     ...The club offered season ticket holders a refund when appointing unproven
                      Glenn Roeder as manager in 2001...
...Although popularly known as Upton Park, the club's stadium is officially the 'Boleyn Ground'...
```

RIVALS

On the face of it, West Ham's history of uncompromising/lunatic supporters and its reputation for fielding hard-as-nails players (from Frank Lampard senior, through Neil Ruddock, to the loyal but certifiable Julian Dicks), mark the club out as one that should have plenty of enemies. But strangely, it's almost a case of 'no-one hates us, we don't care'. With Tottenham drawing the majority of bad feeling from other London clubs, West Ham are left comparatively in the cold. For Charlton and Tottenham, The Hammers are considered fairly low grade rivals. For Chelsea, they have fallen off the radar completely after a few 70s' pitched battles, and even near neighbours Leyton Orient (who should, by the pattern of smaller clubs hating more prestigious near neighbours, loathe them) direct more ire towards Southend United, 30 miles to the east.

MILLWALL ☠☠☠

TOTTENHAM ☠☠☠☠

With others ambiguous towards West Ham, the view of Hammers' fans is even more confusing. Many point to Tottenham as the number one rivals, although Spurs have a strong tendency of being disliked by supporters of many other London clubs. The social contrast between east and west London should be fertile ground for pronounced dislike between West Ham and Chelsea. Chelsea's overt attempts to spend their way into the big time doesn't go down well in the rest of the capital, though the strength of feeling has lessened since the 70s when the ritual attempt to 'take the Shed' had become West Ham's main off the pitch ambition. But recently, Chelsea's new-found family orientation has left them viewed with neutrality.

SUPPORTERS' **VFM** 47%

PERFORMANCE AGAINST RIVALS
MILLWALL

WON 50%
LOST 20%
DRAWN 30%

In some respects, it is an unusual rivalry because of the differing fortunes of the two sides. During the 80s, when the trouble was perceived to have been at its worst, the two clubs were only in the same division for a single season (1988-89). They also met twice in 1978-79, but you have to go back to 1947 (at a time when most of the respective clubs' areas had been destroyed by the Lufftwaffe) to find them in the same League. They were finally flung together in Level One in 2003-2004, culminating in one of the worst recent hooligan incidents at The New Den when the sending off of Alan Pardew triggered arguably the worst stadium violence of the season. The police operation for that one game cost £270,000, making it the most expensive in British football history.

LOVE/HATE

Paul Ince was accused of using the media to aid his dream move to Manchester United. In 1989, he let himself appear in the tabloids beaming in his 'new' United kit. However, West Ham, whom he played for at the time, were in the dark over the move. The price leaped, and although Ince got his wish eight weeks later, it left a sour taste in the mouth in east London and got Ince pilloried elsewhere as well. History repeated itself with the tug-of-war for Rio Ferdinand with Leeds.

CHANTS

Written in 1919 by Kenbrovin and Kellette,

'I'm Forever Blowing Bubbles'

was adopted by West Ham fans in the late 20s. An exceedingly unlikely football song, the lyrics reveal a dreary analogy:

'then like my dreams they fade and die'.

'YOUR GROUND'S TOO BIG FOR YOU!'

RATING

100

80

60

40

20

0

ATTENDANCE AS A PERCENTAGE OF CAPACITY
89%

DOH!!

Harry Redknapp's ceaseless player trading led to a handful of spectacular turkeys. Floran Raducioiu, costing £2.4 million in 1996, was found browsing the shelves of Harvey Nichols rather than travelling for a match at Stockport. Six appearances later, he was resold for £1.6 million.

Notoriously, Redknapp signed Marco Boogers from Sparta Amsterdam for a mere £1 million in 1995, though he hadn't actually seen Boogers play in the flesh. However, he had managed to sneak a look at his purchase on a few video clips. Having come on as a sub during his second West Ham game, the Dutchman immediately committed one of the most atrocious fouls in living memory, a snow-plough tackle on Manchester United's Gary Neville. He then vanished. Tracked down to a caravan park in Holland, he ended up on a free transfer to Groningen.

WIGAN ATHLETIC

Recommended website: **www.chilvers1.demon.co.uk/Wafc.htm**

WHO ARE YA?

On paper, Wigan Athletic probably shouldn't exist, let alone have reached the heights of Premiership contention. Surrounded by other League clubs, including five Premiership sides within easy travelling distance, and representing a town where rugby league is huge, previous attempts at setting up a football club were dogged by lack of support. JJB Sports chain owner Dave Whelan has taken a massive gamble in funding Wigan. When the club moved into their new 25,000 seater stadium their gates were barely a quarter of the ground's capacity, with 9,000 spaces reserved for away fans. No side has ever managed to actually fill it, though Preston North End made a good fist of trying when bringing approximately 7,000. Whelan's double dare was to take over both the football and rugby league club (Wigan Warriors) and decamp them into the same stadium. This seemed a reasonable move, seeing that Wigan's previous rugby ground, Central Park, (as its name suggests) was on a juicy piece of real estate that proved too much for Tesco to resist.

IN and AROUND

Wigan has more pie shops and bakeries per head of population than any other British town

Wigan have a reputation for performing better on their travels. Aside from their churned up pitch, the skew could also be explained by the fact that although their home games have understandably suffered from a lack of atmosphere, Wigan's away support makes a hell of a racket. The 8,000 that followed the club to the Auto Windscreens Shield Final in 1999 virtually blew the ball into Millwall's net. The club has a strong London-based fan club of ex-pats, guaranteeing a good away turnout in the capital and South-East.

CELEBRITY FANS
STUART MACONIE -
Journalist/Broadcaster
RICHARD ASHCROFT -
The Verve
MIKHAIL GORBACHEV -
Ex-Soviet President

Wigan pioneered the signing of overseas players to lower division clubs. The acquisition of the 'three amigos', Martinez, Seba and Diaz from Spain, was unheard of for a Level Three club in 1995. Staggered that they had pulled off such a scoop, the Board was understandably nervous about introducing them to the delights of Wigan's local culture. But greeted with fans parading sombreros and moth-eaten donkeys collected from previous trips to the Costas, the signings proved to be the turning point for the club.

The unlikely association of Mikhail Gorbachev with Wigan Althletic dates back to a pre-season friendly with a Russian side in 1969. Gorbachev got a pass-out to attend the game in his capacity as Metallist Kharkov club secretary. In 1987, a British journalist reported that the then President lifted the block on BBC broadcasts to the Soviet Union in order that he could follow the football results. The Russian embassy tactfully declined to confirm or deny the story.

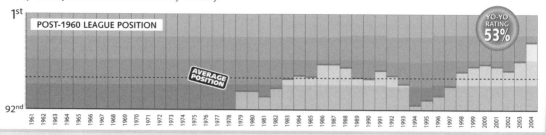

1st

POST-1960 LEAGUE POSITION

YO-YO RATING 53%

AVERAGE POSITION

92nd

1961 1962 1963 1964 1965 1966 1967 1968 1969 1970 1971 1972 1973 1974 1975 1976 1977 1978 1979 1980 1981 1982 1983 1984 1985 1986 1987 1988 1989 1990 1991 1992 1993 1994 1995 1996 1997 1998 1999 2000 2001 2002 2003 2004

PROGRESS REPORT

Wigan's steady climb in the years following their election in 1978 was quickly undone. When Dave Whelan bought a controlling share in 1995, the side was near the foot of Level Three, making his predictions of imminent Premiership action sound like the usual dronings of a hopelessly deluded individual with more money than sense. But in less than 10 years, The Latics are knocking on the door.

...Last club to be admitted to League by election process (1978)...Bolton's Reebok stadium is closer to Wigan town centre than Bolton...The JJB Stadium is built on a former sewerage works...

RIVALS

As relative newbies to the football league, Wigan have the dubious luxury of being hated by almost nobody, though they seem to loathe everyone. Ask Wigan fans to list their rivals and you get a recitation of about half Britain's League teams. Historically Bolton were the foes, and still are with older supporters, though younger fans tend to point more towards Preston North End. As is often the way with brewing rivalries, the two have followed each other around the divisions in recent years. Oldham get up their noses as they claim to be the 'original' Latics (also Wigan's nickname) and are baited with chants of 'You're just a small club in Yorkshire'. Otherwise, Burnley, Blackpool, Millwall and Stoke all get a mention. Wigan have a hard core of fans who are not averse to a bit of aggro, most notoriously at the game with Stoke City at the Britannia Stadium in 1999. Wigan fans swear blind that they abided by the minute's silence in honour of Sir Stanley Matthews, but the resulting scenes were amongst the worst stadium disorder in recent years.

PRESTON NORTH END

BOLTON

But what really annoys Wigan fans is the Rugby League Club, variously known as the 'lodgers' or 'squatters'. (Although popularly thought of as shared, the fine print reveals that it is Wigan Athletic who own the JJB - the Wanderers are tenants). There are few inhabitants who feel loyal to both clubs - you're one or the other. It doesn't help that the players of the 'fat man's sport' tear up the pitch. With Whelan also owning Orrel Rugby Union club, there is even the prospect of a third team coming to join the fun at the JJB. The football fans are peeved at the assumption that the town is rugby dominated and point to the fact that in 2003/04 Athletics' average gate was better than Wigan Warriors. There is some hostility towards the local press, particularly the Wigan Evening Post, whose habit of covering Australian Rugby League during the British close season seems to smack of lazy 'living in the past' journalism dominated by rugby writers. The memory of the rugby club refusing to share its old Central Park also was at the root of the bad feeling.

WIGAN WARRIORS

SUPPORTERS
VFM
100%

PERFORMANCE AGAINST RIVALS
BOLTON

WON 40%
LOST 40%
DRAWN 20%

LOVE/HATE

The infamous 'hand of Goat' goal denied Wigan a play-off win in 1999. At 0-0, Manchester City's *Shaun Goater* forced the ball home - clearly with help from his arm, ensuring his future notoriety in Wigan.

CHANTS

♪ ** ♫ * !

Wigan fans indulge in some extreme self-parody as an 'answer' to opposing songs about Northern life. Their reply is a peculiar confirmation of stereotypes:

'we come from Wigan and we live in mud huts'.

'YOUR GROUND'S TOO BIG FOR YOU!'
RATING

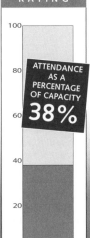

ATTENDANCE AS A PERCENTAGE OF CAPACITY
38%

100
80
60
40
20
0

DOH!!

The JJB's pitch frequently shows signs of serious wear and tear, finding the battering of both the football and rugby teams rather more than it can take. The alarm of supporters seems justified: their push for the Premiership in 2004 faltered with a run of three months without a win at home, culminating in an excruciating 90th minute goal by West Ham, dumping them out of the play-off places.

WOLVERHAMPTON WANDERERS

Recommended website: **www.wolves-mad.co.uk**

WHO ARE YA?

A Swedish based unofficial club website's ticker finally stopped on 27th April 2003 – noting that it had been 6,923 days, 18 hours, 15 minutes and 19 seconds that Wolves had spent in the wrong division. But having finally got there in 2003-2004, they never made it out of the starting blocks and, like bitter rivals West Brom the season before, hardly got a taste of the big time before it was all over. The agony was compounded by a series of five consecutive matches towards the end of the season in which they conceded important injury-time goals.

The fastest way to nark a Wolves' fan is to refer to their 'orange' shirt – they're gold. Or at least they're supposed to be, as their shade has sometimes bordered on brown. Molineux has lost little of its atmosphere to its conversion to all-seater, possessing the design quirk of two touchline stands that are slightly oval in shape.

CELEBRITY FANS
DENISE LEWIS
Heptathlon Olympic Gold Medallist
KEVIN ROWLANDS
Frontman - Dexy's Midnight Runners
EDWARD ELGAR
Composer

Wolverhampton is worshipped by those with robust dental work – as pork scratchings are the locally manufactured delicacy

The local psyche is largely shaped by the trials of the football club. Years of angst over the team have translated into a permanent state of mind, to the extent that one fan commented that achieving Premiership status felt almost unnatural because they wouldn't have anything to moan about any more. Wolverhampton tends to rank very low in surveys of towns with happy populations. It must have descended into abject misery when, in 2002, Wolves' 11-point lead at the top of Level One was eroded by West Brom, leaving Norwich to dump Wolves out of the play-offs, who in turn got beaten in the final by secondary hates Birmingham City. This left Wolves as the only major West Midlands club outside the Premiership. Wolves' fans occasionally have to remind the opposition of their geographical identity with the chant 'We are not Brummies'.

Such was fans' desperation during the dark times, they even borrowed Derby's legend of a gypsy curse being placed on the ground.

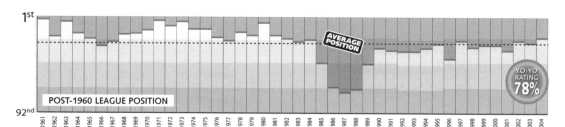

1st

AVERAGE POSITION

YO-YO RATING 78%

POST-1960 LEAGUE POSITION

92nd

1961 1962 1963 1964 1965 1966 1967 1968 1969 1970 1971 1972 1973 1974 1975 1976 1977 1978 1979 1980 1981 1982 1983 1984 1985 1986 1987 1988 1989 1990 1991 1992 1993 1994 1995 1996 1997 1998 1999 2000 2001 2002 2003 2004

PROGRESS REPORT

For twenty years prior to 1984, Wolves' league record was a very static tale of moderate old First Division placings, with the addition of a couple of League Cups in 1974 and 1980. The rate of the catastrophic fall that saw them relegated in three successive seasons from 1984 to 1986 has only been matched by Bristol City, who performed the same trick between 1980 and 1982. Rock-bottom was reached in November 1986, whilst in Level Three, with a defeat in the FA Cup by non-league Chorley. Their post-1960 average has settled uneasily in the higher reaches of Division One. Having made quick progress back to Level One, it was an agonising wait of 11 years to reach the Premiership.

```
...Played in the 'H' Cup final of 1908, when the Wolves' scorers were Hunt, Hedley and
Harrison, with a reply for Newcastle by Howie...Have won all four English Divisions...
...Started a men's health clinic outside Molineux...
```

RIVALS

Most rivalries are given the edge when one club is going through a purple patch, leaving their neighbours struggling i.e. Blackburn and Burnley. But there are special problems when both sides are seen to be underachieving. Wolves suffered badly from losing its floating supporters, but keeping its hooligans. (Attendances were as low as 5,000 for home games in Level Three). With an up-turn in fortunes for both, their league positions have followed a very similar path, with both recently perched precariously between the Premiership and Level One. The ultimate insult from West Brom was the suggestion that, having proved their footballing superiority, they would increasingly turn their attentions to Villa.

WEST BROM

BIRMINGHAM

The intensity of the rivalry between the two is not always accepted as natural – with some from both clubs feeling it has gone too far. It is said that for many the result against the Baggies matters above everything else, including final league position. But at the other end of the confrontation scale, a significant minority in the area are happy to cheer on other West Midlands' teams when appropriate. There is a solid argument for a bit more Black Country unity. Along with the southwest and East Anglia, the local accent tends only to be heard in the mainstream media when there are comic overtones. Already having to endure Frank Skinner, the BBC added to the pro-West Brom TV camp when drafting in Adrian Chiles as *MOTD* presenter. His OTT fixation with the Baggies broke the convention that sport's presenters are relatively neutral.

SUPPORTERS' VFM 61%

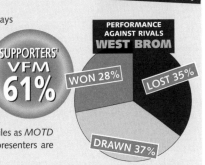
PERFORMANCE AGAINST RIVALS
WEST BROM

WON 28%
LOST 35%
DRAWN 37%

The ritual aspect of anti-West Brom chanting has been helped by the Wolves team coming onto the field to the strains of The Liquidator (originally a Baggies song). Each rendition unfailingly leads to a hail of obscenities against their rivals. West Brom complain that the playing of the song amounts to an 'official endorsement' to stir up hatred. But perhaps Molineux's most famous aggro occurred when their mascot Bully had an on-pitch fight with West Brom's Three Little Piggies. The video of the altercation shows Bully landing a solid right hook, though to the neutral observer, he seems to be on the retreat. Sadly Wolves generally like Walsall, but the friendliness is flung back in their face, as they far prefer Villa.

With a greater proportion of hard-core troublemakers, there was frequent havoc when they were visiting smaller clubs during the dark days, which has done little for their long term reputation.

LOVE/HATE

Steve Bull's ♡ first game for the club in November 1986 almost exactly coincided with their recovery from the depths. Wolves' all-time record scorer, with 306 goals, resolutely refused to sign for a top-flight club, probably damaging his England career in the process – but the sacrifice perhaps makes him the ultimate 'fans' player'. Ironically, he was signed from West Brom.

CHANTS

To the tune of the Rolling Stone's *'Satisfaction'*, the Molineux disenchanted sang

'Wolves can't get no....Premier League action'.

'YOUR GROUND'S TOO BIG FOR YOU!'
RATING

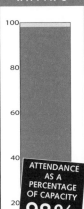

ATTENDANCE AS A PERCENTAGE OF CAPACITY
98%

DOH!!

On 2nd March 2002, with Wolves eight points ahead at the top of Level One, the club was happy to start taking payment for the sales of Premiership season tickets. In the last nine games, they picked up just ten points to leave them in third. Fans could only look forward to refunds as Birmingham and West Brom went up.

WREXHAM

Recommended website: **www.red-passion.com**

WHO ARE YA?

Here we go again with one last spin of the familiar CD: lack of support, hostility towards chairman, worries over relocation. The one difference with Wrexham is that their on-field performance is a cut above the backroom antics. Even to hardened optimists, their promotion to Level Two in 2003 came as something as a surprise.

Conventional wisdom has it that north Wales should be able to support a League team, whereas the south is too rugby dominated to bother too much about the round ball. But the generalisation is about as helpful as Tony Gubba's classic 'west Londonism', "they'll be singing in the valleys tonight" following Wrexham's mauling of Arsenal in the FA Cup of 1992. They may well have been singing in the valleys, but since they are 90 miles to the south it was unlikely to have anything to do with Wrexham's triumph.

Wrexham's problem has more to do with the proximity of Liverpool. Historically there has been some two-way traffic of fans. In 1997, FIFA closed one of the quaintest international loopholes by barring winners of the Welsh Cup from European competition. Prior to this, Wrexham had taken some huge continental scalps and associated paydays, the most spectacular being the 1-0 win over mighty Porto in 1984. The crowds at the Racecourse were undoubtedly swelled by glory-seekers from over the border. To this day, there are still gripes that the BBC coverage of their European exploits amounted to no more than a condescending 'well done to the Welsh minnows' as the scores were being read out.

IN and AROUND

Nearby Buckley was the focus of the media scrum surrounding Judith and John Kilshaw and their temporary residents, twin babies acquired from a shady lady in the US. The delightfully gobby Mrs Kilshaw sang at a concert in aid of Wrexham FC. She claimed her voice was "alright once I've had a few pints".

Rugby has been a mixed blessing. The development of the National Stadium in Cardiff robbed Swansea of the chance to host Wales' internationals. But in return, their dilapidated Racecourse Ground was granted a costly facelift in preparation for the Rugby World Cup of 1999.

Their current chairman is a property developer (gulp) from Manchester (double gulp). Relations between the supporters' trust and Alexander Hamilton are roughly as you'd imagine, 'We need to make it unpleasant for him to own Wrexham FC'. He followed on the heels of Mark Guterman, another property man with a similar popularity rating, who, with a twist to the usual phrase, dubbed Wrexham a 'sleeping medium-sized club'.

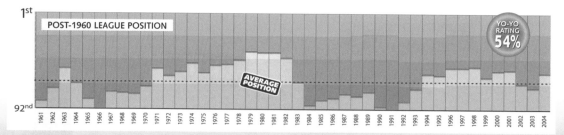

POST-1960 LEAGUE POSITION

1st — 92nd

YO-YO RATING 54%

AVERAGE POSITION

1961 1962 1963 1964 1965 1966 1967 1968 1969 1970 1971 1972 1973 1974 1975 1976 1977 1978 1979 1980 1981 1982 1983 1984 1985 1986 1987 1988 1989 1990 1991 1992 1993 1994 1995 1996 1997 1998 1999 2000 2001 2002 2003 2004

PROGRESS REPORT

Wrexham had a slice of luck when propping up the whole Football League in 1991. They were saved by the decision to revert back to 92 League clubs (it had been 91 for a spell), so there was no relegation out of Level Three. Though their post-1960 average is just ensconced within Level Two, their troughs have being alarmingly deep.

...Reached quarter-finals of Cup-Winners' Cup in 1976...Launched their own credit card...
...Captained by Alex Ferguson's son, Darren...

RIVALS

With Chester and Shrewsbury regaining their League status in 2004, Wrexham's regional isolation is not as intense as it was, but there's still a lack of anyone to pick on. The comparison between Wrexham and their disliked neighbours doesn't make for comfortable reading. At 4,400, Wrexham's average attendance in Level Two wasn't much greater than the gates Shrewsbury were achieving in the Conference.

SHREWSBURY ☠☠☠☠☠

CHESTER CITY ☠☠☠☠☠

Feelings towards Cardiff are generally negative. Wrexham have tended to be a more authentic source of Welsh nationalism, and they feel irritation that Sam Hammam has hijacked the 'pride of Wales' tag for his own artificial ends. *'Men of Harlech'*, popularised in the film *Zulu*, has been a favourite at the Racecourse, though, to their annoyance, the song is now associated more closely with Cardiff. It was a road that Wrexham were travelling down, with a name change from the Robins to the Red Dragons.

CARDIFF ☠☠☠☠

SUPPORTERS' VFM 73%

PERFORMANCE AGAINST RIVALS CHESTER

WON 40% · LOST 30% · DRAWN 30%

The club has made efforts to ban troublemakers from the ground, but disorder got transplanted elsewhere, with police in Manchester city centre faced with serious trouble between Oldham and Wrexham fans in 2001. There was evidence that the banning orders were effective, as the home game between the two was completely trouble-free, with an estimated 160 officers left twiddling their thumbs amidst cries of 'overkill' for a crowd of 3,963, leaving Wrexham to pick up the hefty tab.

The relationship with Liverpool is up and down. It niggles Wrexham fans that they are surrounded by 'plastic scousers' who live and work in North Wales but whose football allegiances lie in Merseyside. Liverpool have recently been cosy to Chester, playing reserve games at The Deva. But a mysterious fall-out saw them choose to go to the Racecourse for a pre-season friendly in 2004, 'reneging' on an agreement with Chester. This gifted Wrexham a £150,000+ turnstile cash boost and caused some mirth when Chester told Liverpool they could take their reserves somewhere else.

Wrexham's efforts to deter the lunatic fringe have been largely successful, though they have managed to cause problems away from match days. In the summer of 2003, a group of 200 youths rioted in an incident connected with a few Kurdish refugees moving into the area, including a proportion of the club's rougher followers in ski-masks.

'YOUR GROUND'S TOO BIG FOR YOU!' RATING

ATTENDANCE AS A PERCENTAGE OF CAPACITY 28%

LOVE/HATE

Mark Guterman came to the club with a reputation for ruining Chester City – a mixed blessing when taking over as chairman at Wrexham. He failed to soothe the faithful by declaring 'I was not born a Chester fan'....so Wrexham through and through? Not quite, 'I'm a Manchester United fan'.

CHANTS

'Oh fluffy sheep...are wonderful,
oh fluffy sheep are wonderful.
They're white, fluffy and Welsh,
oh fluffy sheep are wonderful.'

Purely platonic you understand

DOH!!

In 2004, an inspector from the Performing Rights Society (the people who collect royalties on behalf of record companies) caught the club playing songs over the tannoy without a licence. Wrexham had to fork out £1,300 in court costs, a high price to pay considering the inspector noted that their idea of 'pre-match entertainment' was Gareth Gate's 'Spirit in the Sky'.

WYCOMBE WANDERERS

Recommended website: **www.chairboys.co.uk**

WHO ARE YA?

As recently as 1987 Wycombe were making journeys to the like of Bognor Regis Town, in the Isthmian League (one below the Conference). For most of their history, they seemed to shun the ambition of getting into the League, resolutely hanging on to their amateur status. But when they summoned up the nerve, they were like an express train. Ditching their old Loakes Park Ground in 1990 with its obligatory non-league slope (an 11ft difference in height between the goal lines), Martin O'Neill presided over a five-year spell that took them within a whisker of Level One. After his departure, the club disappeared into a Level Two black hole, seemingly never to be heard of again, (along with Brentford).

CELEBRITY FANS
ALAN PARRY
Football Commentator

They popped up in 2001, with one of those evergreen FA Cup tales when appearing in the semi-final against Liverpool. Their place had been secured by a late sixth round goal against Leicester by Roy Essandoh, a Belfast-born, Ghana-raised striker from Finland. A plea for a forward had been posted on the club's internet site and when the story was picked up by Teletext, Essandoh's agent offered his services. Signed on a two-week contract with Wycombe, he was said not to have known his colleagues' names as he had not attended a training session. After rising to head the winner, he got his name on the team sheet for the Liverpool clash and was very happy to walk away with Sammy Hypia's shirt. In 2004, he was in the Conference with Gravesend.

High Wycombe is becoming increasingly known as the chav capital of the UK

The reign of Lawrie Sanchez was marked with some disgruntlement from fans who would have far preferred the ball to be elegantly travelling along the ground rather than the sort of style Sanchez was used to in his playing days at Wimbledon. A symptom of his 'boot and hope' technique was the taped drumming that was blasted over the PA whenever the team won a corner. But the worst fans/club stink erupted when a change of kit design was bludgeoned through. Wycombe's traditional startling dark and light blue quartered strip has a slight 19th century feel. But in 1996, keen for a commercial spin-off, the club gave supporters the chance to vote on two choices, both equally hated. Forced into a 'no win' act of democracy, they opted for a semi-quartered affair where the dark blue portion was striped (roughly as if Coventry City had been run over by an out of control contraption that paints the lines on roads). A 'Just say no' campaign was launched and with supporters boycotting the new kit, the paltry sales' figures forced the club's hand. They caved in 18 months later and the favoured version was reintroduced.

Compared to other clubs, Wycombe should be immune to board v supporter bust-ups as major decisions are taken by members, who, for a quid, include any season ticket holders of three years' standing.

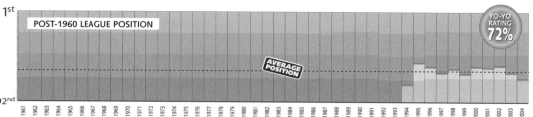

1st

POST-1960 LEAGUE POSITION

YO-YO RATING **72%**

AVERAGE POSITION

92nd

1961 1962 1963 1964 1965 1966 1967 1968 1969 1970 1971 1972 1973 1974 1975 1976 1977 1978 1979 1980 1981 1982 1983 1984 1985 1986 1987 1988 1989 1990 1991 1992 1993 1994 1995 1996 1997 1998 1999 2000 2001 2002 2003 2004

PROGRESS REPORT

Having won their League status in 1993, Wycombe weren't hanging around in Level Three, and went up again the following year. Their peak was reached the following season, 1995, with sixth place in Level Two. They then stagnated with nine middling years in Level Two before taking the plunge back to Level Three in 2004.

```
          ...Called themselves Wanderers in honour of first winners of the FA Cup...
...Were the only professional club ever in Buckinghamshire (until pesky MK Dons came along)...
   ...Jack Charlton said his Middlesbrough team would 'murder' them in a 1975 Cup tie
                    (they scraped through 1-0 after a goalless draw)...
```

RIVALS

Wycombe maintain a serious rivalry with Colchester United, bubbling away for around 20 years despite the significant geographical gap between the two.

COLCHESTER UNITED

The ill feeling probably started after fisticuffs in 1985 when Colchester (then in Level Three) were knocked out by non-league Wycombe. The two went to the wire for the Conference title of 1992, with Colchester edging it on goal difference after a 'fluky' win at Adams Park. Having had the home end stormed by an Essex mob, they watched Wycombe go down to a late goal when the opposing keeper got a clearance from his own box to sail into their net. Wycombe felt that the fractiousness was made worse by the sudden appearance of some squaddie-types based around Colchester who attached themselves to the side, giving the club a 'thuggish' hardcore of supporters that made them 'extremely easy to hate'.

In 1999, Wycombe become involved in a dog-fight to avoid relegation to Level Three when in March the two met at Adams Park. Things got seriously hectic as soon as the whistle was blown. On three minutes, the visitors had the ball in the net, triggering a pitch invasion. After order had been restored, it was promptly given offside. But referee Fraser Stretton was not to remain in Wycombe's good books. Leading 2-1 as the 90th minute ticked by, the board went up indicating there were seven minutes to be added. Wycombe swear that a penalty award to Colchester came in the 99th minute. David Gregory put it away causing extreme grinding of teeth as he had performed the same last minute trick in their home game in September, on that occasion scoring a winner to give his side a 2-1 victory.

SUPPORTERS' VFM 61%

PERFORMANCE AGAINST RIVALS
COLCHESTER

WON 29%   LOST 29%   DRAWN 42%

READING

Reading are seen as having snobbish fans, a snobbish chairman and a ridiculously overblown stadium (that you can't smoke in). And they let their own 'crappy' band in but refuse admission to opposing musical instruments.

LOVE/HATE

No hard feelings whatsoever towards *Martin O'Neill* ♡. *Alan Smith* comes high on the dislikes' list. No, not that one...but their manager in 1995-96. The name *Fraser Stretton* is difficult to forget as it is, but it lingers in Wycombe's 'Room 101' after not only the 1999 derby, but also his abandonment of a fixture at Peterborough two years earlier, due to ice (Wycombe protest it was perfectly playable). Wycombe were winning 2-0.

CHANTS

The offer of *'Shall we sing a song for you?'* is rarely taken up, but Wycombe fans were feeling so sorry for their opponents from Nottingham, whom they were beating 3-0, they did their best to lift them with spirited chants of *'County...County'*.

'YOUR GROUND'S TOO BIG FOR YOU!'
R A T I N G

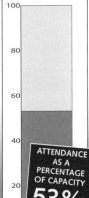

100
80
60
40
20
0

ATTENDANCE AS A PERCENTAGE OF CAPACITY
53%

DOH!!

As a novel form of half-time entertainment, the club organised a group of sky-divers to land on the pitch. Their downwards progress was significantly longer than anticipated and they finally touched down at 4.10pm, delaying the kick off to the second half. One failed to make the ground at all and was later discovered in local woods.

YEOVIL TOWN

Recommended website: **www.ciderspace.co.uk**

WHO ARE YA?

When Yeovil emerged from the Conference in 2003, nobody begrudged them their newly found status. They were the darlings of non-league football, having dispensed with a record 20 League teams in their FA Cup giant-killing history. They have attracted plenty of admiration as an 'authentic' non-league success story, in contrast to one or two others who have gained promotion from the Conference. Their reputation as being the side League teams weren't keen to meet began with a 2-1 victory over Sunderland in the 4th round of the 1948-49 FA Cup. This was only the second time (out of seven in total) that a side from the highest division had been beaten by non-league opponents.

CELEBRITY FANS

NOBODY YOU'RE LIKELY
TO HAVE HEARD OF

The notorious sloping pitch of the old Huish ground (now a Tesco) not only gave League sides a major headache, but also guaranteed the club could count on plenty of mainstream coverage as it gave visiting reporters an excellent off-the-shelf story. The away side's fans were sometimes disappointed that the slope wasn't very evident from the stands (though it came to life if you were actually on the pitch). Yeovil's green and white strip makes them members of an exclusive club of greenies. The fact that it is customary to consider the colour distinctly unlucky for a football team has caused a certain amount of bonding between similarly clad sides. At a League fixture away at Carlisle, the few Yeovil fans who could face the trip were bolstered by a contingent of 20-30 Celtic supporters keen to express their solidarity. The 'green bogey' probably isn't such an issue in recent years, with the likes of Plymouth, Celtic, Cameroon and Nigeria enjoying enough success to suggest it might even be a bonus.

IN and AROUND

Yeovil's largest employer is Westland Helicopters, best known for being at the centre of a defence procurement row between Margaret Thatcher and Tory grandee Michael Heseltine. In 1986, during the middle of a Cabinet meeting, he retreated in turmoil to the loo, finally emerging to stride outside to issue his resignation statement to a surprised lone TV cameraman.

The club pioneered an interesting technique for trying to boost revenue – simply play as many games as possible. During the 70s in particular, with the purse strings ultra-tight, Yeovil entered any and every competition, leading to a bewildering array of fixtures in minor floodlit competitions and obscurities such as the Anglo-Italian Cup, ensuring that some members of the squad were forced to play 70 fixtures per season.

Yeovil's unofficial website *www.ciderspace.co.uk* deserves a mention as the most exhaustively comprehensive football site currently in existence, with an editorial of 'War and Peace' proportions and scores of photos from every one of their fixtures. With something to spare, it tops our list of best sites.

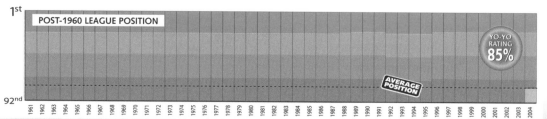

POST-1960 LEAGUE POSITION

1st

92nd

YO-YO RATING 85%

AVERAGE POSITION

1961 1962 1963 1964 1965 1966 1967 1968 1969 1970 1971 1972 1973 1974 1975 1976 1977 1978 1979 1980 1981 1982 1983 1984 1985 1986 1987 1988 1989 1990 1991 1992 1993 1994 1995 1996 1997 1998 1999 2000 2001 2002 2003 2004

PROGRESS REPORT

Despite their impeccable non-league pedigree, Yeovil had a mixed time in the Conference. After entering the unofficial Fifth Division in 1988 they sunk back down to the Isthmian for two seasons from 1995. Their next spell was more promising; a second and third place in 2000-2001 and 2001-2002. They breezed through the season, winning the Conference with a record 17-point margin. Their first League campaign continued the progress with a more than respectable eighth place.

```
        ...Were the first non-league team to feature as a Subbuteo side...
   ...Beat Czechoslovakia 8-3 (1933)...Competed in FA Cup game with biggest attendance
             (outside final), 81,000 v Manchester United in 1948...
```

RIVALS

As the only League club in Somerset, and with a considerable trek to get to other centres of football civilisation, Yeovil have yet to establish any significant new enemies since acquiring their Level Three status. Their main current hates are a hangover from their Conference days, namely Rushden and Diamonds who have gained the ire of many. But Yeovil's anti case is stronger than most, as they can legitimately claim a significant non-league heritage, in stark contrast to R&D with their almost absurdly rapid rise to prominence. Their fans are charged with being glory-hunting defectors from Kettering Town, a team they now profess to hate. R&D fans are also said to have the irritating habit of excusing any poor results by claiming that they are such a major club that other sides raise their game against them.

RUSHDEN & DIAMONDS
☠️☠️☠️☠️☠️

WEYMOUTH
☠️☠️☠️☠️☠️

Although not really much of an issue now, their rivalry with Weymouth is far more interesting than it sounds. The two almost come as a pair, managing to broadly match each other's status for over 110 years, playing a massive number of fixtures in the process, starting off in the Somerset Senior League and Dorset District League. They first locked horns in 1891, resulting in a blood-curdling 7-0 victory for Weymouth. In fact, the early fixtures were conspicuous by their lack of draws and, more significantly, their severely lop-sided scorelines. Yeovil got their own back with a 9-1 victory in 1907-08, only to be on the receiving end of a 7-1 five years later. This constant yo-yoing of results contributed to constant attempts at revenge.

**SUPPORTERS'
VFM
78%**

**PERFORMANCE AGAINST RIVALS
WEYMOUTH**

WON 33%

LOST 67%

As interest in the fixtures grew, both clubs seemed to realise they were on to a good thing, and became intent on capitalising on the large attendances by arranging as many games as possible. In the early 50s, the matches attracted gates of up to 11,000 (huge by non-league standards). With some luck and a degree of judgement, the two contrived to meet 11 times in two seasons. The atmosphere was ratcheted up a few notches, when in a FA Cup qualifying tie in 1973, Yeovil's stalwart keeper, Tony Clark, was left in a heap after an appalling Weymouth challenge, ending his unbroken run of 232 games for Yeovil. The two clubs had a 20-year tussle together in the Southern Premier League in which they notched up four championships between them and were rarely out of the top ten. Although Weymouth are named by the majority of Yeovil fans as number one rivals, they went their separate ways in the late 80s and have only had one competitive fixture since. Game, set and match to Yeovil after a century of trying.

Despite their recent difficulties, or more likely because of them, Weymouth pulled off a minor scoop when getting themselves featured on BBC's *Football Stories* documentary. They are currently in the Dr Martens Premier.

'YOUR GROUND'S TOO BIG FOR YOU!'
R A T I N G

CHANTS

Various cider-celebrating, and most probably cider-induced, songs are popular, belted out in a suitably hammed-up West Country accent. Away fans are treated to the rarely heard exaltation of

'C'mon you Greens'.

LOVE/HATE

Yeovil's good reputation is only marred by the musings of someone using the cover of the name *Yeovil_Massive*. He is widely considered the most irritating internet poster in the brief history of the medium.

100

80

60

40

20

**ATTENDANCE AS A PERCENTAGE OF CAPACITY
68%**

DOH!!

In 1999 as Warren Patmore was gearing up for the landmark of his 100th League goal for Yeovil, he started to fantasise about his goal celebration should he score in the next match with Leek Town. Plan A was to join the queue at the hot-dog stand (since he tended to get stick for his weight). This was ruined as it was inconveniently moved. So he decided on a simplified celebration whereby his mates would rush to the front of the stand. On netting the required goal, he ran deliriously to the rendezvous point. They didn't arrive at the ground until five minutes after he'd scored.

VALUE FOR MONEY

Reading 100	Crewe Alexandra 61
Wigan Athletic 100	Darlington 61
Plymouth Argyle 98	Stoke City 61
Birmingham City 96	Wolverhampton Wanderers 61
Arsenal 94	Wycombe Wanderers 61
Bolton Wanderers 94	Huddersfield Town 59
Hull City 94	Lincoln City 59
Chelsea 88	Rushden & Diamonds 59
Preston North End 88	Scunthorpe United 59
Colchester United .86	Southampton 59
Hartlepool United .86	Rotherham United 57
Charlton Athletic 84	Macclesfield Town 55
Fulham 84	Bradford City 53
Manchester City 84	Bristol City 53
Middlesbrough 84	Sheffield United 53
Portsmouth 84	Stockport County .53
Doncaster Rovers .82	Walsall 53
Millwall 82	Boston United 51
Newcastle United .78	Chester City 51
Tranmere Rovers 78	Leyton Orient 49
Yeovil Town 78	Liverpool 49
Gillingham 76	Manchester United 49
Everton 73	Nottingham Forest 49
Sunderland 73	Oxford United 49
Torquay United 73	Port Vale 49
Wrexham 73	Coventry City 47
Brentford 71	Northampton Town 47
Cardiff City 71	Oldham Athletic 47
Norwich City 71	Southend United .47
Queens Park Rangers 71	Swindon Town 47
Bournemouth 69	West Ham United .47
West Bromwich Albion 69	Luton Town 45
Rochdale 67	Brighton and Hove Albion 43
Tottenham Hotspur 67	Kidderminster Harriers 43
Watford 67	Sheffield Wednesday 43
Aston Villa 65	Notts County 41
Blackburn Rovers .65	Bury 39
Burnley 65	Cheltenham Town 39
Chesterfield 65	Shrewsbury Town 31
Derby County 65	Blackpool 29
Ipswich Town 65	Cambridge United 29
Mansfield Town 65	Grimsby Town 29
Peterborough United 65	Leicester City 29
Barnsley 63	Bristol Rovers 27
Crystal Palace 63	Leeds United 27
Swansea City 63	Milton Keynes Dons 27

YOUR GROUND'S TOO BIG FOR YOU

Manchester United	100%
Newcastle United	100%
Charlton	100%
Arsenal	99%
Portsmouth	99%
Southampton	99%
Manchester City	98%
Wolverhampton Wanderers	98%
Birmingham City	97%
Chelsea	97%
Everton	97%
Tottenham Hotspur	96%
Bolton Wanderers	95%
Leicester City	95%
Liverpool	94%
Doncaster	93%
Leeds United	91%
Brighton and Hove Albion	90%
West Ham United	89%
West Bromwich Albion	88%
Middlesbrough	87%
Aston Villa	85%
Fulham	85%
Ipswich Town	82%
Nottingham Forest	81%
Gillingham	80%
Blackburn Rovers	78%
Cardiff City	78%
Norwich City	77%
Queens Park Rangers	77%
Crewe Alexandra	76%
Hartlepool United	75%
Bournemouth	72%
Watford	72%
Sheffield United	70%
Walsall	70%
Northampton Town	69%
Preston North End	69%
Yeovil	68%
Hull City	67%
Rushden & Diamonds	67%
Crystal Palace	66%
Derby County	66%
Luton Town	66%
Coventry City	64%
Rotherham United	64%

Plymouth Argyle	63%
Reading	63%
Blackpool	62%
Bristol Rovers	61%
Bristol City	60%
Milton Keynes Dons	60%
Cheltenham Town	56%
Sheffield Wednesday	56%
Sunderland	56%
Burnley	55%
Torquay United	55%
Swindon Town	54%
Wycombe Wanderers	53%
Mansfield Town	52%
Millwall	52%
Stoke City	52%
Swansea City	53%
Chesterfield	51%
Oxford United	50%
Grimsby Town	48%
Oldham Athletic	48%
Colchester United	47%
Kidderminster Harriers	47%
Shrewsbury Town	46%
Stockport County	46%
Tranmere Rovers	46%
Boston	45%
Bradford City	45%
Lincoln City	45%
Chester City	44%
Brentford	43%
Huddersfield Town	43%
Scunthorpe United	42%
Barnsley	41%
Cambridge United	41%
Macclesfield Town	38%
Wigan Athletic	38%
Leyton Orient	37%
Southend United	37%
Peterborough United	34%
Rochdale	32%
Port Vale	31%
Notts County	29%
Wrexham	28%
Bury	24%
Darlington	20%

NUTTER RATING

Cardiff City	5 stars	Sunderland	3 stars
Lincoln City	5 stars	Bolton Wanderers	3 stars
Stoke City	5 stars	Norwich City	3 stars
Swansea City	5 stars	Manchester United	3 stars
Swindon Town	5 stars	QRP	3 stars
Wigan Athletic	5 stars	Bury	3 stars
Port Vale	5 stars	Middlesbrough	3 stars
Wrexham	5 stars	West Ham United	3 stars
Bristol City	5 stars	Crystal Palace	2 stars
Shrewsbury Town	5 stars	Preston North End	2 stars
Brighton & Hove Albion	5 stars	Aston Villa	2 stars
Millwall	5 stars	Bradford City	2 stars
Luton Town	5 stars	Northampton Town	2 stars
Chesterfield	5 stars	Walsall	2 stars
Rotherham United	5 stars	Everton	2 stars
Hartlepool United	5 stars	West Bromwich Albion	2 stars
Mansfield Town	5 stars	Stockport County	2 stars
Burnley	5 stars	Newcastle United	2 stars
Boston United	4 stars	Tottenham Hotspur	2 stars
Chester City	4 stars	Crewe Alexandra	2 stars
Birmingham City	4 stars	Liverpool	2 stars
Peterborough United	4 stars	Milton Keynes Dons	2 stars
Grimsby Town	4 stars	Doncaster Rovers	2 stars
Manchester City	4 stars	Blackpool	2 stars
Leeds United	4 stars	Colchester United	2 stars
Oldham Athletic	4 stars	Rushden & Diamonds	1 star
Sheffield United	4 stars	Ipswich Town	1 star
Portsmouth	4 stars	Gillingham	1 star
Nottingham Forest	4 stars	Blackburn Rovers	1 star
Cambridge United	4 stars	Bournemouth	1 star
Wolverhampton Wanderers	4 stars	Cheltenham Town	1 star
Barnsley	4 stars	Tranmere Rovers	1 star
Leicester City	4 stars	Yeovil Town	1 star
Huddersfield Town	4 stars	Southampton	1 star
Darlington	4 stars	Leyton Orient	1 star
Rochdale	3 stars	Watford	1 star
Plymouth Argyle	3 stars	Fulham	1 star
Derby County	3 stars	Notts County	1 star
Coventry City	3 stars	Arsenal	1 star
Scunthorpe United	3 stars	Southend United	1 star
Hull City	3 stars	Brentford	1 star
Oxford United	3 stars	Charlton Athletic	1 star
Chelsea	3 stars	Torquay United	1 star
Sheffield Wednesday	3 stars	Kidderminster Harriers	1 star
Bristol Rovers	3 stars	Wycombe Wanderers	1 star
Reading	3 stars	Macclesfield Town	1 star

PICK OF THE BEST WEBSITES

1 www.ciderspace.co.uk . . . . .Yeovil Town
2 www.codalmighty.com . . . . .Grimsby Town
3 www.mehstg.co.uk . . . . .Tottenham Hotspur
4 www.park-road.u-net.com . . . . .Burnley
5 www.chairboys.co.uk . . . . . .Wycombe Wanderers
6 www.readytogo.net . . . . .Sunderland
7 www.boyfrombrazil.co.uk . . . . .Bradford City
8 www.hof.org.uk . . . . .Millwall
9 www.hatternet.com . . . . .Luton Town
10 www.y3kshakers.co.uk . . . . .Bury

Other publications from Aesculus Press

The Essential Football Fan
by Duncan Adams (£9.95)
The definitive guide to the Premier and Football League grounds. Like its counterpart, *The Essential Scottish Football Fan*, a must for travelling and stadium enthusiasts.

The Essential Scottish Football Fan
by Duncan Adams (£6.95)
The definitive guide to the Scottish Premier and Football League grounds. Like its counterpart The Essential Football Fan, a must for travelling and stadium enthusiasts.

Successful Football Betting
by Geoff Harvey (£9.95)
This ground-breaking book focuses on changing the mind-set of the football punter and lucidly describes how to spot, and exploit, areas of bookmaker vulnerability.

AESCULUS PRESS LTD

Other publications from Aesculus Press

Successful Matched Betting
by Geoff Harvey (£9.95)
The phenomena of betting on the exchanges explained in detail. The author details the basics and then goes on to explore the many areas where strategies can be applied to maximise returns.

Winning Without Thinking
by Nick Mordin (£12.95)
From one of the truly original writers in horse race betting, the ultimate guide to racing systems. Also available in hardback, complete with extensive appendices (£18)

Betting for a Living
by Nick Mordin (£12.95)
Fully revised. Quite simply the most authoritative horse race betting book ever written in the UK. Nearly 25,000 copies sold.

Other publications from Aesculus Press

Mordin on Time
by Nick Mordin (£9.95)
The bible of constructing speed ratings which, uniquely, can be applied to any country in the world.

Against the Crowd
by Alan Potts (£8.95)
The techniques and methods of a professional punter full of valuable insights on how to become - and stay - a winner.

The Inside Track
by Alan Potts (£12.95)
There are no systems, no rules and no guarantees in this book, yet there is plenty of material that will challenge accepted beliefs and persuade readers to think in new ways about their betting.

AP
AESCULUS
PRESS LTD

Other publications from Aesculus Press

100 Hints for Better Betting
by Mark Coton (£9.95)
From the originator of the ground-breaking *Pricewise* column in the Racing Post, this title shows how to capitalise on basic insights familiar to all punters, as well as identifying many bad habits which often spoil betting.

Racing Around Britain
by Stephen Cartmell (£12.95)
Whether an occasional or regular Racegoer, this title will enhance the rich and varied experience of a day at the races. A highly entertaining guide and travelogue.

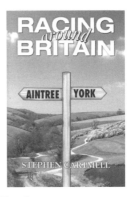

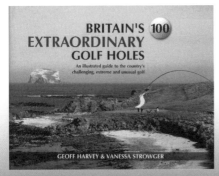

Britain's 100 Extraordinary Golf Holes
by Geoff Harvey and Vanessa Strowger (£19.95)
A collection of the country's most challenging, eccentric and unusual golf holes, together with oddities, curiosities and bizarre tales from Britain's 4,000 courses. With over 300 stunning colour photographs, a book to captivate the imagination of golfers everywhere.